ANIME

*

from *Akira* to *Princess Mononoke*

Experiencing Contemporary Japanese Animation

Susan J. Napier

palgrave

ANIME FROM AKIRA TO PRINCESS MONONOKE © Susan J. Napier, 2001

First published 2000 by
PALGRAVE
175 Fifth Avenue, New York, N.Y.
Companies and representatives throughout the world

PALGRAVE is the new global publishing imprint of St. Martin 's Press LLC
Scholarly and Reference Division and Palgrave Publishers Ltd (formerly Macmillan Press Ltd).

ISBN 0-312-23862-2 hardback
ISBN 0-312-23863-0 paperback

Library of Congress Cataloging-in-Publication Data

Napier, Susan Jolliffe.
   Anime from Akira to Princess Mononoke : experiencing contemporary Japanese animation / Susan J. Napier.
      p. cm.
   Includes bibliographical references and index.
      ISBN 0-312-23862-2 — ISBN 0-312-23863-0 (pbk. : alk. paper)
      1. Animated films—Japan. I. Title.

NC1766.J3 N37 2001
791.43'3—dc21

                                        00-051473

Design by Acme Art, Inc.

First edition: May 2001
10 9 8 7 6 5 4 3 2 1

Printed in the United States of America.

For Julia
Moon Prism Power!

CONTENTS

ACKNOWLEDGMENTS

One day in 1989 a student lingered after my Japanese class to show me one of the Japanese comic books (manga) he had frequently brought up in class discussion. Expecting something simple and upbeat along the lines of my childhood favorite, *Superman*, I was surprised, then transfixed. The comic he showed me, *Akira*, was a complex evocation of a twenty-first century dystopian Japan, dominated by beautifully rendered images of surpassing bleakness. Thanks to the manga, I was inspired the next year, while teaching in London, to go to the British premier of *Akira* and was again transfixed, gradually becoming aware that I was seeing something both wonderful and different.

So my first acknowledgment must be to the student who first showed me *Akira* and to all the students and anime fans over the last 11 years who have shared with me their favorite manga and anime and their thoughts about them. I want particularly to thank Jonathan Nawrocki, Peter Siegenthaler, Kara Williams, Brian Ruh, and Alex Aguila, who have been especially helpful at various stages in the research of this book.

Perhaps it was no coincidence that the premier of *Akira* was followed shortly thereafter by what I believe was the first conference on Japanese Popular Culture ever organized in the West. I must thank most deeply its organizers, Beth Berry and John Treat, who invited me to give a paper there. The paper turned out to be on *Akira* and the enthusiastic response at the conference made me realize that this was a research topic worth pursuing at far greater length.

Venturing to write a book-length discussion of anime was really journeying into undiscovered country. I could not possibly have done it without the generous awards from three institutions, the John Simon Guggenheim Memorial Foundation, the Social Science Research Council, and the University of Texas, whose awards gave me the time to leave the teaching world temporarily behind. I cannot thank enough the friends/colleagues/mentors who helped me obtain these awards: Anne Allison, Helen Hardacre, Patrick Olivelle, Sharalyn Orbaugh, Miriam Silverberg, Arthur Stockwin, and Ezra Vogel. Others who helped along the way are Sharon Kinsella, Livia Monnet, Jay Rubin, Robert Khan, Henry Smith, Ian Reader, Alex Smith, Kotani Mari, and Takayuki Tatsumi. As always, I would like to thank my two most important mentors, Howard Hibbett and Asai Kiyoshi, who have remained marvelously supportive, especially considering how far I seemed to have traveled from the study of "pure literature."

Along the way I also made some exciting new friends in the anime community. I am grateful and honored by Helen McCarthy's enthusiasm for the book. I also want to thank Marc Hairston for his consistent support and interest in the project.

The editing of this book was a whole other journey in itself. I would like to thank Robert Luskin for his help in the initial stages and with the statistical surveys used in the Appendix. As for my editors at Palgrave—Anthony (Toby) Wahl, Alan Bradshaw, and Annjeanette Kern—they are in a class by themselves, the very best. I must especially extend my heartfelt gratitude to Toby, whose consistent support and enthusiasm for the project, combined with editorial brilliance and (perhaps even more important) saintlike patience, made him the perfect editor.

Lastly I want to thank the people closest to me whose lives were most touched by anime (whether they wanted it to be or not). I want to thank Bill Barlow for his consistent interest, not to mention his willingness to attend anime conventions. And I want to thank my daughter, Julia, who lived through too many weekends of my writing and not playing with her, and to whom this book is dedicated.

PART ONE

*

INTRODUCTION

CHAPTER ONE

WHY ANIME?

THERE ARE MANY ANSWERS to the question that titles this chapter, as the rest of this introduction will demonstrate, but for now it is worth exploring the question itself. Japanese animation, or "anime," as it is now usually referred to in both Japan and the West, is a phenomenon of popular culture. This means that much (some would argue most) of its products are short-lived, rising and falling due to popular taste and the demands of the hungry market place. Can or even should anime be taken as seriously as the extraordinary range of high cultural artifacts, from woodblock prints to haiku, that Japanese culture is famous for? Can or should anime be seen as an "art," or should it only be analyzed as a sociological phenomenon, a key to understanding some of the current concerns abounding in present-day Japanese society?

These are legitimate questions. As John Treat, one of the major scholars in this area, notes in his ground-breaking introduction to *Contemporary Japan and Popular Culture*:

> To worry about the relation of the popular to high or official
> culture is to think about the perennial problem of value: perennial
> first because value is so exasperatingly mercurial . . . and second
> because its determination only deflects us from understanding
> how cultures high, low and in-between exist in discursive and
> material relations of exchange, negotiation and conflict with each
> other."[1]

The "culture" to which anime belongs is at present a "popular" or "mass" culture in Japan, and in America it exists as a "sub" culture. However, as Treat's point about the mercuriality of value suggests, this situation may well change. Indeed, in Japan over the last decade, anime has been increasingly seen as an intellectually challenging art form, as the number of scholarly writings on the subject attest.

Furthermore, anime is a popular cultural form that clearly builds on previous high cultural traditions. Not only does the medium show influences from such Japanese traditional arts as Kabuki and the woodblock print (originally popular culture phenomena themselves), but it also makes use of worldwide artistic traditions of twentieth-century cinema and photography. Finally, the issues it explores, often in surprisingly complex ways, are ones familiar to readers of contemporary "high culture" literature (both inside and outside Japan) and viewers of contemporary art cinema. Anime texts entertain audiences around the world on the most basic level, but, equally importantly, they also move and provoke viewers on other levels as well, stimulating audiences to work through certain contemporary issues in ways that older art forms cannot. Moreover, precisely because of their popular reach they affect a wider variety of audiences in more ways than some less accessible types of high cultural exchange have been able to do. In other words, anime clearly appears to be a cultural phenomenon worthy of being taken seriously, both sociologically and aesthetically.

The following anecdote illustrates the often surprising ways anime affects its audience. In 1993 the Japanese critic Ueno Toshiya made a visit to the city of Sarajevo in war-torn Serbia. Wandering through the bombed-out city, he encountered an unexpected sight. In the middle of the old city was a crumbling wall with three panels. On the first was drawn a picture of Mao Zedong with Mickey Mouse ears; the second had a slogan for the Chiappas liberation group, the

Zapatistas, emblazoned on it. But when he came to the third he was "at a loss for words. Incredibly, it was a large panel of a scene from Otomo Katsuhiro's *Akira*. Against the crumbling walls of the collapsing group of buildings, that 'mighty juvenile delinquent' Kaneda was saying 'So it's begun!'"[2]

Ueno's story is a thought-provoking one. Unquestionably a masterpiece of technical animation, *Akira* is also a complex and challenging work of art that provoked, bewildered, and occasionally inspired Western audiences when it first appeared outside Japan in 1990. However, it is not a work whose image might have been expected to appear on a wall in Sarajevo three years later as an icon of political resistance. At the time of *Akira's* first appearance in the West, animation was generally regarded as a minor art, something for children, or, perhaps, the occasional abstract, art-house film. Animation from Japan was marginalized even further. If audiences took note of it at all, it was to fondly remember watching *Speed Racer* after school on television, often without realizing its Japanese origin. The notion that a sophisticated Japanese animated film could cross international borders to become a political statement in a war-wracked European country would have been deemed bizarre at best and most likely absurd.

Things have changed. Whereas Japan has been known for such "high cultural" products as haiku, Zen, and the martial arts, the Japan of the 1990s began to develop a new export, animated films and videos—anime, a Japanese abbreviation of the English word "animation." Anime has now entered the American vocabulary as well, to the extent that it has appeared in recent years in a *New York Times* crossword puzzle.

Through anime Japan has become an increasingly significant player in the global cultural economy. Indeed, one scholar has gone so far as to label anime Japan's "chief cultural export."[3] As a 1997 cover story in the Japanese version of *Newsweek* makes clear, anime's reach extends around the world. Its products are popular in countries such as Korea and Taiwan, and also in Southeast Asia, where the children's animated series *Doraemon* became a big hit in Thailand in the early 1990s. Anime has also penetrated Europe, from the United Kingdom, where *Akira* was a top-selling video in the year after its release, to France, a country not known for its generosity to non-native cultural products, which in the mid 1990s carried over 30 hours a week of Japanese cartoons. In America as well, anime's popularity has grown enormously in the last decade. While even a few years ago it was known only to small subgroups among science fiction fans, anime is increasingly•moving to at least a marginal niche in the mainstream. Whether it will ever be totally integrated into Western pop culture is still debatable. Indeed, a strong part of its appeal, as will be seen, is its difference from the Western mainstream.

Despite (or thanks to) this difference, anime clubs continue to attract growing numbers of members. Anime is shown on the Sci-Fi Channel, is available at such mainstream video venues as Blockbuster Video, and has a whole section devoted to it at Virgin Megastore in London. Anime's influence also extends beyond Japanese exports of actual tapes and videodiscs to include everything from the *Pokemon* toy give-away in 1999 at Kentucky Fried Chicken (a product tie-in with the extremely popular children's animated television show) to American museums where anime-inspired artists such as Yanobe Kenji have received favorable critical comment. Perhaps anime's "greatest" moment of transcultural recognition so far was a cover story about *Pokemon* in *Time* (November 22, 1999) that included a special section on anime in general.

What exactly is anime? To define anime simply as "Japanese cartoons" gives no sense of the depth and variety that make up the medium.[4] Many definitions in the West attempt to explain anime by comparison to American animation, specifically Disney. Thus, the *Time* article attempts to answer the question by suggesting that in comparison to Disney "anime is all kinds of differents . . . Anime is kids' cartoons: *Pokemon* yes, and *Sailor Moon* . . . But it's also post-doomsday fantasies (*Akira*), schizo-psycho thrill machines (*Perfect Blue*), sex and samurai sagas—the works."[5] If anything, *Time's* focus on the more extreme visions of anime actually minimizes the variety of the form, since anime also includes everything from animations of children's classics such as *Heidi* to romantic comedies such as *No Need for Tenchi*. Nor do the insistent comparisons with Disney permit the appreciation of the fact that anime does not deal only with what American viewers would regard as cartoon situations. Essentially, anime works include everything that Western audiences are accustomed to seeing in live-action films—romance, comedy, tragedy, adventure, even psychological probing of a kind seldom attempted in recent mass-culture Western film or television.

It is not surprising, therefore, that animated works are a major part of the output of Japanese studios. Japanese television studios produce around 50 animated series a year and a comparable number of OVAs (Original Video Animation). Animated films are also far more important in Japan than in the West, amounting to "about half the tickets sold for movies."[6] In fact, in 1997 *Princess Mononoke* broke all box office records to become, briefly, the highest-grossing film of all time in Japan, and it remains to this day the highest-grossing Japanese film ever.

Unlike cartoons in the West, anime in Japan is truly a mainstream pop cultural phenomenon. While rabidly fanatical fans of anime are called by the pejorative term *otaku* and looked down upon by conservative Japanese society, anime is simply accepted by virtually all the younger generation of Japanese as a cultural staple. Viewers range from little children watching *Pokemon* and other child-oriented fantasies, to college students or young adults enjoying the harder-edged science fiction of films like *Akira* and its many descendants, such as the bleak *Evangelion* series. Sometimes, as was the case with *Princess Mononoke* and other films by its director, Miyazaki Hayao, anime cuts across generational lines to be embraced by everyone from children to grandparents.

Images from anime and its related medium of manga (graphic novels) are omnipresent throughout Japan. Japan is a country that is traditionally more pictocentric than the cultures of the West, as is exemplified in its use of characters or ideograms, and anime and manga fit easily into a contemporary culture of the visual. They are used for education (one manga explains the Japanese economy), adornment (numerous shirts are emblazoned with popular manga and anime personages), and, of course, commercial enterprise. When the hit television and manga series *Sailor Moon* was at its most popular in the mid 1990s, pictures of its heroine Serena (*Usagi* in the Japanese version) peered down ubiquitously from billboards, while *Sailor Moon*–related paraphernalia—everything from "moon prism power wands" to bath towels—were snapped up by devoted fans of the series, largely young girls who were attracted by the characters' unique combination of cuteness and fantastic powers.

On a more ominous note, Japanese society has on occasion convulsed into what the sociologist Sharon Kinsella has described as a "moral panic" regarding the *otaku* culture, as it determined anime and manga to be socially unhealthy.[7] The first time this occurred was in the 1980s when a young man accused of murdering four little girls was found to be an avid watcher of violent pornographic anime. More recently, the Japanese media, indulging in an orgy of blame-finding for the disastrous sarin gas subway attack in 1995 by the cult group Aum Shinrikyō, claimed that many of Aum's "best and brightest" followers were also avid fans of apocalyptic science fiction anime.

Reasons to study anime within its Japanese context should by now be obvious. For those interested in Japanese culture, it is a richly fascinating contemporary Japanese art form with a distinctive narrative and visual aesthetic that both harks back to traditional Japanese culture and moves forward to the cutting edge of art and media. Furthermore, anime, with its enormous breadth of subject material, is also a useful mirror on contemporary Japanese society, offering an array of insights into the significant issues, dreams, and nightmares of the day.

But anime is worth investigating for other reasons as well, perhaps the most important being the fact that it is also a genuinely global phenomenon, both as a commercial and a cultural force. Commercially, it is beginning to play a significant role in the transnational entertainment economy, not only as an important part of the Japanese export market, but also as a small but growing part of the non-Japanese commercial world, in terms of the increasing number of non-Japanese enterprises that deal with anime. These range from small video rental operations in big cities throughout the world to mail order houses up to and including such behemoths as Amazon.com (which has a special anime section) and most famously the mammoth Walt Disney Enterprises, which, in 1996, made a deal with Studio Ghibli, Japan's most well-known animation studio, to distribute its products in America and Canada. To be sure, its international commercial impact is still small compared to the global returns on a successful Hollywood blockbuster, but anime and its related products are increasingly drawing attention from marketers around the world.[8]

Investigating anime as a cultural force is even more fascinating than inquiring into its commercial aspects, as it brings insight into the wider issue of the relationship between global and local cultures at the beginning of the twenty-first century. In a world where American domination of mass culture is often taken for granted and local culture is frequently seen as either at odds with or about to be subsumed into hegemonic globalism, anime stands out as a site of implicit cultural resistance. It is a unique artistic product, a local form of popular culture that shows clear indications of its Japanese roots[9] but at the same time exerts an increasingly wide influence beyond its native shores.

Westerners raised on a culture of children's cartoons may find anime's global popularity surprising. Noted scholar Arjun Appadurai has suggested that "the most valuable feature of the concept of culture is the concept of difference,"[10] and certainly one salient aspect of anime, as *Time*'s disquisition makes clear, is its insistent difference from dominant American popular culture. As Susan Pointon astutely comments, "[W]hat is perhaps most striking about anime, compared to other imported media that have been modified for the American market, is the lack of compromise in making these narratives palatable."[11] This is not only true in regards to the many specifically Japanese references within the narratives, but also in regards to narrative style, pacing, imagery, and humor, not to mention emotions and psychology, which usually run a far wider gamut and often show greater depth than do American animated texts.

Anime is uncompromising in other ways as well. Its complex story lines challenge the viewer used to the predictability of Disney (or of much of Hollywood fare overall, for that matter) while its often dark tone and content may surprise audiences who like to think of "cartoons" as "childish" or "innocent." Indeed, what appears to be the single most-asked question about anime in America, "why is anime so full of sex and violence?,"[12] is an inquiry that, while betraying an ignorance of the complexity and variety of the art form, is still significant in that it reveals the bewilderment of Western audiences in confronting so-called adult themes within the animated medium.[13]

Given its apparently uncompromising "otherness," why has anime succeeded so remarkably as a cross-cultural export? The short answer to this, culled from many interviews with anime fans in America, Europe, and Canada, would have to do with the fact that the medium is both different in a way that is appealing to a Western audience satiated on the predictabilities of American popular culture and also remarkably approachable in its universal themes and images. The distinctive aspects of anime—ranging from narrative and characterization to genre and visual styles—are the elements that initially capture Western viewers' attention (and for some viewers these may be the main keys of attraction), but for others it is the engrossing stories that keep them coming back for more.

Up to this point, much of the academic discourse about anime has centered on its visual properties; understandably so, given that this is what most obviously differentiates animation from live-action cinema. It is also important to emphasize how the visual style of anime is significantly different from mass-audience American cartoons. As anime critics Trish Ledoux and Doug Ranney point out, even early 1970s Japanese animated television series "absolutely overflow with tracking shots, long-view establishing shots, fancy pans, unusual point-of-view 'camera angles' and extreme close-ups . . . [i]n contrast [to] most American-produced TV animation [which] tends to thrive in an action-obsessed middle-distance."[14]

However, Japanese animation merits serious consideration as a narrative art form, and not simply for its arresting visual style.[15] Anime is a medium in which distinctive visual elements combine with an array of generic, thematic, and philosophical structures to produce a unique aesthetic world. Often this world is more provocative, more tragic, and more highly sexualized (even in lighthearted romantic comedies) and contains far more complicated story lines than would be the case in equivalent American popular cultural offerings.

Much of this book will be an investigation into the themes, imagery, and ideas of some of the more memorable anime created over the last two decades, the period of the so-called anime boom, in an attempt to understand what makes anime the distinctive art form that it is. It should be stressed that not all of the texts to be considered are masterpieces (as with any entertainment medium, much that is produced is simply commercial fodder), but each work that I have chosen to discuss will ideally help to reveal some of the more fascinating and distinctive features of the anime world and ultimately illuminate the reasons behind its increasingly global appeal. This is an appeal that is strongly related to the increased importance of such contemporary issues as technological development, gender identity and relations between the sexes, and the problematic role of history in contemporary culture.

It may be that animation in general—and perhaps anime in particular—is the ideal artistic vehicle for expressing the hopes and nightmares of our uneasy contemporary world. Even more than live-action cinema, animation is a fusion of technology and art, both suggesting in its content and embodying in its form new interfaces between the two. It is perhaps no accident that two of anime's most popular genres, the cyberpunk and the so-called *mecha* genres, are within science fiction. Cyberpunk, well known from such Western science fiction classics as William Gibson's *Neuromancer* (a major influence on Japanese science fiction in general), is a genre focusing on dystopian futures in which humans struggle in an overpoweringly technological world where the difference between human and machine is increasingly amorphous. *Mecha* (a shortening of the English word "mechanical") privileges a favorite form from Japanese popular culture, the robot. Although in such classics as Tezuka Osamu's *Astro Boy* the robot is drawn in a positive light, more recent *mecha* often feature humanoid machines in a more ominous mode.

Both these genres are particularly appropriate ones for our increasingly high-tech world. As J. P. Telotte says of Western science fiction film:

> In a near fixation on the artificial, technologized body—the robot, cyborg, android—the [science fiction] genre has tried to examine our ambivalent feelings about technology, our growing anxieties about our own nature in an increasingly technological environment and a kind of evolutionary fear that these artificial selves may presage our own disappearance or termination.[16]

It is not only anime's references to technology that make it such an appropriate art form for the turn of the millennium. In its fascination with gender roles and gender transgression—seen in lighthearted terms in romantic comedies or *shōjo* (young girl) narratives and more bleakly in occult pornography—anime encapsulates both the increasing fluidity of gender identity in contemporary popular culture and the tensions between the sexes that characterize a world in which women's roles are drastically transforming. Perhaps many of anime's most important characters are female because it is so often the female subject who most clearly emblematizes the dizzying changes occurring in modern society.[17] Anime texts also explore (sometimes implicitly and sometimes explicitly) the meaning of history in contemporary society. These works usually involve a specifically Japanese context, such as the period of samurai warfare, but even the most specific texts, like *Grave of the Fireflies,* set in the waning days of World War II, implicitly suggest larger issues, including the political nature of historical memory. Most recently, Miyazaki's historical epic *Princess Mononoke* problematized the nature of historical identity in relation to the modern world through its complex mixture of fantasy and fact.

Indeed, anime may be the perfect medium to capture what is perhaps the overriding issue of our day, the shifting nature of identity in a constantly changing society. With its rapid shifts of narrative pace and its constantly transforming imagery, the animated medium is superbly positioned to illustrate the atmosphere of change permeating not only Japanese society but also all industrialized or industrializing societies. Moving at rapid—sometimes breakneck—pace and predicated upon the instability of form, animation is both a symptom and a metaphor for a society obsessed with change and spectacle. In particular, animation's emphasis on metamorphosis can be seen as the ideal artistic vehicle for expressing the postmodern obsession with fluctuating identity. What animation scholar Paul Wells describes as "the primacy of the image and its ability to *metamorphose* into a completely different image,"[18] is a function of animation that has powerful resonances with contemporary society and culture.

Such a protean art form as anime is impossible to completely sum up in a single book and I shall not attempt to do so. Rather, I intend to look at a variety of anime in terms of three major expressive modes that I have termed the apocalyptic, the festival, and the elegiac. The next chapter will discuss how these modes fit into Japanese cultural norms, but they also exist in more autonomous terms. The apocalyptic is perhaps the most obvious mode, since a vision of worldwide destruction seems to be a staple across all cultures. It is certainly a major part of American film culture, ranging from the alien invasion cinema of the 1950s to the late 1990s spate of end-of-the-world films such as *Armageddon* or *End of Days.* As will be seen, however, the apocalyptic can range beyond material catastrophe (although this is well represented in an enormous number of Japanese anime), to include more intimate forms of apocalypse, such as spiritual or even pathological ones. The flexible visuals available to animation make apocalypse a natural subject for the medium, but it is in the interplay of character that anime offers its most distinctive visions of apocalypse.

Perhaps equally important in anime is the mode of the festival. "Festival" here is used as a direct translation of the Japanese term "*matsuri*" but the term "carnival" as theorized by Mikhail Bakhtin has very similar connotations. According to Bakhtin the "carnival sense of the world" is one predicated on "*the pathos of shifts and changes, of death and renewal.*"[19] This privileging of change is at the heart of animation, but animation's narrative structure and themes can also be carnivalesque. In Bakhtin's view carnival is a liminal period of topsy-turvy that expresses "the *joyful relativity* of all structure and order, of all authority and all (hierarchical) position." For a brief moment norms are transgressed or actually inverted. The weak hold power, sexual and gender rules are broken or reversed, and a state of manic intensity replaces conventional restraint.[20] Comedies are usually the most obvious sites of the carnival/festival mode, and it may be suggested that sex-reversal comedies such as *Some Like It Hot* in America or *Ranma 1/2* in Japan are particularly carnivalesque in their implicitly transgressive antics. Again, the visual flexibility of animation, with its intense palette of colors and ability to transform figures, shapes, and even space itself, also makes the medium peculiarly suited to the extreme and sometimes grotesque mode of the festival.

The elegiac mode, with its implications of loss, grief, and absence, may at first seem a less obvious mode to Western viewers, who are used to emotions being painted with broad brush in animation. Even in live-action films the elegiac may not be so wide a category in the West, although movies like *The Way We Were,* with its mourning for a more innocent romantic time, or even *Blade Runner,* with its privileging of genuine emotional response in reaction to growing dehumanization, might be considered candidates. In Japan, the elegiac—in terms of a lyrical sense of mourning often connected with an acute consciousness of a waning traditional culture—is an important element in both anime and live-action cinema. Although it is important to acknowledge the immense range of anime—its fascinating variety of genres, its mixture of traditional and modern elements, and its disparate assemblage of subjectivities—it is also rewarding to see how the modes of apocalypse, festival, and elegy continually appear, reworking and recombining themselves across the broad tapestry of contemporary animation.

To return once more to the question asked at the beginning of this chapter, "Why anime?," there now should be enough evidence to show the value in studying this complex and fascinating medium. As a form of popular culture, anime is important for its growing global popularity but it is also a cultural form whose themes and modes reach across arbitrary aesthetic boundaries to strike significant artistic and psychological chords. Furthermore, the three modes used to examine anime are ones that go beyond any distinction between "high" and "low" culture or beyond any nation-specific site to illuminate in a timely fashion some of the major issues of global society at the turn of the millennium.

CHAPTER TWO

ANIME AND LOCAL/GLOBAL IDENTITY

THE DEVELOPMENT OF ANIME IN JAPAN

TO WESTERNERS it may seem surprising that an artistic form that has been known to them largely as children's entertainment could encompass so many varieties. To understand the reasons behind this variety, we need to understand something of the history and role of anime in Japanese society. First of all, it is important to appreciate just how significant a force anime is in contemporary Japanese media. In 1988 roughly 40 percent of Japanese studio releases were animated. By 1999, as the previously mentioned article in *Time* notes, at least half of all releases from Japanese studios were animated.[1] Animation on television is a continuous presence, beginning with children's shows in the morning, continuing through family viewing hours in the evening, and taking on a significant presence in the late-night market (after 11:00 P.M.), where edgy animated shows aimed at late teens and twenty-somethings are major offerings. From the early 1980s anime also became an important player in the video market, where OVAs constitute a high proportion of video sales and rentals.[2]

Of course, animation was not always such an important part of the Japanese popular culture industry. For a long time it was overshadowed by Japan's superb live-action cinema and existed only as a fairly marginal and largely child-oriented alternative. To some extent, animation's rise in Japan is in an inverse relationship with the decline of the Japanese film industry, which, in the fifties and sixties, was one of the greatest in the world. Unfortunately, the 1950s decade of film masterpieces, exemplified in the works of Kurosawa Akira, Ozu Yasujiro, and Mizoguchi Kenji, was also the decade in which film attendance peaked in Japan. Japanese filmmakers have continued to create important and provocative works, but they are now increasingly in competition with both television and American imports.

While Western animated films had appeared in Japan as early as 1909, and Japanese animators began to create their own work by 1915, animation as a commercial art form really got started in the postwar period with popular, feature-length animated films produced by studios such as Toei, a company primarily famous for its live-action films.[3] Perhaps the most important date in Japanese animation history, however, is 1963, the year that Japan's first animated television series, Osamu Tezuka's legendary *Astro Boy* (Tetsuwan Atomu), appeared. The story of a little-boy robot, built by a brilliant scientist as a replacement for his dead son, was an immediate success, as much for its exciting and often affecting story line (the first in what would be a long line of animated features about humanoid robots) as for its spare but effective graphic design. Tezuka followed *Astro Boy* with the color series *Kimba the White Lion* (Janguru taitei, 1964), which also became a major hit, and, by the late 1960s, animated television series were securely established in Japan.[4]

Tezuka himself was a strong admirer of Disney animation, as were many of Japan's pioneer animators. Even today Japanese animators are strongly aware of American animation. But, virtually from the start, postwar Japanese animation has tended to go in a very different direction, not only in terms of its adult orientation and more complex story lines but also in its overall structure. It is important to emphasize the link between television and Japanese animation in terms of anime's narrative structure and overall style.[5] The weekly television format of most series gave rise to certain narrative structures, most notably serial plots, which allowed for longer, more episodic story lines than a cinematic format would have done. This serial quality was also reinforced by animation's connection with the ubiquitous manga, which emphasized long-running episodic plots as well.

The animation industry's connection with television was also crucial in relation to its ability to attract talented people. Riding the wave of television's increasing popularity in the mid-sixties, animation offered openings to a large pool of gifted young animators at a time when live-action cinema seemed to offer fewer opportunities to ambitious artists. Buffeted by the increasing dominance of Hollywood on the one hand and the expansion of television viewing on the other, Japanese live cinema had begun to play it safe. While brilliant directors such as Imamura Shōhei, Itami Jūzō, and, most recently Kitano "Beat" Takeshi, still appear, the typical Japanese film product of recent decades tends to be highly formulaic action films or softcore pornography. Donald Richie, the dean of Western commentators on Japanese film, sums it up when he writes that from the 1970s on "distrust of the new and the original became even more intense."[6]

While this gloomy assessment has been contradicted by the rise of some exciting new filmmakers in the last decade (and the production of some brilliant works from older directors such as Imamura), for a long time it was clear that opportunities for the "new" and "original" were far more likely to be found in the fast-developing—and increasingly commercially important—field of animation. Minamida Misao points to the "sense of new things in a medium full of liberating possibilities," that made the early days so exciting to young animators. He also points out that anime offered a way of going "beyond the framework of [conventional] Japanese entertainment."[7]

By the late seventies, anime in the cinema was also an important trend, although the films were usually tied in with long-running television series. One example is the classic *Space Battleship*

Yamato (Uchū senkan Yamato, 1973), a film based on a television series of the same name. The series was so popular that it inspired long lines outside the theaters the day before the film even opened. Since the early 1980s the OVA market has not only boosted sales at home but has also helped to increase the overseas sales prodigiously. By the end of the 1990s it was clear that anime was an important element of Japan's contemporary culture.

Also, by the 1990s intellectually sophisticated anime were increasingly appearing. The two most important of these were Anno Hideaki's television series *Neon Genesis Evangelion* (Shinseiki Ebuangerion, 1996-1997) and Miyazaki Hayao's film *Princess Mononoke* (Mononokehime, 1997). In each case the work's enormous popularity was equaled by intellectually challenging themes and ideas that stimulated a plethora of scholarly articles, not only about the respective works but also about anime itself. It was clear that anime was finally being recognized, by Japanese commentators at least, as a cultural product genuinely worthy of intellectual study. One particularly interesting example of such a study is Minamida's attempt to define the almost forty years since anime began in terms of a series of transitions of narrative, performative, and even intellectual styles. Working chronologically, he starts with what he calls the "dawn" of anime, treating relatively simple works, such as *Astro Boy,* which privilege black and white characterizations and adventure stories and which concern "love, courage, and friendship." He ends in the 90s, discussing what he considers to be the almost overripe "maturity" that characterizes such complex philosophical works as *Ghost in the Shell* and *Neon Genesis Evangelion,* the profound existential concerns of which would be remarkable even in most live-action films.[8]

But what is perhaps most interesting about Minamida's analysis is his willingness to take anime seriously as a cultural form that deserves intellectual explication. This is in significant contrast to American writing on Western animation, which still tends to look at either the terms of its visuality or its sociological role. The reasons behind this difference are not hard to discover. Simply put, the West does not have the wealth of animated texts to draw on that Japanese scholars do.

ANIME AND JAPAN'S CULTURAL HERITAGE

Why should animation exercise such a powerful hold on Japanese popular culture? The reasons can be found both in Japan's distinctive cultural heritage and in certain key economic realities of art and commerce in the late twentieth century. The most salient economic reality in anime's development is probably the increasing domination of the global film market by Hollywood. While excellent Japanese films are still being produced, they are forced to compete for market share against a flood of American blockbusters. As film writer Stuart Galbraith noted in 1994, "Today it is common to find seven of the top ten box office attractions in Japan to be American movies, and the number of Japanese made films has gone down to a tiny portion."[9] There are exceptions to this situation and some of the most important ones have been animated. For example, in 1988 *Akira* beat out *Return of the Jedi* to become the number one film in Japan. More recently Miyazaki's epic *Princess Mononoke* became the number one film in Japanese box-office history (until it was bested by *Titanic*). Produced for infinitely less money than the Hollywood hits, the two Japanese works are marvels of creativity and imagination. It is clear that animation is perhaps the major area of film in Japan that has strong commercial and artistic potential. It makes sense that filmmakers should put money and effort into an art form that does not directly compete with the Hollywood behemoth but that still appeals to a broad audience.

The cultural reasons behind anime's popularity are more complex. Undoubtedly, one of the most obvious is the relation between anime and the twentieth-century Japanese culture of manga. Although the word "manga" is often translated into English as "comics," manga are not only distinctively different from American comics but they also exercise considerably wider influence in Japanese society than their American equivalents do in theirs. The reasons behind this are twofold. First is their variety of subject matter. Even more so than anime, manga cover a dazzling range of topics. These can include child-oriented fare, such as the sports club stories aimed at boys or the highly inventive, beautifully drawn *shōjo* manga produced for young girls, as well as a vast variety of manga for adults ranging from etiquette journals to the so-called Ladies Comics (*Reideezu komikku*), which are actually explicitly erotic comics targeted at women.

The second reason behind manga's influential role in contemporary society springs from the first. The wide range of manga ensures that virtually everyone reads them, from children to middle-aged salaried workers. Indeed, some estimates go so far as to suggest that 40 percent of material published in Japan is in manga form. As Frederik Schodt, the dean of writers on manga in the West, puts it, "Japan is the first nation on earth where comics have become a full fledged medium of expression."[10]

It is important to understand the connections between anime and the rich and fascinating world of manga. The most obvious one is that of visual style. Although it might be an oversimplification to say that "anime could be considered . . . a kind of animated comic strip,"[11] it is certainly true that there are many pictorial similarities between the two media. Furthermore, as animation scholar Luca Raffaelli suggests, the distinctive cuts, which rely on the viewer's imagination to move the animated story along, undoubtedly come from the unique manga form of visual narration that is very different from the more dialogue-intensive Western comics and graphic novels.

The other crucial link between the two media is the fact that many, if not most, anime are based on stories that appeared first in manga.[12] These anime versions are often quite different from the original, not only because of the different media involved but also because they are frequently directed by people not related to the original manga, sometimes to the indignation of the manga fans. (Oshii Mamoru, for example, tells the story of how his film *Beautiful Dreamer,* based on the immensely popular comic and television series *Urusei Yatsura* by Takahashi Rumiko, earned him the anger of fans to such an extent that some included razor blades in their letters to him.[13]) However, even when an anime is directed by a manga's own writer, the format, time limits, and design strictures of film inevitably lead to significant changes between the texts, as is obvious if we look at such works as Ōtomo Katsuhiro's *Akira* or Miyazaki Hayao's *Nausicaä of the Valley of the Winds.* The print versions of each work allowed space for numerous other characters and for a far more complex story line, while both films used pacing, music, and extraordinary visuals to permit the viewer a truly visceral experience.

The above examples suggest some of the major differences between anime and manga, but it is important to note that both media share a common heritage in a culture that most scholars agree privileges the visual far more than does that of the West. Most commentators on manga suggest that the origins of the form go back at least to the Edo period (1600-1868), and some see its origins even earlier, in the Zen cartoons of the medieval period and the comic animal scrolls of the tenth century. Certainly Edo period works have images that appear to have direct links to both manga and anime, particularly with the kibyōshi, illustrated books with an often humorous and/or erotic content, and the woodblock prints known as ukiyo-e, which featured not only actors and courtesans of the demimonde but, as time went on, increasingly grotesque and imaginative subjects such as demons, ghosts, and extremely creative pornography.[14]

Although it would be impossible to say for certain how much today's animators are consciously influenced by the visual trove of their traditional culture, it seems safe to say that their culture's tradition of pictocentrism is definitely an influence behind the ubiquitousness of anime and manga. Certainly some images from earlier periods would not seem out of place in contemporary anime or manga. Anyone who has seen Hokusai's astonishing 1824 print, *The Dream of the Fisherman's Wife,* which depicts a naked woman lying back with two octopuses sucking her genital area and her mouth while their tendrils coil around her body, cannot help but make a connection between that and the notorious "tentacle sex" scenes occurring in some of anime's more sadistic pornography.

Grotesque images of this sort were particularly common in works from the so-called Bakumatsu (end of the shogunate) and Meiji periods (1868-1912), transitional epochs when Japan was opened to a tidal wave of Western influence at the same time as the culture struggled to preserve its traditions.[15] As art historian Melinda Takeuchi documents,

> [t]he depiction of supernatural themes reached an apogee during the nineteenth century, an age when artists vied with each other to satisfy the public's quickened appetite for images of the bizarre and the macabre. In response to the challenge, illustrators turned back into their cultural past, outwards towards the art of other lands, and inwards to the realm of the imagination.[16]

In many ways this description might well be an apt one for today's animators and manga artists who, even if they do not necessarily work in the modes of the bizarre and the macabre, certainly use an enormous range of cultural references as they explore the realms of their own creative imaginations.

ANIME AND GLOBAL CULTURAL IDENTITY

Perhaps the final reason behind anime's hold on Japanese culture has to do with its participation in global culture. By the late 1990s it was clear that anime both influenced and was influenced by a plethora of Western cultural products. As film scholar Susan Pointon writes of Japanese anime videos:

> It is impossible to ignore the constant cross-pollination and popular cultural borrowing that complicate and enrich anime texts. The creators for the most part are young Japanese artists in their twenties and thirties who have been exposed since birth to Western influences. Despite their Japanese overlay, many of these videos pay generous and excessively scrupulous homage to sources as diverse as American television cop shows of the seventies, European GlamRock fashions of the eighties and French New Wave cinema from the sixties.[17]

Pointon's statement concerning the "constant cross-pollination" occurring between anime and Western popular cultural texts is an important one. For most Japanese consumers of anime, their culture is no longer a purely Japanese one (and indeed, it probably hasn't been for over a century and a half). At least in terms of entertainment, they are as equally interested in and influenced by Western cultural influences as they are by specifically Japanese ones. A similar process is happening in the West as many youths open up to a more international entertainment culture. This relates to a further point Pointon makes, concerning the need to approach contemporary media cultures as "'zones' and 'intersections' where the elements of different cultures collide and mutate."[18] Despite its indisputably Japanese origins, anime increasingly exists at a nexus point in global culture;

this position allows it to inhabit an amorphous new media territory that crosses and even intermingles national boundaries.[19] And this is clearly one of its attractions.

Film scholar Mitsuhiro Yoshimoto has commented that:

> [O]ne of the highly contested issues among those who study the formation of global image culture concerns the connection between global circulation of images and regional boundaries . . . The relevant question is where the image is to be situated in this new global dynamic. Are globally circulated images simply subsumed under the bifurcating tendency of simultaneous globalization and against globalism and localism, or do they reinforce instead the identities of nation-states as a counterforce against globalism and localism?[20]

The answer to this question in terms of anime is a complex but thought-provoking one. First, the appropriate answer to the question of whether anime is being "subsumed" into global culture seems to be "not yet," even though anime's influence is increasing in American popular culture. For example, many anime fans have seen what they believe to be heavy "borrowing" in Disney's 1994 *Lion King* from the Tezuka Osamu classic *Kimba the White Lion*.[21] More recently, John Lasseter, the director of the immensely popular *Toy Story* animated films, has acknowledged the influence and inspiration of the great anime director Miyazaki Hayao.[22] As has already been discussed, however, part of anime's appeal is its "differentness," and this seems likely to remain the case for a long time to come, given how Japanese society remains in certain respects quite dissimilar from that of the West.

The answer to the second part of Yoshimoto's question, concerning whether "globally circulated images" actually reinforce national identity, is an even more complex one. In some ways the content of anime—its particular themes, issues, and icons—is inevitably culturally specific. For example, many anime comedies are set at school, since education is one of the major pivots around which Japanese society revolves. (Many of these comedies are quite subversively inclined toward the educational system, although in a lighthearted way. As with any art form, anime does not simply reflect society, it problematizes aspects of the dominant social culture.) Furthermore, many anime use Japanese historical settings as material for a variety of dramas, comedies, and even fantasies.

But one of anime's most popular genres, science fiction, is the one that is far less likely to be culturally specific. Although many science fiction anime contain significant elements related to contemporary Japanese issues, they are usually played out across "stateless" fantasyscapes of future cities or far-away galaxies. For example the 1970s *Space Battleship Yamato* series simultaneously celebrated such Japanese cultural norms as the notion of collective sacrifice at the same time as it emphasized more transnational values such as universal peace and love. Moreover, as almost every non-Japanese viewer soon notes, the characters in anime often do not look particularly Japanese, instead they participate in what might be called a nonculturally specific anime style. Rather than necessarily reinforcing Japanese cultural identity, it might be at least as appropriate to say that anime narratives, even when they include strong culturally specific situations, problematize the nature of Japanese identity.

In fact, a number of Japanese commentators have chosen to describe anime with the word "*mukokuseki*," meaning "stateless" or essentially without a national identity. Anime is indeed "exotic" to the West in that it is made in Japan, but the world of anime itself occupies its own space that is not necessarily coincident with that of Japan. Unlike the inherently more representational space of conventional live-action film, which generally has to convey already-existing objects within a preexisting context, animated space has the potential to be context free, drawn wholly out of the animator's or artist's mind. It is thus a particularly apt candidate for participation in a transnational, stateless culture.

In a revealing discussion between the critic Ueno Toshiya and the animators Oshii Mamoru and Ito Kazunori, the *mukokuseki* aspect of anime comes up frequently as an expression of what they perceive as Japan's very problematic cultural identity at the start of the twenty-first century. Ueno's position explains anime as a product of what he deems to be Techno-Orientalism, an Othering of Japan by the West that sees it only as a technological dystopia or occasionally as a utopia. Thus, anime may be seen as a dark mirror that reflects Japan to the West and to some extent vice-versa, in that anime also gives Japanese viewers a distinctive vision of non-Japanese worlds. The three commentators are fascinated both by the medium's appeal at home and by its increasing popularity abroad.[23] Groping for an explanation of this popularity, they all seem to agree with a statement made by Oshii that anime is "another world."[24] This "other world," according to Oshii, is created by animators who themselves are "stateless." He supports this point by suggesting that animators do not possess a real "*furusato*" or hometown. The use of the emotionally and ideologically charged word *furusato*, with its lyric evocation of a quintessentially Japanese originary village and landscape, stands in strong contrast to the neutral and abstract *mukokuseki*, suggesting how far anime diverges from traditional Japanese cultural products. For years the *furusato* has been a vital building block in Japan's cultural construction of itself. By rejecting the notion of a *furusato* for the creators of anime, Oshii seems to be implicitly rejecting another precious cultural construct, the notion of Japan's uniqueness.

Another aspect of anime's *mukokuseki* quality in many eyes is the extremely "non-Japanese" depiction of human characters in virtually all anime texts. This is an issue among American audiences new to anime as well, who consistently want to know why the characters look "Western." In fact, while many anime texts do include figures with blond hair, it is perhaps more correct to say that rather than a "Western" style of figuration, the characters are drawn in what might be called "anime" style. This style ranges from the broadly grotesque drawings of characters with shrunken torsos and oversize heads of some anime comedy to the elongated figures with huge eyes and endless flowing hair that populate many romance and adventure stories. And while many of them are blond or light brunette, many have more bizarre hair colorings such as pink, green, or blue.

To Oshii and Ueno this deliberate de-Japanizing of the characters is in keeping with their view of anime as offering an alternative world to its Japanese audience. In fact Oshii suggests that this is part of a deliberate effort by modern Japanese to "evade the fact that they are Japanese,"[25] quoting a provocative statement by the director Miyazaki Hayao to the effect that "the Japanese hate their own faces."[26] Oshii sees the Japanese animators and their audiences looking "on the other side of the mirror," particularly at America, and drawing from that world to create, "separate from the reality of present day Japan, some other world" (*isekai*).[27]

Oshii's statements are not altogether universal, as he himself acknowledges when he admits that Matsumoto Leiji's *Space Battleship Yamato* series has very "Japanese-esque" aspects to it. In fact, virtually all anime contain some Japanese references, from psychology to aesthetics to history. This referencing may be superficial but many works, particularly from Miyazaki's Studio Ghibli, such as *My Neighbor Totoro, Ponpoko,* and *Grave of the Fireflies,* are deeply embedded in Japanese history and culture. Indeed, Oshii's *Ghost in the Shell,* while referencing a dystopian global future and containing many allusions to the Bible, also strongly evokes both Shinto and Buddhist archetypes in its climactic scene.

Oshii's central point, that anime is a world unto itself, however, is essentially correct. The animated space, with its potential for free form creation, is in many ways a realm that exists in counterpoint to the world of modern Japan. Indeed, perhaps the most fundamental reason for animation's popularity in Japan is not just economic constraints and aesthetic traditions but the very flexibility, creativity, and freedom in the medium itself, a site of resistance to the conformity of Japanese society. If this hypothesis is true, it might also explain anime's increasing popularity outside of Japan, for it seems reasonable to argue that this is an appeal that goes beyond the constraints of any specific culture. The very quality of "statelessness" has increasing attraction in our global culture. It is not just Japanese audiences who search for more varied forms of electronic entertainment, who long for an "anywhere," or who are tired of their own faces.

In fact, the popularity of anime, both in Japan and abroad, attests to a new kind of hybridity on the part of a global younger generation that is increasingly electronically conversant with the vast variety of worldwide popular culture. Contrary to Homi Bhabha's vision of "hybridity" in terms of a colonial (or postcolonial) exercise of power and discrimination, this vision of hybridity is an equalizing one. Safe within the stateless fantasy space that anime provides, both Japanese and non-Japanese can participate in trying on a variety of what might be called "postethnic" identities. Although it is true that this fantasy space is the product of the Japanese entertainment industry and may therefore have economic or even politically problematic aspects to it,[28] the anime medium—precisely because it so often highlights characters and settings that are neither clearly Western nor clearly Japanese—offers a space for identity exploration in which the audience can revel in a safe form of Otherness unmatched by any other contemporary medium.

But at the same time as many viewers long for some Other world, many also fear its homogenization into a fantasy space of cookie-cutter themes and theme parks. Perhaps for this reason a basic human fascination with "difference" seems, if anything, to have increased with the entrance into a new and even more complex millennium.[29]

ANIME AND JAPANESE CULTURAL IDENTITY

In order to understand this new hybridized space more fully, it is first necessary to understand anime in relation to the context of Japanese cultural identity. For, while anime has been enormously influenced by global culture, it remains an original product of the concatenation of circumstances that have created the culture of modern Japan. This is a society that even today remains unique, not only for its distinctive culture but for the fact that it is still the only non-Western society to have successfully industrialized virtually every aspect of its economy. Despite the many successes of its Asian neighbors, Japan stands alone as a country that can accurately be described as modern—or indeed postmodern—from a Western point of view.

It is also a society that, in ways both positive and negative, is almost larger than life. The positive is deeply impressive. Not only was Japan the first non-Western nation to modernize successfully, but also it succeeded so well that, during the 1960s and 70s, it became a model for other developing nations. Today it is the world's second-largest economy. Despite some lacks in the social and environmental infrastructure, the standard of living is high, the citizenry is exceptionally well educated, and 90 percent of Japanese consider themselves "middle class." Its arts, from the traditional to the contemporary, are renowned around the world. It is the only Asian country to have two Nobel Prize winners in literature. During the 1980s it seemed that Japanese society, with its superb bureaucracy, efficiently functioning government, and high technological expertise existed as a utopian alternative to what many perceived as the corrupt and decadent societies of the West.[30]

The negative is nightmarish, however. The past 11 years have seen the longest collapse of any stock market in the world since the Great Depression. Japan is still the only country on earth to have suffered atomic bombing, an experience that continues to affect the society today and that has created for many a collective sense of victimhood. Many of its citizens maintain an ambivalent attitude toward America, whose occupying troops in 1945 were the first in Japan's entire history to breach the country's defenses, an event that cast a long shadow over Japan's efforts at constructing its own postwar identity. At the same time Japan's relations with its neighboring Asian countries remain tense because of an unwillingness on the part of the Japanese government to acknowledge past war crimes during its war of aggression in Asia in the 1930s and '40s. In 1995 many Japanese eyes were suddenly opened to the dangers of the modern age when the heart of Japan's capital endured a nerve gas attack by an apocalyptic cult, Aum Shinrikyō, a cult that still attracts adherents today.

The Aum attack is seen by both Japanese and Western observers as a watershed in postwar Japanese history, encapsulating the dark and complex currents that were roiling beneath what many Japanese wanted to believe was still a utopian society. In addressing the reasons behind the attractiveness of Aum and other cults for contemporary Japanese, Ian Reader gives a useful list of the difficult issues confronting Japanese society:

> The stresses and pressures of the education system, which . . . trains people to do little other than pass examinations, the increasingly competitive nature of a society which appears only to emphasize material values and appears spiritually sterile, the erosion, in the cities, of a sense of community and of widely shared values, the alienation and isolation of individuals within the city environment, the political weakness and lack of leadership within society and the perceived weakness of the older religions which have failed to provide moral guidance are all contributory factors.[31]

This complex cultural background, sometimes heady, sometimes traumatic, is brilliantly expressed in anime's range of modes, themes, and imagery. Given the dark events that have permeated Japan's twentieth century, it is hardly surprising that many of anime's most important texts, from Miyazaki Hayao's 1985 *Nausicaä* to Anno Hideaki's 1997 *Evangelion,* are not simply dystopian but deeply apocalyptic, suggesting a society with profound anxieties about the future. The end of the world is an important element in postwar Japanese visual and print culture. Postwar writers such as Ōe Kenzaburō, Abe Kōbō, Murakami Ryū, and Murakami Haruki, have presented literary visions of apocalypse, from nuclear war to a purely psychological endtime. The apocalyptic is also a frequent feature in live-action film, from obvious sci-fi fantasies such as the long running *Godzilla* series to the more complex explorations in the films of Kurosawa Akira, such as the relatively realistic *Record of a Living Being* (*Ikimono no kiroku,* 1955) and his sumptuous late fantasy *Dreams* (*Yume,* 1990). Anime's visual effects, however, seem to lend them themselves particularly well to the apocalyptic, since all kinds of destruction can be easily represented in animation without reliance on costly special effects.

While some of these apocalyptic anime, such as the films of Miyazaki, contain visions of hope and rebirth, most of anime's apocalyptic fare is much darker, centering on the destruction of society and the planet itself. Clearly, the most obvious reason behind the high incidence of apocalyptic scenarios is the atomic bomb and its horrific aftereffects. There are other factors, however, either culturally specific or simply specific to the twentieth century, that contribute to the pervasive darkness of many anime. These include the increasingly alienating aspects of an urbanized industrialized society, the gap between generations, and the growing tensions between the genders, as men lose dominance and women play a wider role outside of the family. More specific to Japan, however, is the decade of economic problems that began with the collapse of the stock market in 1989. The perceived failure (or at least inadequacy) of Japan's postwar economic success has led to an increasing disenchantment with the values and goals that much of postwar Japan has been built on. Although this disenchantment is very obvious in youth culture, which celebrates the ephemeral fashion of the *shōjo* (young girl) and the culture of *kawaii* (cuteness), disillusionment has permeated throughout society, leading to record-breaking suicide rates across the generations. The many apocalyptic anime seem to be expressions of a pervasive social pessimism. Thus, more recent apocalyptic anime, such as *Evangelion*, link violent apocalyptic tropes with intense psychoanalytical probing into dysfunctional psyches to produce a memorable vision of what might be called "pathological apocalypse."

But there is another aspect of Japanese society, both traditional and modern, that anime captures: what I have called the notion of "festival" or its Japanese equivalent, "*matsuri*." The *matsuri* is an integral element of Japanese religious and social life, a celebration of "the realm of play and ritual."[32] Similar to carnival in the West, the liminal space of the festival allows for a kind of controlled chaos, in which "people behave in extraordinary ways, once freed from ordinary time and everyday order,"[33] or, as anthropologist John Nelson says of the *shukusai,* or night festival, there are "aspects of carnival, bacchanalia, and even protest."[34] While some observers emphasize that the Japanese festival is less out of control than the Western carnival and is more concerned with a (temporary) leveling of the social order than its complete reversal, the two forms seem very similar in celebrating a spirit of anarchy that offers a brief playful respite from conformity. In Japan this often involves both sexual and violent themes, usually expressed in the form of a performance for the gods of Shinto, Japan's native religion. As critic Ian Buruma describes *matsuri*, "Pain and ecstasy, sex and death, worship and fear, purity and pollution are all vital elements in the Japanese festival." Buruma goes on to suggest that:

> ... it is this theater of the gods (*matsuri*) that forms the basis of the popular culture in Japan. This primitive, often obscene, frequently violent side of Japanese culture has persisted to this day, despite the frequent disapproval of its raunchier manifestations and the superimposition of more austere and alien forms.[35]

Although anime can have its "austere" side as well, it is certainly true that many works, in their wild humor, grotesque exaggeration, playfulness, sexual content, and violent themes powerfully express this spirit of the festival.

As with apocalypse, the festival mode is frequently found in live-action Japanese films, ranging from the chaotic history of Imamura Shōhei's *Eijanaika* to anarchic comedies such as Itami Jūzō's *Tampopo* or Morita Yoshimitsu's *Family Game,* all of which brilliantly play off of the stereotypical notions of the Japanese as a repressed and quiet people and offer a vision of social and familial disorder. But, as is also true of the apocalyptic mode, animation can add its own special touch to the trope of festival. As with the festival space itself, the space of animation is one that allows for experimentation, fluidity, transformation, and ultimately an entry into a world more radically Other than anything in conventional live-action cinema. The immensely popular television series *Ranma 1/2* and *Urusei Yatsura* of Takahashi Rumiko are comic examples of the festival mode, while fantasy series such as *Saber Marionettes* bring festive anarchy into historical adventure. Intriguingly, the festival mode is often linked to female characters, such as the alien Lum in *Urusei Yatsura* and the giggling but powerful superheroes of *Sailor Moon.* Because Japanese women are still relatively disempowered, the overturning of the stereotype of feminine submissiveness may create a particularly festive resonance. In the animated space, female characters seem to glory in manifestations of power still denied them in the real world.

Anime is not always frenzied and intense, however. The medium also exhibits the lyric and the elegiac mode. The word "elegiac" literally refers to a poem about death written in a style of lamentation and may be taken in a wider sense to refer to a mood of mournfulness and melancholy, perhaps mixed with nostalgia. This wistful mood is an important element in Japanese cultural expression. As anthropologist Marilyn Ivy has shown,[36] contemporary Japanese society shows a strong consciousness of the "vanishing" of many links with tradition, and it is consequently not surprising that some of the greatest works of postwar culture, such as many of the works by the novelist Kawabata Yasunari or the brilliant films of Ozu Yasujiro, may be seen as elegiac. But the elegiac also has links with the long lyric tradition in premodern Japanese culture, in which poetry and romance celebrated the beauty of transience and the bittersweet pleasure that can be derived from the passing of love, youth, and beauty. In the past this mode has been frequently linked to the natural world, the seasons and change of which best epitomize the feeling of transience. Thus, the classical Japanese expression of ephemerality, "*mono no aware*" (the sadness of things), is often connected with natural objects like the cherry blossoms or water imagery.

For example, perhaps the single most lyrical sequence in anime occurs in a scene in Oshii Mamoru's masterpiece *Ghost in the Shell* (Kōkaku kidōtai, 1995) in which water imagery is an important element. In a slow-paced sequence the viewer sees the female protagonist, the cyborg Kusanagi Motoko, in a series of long shots as she travels alone down a city canal in a boat, through drenching rain. By this point the audience has heard Kusanagi give a surprisingly articulate monologue concerning her fears and uncertainties as to whether she actually possesses a human soul. This wordless series of images is even more memorable, however, as it captures her vulnerability, alienation, and fragility through a brilliant combination of beautiful music and images of crowds, water, and rain that are reminiscent of woodblock prints by Hiroshige. The elegiac usually includes a sense of mourning, and this vision of the cyborg pondering her problematic humanity alone among a bustling group of humans suggests a profound sense of loss in relation to the modern world.

As is obvious from the above example, the elegiac mode exists in a variety of genres within anime. It can be found linked to the apocalyptic in Oshii's *Urusei Yatsura Beautiful Dreamer,* but is more likely to be found in such anime romances as Kondo Yoshifumi's *Whisper of the Heart* and Takahata Isao's *Only Yesterday,* which are essentially celebrations of youth, innocence, and nostalgia for a disappearing past. A more literal version of the elegiac mode is Takahata's *Grave of the Fireflies,* which revolves around two siblings' experiences during World War II, focusing in particular on the illness and death of the little sister. While the elegiac mode is perhaps less central to anime than the modes of either apocalypse or festival, it still has considerable influence, adding poignancy to even the most comic or adventurous anime texts. Even the ominously existential *mecha* blockbuster *Evangelion* contains a lyrically pastoral scene in Episode 3 in which its main protagonist, Shinji, briefly escapes to the countryside.

In my view the three modes of apocalypse, festival, and elegy are the most significant ones in anime, but it is important to remember that anime is an immensely wide-ranging popular cultural form. Anime mines all aspects of society and culture for its material, not only the most contemporary and transient of trends but also the deeper levels of history, religion, philosophy, and politics. At its best, anime can be highly creative, intellectually challenging, and aesthetically memorable. But even at its most pedestrian, the incredible variety of animated works can offer rich insights into a complicated and sometimes agonized culture.

In other words, Japanese animation is far more than simply an escape valve for the masses. It is also far more than simply a "reflection" of contemporary Japanese social currents or "compensation" for Japanese social anxieties. Indeed, while certain anime, most notably romantic comedies, do seem to provide a compensatory function, others offer explicit alternatives to social norms. Popular youth-oriented anime series such as the 1980s *Cutey Honey* and the 1990s *Sailor Moon* show images of powerful young women (albeit highly sexualized in the case of *Cutey Honey*) that anticipate genuine, although small, changes in women's empowerment over the last two decades and certainly suggest alternatives to the notion of Japanese women as passive and domesticated. At a more complex level, films such as *Princess Mononoke* actually work to resist and even confront certain public stereotypes, inspiring huge numbers of moviegoers to look at some of the myths of modern Japan in a more critical way.

This subversive aspect of anime is a prominent element in comparison with much of American popular culture. Critics such as Douglas Kellner have suggested that in America, "mass culture . . . articulates social conflicts, contemporary fears, and utopian hopes and attempts at ideological containment and reassurance."[37] While it is certainly true that anime does some of this, much of the best of anime resists any attempt at "ideological containment" and, given the dark tone of many of its most memorable texts, could well be considered a cinema of "de-assurance" rather than one of "reassurance," which film scholar Robin Wood asserts is the dominant tone of most Hollywood films.[38] Even in its less overtly apocalyptic mode, anime tends toward open ended, often tragic story lines, which sometimes include the death of the hero(es), and they are often told within a narrative framework that is deeply critical of contemporary technology and society. While it is also true that anime contains more upbeat fare with at least marginal "happy endings," even these are often more complex and less obviously one-note than the equivalent American sitcom.

Anime's immense range enforces that there is no single anime style and that the "difference" it presents is far more than a simple division between Japan and not-Japan. Anime thus both celebrates difference and transcends it, creating a new kind of artistic space that remains informed and enriched by modes of representation that are both culturally traditional and representative of the universal properties of the human imagination.

PART TWO

*

BODY, METAMORPHOSIS, IDENTITY

AS THE INTRODUCTORY CHAPTERS HAVE SHOWN, issues of cultural identity are a central aspect to a discussion of animation, not only in terms of its reception at home and abroad, but within the medium itself in terms of what it chooses to represent. The very "imaginary" quality of animation allows it to explore these issues in different and perhaps far more creative forms than would be possible in live-action cinema, as the spirited discussion over the non-Japaneseness of human figures in anime suggests. What Scholar J. P. Telotte says about the "robotic fantasy" in American cinema is appropriate for the "animated fantasy" as well, that as an art form it presents "the seductive view of the self as fantasy, able to be shaped and reshaped, defined and redefined at our will."[1]

Indeed, what animation can do to the human body is one of the most interesting and provocative aspects of the medium. Anime representations of the human figure range across an extraordinary variety of types (and archetypes), implicitly promising a vast range of fictional identities for the viewer to revel in. The animated space becomes a magical tabula rasa on which to project both dreams and nightmares of what it is to be human, precisely as it transforms the human figure.

The following chapters explore anime's relation to the body in terms of a variety of genres: the comic, the apocalyptic/horror, the pornographic, and the *mecha* or technological; and it is seen in relation to one of the most important devices in animation, the process of metamorphosis. This is not only to examine the truly awe-inspiring range of body types and archetypes that anime can offer but also to explore the ways in which the body works within each narrative to highlight some of the most explosive issues of Japanese identity. These issues include the schism between generations, the tension between the genders and related issues of masculinity and femininity, the increasingly problematic relationship of human to machine, and the position of Japan vis-à-vis the modern world. Furthermore, although some of these issues are unique to Japan, many more have roots within the technologized global culture of the contemporary world.

Resonant with a complex and ever-changing contemporary society, the animated body is perhaps best understood in relation to the process of metamorphosis. As Paul Wells suggests in his book on animation, metamorphosis may be "the constituent core of animation itself."[2] Since movement is at the heart of animation, animation can and does emphasize transformation in a way that simply no other artistic genre is capable of doing. Even contemporary live-action films with their superb special effects have a jerky uneasy quality when compared with the amazing fluidity of the animated image. As Wells says, "Metamorphosis [in animation] . . . legitimizes the process of connecting apparently unrelated images, forging original relationships between lines, objects etc., and disrupting established notions of classical story-telling . . . [I]n enabling the collapse of the illusion of physical space, metamorphosis destabilizes the image, conflating horror and humor, dream and reality, certainty and speculation."[3]

Part of the pleasure of watching animation is being invited into that destabilized and fluid world. Metamorphosis, known as *henshin* in Japanese,[4] occurs frequently in, and is perhaps even omnipresent throughout, this world, affecting an enormous variety of images from landscape and the natural world to machinery and architecture. The favorite object of transformation is clearly the body, however.

What Scott Bukatman says of superhero comics in America is highly appropriate, both for Japanese comics and for anime as well:

> The body is obsessively centered upon. It is contained and delin-
> eated, becomes irresistible force and immovable object. The body
> is enlarged and diminished, turned invisible or made of stone,
> blown to atoms or reshaped at will. The body defies gravity, space,
> and time . . . [T]he body takes on animal attributes; it merges with
> plant life and melds with metal. The body is asexual and homosex-
> ual, heterosexual and hermaphroditic.[5]

In Japanese animation and comics this protean transforming body is sometimes grotesque (the *Guyver* series, *Akira*), sometimes alluring (*Sailor Moon, Cutey Honey*), but always memorable. From cyborgs to superheroes on the positive side, and from mutants to monsters on the negative, a great many anime texts focus on the process of bodily change. In this fantastic mode, ranging from science fiction to occult pornography, the body interrogates the dominant constructions of identity in modern society—be they gender-based or even human species-based. Some anime texts even go beyond the body to suggest new forms of identity. For example, the cyberpunk masterpieces *Akira* and *Ghost in the Shell,* while initially focusing on the metamorphic potential of the body, ultimately end up privileging the absence of the body. Each film ends with its protagonist potentially giving up his or her corporeal self to move into a transcendent, noncorporeal state of being.[6]

The following chapters examine the transforming body within a variety of anime texts, from the martial arts comedy *Ranma 1/2* and hardcore pornography of such works as *La Blue Girl* to classic *mecha* (robotic or technologically themed anime) like *Ghost in the Shell.* The texts contain other commonalities as well. Although ranging across a broad continuum of genres, they all take place within either a fantastic or a science fiction framework. Indeed, what is called here porno-graphic anime might be more appropriately termed: science fiction and occult animation with explicitly sexualized imagery and themes. Conversely, even the "hard" robotic science fiction animation contains a paradoxical sexual subtext in its implicit problematization of sexual and gender boundary-crossings. The *mecha* genre also contains aspects of the occult and the gothic as well, as can be seen in *Ghost in the Shell* and *Evangelion*. Furthermore, all of the works discussed participate in the modes of apocalypse, festival, and elegy, with occult pornography sometimes participating in all three modes at the same time. Perhaps most important, because of their literally "fantastic" settings and imagery that allow visual imagination free rein, these genres contain some of the most memorable explorations of the body and identity available in animation.

CHAPTER THREE

AKIRA AND *RANMA 1/2:* THE MONSTROUS ADOLESCENT

AKIRA: REVENGE OF THE ABJECTED

> One of the major changes in the representation of the monstrous is
> that it has been increasingly represented as coming from within.
> —Barbara Creed, *The Monstrous Feminine*

DESPAIR AND A FEELING OF ENTRAPMENT are emotions often associated with adolescence. They are also frequently emotions projected onto the adolescent body, an object that becomes the site of a welter of contradictory feelings, from tremulous hope to savage disappointment. This chapter discusses two forms of the representation of the adolescent body in Japanese animation, the confused and terrifying figure of Tetsuo in Otomo Katsuhiro's 1988 tour de force *Akira* and the confused and comic figure of Ranma in the popular late 1980s and early 1990s television series *Ranma 1/2*. Although very different from each other in style and tone, both texts privilege the notion of the adolescent body as a site of metamorphosis, a metamorphosis that can appear monstrous both to the figure undergoing it and to the outside world. What makes the two works fundamentally different, however, is the protagonists' basic attitudes toward metamorphosis. In the case of Tetsuo, he sometimes resists the transformation but also at times nihilistically glories in it, and ultimately asserts his monstrous new identity unflinchingly at the film's end. Ranma's reaction to his transforming body is very different. He continually denies it, searching for a return to "normality" that is forever comically (but perhaps for him tragically) elusive.

Although each anime can and should be enjoyed for its own brilliance, they are also interesting as implicit comments on Japanese society. While Tetsuo's marginal status in *Akira* may at first seem far from the conventional view of Japan as a largely homogenous nation, his character actually evokes a less obvious but deeply significant side of Japanese national self-representation, that of the lonely outcast. As scholar Marie Morimoto describes this identity, "Dominant themes in Japanese cultural self-representation have long been those of uniqueness, isolation, and victimization—hence of a lone nation struggling against all odds."[1] *Akira* appeared in 1988, a time when Japan had reached what has perhaps been its postwar peak of international influence and (mis)recognition, a period when many nations felt threatened by what they saw as Japan's emerging superpower status.[2] Tetsuo's monstrousness can thus be coded in ideological terms as a reflection of Japan's own deep-seated ambivalence at this time, partly glorying in its new identity but also partly fearing it. In certain ways *Akira* opens up a space for the marginal and the different, suggesting in its ending a new form of identity.

It is fitting that we begin our discussion of anime texts with *Akira*, not only because it foregrounds some of the most important themes of this book, such as identity, body, apocalypse, and the festival, but also because it is one of the most famous anime ever made. *Akira* was number one at the box office the year of its release in Japan, even beating out *Return of the Jedi*. Released in America and Europe the following year, it became both a critical and a cult hit and in many ways can be seen as the film that started the anime boom in the West. The film's adult themes of dystopia and apocalypse and its superbly detailed, viscerally exciting animated style amazed Western audiences.[3] *Akira* was also a long-running manga series. Even though the film and manga contain some important differences, the two texts are alike in their edgy dark intensity, encapsulated in the film's antihero, Tetsuo.

Within its visceral spectacle of human destruction, however, is a not-unfamiliar horror film trope of a youth who, made subject to sinister outside powers, is transformed into a monstrous creature, capable of doing great harm to others and to himself. In this case the youth, Tetsuo, is a member of a gang of down-and-out hot rodders (*bosozoku*) who cruise the streets of post–World War III Neo Tokyo looking for action. One of the weaker members of the gang, Tetsuo is initially only noticeable because of his friendship with the gang's leader, Kaneda. Reared together with Tetsuo in an orphanage, Kaneda has always come to the aid of his weaker friend, a situation that, it becomes clear later, has bred a contradictory mixture of dependence and resentment in Tetsuo. A revealing early scene shows Tetsuo attempting to jump-start Kaneda's enormous red motorcycle, only to be laughed at by his stronger comrade.

Film scholar Jon Lewis describes the motor cycle as "the phallic symbol of power and authority"[4] in countless teen films, but, while this is true in *Akira* as well, the motorcycle is also an agent of change, a symbol of subversive flexibility against a monolithic and indifferent state. The vigorous but fluid movement of the motorcycles serves as a kinetically realized contrast with the unmoving structure of power and authority, represented by the enormous massed buildings that rise threateningly in the face of the bikers' charge. The emphasis on movement may also evoke a premodern group of marginals, the so-called *ronin* (literally "wave man"), masterless samurai who roamed Japan in the Edo period and who also worked outside the power structure.

Tetsuo's inability to control Kaneda's motorcycle underlines his weakness and dependence at the beginning of the film, but this soon changes. During a frenzied motorcycle ride Tetsuo encounters a strange, wizened creature beside the enormous dark crater of what used to be "old Tokyo." The viewer later learns that the creature is a psychic child, one of a group of children who, as the result of government experiments with telekinesis, has been frozen into a kind of unnatural aged childhood, imprisoned by his powerful psychic energies. Tetsuo's encounter with the psychic mutant triggers his own immense telekinetic energies, and it is the saga of his growing powers, developing against a dystopian background of civil chaos, religious revivalism, and government oppression that forms the core of the film's narrative. Taken captive by government scientists who experiment on him in an attempt to further develop his powers, Tetsuo soon escapes, wreaking havoc everywhere as he flees across the city in search of "Akira" the entity rumored to be the most powerful of the group of child mutants. In the film's visually brilliant climax we see Tetsuo undergoing a series of mutations as he engages in an all out battle with his former friend Kaneda as well as with what appears to be virtually all of the Japanese Self Defense Force, which is called out to stop him. Ultimately, after going through a variety of increasingly disturbing metamorphoses and destroying much of Neo Tokyo, Tetsuo disappears, apparently taken away by "Akira" and the other psychic mutants.

The film resists closure, however. An ominous earlier episode shortly before his disappearance shows scientists analyzing Tetsuo's psychic patterns and discovering what might be a new universe forming out of them. As Tetsuo's former comrades begin to breathe a sigh of relief, therefore, we hear in voiceover the words, "It's begun." Tetsuo's former comrade Kaneda sees a radiant white dot come down from the sky and closes his hand on it, whispering, "Tetsuo." The film ends with the view of a human eye emitting a dazzling white radiance and a final voiceover, the words "I am Tetsuo."

Tetsuo's unhappy antiheroism represents a form of all-out adolescent resistance to an increasingly meaningless world in which oppressive authority figures administer the rules simply to continue in power. This bleak characterization clearly struck a chord in its Japanese audience. In fact, the brooding figure of Tetsuo became the inspiration behind the filmmaker Tsukamoto Shinya's two avant-garde science fiction films, *Tetsuo I* and *Tetsuo II,* both of which were essentially homages to a particularly dark form of body metamorphosis.

The film's dark subject matter also met with a favorable reception beyond the borders of Japan and it is a perennial favorite among Western viewers' "Top Ten Anime" lists. Clearly, the theme of stubborn adolescent resistance is one that resonates in many corners of global society as Ueno's anecdote concerning *Akira* in Sarajevo, quoted at the beginning of this book, richly illustrates. It should also be acknowledged that a large part of the film's appeal comes from what film critic Tony Rayns describes as "the sheer quality and vigor of the animation itself."[5] It is this combination of brilliant animation with a fascinating, if not incredibly complex and bleak, narrative that has made the film so popular with both domestic and foreign audiences.

Focusing on one of the film's dominant themes, metamorphosis, *Akira* can be looked at on two levels: as a fresh expression of an alienated youth's search for identity and as a cyberpunk meditation on apocalypse. For now, the focus will be on a more personal form of destruction (and perhaps resurrection), what film scholar Peter Boss calls an "intimate apocalypse," the "sense of disaster being visited at the level of the body itself."[6] This, in turn, is related to psychoanalyst Julia Kristeva's notion of abjection, in terms of separation from/ identification with the maternal, as Tetsuo's disaster ridden body crosses gender boundaries to implode into a grotesque scene of birth.[7]

The film fits into a comparatively recently identified subset of the horror genre, a subgenre that has been identified as "Body Horror." As Kelly Hurley defines it:

> "Body Horror" [is] a hybrid genre that recombines the narrative and cinematic conventions of the science fiction, horror, and suspense film in order to stage a spectacle of the human body defamiliarized, rendered other. Body horror seeks to inspire revulsion—and in its own way pleasure—through representations of quasi-human figures whose effect/affect is produced by their abjection, their ambiguation, their impossible embodiment of multiple, incompatible forms.[8]

Akira works remarkably well in this subgenre, for the film's last fifteen minutes or so contain an extraordinary vision of almost unwatchable excess as Tetsuo's mutations become increasingly grotesque. Although hideous, these metamorphoses are also truly spectacular (in the postmodern sense of spectacle) leaving the viewer shaken by feelings of both horror and exhilaration. On a more traditional level, they can be seen as memorably emblematizing the crisis of the alienated adolescent, isolated, vengeful, frightened, and, at a deep level, monstrous both to himself and others.

The film's primary subtext is the tension between the two related but contradictory concepts of power and control (the English word "control"—or "kontororu," as it is pronounced in Japanese—is used frequently throughout the film), concepts that have deep resonance for the adolescent developing from child to adult. At the beginning of the film the oppressive male adult authority structure of government, military, and the scientific establishment (not so different than contemporary Japan, although more extreme) wield all control. However, by *Akira*'s end, we see the total diminishment of authority as, one by one, the representatives of the establishment admit that they can no longer control what is happening around them; this is seen especially in the body of Tetsuo, who they had hoped to use as an experimental guinea pig. While the power of authority diminishes, the young man's power grows, but even he is unable to control it in the end. Total bodily transmogrification into a form of Otherness hinted at in the film's ending is the final price Tetsuo has to pay. Before this occurs however, the viewer is treated to (or subjected to) an awesome spectacle of corporeal mutation that conforms well to Hurley's general description of what happens to the human subject in body horror: "The narrative told by body horror again and again is of a human subject dismantled and demolished; a human body whose integrity is violated, a human identity whose boundaries are breached from all sides."[9]

Tetsuo's metamorphosis is both a literal and a symbolic one: from ordinary human boy to monstrous creature to, perhaps, a new universe; in other words, from impotence to total power. Tetsuo's new powers may also symbolize his development from adolescent into adult, especially since at the film's end he is identified by language rather than image, thus suggesting his entry into the Symbolic order. However, this form of "adult" identity appears to be totally uncontrollable in its arrogation of power, not to mention wholly lacking in any spiritual or moral development.[10]

Furthermore the grotesque visual tour de force of the film's climactic scene casts doubt on any positive interpretation of Tetsuo's newfound identity. These transformations begin with Tetsuo losing his arm in a laser attack by a government satellite.[11] Until this point Tetsuo mostly glories in his new powers and in his ability to destroy humans, buildings and anything else in his path, but the loss of his arm forces him to use his powers on himself. Clearly in enormous pain, Tetsuo telekinetically constructs a new arm, a hideous append-age consisting mainly of veinlike tentacles that grow increasingly longer and larger. Unable to stop the mutations of his arm, Tetsuo uses it to engulf the enigmatic military figure known as the Colonel, who has come to take him back to the government laboratory. The arm goes on to engulf Tetsuo's girlfriend Kaori and his friend Kaneda, although in the case of these two it is uncertain whether this is an attack or a cry for help.

This uncertainty is based on the fact that, as his mutations continue and begin to take over his whole body, Tetsuo's aspect changes from cocky self confidence ("I never knew I could have such power!" he exults at one point) to frenzied desperation. Totally defamiliarized from the wistful adolescent punk he used to be, Tetsuo transforms into a grotesque gigantic infant whose oozing pink flesh seems to overflow the screen. His newly infantile physical condition is matched by a return to his emotional dependency on Kaneda. Whereas previously he had triumphantly shouted his independence, crowing to Kaneda, "I don't need your help anymore," in these final scenes of metamorphosis, he cries out again to Kaneda as he had when they were children. Even Kaneda cannot save him, however. He is left alone to acknowledge for the first time his newfound identity in his final statement, "I am Tetsuo."

Tetsuo's transformations can be viewed as a particularly grue-some form of combined primal and birth scenes: The phallic tentacular arm that expands and contracts ultimately seems to lose itself into an oozing feminine pinkness, which in turn becomes a gigantic baby. This horrifying "birth scene" echoes cinema theorist Barbara Creed's statement that the act of birth is seen as grotesque "because the body's surface is no longer closed, smooth, and intact, rather it looks as if it may tear apart, open out, reveal its innermost depths."[12] This scene also seems to be a classic example of Kristeva's notion of abjection, in which the (male) infant finds the mother's body simultaneously horrifying and erotic. The abject is a state that exists on the borderline of identity between mother and infant, and in order for the infant to attain subjectivity, it is necessary for him to abject the maternal. In Tetsuo's transformation there is, of course, no actual "mother" (significantly, *Akira* contains virtually no representations of a maternal figure or even of any adult female characters). Instead, the moist pink oozing mass that eventually becomes the infant can be seen as the as yet unabjected maternal within Tetsuo himself, an orphan who may at last be finding or perhaps "creating" his lost mother.[13] Oozing across all the normal borders of identity, it is no wonder that Tetsuo's mutating form becomes an object of both horror and fascination. Given access to the secret depths of the body, and being allowed to see the transgressions of the body's boundaries, the viewer cannot quite look away.

The participation of the viewer is important here because, on one level, Tetsuo's transformation may be read in purely cinematic terms as a visual "frenzy of metamorphosis." Tetsuo's "eruptive body" (to borrow popular culture specialist Scott Bukatman's term)[14] becomes an orgiastic spectacle of hideously transmogrifying body shapes that leave the viewer both repulsed but, on some level, perhaps, exhilarated, as the viewer loses him or herself into the overwhelming body catastrophe transpiring on the screen. As film scholar Philip Brophy says of the grotesque transformation scene in the American film *The Beast Within,* "[t]he horror is conveyed through torture and agony, of havoc wrought upon a body devoid of control. The identification [by the viewer] is then leveled at that loss of control—the fictional body is as helpless as its viewing subject."[15] This feeling of helplessness can be perversely pleasurable for the viewer who can enjoy the extremity of the spectacle from a safely detached distance.

But Tetsuo's story is not only a postmodern celebration of spectacle and boundary transgression. It needs also to be read as a deeply ambiguous rite of passage story. Tetsuo's outsider status, his rivalry with Kaneda, and his negative attitude toward authority position him as a classic alienated teenager whose mutations are also visual expressions of his own adolescent angst. Again, Kristeva's notion of abjection, this time in the sociocultural sense of the expulsion from the body politic of what is marginal, outcast, or simply "unclean," is useful here since Tetsuo and his friends (and the original mutant subjects) are all coded as social excrescences. It is worth remembering that Tetsuo's first encounter with the mutants is beside the crater of old Tokyo. This "hole" has many associations with the abject. As a crater from a nuclear bomb it brings up links with death and destruction, unwelcome intrusions into the empty glittering world of Neo Tokyo. Psychoanalytically, the crater may be read in terms of both the vagina and the anus. Coded as the female organ, the crater evokes the dryness and emptiness of atrophy and absence, once again underlining the absence of the maternal throughout the film. Coded as the body orifice associated with excretion, the crater is a metonym for the status of the bikers and the mutants, children and adolescents necessary only as fodder for the industrial and scientific demands of their dystopian world.

In many regards Tetsuo conforms well to Bukatman's description of the outcast mutants of American comic books: "While they want to fit in, mutants know their birthright is to exist 'outside' the normative. They are categorical mistakes of a specific type; they are, in short, *adolescents*."[16] This characterization is also appropriate for Tetsuo's story as a whole, which is a classic example of the adolescent fascination with what Freud calls the "omnipotence of thought,"[17] the ability to use psychic powers to change the world around oneself, a world that is seen as disappointing, rejecting, and dangerous. Thanks to his newly found telekinetic powers, Tetsuo can indulge in wish-fulfilling vengeance on the world that has disappointed him. As Bukatman says of the outsider mutant's attitude toward the social system, "At issue is not whether our social system is well- or ill-articulated; at issue is the mapping of the adolescent subject onto a social order that is *perceived by that subject* as arbitrary, exclusionary, and incomprehensible."[18]

Ultimately, Tetsuo manages to revenge himself on the social order (and implicitly on his parents who abandoned him to the orphanage), succeeding in virtually destroying it in the violence and explosions that strew the second half of the film. Given the generally safe and contained nature of Japanese society, this orgy of destruction is especially interesting. While Tetsuo, in his down-and-out biker identity, is clearly not a "normal" teenager (if there are any left in the film's dystopia), it seems likely that his anger and vengefulness may have touched a chord among the viewing public who made the film such a popular hit. Even among those viewers who were no longer adolescent, the image of a youth going up against and destructively triumphing against a repressive society that in certain ways was a daring but not totally distant defamiliarization of today's Japan, is likely to have had a cathartic effect.

Tetsuo's "accomplishments" come at a cost, however. His powers and the newfound arrogance that come with them alienate his few remaining friends and in the end, like so many of the protagonists of horror films, he is utterly alone. His "intimate apocalypse" has been vengeful not only to others but to his core identity as well. The eye that stares out at the audience at the film's end may suggest a new form of vision but, given the nihilistic events of the film's narrative, it seems reasonable to imagine that the final vision is a cold one, detached from any human concerns. The movie's nihilistic celebration of abjection and finally of extinction suggest no hope for change within the actual fabric of society.

RANMA 1/2: "DON'T YOU KNOW THE DIFFERENCE BETWEEN A BOY AND A GIRL DADDY?"

Segregating the sexes during childhood and defining the contexts and nature of their encounters later on, Japanese society defines gender roles with adamantine rules. In the realm of the imaginary, the strict roles encapsulating male and female are broken, being transgressed in fantasies which can be singly and variously violent, sadistic, maudlin, sentimental or comical . . .

—Nicholas Boronoff, *The Pursuit and Politics of Sex in Japan*

. . . identification is always an ambivalent process. Identifying with a gender under contemporary regimes of power involves identifying with a set of norms that are and are not realizable, and whose power and status precede the identifications by which they are insistently approximated. This "being a man" and this "being a woman" are internally unstable affairs. They are always beset by ambivalence precisely because there is a cost in every identification, the loss of some other set of identifications, the forcible approximation of a norm one never chooses, a norm that chooses

us, but which we occupy, reverse, resignify to the extent that the
norm fails to determine us completely.

—Judith Butler, *Bodies that Matter*

While *Akira* turns its back on normality to present an extravagant
spectacle of the monstrous, *Ranma 1/2,* our next work to be discussed,
portrays its eponymous hero as frenziedly seeking the normal. Both
Akira and *Ranma 1/2* play on the motif of the changing adolescent
body but while *Akira* presents the changing body as menacing, *Ranma
1/2* uses it largely for comic effect. To put it another way, *Akira* is
fundamentally apocalyptic, although it participates in the festival
mode, while *Ranma 1/2,* although containing episodes of destruction
and even elegiac interludes, is largely a celebration of the festival. Both
texts feature adolescent protagonists who deal with such classic
adolescent issues as isolation, jealousy, and generational conflict,[19]
constructed around the motif of uncontrollable metamorphoses. However, in keeping with *Ranma 1/2*'s festival mode, and in sharp contrast
to *Akira*'s vision of Armageddon, *Ranma*'s metamorphoses threaten but
never completely overturn the social structure. Furthermore, the
metamorphoses in *Ranma 1/2* are gendered ones, from male to female
or vice versa, which raises issues of sexual identity that Tetsuo's lonely
monstrousness only subtextually evokes.[20]

Like *Akira*, *Ranma 1/2* is based on a long-running comic book
series (by the immensely popular female artist Takahashi Rumiko) and
has inspired feature-length movies as well. For our purposes we will
concentrate on the long running animated television series. Since the
series went on for many episodes, a slightly different form of analysis
is called for than with an epic film such as *Akira*. Due to the episodic
nature of television comedy there is far less emphasis on character
development or an overall story line (although many might argue that
Akira is not nearly as structured as an American science fiction or
horror film would be). What is emphasized in *Ranma 1/2* are certain
comic tropes such as pursuit, mistaken identity, and usually amusing,
sometimes poignant, character interaction.

Popular in the late 1980s and early 1990s, the series is an
imaginative comic romance that plays with gender (mis)identification
through a fantasized form of transsexuality. Ranma Saotome, the hero

of the series, is fated to transfer back and forth between male and female, due to the workings of an arbitrary curse. Unlike the protagonists of such famous Western treatments of cross dressing as *Tootsie* or *Yentl,* Ranma has no choice in the matter. He is a literal representation of Butler's vision of the "norm that chooses us."[21] Unfortunately for Ranma, two norms choose him, and his very public and haphazard boundary-crossing between male and female creates confusion not only for him but also for those around him. They are uncomfortably aware of a threatening destabilization of social boundaries without necessarily understanding the reasons for their own discomfort. *Akira* plays with boundaries in order to break them, but *Ranma 1/2* plays with them to a different, ultimately conservative, effect. Despite its emphasis on boundary transgressions, humorous generational reverses, and explicit (although humorous) sexual content (both reminiscent of the festival and the carnival), *Ranma 1/2's* transgressions are always contained within the realistic space of the "normal" world. While boundaries are crossed and re-crossed to often riotous effect, the inevitably more conservative format of a weekly television series ultimately leads to a conservative resolution in which, at the end of each episode, the boundaries are reinscribed into the conventions of heterosexual hierarchical society.

Ranma 1/2 operates on at least two levels: the issue of constructing gender identity at the individual level and the public level of society's expectations for gender norms, both of which are played out in the series through a range of imaginative visual tropes and action sequences that consistently work to destabilize the "normal." Because *Ranma 1/2* is a comedy, these forms of destabilization are frequently very funny, as Ranma makes his/her way across a somewhat unconventional but still familiar contemporary landscape of school and family, unwittingly spreading confusion and sometimes outright craziness at every turn. At times the very wildness and unexpectedness of the comedy can lead to moments of liberating self-knowledge on the part of its protagonists. At other times, however, the series seems to be more in-line with such Western gender bending comedies as *Some Like It Hot* or *I Was A Male War Bride* in which gender crossing is held up only as an amusing performance that temporarily disturbs but never actually unsettles society's basic assumptions about the genders.[22]

In contrast to the cyberpunk future of *Akira, Ranma 1/2* is set in a fairly realistic teenage world, into which a bizarre or alien element suddenly interjects itself. In the case of *Ranma 1/2*, it is the hero who is the "alien," but his marginalization is of a very different sort than that of Tetsuo. Ranma is simply a regular high school boy who falls into a magic spring while practicing martial arts with his father. The magic of the spring causes him to turns into a girl when touched by cold water and to return to male form when touched by warm water. Ranma's father, Mr. Saotome, is also magically cursed by falling into a spring that turns him into a giant panda, a condition that is also alleviated with hot water. Since rainy days, hot baths, and ponds or pools abound in the series, the opportunities for inadvertent metamorphoses are plentiful. It is important to note, however, that Mr. Saotome's panda guise causes little consternation. It is Ranma's gender transformation that is the key narrative impetus in the series.

Most of the series' action takes place in urban Japan, principally around the dōjō (martial arts hall) owned and resided in by the Tendō family (a father and his three daughters, with whom Ranma and his father seem to be permanent guests) and the Furinkan high school, which Ranma attends along with the Tendō daughters. Of the daughters, the youngest, Akane, is the most fully developed character. Like Ranma, she too is a brilliantly gifted martial artist, but she is also a tomboy who insists that she hates boys, although they constantly flock to her beauty.

The opening episode of *Ranma 1/2* is worth looking at in some detail as it displays some of the most prominent tropes and tensions maintained throughout the series. In the opening scene the "camera" follows what appears to be a young girl in Chinese dress and pigtails as she argues with a giant panda while they walk down a rainy street. As agitated onlookers scatter, the panda picks up the girl and slings her over his shoulder. The action cuts to the Tendō's Japanese style house complete with a traditional pond. They are anxiously awaiting the arrival of their father's old martial arts companion, Mr. Saotome, and his son Ranma. Mr. Tendō tells his daughters that he hopes that Ranma might choose one of them to marry and thus carry on the "Tendō family tradition." The girls are curious but skeptical, especially Akane—she is introduced in a scene where she is being warned by her older sister that "the boys" will think she is "weird" if she continues her absorption in martial arts. Akane resists the idea of a fiancé chosen by her father, arguing that the daughters should have a say in whom they are going to marry.

As they talk, the doors open and the giant panda and Chinese girl appear, much to everyone's consternation. The girl announces that she is Ranma and Mr. Tendō, choosing to believe that "she" is a boy, folds her in a close embrace only to become uncomfortably aware that "he" has breasts. His daughters laugh sardonically and one of them, poking Ranma's breasts, asks "Don't you know the difference between a boy and a girl, Daddy?"

The rest of the episode consists of the Tendō family's gradual realization that this may be a difficult question to answer since Ranma is also a boy. Akane, who is at first pleased that Ranma is a girl and suggests that they be friends, is the first to discover Ranma's duality. She goes into the family bath only to discover Ranma, who has been changed back into boy form by the bath's hot water. Shrieking "pervert!" she runs naked from the bath, followed by Ranma. Ranma explains the story of his and his father's change but the girls are more amused than sympathetic. Akane's older sisters laughingly suggest that "Akane would be the wisest choice [for marriage] since she hates boys . . . and Ranma's half a girl." Akane, however, is affronted by the suggestion, calling Ranma a pervert for having seen her naked. He points out that, "You took a pretty good look at me [while I was naked]. And anyway, it's no big deal to see a naked girl since I see myself plenty of times, and *I'm* better built to boot." Akane becomes even angrier and Ranma mournfully thinks to himself "So much for being friends when she found out that I'm a boy." The episode ends with Ranma (now in female form) and Akane once again confronting each other nude in the bathroom. The two stalk off in silence and go to complain to their respective family members.

In this opening episode (and in many of the best episodes of the series) the narrative is structured around a series of reversed expectations through which both characters and audience are consistently surprised, and, in the case of the characters, often outraged. Appropriate to the world of the festival, normal social conventions are consistently undermined. What is anticipated to be a traditional reunion among old friends becomes a bizarre and disturbing event. Taking a bath leads to a frightening and unexpected encounter. And a boy makes fun of a girl's body by telling her that his body is "better built." This kind of complex plot, replete with humorous surprises involving gender transgression, is one that is familiar to Western audiences as well, at least as far back as the time of *Twelfth Night*. Like the Shakespearean comedies and many others up until recently, the comic and fantastic nature of the plot, while thoroughly enjoyable on the surface, is also one that serves to hide or displace some important and serious issues of power and identity.

Thus, the comic high points of this opening episode are often predicated on a variety of tensions around which the series revolves. The most important of these have to do with gender identification on both a personal and a public level. At the personal level, the viewer watches the appealing characters of Ranma and, at certain moments, Akane as they attempt to construct their gender identities while navigating the confusing tides of adolescence. At the public level, the series shows the gender norms that society attempts to impose upon them through the agencies of school and family. Issues of sexual identity, generational conflict, and societal confusion, are all invoked through Ranma's constant and haphazard transformation as he becomes variously an object of fear, derision, puzzlement, and, most often, desire.

Examining *Ranma 1/2* first from the point of view of individual development, it is worthwhile to consider cultural studies scholar Elizabeth Grosz's description of adolescence and the body in *Volatile Bodies* where she asserts that

> [adolescence] is the period that the subject feels the greatest discord between the body image and the lived body, between its psychical idealized self-image and bodily changes . . . The adolescent body is commonly experienced as awkward, alienating, an undesired biological imposition.[23]

Ranma's "discord" between image and reality is literally enacted for him in his constant transformations and is further emphasized by the reactions of those around him who, as we saw in the first episode, become puzzled, shocked, or even angry upon witnessing his metamorphoses. On the most general level, we can see this discord as going beyond body or even gender construction and instead expressing simply the agonies attendant on the construction of identity in adolescence. Stripped of its fantasy elements, the opening episode can be viewed as a classic encapsulation of some of the problems attendant on growing up, adolescent loneliness, in particular. Neither boy nor girl, Ranma occupies a liminal space that, although played for comedy, is actually a forlorn and isolated one. Unlike the typical narcissistic adolescent who simply *feels* "different," Ranma *knows* he is different, and therefore isolated. Or as he puts it at the end of the episode, "Friends, she says: so much for being friends when she found out that I'm a boy."

Ranma's statement of disappointment brings us back to the body confusion that expresses his alienation and raises the question *why* can't Akane be friends with him now that she knows he's a boy. The answer lies in the strict gender construction on which his and Akane's world is based. As Boronoff says in the quotation at the beginning of this section, "Japanese society defines gender roles with adamantine rules." In fact, these adamantine rules are not restricted to Japan (although it is true that the sexes are more segregated there than in the West) but are universal ones that bear particular weight during the tumultuous period of adolescence. Despite the carnival-esque nature of the situations they are thrust into, neither Akane nor Ranma himself can go beyond the rules of the real world, particularly because they are adolescents, a stage where ambiguity can be alluring but at the same time is deeply frightening. To quote Grosz again, "it is only in adolescence that it becomes clear that the subject has a sexual, i.e., genital, position *whether this is wanted or not*."[24] The unfortunate Ranma who was presumably just beginning to come to grips with the male sexual subject position is now forced to express the female one as well and in extremely graphic and often humiliating terms.

Thus, although references to genitalia are conspicuous by their virtual absence in *Ranma 1/2,* the sexual signifier of breasts is constantly invoked throughout the series to denote that something is "wrong." This is clear in the opening episode where Mr. Tendō attempts to ignore the strange fact that he has a giant panda and a Chinese girl in his living room by embracing the "male" Ranma, only to fall into a faint at the evidence of Ranma's breasts, a sexual signifier that he is simply unable to process into his orderly world. Even more telling is Ranma's flashback to his initial discovery of his female transformation. In that scene Ranma rises from the spring, tears open his shirt, stares at his breasts in shock, and shrieks.

The fact that breasts, the signifier of femininity, mark the alien is significant. Although it is true that many gender bending comedies emphasize men with false breasts for comic effect, in Ranma's case his breasts are not only comic but—initially at least—horrifying as well.[25] It is interesting to note that the other consistent metamorphoses occurring throughout the early part of series are also enacted *only* by men. Ranma's father becomes a panda, a guise in which he seems quite comfortable, since the viewer often sees him in panda form happily reading his newspaper while munching on a stick of bamboo. Ryōga, one of Ranma's competitors transforms into an adorable miniature pig, unhappily at first, but he becomes increasingly philosophical about it as he realizes that this allows him to sleep with Akane. It is clear therefore that the male is the norm, and it is the female that is one of a variety of attributes (including panda-ness, pig-ness) that signify difference. Furthermore, being female is coded as being inferior to either a pig or a panda.

Whereas turning from female into male is usually seen in many fantasies as a means of empowerment, Ranma's transformation from male to female is clearly coded as negative. As scholar Rebecca Bell-Metereau puts it in her discussion of androgyny and cross-dressing in Western film, "[I]mpersonating a woman involves anxiety over loss of power, because it means that the male must identify with a typically lower-status figure."[26] In the first episode, for example, Ranma's father tosses him into the Tendō's pond, shouting "you have betrayed the honor of this house." Later on in the same episode his father is even more direct shouting, "Ranma, you sound like a girl!" He then picks up Ranma-as-boy and throws him into the pond again, presumably to have Ranma's form correspond to his "girlish" behavior. Ranma's very identity as a martial artist is threatened as well, because he is shorter and physically weaker as a girl. In a later episode Ranma is forced to enter in a martial arts competition while stuck in girl form. Although he wins in the end, his friends have little confidence in him because they are aware that even his martial arts expertise may not make up for his female limitations. Ranma's girlishness thus adds an extra tension to an already intense action sequence.

Ranma-as-girl is a problematic figure. Physically weaker than the boy Ranma, a disappointment to his father, a puzzlement to his peers, rejected by a girl he likes (Akane), Ranma-as-girl is the fantastic embodiment of certain key adolescent fears. Perhaps one of the most terrifying of these fears is what literary scholar Eve Sedgewick calls "homosexual panic," the fear of the heterosexual male that he is really homosexual. This fear is played out in a variety of episodes throughout the series.

The first and most obvious example occurs in the second episode of the series, when Ranma first enters high school. Ranma attempts to rescue Akane from the loathsome attentions of Kuno, a pompous upperclassman who is also a master kendo swordsman. Unfortunately, Ranma turns into a girl while in the midst of a martial arts fight with Kuno and Kuno falls in love with "the pig-tailed girl" not realizing that "she" is actually the boy he is trying to fight. Kuno's confusion and Ranma's embarrassment come to a head when Ranma meets Kuno after school the following day for what Ranma expects to be fight. Instead of bringing his sword, however, Kuno offers flowers to Ranma-as-girl, telling him "I love you." As for Kuno's feelings toward Ranma-as-boy, he has taken an active dislike, taunting him for his cowardice and asserting "that man is no man."

The episode after this encounter with Kuno opens with a dream sequence in which Ranma imagines himself naked in the bath in his male form and confronting Kuno, who tells him, "I love you." Shouting, "Look at me you fool, I'm a guy," Ranma suddenly falls into a swimming pool where the cold water turns him into a female. Naked in the pool Ranma imagines that he is surrounded by a circle of naked Kunos who chant to him "I love you. I would date you." Waking up covered with sweat, Ranma thinks "That Kuno's sick!"

Once again, this episode is played for comedy with the rather effete and pompous Kuno being the butt of the joke. The fear of homosexuality that is the episode's subtext however, lends it a slightly more serious tone than many episodes in the series. When Kuno shouts "that man is no man" the obvious joke is again on Kuno because he is unknowingly technically correct, since Ranma is half woman as well. But the unconscious joke is on Ranma who projects his own fears of being "sick" (i.e., not heterosexual) onto Kuno. In addition, when Ranma tries to assert his masculinity in his dream (nightmare), his own body betrays him, nakedly revealing its essential femininity to an equally naked Kuno who circles him in a threatening and engulfing manner. It is hardly surprising that Ranma wakes up covered with sweat.

Even more potentially disturbing is a much later episode, "*Watashi te Kiree? Ranma no onna sengen*" ("Am I Pretty? Ranma's Declaration of Womanhood") in which Ranma loses control of both his body and his mind in a manner that links him explicitly to both homosexuality and androgyny. Struck on the head by Akane, Ranma loses all memory of himself as a boy and believes that he is a girl, who unaccountably sometimes takes on the form of a boy. In his new mental state Ranma becomes parodically feminine. Being forced to hang up boys underwear (his own), Ranma bursts into tears but is delighted when Akane invites him to go shopping. At the department store, however, he creates a scene when in his male form he picks up a bra and models it, asking Akane "Do you think this will look good on me?," which causes the other customers to turn on them in horror. As a final humiliation, Ranma tries to use the men's room but is too embarrassed to urinate. Later on at home, he faints at the sight of blood, and that night comes into Akane's room "too frightened" to be able to sleep by himself.

The extremely broad sexual stereotyping of this episode is emphasized in the Japanese language version by the exaggeratedly feminine language Ranma now uses. Given that Ranma usually speaks quite roughly when in either male or female form, the emphatic feminine language is particularly disconcerting to his family and friends. At one point, Akane even angrily says, "Stop talking like a faggot!" (okama mitai na hanishikata yamenasai—the English dubbing has "stop speaking so affectedly" but the Japanese version uses the explicit term "okama," a slang term for homosexual). The episode veers away from dealing with homosexuality per se, however, and instead develops into an intriguing and even refreshing treatment of androgyny. Ranma-as-girl insists that she truly feels much more at home as a girl, asserting that, "The real me has awakened and the other person was just fake memories."

Ranma does seem to throw himself into femininity, becoming a truly sweet and obliging person. While Ranma's father and Mr. Tendō become increasingly reconciled to Ranma's new girl persona, especially after he cooks them a delicious meal, Akane grows more and more distraught. Ultimately, she ends up weeping for the old "nasty"

Ranma to return. Fortunately for Akane, Ranma ends up hitting his head again and turns back into his male self and she shrieks in delight "Oh Ranma, you've come back."

The episode is an interesting one not only for its exceptionally broad pandering to traditional gender stereotypes but also for how much Ranma seems to thrill in being a girl. While his hesitant characterization of "the real me" as feminine is of course played for laughs, it also at least momentarily points to an insistent bisexuality or even androgyny at the heart of *Ranma 1/2*. One of the pleasures of this series is the fact that male and female viewers can play with the idea of taking on masculine and feminine roles. The fact that both fathers actually come around to *accepting* Ranma as a girl is a particularly interesting reversal, especially when we recall earlier episodes in which his father seemed about to disown him because he had changed into a girl. In intriguing contrast, this episode actually shows the two fathers agreeing that the new "all girl" Ranma might actually work to "balance out" Akane's tomboyishness creating a more harmonious collective family. Despite the initial annoyance at his "homosexual" style language, this episode seems to suggest the availability of a wider continuum of sexual choices than the final inevitably conservative affirmation of boundaried heterosexuality ("Oh Ranma, you've come back") would seem to offer.

The only person who is really bothered by Ranma's new femininity is Akane and it is interesting to examine her character in relation to these questions of homosexuality and androgyny. It is clear that Ranma is not the only character with a confusing gender identity in the series. This is obvious from the first episode in which her sister, finding her practicing martial arts alone in the training hall, tells her, "No wonder the boys think you're odd." Akane responds, "At least I don't only think about boys." Akane is in many ways Ranma's feminine "double," both mirroring and distorting his own gender identity problems. Although she is attractive and feminine (and without overtly masculine speech patterns), Akane is clearly shown as "different," not only from her sisters, but also from the other high school girls. In fact, her devotion to the martial arts causes severe problems. In an amusingly outrageous sequence in the second episode, Akane is seen confronting all the boys in her high school as she enters the schoolyard. She is forced to defend herself against a vast array of attacks by athletes in virtually every field, from sumo wrestlers to tennis players, all of whom are competing in order to win the chance to "date" her. Akane's only response is to take on and defeat every one of them, all the while intoning "I *hate* boys! I *hate* boys."

Akane's gender coding is thus in some ways more extreme than that of Ranma who, even as a boy, seems to like girls. However, she is carefully presented as having feminine aspects as well. One of the series subplots involves Akane's unrequited love for the family doctor, Dr. Tofu, who is passionately in love with her elder sister. As the series progresses, Akane's unrequited love for Dr. Tofu begins to dissipate and there are increasing suggestions that she and Ranma are beginning to appreciate each other. Well before the "Am I Pretty?" episode, Ranma is shown as becoming more sensitive and kind, especially where Akane is concerned, and Akane, while often furious with him, occasionally acknowledges his sensitivity.

While, as Butler says, "there is a cost to every identification," sometimes there may be a benefit as well. The two protagonists' implicit identification with the opposite sex opens up the potential for genuine self-knowledge and even, in Ranma's case at least, empathy for the opposite sex. As the series develops, Ranma overcomes the problems of his physical weakness as a girl by relying more on strategy than physical strength. In various episodes he learns to use his female attractiveness for manipulative purposes and in a later episode (Episode 15) he even begins to enjoy indulging his fondness for sweet deserts, a partiality coded as feminine in Japan. Although it is never explicitly suggested that Ranma is growing more in touch with his feminine side, his behavior appears to develop what would traditionally be considered a more feminine style.[27] Furthermore, while Ranma-as-girl is essentially negatively coded by society, it is Ranma-as-girl who engenders all the narrative excitement, adding an intriguing note of androgynous fantasy to what otherwise might be a more standard martial arts comedy.

In fact, Ranma-as-girl in her Chinese clothes and pigtail is very attractive, perhaps because her Sinicized accoutrements are a displaced reflection of the more profound Otherness of Ranma's primary masculine sexuality. As both male and female, Ranma suggests an extremely appealing form of androgyny, one that recalls the so-called *bishōnen* ("beautiful boy" comic books), which often contain explicitly homosexual encounters while at the same time being largely targeted at young female readers.[28] The *bishōnen* comic books are only one example from a larger fantasy world in Japanese culture in which androgyny and gender-crossing are staple tropes.[29] What Boronoff calls the "realm of the imaginary" includes such famous cultural institutions as the all-male kabuki theater where *onnagata*, or female impersonators, were traditionally raised from boyhood to be more womanly than a woman. A more contemporary example of gender-bending fantasy would be the renowned Takarazuka acting troops, in which women take all the parts in plays that themselves often revolve around plots based on comic books including *bishōnen* comics.[30] What is unusual about *Ranma 1/2*, however, is that the protagonist's particular "realm of the imaginary" keeps colliding with the "real world" of high school and family. This provides a different kind of tension in the series that the more purely fantastic treatments do not.

The relation between body image and desire is paramount in Ranma's relations with the outside world. His public transformations ensure his objectification by others in a variety of ways. To his father his transformations make him an object of embarrassment. To others they are a source of fascination and he becomes an object of desire. Kuno no doubt finds the "pig tailed" girl particularly attractive because of her mysterious provenance and tendency to disappear abruptly. Many others find him/her an object of intense desire as well. Indeed, much of the action in subsequent, increasingly broad episodes consists of Ranma fleeing various male and female figures who have fallen madly in love with one or the other of his identities. The mad pursuit of the ever-transforming Ranma, and the ambiguously gender-coded Akane is evocative of Shakespearean comedy in which cross-dressing becomes a catalyst for a variety of misidentifications and misadventures.

As in Shakespeare, Ranma's changes usually set into motion an intense amount of narrative activity revolving around pursuit and competition. The object of pursuit/competition is usually Ranma, although sometimes also Akane. At other times it is Ranma himself pursuing the ultimate prize, the magic that will turn him back into a boy permanently. Later in the series, the theme of pursuit and desire widens to include Happosai, an old man who, despite being introduced as Mr. Saotome and Mr. Tendo's martial arts master, is usually presented as a shrunken old lecher in pursuit of panties and bras.

Competition, the other hallmark of the series, appears as various forms of martial arts or athletic tournaments. The series contains an inordinate number of scenes of frenzied activity as one or more of the characters is either chased by a huge crowd or forced to perform in increasingly bizarre forms of competition including even a martial arts ski tournament. Accompanied by fast-paced music, the images speed by at a dizzying pace, but the prize (Ranma, Akane, panties, magic potions) is never permanently won, allowing for ever more bizarre variations on the theme.

The series' twin themes of pursuit and competition can also be read as comic and/or fantastic exaggerations of contemporary Japanese society. While the frenzied but essentially aimless motion of the bikers in *Akira* underlined the contrast between them and their immovably dystopian society, the privileging of movement in *Ranma 1/2* suggests a parody of the intensely pressured real world of contemporary Japan in which everyone—workers, students, housewives—is in constant pursuit of some ever-receding goal.

Although played as festive comedy, the underlying sense of oppressive pressure is hard to avoid. Thus, the scene in which the entire spectrum of athletes vies for Akane mixes the themes of competition and pursuit in a scene that is both ferociously comic but also strangely unsettling in its fantastic exaggeration; every time Akane dispatches one pursuer/competitor another takes his place. Interestingly, many of the series' episodes revolve around competition among girls who compete as ruthlessly (and sometimes more craftily) than the boys.

Perhaps the most consistent display of competition, however, is between the generations, specifically between Ranma and his father, who are constantly fighting. Much of this is clearly for humorous effect as Ranma and his father throw each other into water and switch constantly back and forth between male and female and human and panda. But the sharply clear note of rivalry is impossible to ignore, as when Mr. Saotome complains that his son has disgraced him by being a girl and Ranma appropriately ripostes, "who are you to talk? . . . My old man is a panda!"

While far removed from the rage that Tetsuo turns on authority figures in *Akira*, this riposte still suggests some deep divisions between the generations, especially in relation to the father. The fall in the stature of the father since World War II has been a staple theme in much of Japanese culture both high and popular, and both the passive panda Mr. Saotome and the amusingly inept Mr. Tendō are honorable descendants in a long line of inadequate father figures.[31] In this regard it is interesting that so much of the conflict between father and son takes place in the traditional setting of the dōjō. The house, hall, and garden are all exemplary models of traditional Japanese culture and the contrast between their traditional serenity and the constant thumping, transforming, and splashing of father/panda and son/ Chinese girl makes for superb comic dissonance while also evoking the unsettling strangeness of change that has penetrated even into the most traditional corners of Japan.

Faithful to its comic form *Ranma 1/2* always manages, if only barely, to contain the chaos each episode unleashes. The tropes of adolescence such as generational conflict, competitive pressures, and struggles with identity construction that we saw dealt with so darkly in *Akira* are given a lighthearted treatment here. While *Akira* showed the cathartic destruction of what was left of the world of adult authority, *Ranma 1/2* shows its farcical subversion. Despite their very strong differences in tone, however, both *Akira* and *Ranma 1/2* revolve around the exultant privileging of change. This change is exemplified in the work's fundamental visions of bodies out of control whose memorable transformations are presented in each work as simultaneously exhilarating and threatening. Ultimately *Ranma 1/2*'s narrative framework allows the threat to dissipate, while *Akira*'s open-ended text suggests possibilities of ominous empowerment, but both texts allow the viewer to entertain, if only briefly, a pleasure predicated in going beyond the fetters of the physical.

CHAPTER FOUR

CONTROLLING BODIES: THE BODY IN PORNOGRAPHIC ANIME

The womb is the source of all energy and life for a female ninja. If you control the womb, you control the woman.

La Blue Girl

I'm going to change.

Cutey Honey

BEFORE BEGINNING THE DISCUSSION about sexually explicit anime (what will be referred to as the pornographic genre here) it should first be understood that, while not totally mainstream, pornography is nevertheless a major current within the world of anime. Contrary to Western stereotypes, Japanese pornographic anime is both thematically wide-ranging and narratively complex. Although enveloped in a hardcore sexual framework, the pornographic anime goes beyond the sexual in terms of plots, themes, and settings. Often, sexually explicit situations are integrated into dense narratives that are usually related to the fantastic, the occult, or science fiction. As such, pornography not only brings up obvious questions of gender construction and interaction, but also less obvious ones as well, such as the relation of gender, power, and control to technology, tradition, and transition.

More than any other genre (with the possible exception of horror, with which it is often linked),[1] pornography brings the body to the fore, not only in terms of sexuality but also in relation to aesthetics, gender, and social identity. The related themes of power and domination are played out in the interaction of male and female bodies, although these themes are worked through in a fashion that is often highly problematic. Although the genre also contains many examples of "normal," i.e. nonviolent, sexuality, Japanese pornography sometimes seems to privilege the image of the female body in pain, usually with graphic scenes of the torture and mutilation of women.

Much work remains to be done on the motivation behind these disturbingly frequent scenes, but, just as with slasher films in the West, it is impossible to reduce all Japanese pornography to a simple vision of brutal male dominance. Even the most appallingly violent films, such as *La Blue Girl* or *Twin Dolls,* show a more complex vision of male-female interaction than one of simply dominance and submission. As popular culture scholar Douglas Kellner says of Hollywood films, "[E]ven conservative ones . . . put on display hopes and fears that contest dominant hegemonic and hierarchical relations of power . . . [They] put on display both the significant dreams and nightmares of a culture and the ways that the culture is attempting to channel them to maintain its present relations of power and domination."[2] Kellner's point is an important one for interpreting all forms of popular culture, but what is most interesting in the texts examined here is that they often show the *failure*—or at least the confusion—of those attempts to uphold the power structure.

Despite such assertions by critics of manga and anime that "[m]en are always depicted in full control seeking the ultimate pleasure from women,"[3] the reality is far more diverse, although perhaps equally disturbing. Pornographic animation in Japan may want to show women in positions of abjection and submission, but what it in fact shows is a much more intricate series of contesting hierarchical relations in which men do not always come out on top. In this regard the depiction of both male and female bodies is crucial.

Belying the stereotype of women as being only sex objects, Japanese pornographic animation tends to depict the female body in an often contradictory variety of ways. Frequently, the female body is indeed an object to be viewed, violated, and tortured, but other scenes show women's bodies as awesomely powerful, almost unstoppable forces of nature, although these two visions are hardly antithetical. There are also scenes in which the female body is enjoyed as a partner in joyful, even loving, conventional sexual intercourse. Furthermore, while the female body inevitably remains an object of the male gaze, even the most violent pornography frequently represents it as active and capable of intimidating transformation. Although the women in these films are far from being icons of emancipation, they are no closer to being the passive objects of domination described by many critics.

In contrast, the male body is usually limited to a few very different types, the two most frequent of which are "comic voyeur" and the "demonic phallus incarnate." The first of these body images is not even conventionally powerful but instead constitutes an infantile, passive status. In fact, the only really powerful male figures in many pornographic films are not human. They are, literally, demons.

These body images figure prominently in relation to three representative pornographic films, *Wicked City* (*Yoju toshi*, 1987) *Twin Dolls* (*Injū seisen*, 1995), *La Blue Girl* (*Injū gakuen* La Blue Girl, 1992-1994) and in comparison with a fourth, the more softcore, science-fiction style *Cutey Honey* (*Kiyuchi Hani*, original television series 1973-1974, OVA 94-95). Of the first three, *Wicked City* is by far the most famous, a genuine horror tour de force (given four stars by *Imagi-Movies* and described as a "future-goth noir thriller"), but it is also replete with scenes of stomach-churning violence of the sexual torturing of women. *Twin Dolls* and *La Blue Girl* are far less brilliantly realized than *Wicked City*, although they too share surprisingly complicated and even reasonably engrossing plots.

All three narratives revolve around the notion of demonic interaction with the "real world," although *Wicked City*'s version is the most richly detailed. Based on a novel by Kikuchi Hideyuki, *Wicked City* posits a parallel world, called the "Black World" that has knowingly coexisted with the human world for at least 500 years. The film's narrative tension involves the signing of a peace treaty between the human world and the Black World and the need to protect the one human representative who can deal with the Black World, an elderly man with the Italian-sounding name of Giuseppe who turns out to be a massively endowed old lecher. A handsome government agent named Taki Reizaburo and a beautiful Black World agent named Makie are assigned to protect Giuseppe before the treaty signing.

The plot takes off when Giuseppe escapes to a house of prostitution that turns out to be controlled by Black World resistance fighters who are determined to destroy the peace negotiations. A Black World woman, posing as a prostitute, almost succeeds in killing Giuseppe in an arresting sequence in which he melds into her dissolving body, a literal return to the womb that is as grotesque as it is memorable. Taki and Makie manage to save the ungrateful Giuseppe at the last minute, but Makie is kidnapped by the evil Black World resistance fighters, who proceed to sexually torture her in a series of lengthy and graphically sadistic sequences.

Taki is determined to rescue her and goes into the demonic Other world to do battle in a series of violent scenes, such as the visually stunning sequence in which he confronts a Black World woman who transforms into a giant, moisture-oozing vagina and tries to seduce him. Resisting temptation, Taki ultimately rescues Makie and the two return to the human world, only to apparently be killed in a final violent confrontation with Black Worlders. In the film's climax, however, they are revived and learn the truth about Giuseppe and their own roles. It turns out that Giuseppe has actually been sent to protect Taki and Makie, who are uniquely capable of creating a new race that combines humans and Black Worlders. In a surprisingly tender sequence the two make love after having been brought back from the dead. The ending is an upbeat one in which the pregnant Makie is seen as potentially uniting the two worlds.

In contrast to *Wicked City*, *Twin Dolls*' narrative dispenses with political subplots to concentrate purely on the occult and the sexual.

Its premise is that demons from hell are trying to take over the world through the torture and enslavement of women and the kidnapping of Onimaru, the descendant of one of Japan's greatest gods, Sugawara Michizane. Two high school girls, the Twin Dolls, are themselves descendants of a heavenly ancestress who bequeathed to her descendants skills in the traditional arts of shrine dancing and magic martial arts. They inherit the task of protecting Onimaru, who turns out to be a lecherous midget. Much sexual humor is derived from Onimaru's persistent efforts to see the girls naked. Demons provide the nonhumorous sex in the form of kidnapping, torturing, and raping the high school girls and their friends. Although the demons are eventually quelled, the climax features a lengthy sequence in which the Twin Dolls are tied up and hung over the pit of hell with their legs splayed open while the chief demon, an enormous figure with a penis the size of a baseball bat, tortures and taunts them.

The equally violent *La Blue Girl* intermixes a certain amount of conventional sex within a similar hellish demon-rapist narrative. The film takes place in an isolated mountain village where two female ninjas, Yaku and Miko, go in search of a demonic criminal who is raping young high school girls. The ninjas, specially trained in "sexual magic arts," are also attempting to recover a demonic family sword that has amazing sexual properties itself. The opening scene sets the tone of sexual violence within a traditional setting; the viewer sees what appears to be a temple interior in which nude bodies of women are scattered everywhere, their vaginas covered in blood.

The sex in *La Blue Girl* is not always violent, however. The film actually shows sequences of Yaku enjoying conventional heterosexual sex with one of the local boys who has been spying on them as they bathe in their traditional Japanese inn. The ending of the film is actually somewhat upbeat: Although there is the requisite torture-by-demons sex scene, Miko ends up destroying the demons with the help of her boy sidekick, a kind of junior ninja named Nin Nin, and the local village boys, who ride to the rescue in their souped-up sports cars.

The plots of these films have been detailed here at some length, partly in order to demonstrate some of their more obvious similarities but also to emphasize that pornographic animation in Japan is more than simply a series of bodies coming together. These bodies are embedded within both a narrative and visual context that is worth examining in greater detail.

One striking aspect of all these films is their use of the occult. It is interesting to consider the power of the essentially gothic context of setting and theme. Although *Wicked City* is set in a time close to the present, with the usual film noir venues of bleak, labyrinthine, modern architecture, all three films convey the sense of an occult/gothic Other world, paralleling our own. The traditional European "gothic romance" is one in which "sexuality, elemental passions and fear now moved to the center of the novelist's stage" and it increasingly begins to imply a "whole paraphernalia of evil forces and ghostly apparitions."[4] These works usually take place in "picturesque" settings such as castles, churches, or ruined houses.

Obviously, the Japanese gothic has a somewhat different venue, but it is surprising how much the basic elements, such as an intensely sexual atmosphere, demonic forces, and "picturesque" settings are common both in gothic/occult pornography and in more general gothic anime, such as the OAV series *Vampire Princess Miyu* (Kyūketsuhime Miyu, 1988). The gothic is a clearly nostalgic mode, and it is perhaps not surprising that in the last two films outlined this world is explicitly identified with traditional Japan.[5] The hell depicted in *Twin Dolls* is very similar to ones shown in medieval Buddhist paintings, complete with lakes of blood and jagged mountains (although the huge phallic-shaped stalagmites are perhaps a modern interpolation). *Twin Dolls* also explicitly invokes Japanese history and culture in its references to Sugawara Michizane and in the *hagoromo* costume worn by the Dolls, a reference to a medieval Noh play. Even more significantly, much of the "real world" action in both films takes place in such traditional settings as the country inn where the two ninjas in *La Blue Girl* stay or the *dōjō* (martial arts hall) where the protagonists work out. Even when more modern settings occur, such as the high school where the Dolls study, these are seen mainly as hunting grounds, places from which the demons lure the young students, and are subsidiary to the main setting.

The gothic and the occult are also considered female modes, especially in relation to their privileging of dark interior spaces and fluid, engulfing entities.[6] Traditional Japan has been consistently associated with the feminine in literature and art as well. It makes symbolic sense, therefore, that the Twin Dolls are shrine dancers and Yaku and Miko are ninjas, and even that the agent from the implicitly gothic Black World in *Wicked City* is female. These are female bodies that carry strong cultural resonances. One of the first nude scenes in *La Blue Girl*, for example, takes place in the old-fashioned wooden bath of a traditional Japanese inn, where the two girls discuss their ninja-enhanced sexual abilities. The full moon rises in a scroll-shaped window behind them as they finger each other's bodies in a scene that, except for the more explicit nudity, would not be out of place in an eighteenth century Japanese print. Also smacking of tradition is the interpolation of a voyeur, the figure of the inn's aged proprietor, who peeps at them through the window. The voyeur is an important erotic trope in Japanese culture from at least the tenth century, although the graphic nudity that the proprietor sees in *La Blue Girl* is a very contemporary touch.

Even more replete with tradition are several dance sequences in *Twin Dolls* in which the Dolls cavort in the air, changing from their regular clothes to shrine maiden costumes, with a quick glimpse of their nudity thrown in. The traditional dance itself is actually quite lovely, making for a graceful, strangely poignant scene. The girls weave ribbons woven from the *hagoromo* costume of their heavenly ancestress around themselves while they fly through the air inside their training hall. Liberated from gravity, and apparently unconcerned with any male gaze, the dancers seem both sexual and powerful in their own uniquely female realm.

Another important aspect of the female body is its occult ability to change, a property that has both traditional and contemporary resonances. *Wicked City* is perhaps one of the most striking examples of this. The film contains four major female metamorphoses, three of which may be considered negative, since they exemplify woman at her most sexually powerful and therefore threatening. The film's famous opening sequence revolves around the seduction of the human agent Taki by a woman from the Black World who turns out to possess both spiderlike properties and a literal vagina dentata. In the middle of sexual intercourse the woman's black-stockinged and gartered legs suddenly elongate, insectlike, around the hapless Taki, binding him to her. Even though he escapes, he and the viewer are afforded a glimpse of her teethed vagina, looking remarkably like a metal trap or zipper.

As she scampers down the side of the building after him, she manages to appear both intensely sexual and terrifyingly inhuman at the same time.

Giuseppe's near-assassination by the Black World prostitute mimics Taki's encounter but involves even more ominous imagery. The prostitute's vagina/womb first dissolves into flesh-colored ooze and then opens up and enlarges to literally engulf Giuseppe's small body within it. Unlike the teethed vagina of the previous scene, here it is woman's fluidity, her wet, oozing, engulfing flesh, which is emphasized. Even more frightening than the weaponlike vagina of the spider woman that threatens castration, the female body here clearly threatens incorporation, a total transgression of boundaries.

The third negative metamorphosis occurs near the end of *Wicked City* and combines both sexual and maternal attributes. Taki confronts a Black World demonness whose entire torso turns into a huge red vagina that spews liquid as she moves toward him seductively, asking if he is "man enough" for her. The image of the huge vagina is grotesquely terrifying rather than sexually exciting, however, and it is little wonder that Taki easily resists temptation and goes on to destroy her.[7]

Yaku, in *La Blue Girl* also undergoes a transformation, although this one is somewhat more conventional, as anime metamorphoses go. If Yaku has sex without orgasm during a full moon, she transforms into a werewolf. In the film this power comes to her rescue as she is being sexually tortured by her demonic enemy Kugutsumen, who attempts to make her die from pleasure. Instead she turns into a fearsome (yet still feminine) werewolf and chases him away temporarily. The scene of the Twin Dolls dancing in air may also be seen as a kind of transformation scene, although, significantly, this one is not purely sexual. The light, floating movements of the dance still exude a sense of feminine power, however.

The transformative power of the female body is an important convention in both high and folk culture in Japan.[8] Not only are ghosts in Japan traditionally female, but there is a very popular genre of stories detailing women who were originally animals and who, when caught, return to animal form. The implicitly sexual nature of these stories is made completely explicit in modern pornography and, if anything, is seen as even more threatening. In all of these examples of transformation, we can see how strongly Japanese pornography goes beyond simple fantasies of male dominance and female submission. Women's bodies in these scenes are clearly powerful, more powerful than those of the male, in fact. These anime depict the female body as being in touch with intense, even magical, forces capable of overwhelming male-dominated reality.

However, the potential for female power is deeply undercut in other ways. The most powerful women in *Wicked City*, for example, are all evil and are ultimately destroyed by Taki. Makie is initially positioned as a stronger fighter, and a generally more powerful agent than Taki, but she is soon refigured into a sacrificial victim, giving her body for the sake of her duty to the egregious Giuseppe, and is finally saved by Taki, rather than through her own abilities. No longer a powerful figure in her own right, she has become a means of restoring Taki's ego after his embarrassing encounter with the spider succubus. Her final transformation, the fourth female metamorphosis, moves away from the sexual toward the maternal, as she becomes pregnant with Taki's child. *Wicked City* thus uses the image of female metamorphosis to inscribe itself back into the patriarchal order. Despite the film's brilliant and memorable transformation sequences, its underlying message is what scholar Rosemary Jackson describes as an essentially conservative fantasy.[9] The collectivity is threatened by a series of fantastic others, but ultimately order is restored by the reassuring image of Makie's beautiful body serving its most traditional function.

Women's sexuality is turned back on itself in *La Blue Girl*. While Yaku is having sex with one of the village boys, Miko wanders off in sexual frustration. She encounters Kugutsumen in disguise, wielding an extraordinary instrument, which might be described as an air powered dildo, whose puffs excite her in spite of herself. Although Miko seems to be receiving only pleasure in this scene, there is a clear sadistic subtext. The dildo's real purpose is to attach a kind of homing device into her womb, which will allow the demon to control her. As the demon explains, "The womb is the source of all energy and life for a female ninja. If you control the womb you control the woman." In the case of Miko, this is literally so, as the device compels her to betray Yaku and leads to the two girls' sexual subjugation by Kugutsumen. The womb is thus seen first as a source of woman's strength but ultimately as her basic weakness vis-à-vis men. Women's sexuality can therefore betray a female, even a powerful ninja female.

But the film's final message is contradictory. Miko's "sexual ninja arts" have trained her vagina enough to ultimately expel the controlling device. Awakening from her trance she goes on to destroy the demon using the "Blue Whirlwind" technique, another traditional ninja power. *La Blue Girl* thus shows the woman's body in two antinomic ways: the first is as an object of control and violence by the male and as uncontrollable by the female (hence Yaku's transformation into a werewolf), and the second is as an active vessel of triumphant resistance, although this triumph is aided by tradition (Miko's ninja arts) and the timely arrival of the village boys.

Wicked City's message is also somewhat contradictory, although more conventional than that of *La Blue Girl*. Women can be powerful, but the most powerful ones are clearly evil, and their evil is concentrated in their sexuality. All three Black World women are represented as essentially having vagina dentata or all-devouring wombs, and they are all destroyed in lengthy scenes of graphic violence. In fact, the scene of Giuseppe's small body being engulfed by the prostitute's womb is a classic fantasy of what might be called reverse abjection. The prostitute can clearly be read as a mother figure vis-à-vis the man's tiny body, and their interrupted melding, complete with oozing fluids, can be seen as a kind of reversed birth. This taboo image in turn links with Makie's socially acceptable form of maternity in the film's conservative ending.

Makie initially seems to be a more emancipated figure since she is depicted in nonsexual terms (she has short hair and in the opening scenes she wears a black, masculine-looking suit) as an intelligent and effective agent. But Makie's body also becomes subject to violence through her willingness to sacrifice herself for another. As scholar Barbara Creed notes, "The image of the woman as castrater and castrated is represented repeatedly in the mythology of all patriarchal cultures. She is either the tamed domesticated, passive woman or else the savage, destructive, aggressive woman."[10] This contradictory image resonates both through Japanese folklore and through its high culture. Thus, while folkloric depictions of women often show them as terrifyingly powerful, such as the *yamamba* (mountain witch) who devours lost travelers,[11] premodern Japanese Confucianism positioned women as subservient and domesticated. What is perhaps most disturbing about Makie is that she exemplifies both sides of the image.

A similar dichotomy exists in *Twin Dolls,* in which the protagonists come across as more self-sacrificing than sexual since it is their devotion to duty that leads to their torture by the head demon. The other girl students at their high school, however, are shown as far more sexual beings. One girl in particular, jealous of the Twin Dolls' abilities and attractiveness, ends up being seduced by the head demon and becoming his slave, sexual and otherwise. Interestingly, she is shown craving sex with the mammoth chief demon while the Twin Dolls are shown as resisting to the end. In what may be a subtextual underscoring of the purity of tradition versus the degradation of the contemporary period, the film pits the evil sluttish female, still wearing her high school student uniform, against the Twin Dolls in their shrine maiden robes. Also intriguingly, the Dolls, although tortured, are never depicted as having conventional intercourse with the demon. At the film's end they are still, both technically and symbolically, virgins.[12]

The eponymous heroine of the science fiction OVA and television series *Cutey Honey* makes an interesting comparison to the women in the three occult anime. Created by Nagai Go, a writer and producer famous for his erotic, violent, and often humorous fantasies, the series is actually less violent or overtly sexual than the texts previously discussed. Rather than relying on scenes of intercourse or torture for its sexual content, *Cutey Honey* is an interesting combination of graphic nudity with a form of quasi empowerment on the part of its voluptuous heroine. Honey initially seems more in control than any of the female characters in the other films. A denizen of a near-future dystopia, she is a crusader for good who takes on many disguises in her fight against (inevitably demonic) evil doers. As she herself sums it up, "Sometimes I'm an entertainment reporter, sometimes I'm a Chinese Fighter [martial arts master], sometimes I'm a rock and roll singer, but always there is Honey Flash."

Despite what to some English speakers may seem like obvious sexual referencing, the term "Honey Flash" actually refers to her transformation sequence. Each work in the series contains scenes of Honey metamorphosing (through a magical device implanted in her ample chest) into a variety of identities, each of which carries with it the appropriate attractive accoutrements such as clothing and hairstyles. But this is more than simply a fashion change. In general, these guises are of competent, powerful females; or as Honey's young male sidekick explains, "Honey's really great. She can do anything!"

Two factors subvert this empowering message, however. The first is the fact that Honey is not human. Although she has a kind of pseudo-family who support her crime fighting efforts, as we discover at the end of *Cutey Honey II,* she is actually an android. Her superhuman competence is precisely that, superhuman. Not only is she not a real woman, but also at the end of *Cutey Honey II* her body is temporarily destroyed and she returns as a literal angel, complete with white robe and huge, enfolding wings. For a softcore sexual fantasy, this transcendent ending is certainly a pleasant change from the usual demonic violence. But it is clear that Honey achieves this appealing metamorphosis through self-sacrifice, "dying" in order to save her friends. What might have been a message of female empowerment instead ends up sending decidedly mixed signals. Apparently the best kind of woman is one with an android's body that she is willing to sacrifice.

The other factor undercutting any message of empowerment is found in the gratuitous nudity of Honey's frequent transformation sequences. As Honey metamorphoses into whatever new guise she is going to adopt, the viewer is treated to a set sequence in which her clothes are stripped off her as her nude body rotates, apparently in the air. Next, her new outfit wriggles onto her, ending usually with the strings of her halter top tying themselves around her breasts. The varied camera angles give the impression that the viewer is first disrobing and then dressing her in a ritual series of gestures choreographed to a set piece of music. The transformation from regular person to superhero is of course a staple of science fiction and comic books, but, for anyone who remembers Clark Kent's modest concern over finding a private place in which to change from his secret identity, the public, celebratory, and clearly erotic nature of Honey's metamorphosis is startling. The use of the term "Honey Flash," with its implication of the female genitalia on display, underlines the erotic tone of the metamorphosis even more strongly. The viewer is now able to participate in a way that is both voyeuristic and erotic, not simply by viewing Honey's nude body or even by mentally disrobing and clothing it, but by being able to take part in the almost ecstatic transformation of the body itself. As with Tetsuo's graphic transformation in *Akira,* this process can also be described as "the frenzy of metamorphosis."

Metamorphosis, power, and control of the female body are intimately linked in all four of the films. The Twin Dolls rotate in air, transforming for a time into powerful shrine virgins who dance, warrior style, brandishing their white ribbons. The film's torture sequence negatively deconstructs that very transformation process, however, as the two are again shown in the air, but this time hung suspended on ropes with their legs being pulled apart by the head demon's tentacular hair. The dance/metamorphosis scenes of lightness and autonomy are replaced by images of imprisonment and victimization. The girls are now able to move only at the male's behest, with his hair being a phallic substitute. The female ninjas in *La Blue Girl* are clearly punished, both for their sexuality and their metamorphic abilities. Yaku is unable to transform into a werewolf on her own accord, and she is a victim of her sexual appetites. Miko, her womb taken over due to her own concupiscence, ends up betraying both of them in a torture scene, similar to that in *Twin Dolls,* where the girls are rendered immobile and tortured, only this time with a phallic sword rather than with the demon's hair.

Aside from the evil women of *Wicked City,* only the android Cutey Honey seems able to glory in metamorphosis for its own sake. Interestingly, Honey's final transformation into an angel is not shown, perhaps because of the overtly erotic nature of the transformations until that point. Presumably a sexual angel would be too disturbing. As with the other three works, it is safe to say that *Cutey Honey* sends mixed messages. Despite the regressive and voyeuristic aspects of her characterization, she is still the film's heroine, one worthy of admiration and emulation. Although the viewer is invited to enjoy her body, she is never shown being tortured, and in the film's several violent scenes she more than holds her own. As anime critics Helen McCarthy and Jonathan Clements point out, "Although [Honey's] transformation involves her in a nude scene every time . . . she starts and ends as an attractive, competent, grown-up young female."[13] It is perhaps significant that Cutey Honey 's futuristic world, while certainly noir, is more generic dystopian science fiction than Japanese gothic. As an android in a non-Japanese environment, Honey is more liberated than the women still trapped in tradition.[14]

Overall, the female body in these four animated films seems to be far more than simply an object of sexual desire. The body is seen as powerful, mysterious and frightening, controllable only by demons, and even then only temporarily. In the women's frightening potential for change they reflect some of the serious dislocations Japanese society has undergone over the last decade or so in which women's roles have changed enormously. In the 1980s and 1990s women have grown more independent, both financially and socially, taking on far more identities than the "good wife wise mother" stereotype of Meiji Japan. Like Cutey Honey, women in the theater of the real Japan are "going to change."

In the theater of anime, women's changes are displayed, explored, and interrogated through the mode of the fantastic. Most obviously in *Wicked City* and the werewolf sequence in *La Blue Girl*, these changes take on nightmare proportions. Change is not always negative, however, as long as it is regressive. In *Wicked City* the fearsome metamorphoses of the demon women are matched with the more soothing transformation on Makie's part from powerful agent to sacrificer to mother. Ultimately, the patriarchal hierarchy is reinscribed. *Cutey Honey* and the end of *La Blue Girl* seem, at least potentially, more genuinely subversive of male dominance. On the one hand, Honey revels in her many identities even if, at the end, her most permanent one is that of sacrificial angel. Miko, on the other hand, uses her transformative powers to save herself and her friend, metamorphosing from victim to victor. The film's ending is somewhat downbeat, however: Miko watches in lonely envy as Yaku goes off with one of the village boys. As she turns away, Nin Nin, the lecherous junior ninja, grasps her leg and peers beneath her skirt, telling her that he will "always be there."

THE MALE BODY:
DEMONIC DOMINANCE AND COMIC FRUSTRATION

The image of a woman shackled by a small male who attaches himself to her leg is an interesting way to end a pornographic film, and it highlights the next topic of exploration, the male body. It is actually the portrayals of the male body in pornographic animation that are more potentially subversive to patriarchal culture. While the female body changes are manifold, ranging from glamorous to frightening to traditional, male bodies are largely fixed, and their frozen identities are far from the attractive range of the female ones. The male body in pornography does vary, as is clear in the films discussed above, but the variations are not always empowering.

While the female body in pornography is almost always young, beautiful, and tall, the male body ranges over a variety of types, from the grotesquely demonic to the humorously childlike. However, it is possible to divide the male body into two general types, the comic and the demonic. The first might be called the comic voyeur, who usually has a shrunken, often childlike body with emphasis on the head and especially on such expressive features as the mouth and eyes. Giuseppe, Nin Nin, Onimaru, and the grandfather of Honey's pseudo-family are all examples of this type, whose chief function seems to be to watch longingly from the sidelines.

This emphasis on voyeurism rather than sexual action is an important part of Japanese pornography, both in manga and in anime. Anthropologist Anne Allison has explored the scopophilia endemic in manga, suggesting that the strong emphasis on the male gaze positions males "to be masterful viewers but passive and consuming actors,"[15] an assertion that is underscored by the depiction of the male body in general. Even the strongly hardcore anime, such as *La Blue Girl* or *Twin Dolls,* emphasize voyeurism as much as intercourse and there are as many close-ups of male faces as there are of genitalia.

The comic faces, diminutive bodies and passive positions of so many of the male characters are intriguing in terms of the male identity that they project. Allison performs an interesting analysis of the dynamic of the male gaze in the popular animated television series *Machiko Sensei,* in which the male gaze first "stops" the woman (i.e., freezes her into inaction), making her "an object or image of male viewing,"[16] but then goes on to make the male immobile. In the films discussed here, however, the male is not so much purely immobile as frustrated. Much of the comedy revolves around the voyeur's comic attempts to see, touch, and, ultimately, have sex with women, although they are usually unsuccessful.

It is this image of the ever ready, usually frustrated, grotesquely comic male that is particularly intriguing. While the male gaze itself may have power, many of the males depicted in pornographic animation are virtually powerless. Onimaru in *Twin Dolls* is perhaps the most exemplary representative here. An 18 year old in a tiny body, Onimaru's sexual adventures are relegated to such apparently frustrating activities as peeping from afar, trying to climb up girls' legs, and trying to lift up their skirts. Inevitably, he ends up being beaten by the girls and carried off by his guardian/servant for his pains. Although the viewer sees his massive erections (through his trousers) and his slavering expressions of lust, he is never shown releasing his frustrations through masturbation or actual intercourse. Similarly, Nin Nin, the diminutive ninja sidekick in *La Blue Girl,* although often shown as wild with lust, never actually has intercourse. He does perform cunnilingus on Kugutsumen's female accomplice but is caught and punished by the demonic male.

Giuseppe, while portrayed in a constant state of arousal, is also never shown performing active sex. The most memorable image of him is when Taki and Makie have to literally drag him out of the huge oozing womb/vagina of the Black World prostitute whom he is in the process of dissolving into. This arresting scene highlights not only Giuseppe's concupiscence but also his vulnerability—his aging little body, almost engulfed by the cavernous vagina of the demonic female, looks pathetic and helpless in comparison.

From a Western perspective, scenes of continual sexual frustration in what is certainly hardcore sexual fantasy may be somewhat puzzling. Of all genres, why should hardcore pornography privilege delayed or displaced gratification? There are a number of possible explanations. The first relates to the important position of the voyeur in Japanese erotic culture. Although voyeurism plays an important role in the West as well, it is one of the most significant aspects of sexual fantasy in Japan, as previously mentioned. For example, in the tenth century romances *The Tale of Genji* and *Tales of Ise,* virtually all erotic encounters were presaged by the hidden hero first peeping at the woman who excites his interest. A second explanation lies with the complex relationship between the viewer and anime characters. The comic infantile or aged male body is an inherently unthreatening one. The viewer can both identify with Nin Nin's, Onimaru's, and Giuseppe's lust and feel superior to them. Indeed, it may also be that the viewer identifies and is familiar with their perennial frustration.

The demonic body is in many ways the antithesis of the comic male body. Preternaturally huge, covered with rippling muscles, and inevitably equipped with an enormous penis (and often with phallic tentacles as well) the demon is all action. In important contrast to the comic male whose chief action is ogling, the demon's is penetration of the female, both with the penis and with as many phallic substitutes as possible. For example, the opening scene in *Twin Dolls* shows a crowd of what might be called junior demons, small in stature and lacking genitalia, forcing their horns into their female victims. Even more obvious in its phallic function is Zipangu, the demonic sword in *La Blue Girl*. According to legend, the sword is an ancient one used by a Korean princess for masturbatory pleasure after she has already used it for killing her lovers. Eventually she ends up killing herself by driving the sword up through her vagina into her throat in sexual ecstasy. In the present, however, the sword has taken on a sexual life of its own, enslaving Kugutsumen's female accomplice and attempting to take over Miko's body in the climactic final scene.

It would seem that the only powerful male bodies in pornographic anime are nonhuman ones. Although there are more conventional sexual activities portrayed (*La Blue Girl* shows one of the village boys engaged in clearly satisfying intercourse with Yaku), the male body that consistently gains sexual satisfaction is a nonhuman one, one that in origin, iconography, and substance, is clearly Other—demonic, made of steel, bulging with tentacles.

What does this mean? Is it simply an aesthetic coincidence based on the special powers of animation? Or does it suggest something about Japanese male sexual identity? The answer appears to be "yes" to both questions. The animator's art lends itself to fantasy. The development of tentacles, the huge phalluses, and the horned heads of the little demons are all features difficult to portray in live-action cinema.[17] At the same time they are memorable in ways that depictions of more conventional sexual intercourse are not. There is also the question of censorship. Until fairly recently it was forbidden to show male genitalia in comics, animation, film, or photography. Although this had already begun to change by the time *La Blue Girl* was made, it was still presumably easier to get away with showing nonhuman genitalia in the form of demonic phalluses or phalluslike tentacles.

It is impossible to ignore the social or cultural context in which animation takes place, however. The image of a constantly changing female body is surely related to the change in the Japanese woman's social and political identity over the last few decades. Confronted with more powerful and independent women, Japanese men have apparently suffered their own form of identity crisis. Sumiko Iwao has pointed to some of the most disturbing sociological phenomena related to this male reaction,[18] which include the growth of sexual interest in very young, nonthreatening girls, a phenomenon known as the "Lolita Complex" or *rorikon*. Conversely, the violent and demonic depictions of both men and women in anime are symptomatic reactions to these social changes as well.[19]

The bifurcation of the male body into immobilized shrunken voyeur and enormous, sexually potent demon suggests a real despair over the male identity, not only in a sexual context but in a wider one as well.[20] The male viewer is obviously going to identify, at least at some level, with the sexually interested males in the films, but his choices are limited to goggle-eyed voyeurs and demonic sadists. It seems that the only way a man can imagine himself as sexually potent is to transmogrify his identity into the demonic. While neither of these choices are unique to Japan[21] (although the demonic is clearly stressed more in Japan than elsewhere), the truly remarkable lack of conventional, sexually active males hints that sexual activity and identity are still not integrated into regular life in Japan.

Taki in *Wicked City* is the only male depicted as conventionally "human"—sexually successful and attractive—and it is interesting that he is the one who achieves change in the real world, notably Makie's pregnancy. But he too needs magical help (from Giuseppe, of all people) to finally mate satisfactorily. Intriguingly, he is also one of the few male characters in any of the anime discussed here who achieves orgasm, or so we can assume, since he successfully impregnates Makie. The only other example is the village boy in *La Blue Girl* whom the viewer sees commenting appreciatively that he "came five times."

In general, male orgasm is depicted far less frequently than male frustration or simply endless penetration, no doubt due in part to censorship limitations and also because orgasm might suggest a vulnerable loss of control. The sexual male's combination of frustration and desperate need for control underlines once again the paucity of sexual identities available to the Japanese male. The eternal displacement of orgasm suggests a truly hellish world in which genuine satisfaction can never be achieved. Always erect, the male body, be it comic or demonic, seems to be continually seeking and never finding fulfillment. In contrast, the female body, in its frenzy of metamorphosis, seems finally and frustratingly unavailable, an elusive will-o'-the-wisp whose powerful and ecstatic transformations only underline the frozen and reductive nature of contemporary male identity.

Furthermore, the notion of Otherness is intriguing in a sociocultural context as well. Just as with the female gothic, the sexually active males belong to another, more traditional world. The demons themselves share numerous iconographical similarities with the demons in medieval art (as well as eighteenth and nineteenth century woodblock prints) and their association with a clearly medieval Japanese hell is important as well. The sword in La Blue Girl is of course a traditional medieval sword.

It is possible to see an ideological subtext to anime pornography that goes beyond male/female relations to embrace the issue of overall power in society. In this reading the male demons represent not just some kind of revenge fantasy against the female but against the constricting nature of Japanese society itself. In Japan access to power is often a torturous process beginning with the notoriously challenging examination system and then moving through the glacial advancement to seniority. In his frustration and impotence, the shrunken voyeur figure is an apt alter ego of the average salaryman. Both the powerful demonic male figures and the transforming female figures also offer a form of resistance to the oppressive social order. In fact, both characterizations can be seen as belonging to the abject, a world that is usually coded as female but can also encompass a form of marginalized male who is often associated with sexual violence.[22] The magical Other worlds, from which spring both the negatively presented demons and the metamorphosing females of Wicked City as well as the more positively coded female ninjas of La Blue Girl or Cutey Honey, are related to the uncanny and uncontrollable. They ultimately have little relationship to the real world in which we can assume power relationships go on normally. Therefore unlike the abjected Tetsuo, there is little sense of a satisfying revenge on the mainstream.

Throughout most animated pornography the only appealing "heroes" are the *female* characters who, as we have seen, often triumph against their male interlocutors. At its most radical level, this privileging of the female suggests the possibility of male viewer identification with the metamorphosing female rather than the restricted male. Just as the male viewer of the slasher film may identify with the "final girl" left alive at the end of the movie,[23] it may be that even the most pornographic of anime contains a potential space of androgynous viewer identification.

Androgyny itself finds expression in the pornographic anime discussed, exemplified by the sword Zipangu in *La Blue Girl.* Animated only by sexual desire, the sword appears to be male in its sexual activities as it is shown enveloping the demonic female Kamiri who seems in total ecstasy as a result. But Zipangu is actually an androgyne. As it explains, "the lust of the princess survives in me." This most literally phallic of weapons is actually an instrument imbued with female desire. Perhaps because of this uncanny combination of the sexes, the ninjas perceive the sword as being the most dangerous to them, and at the end of the film Miko's Blue Whirlwind attack rends it into fragments.

The image of androgyny presented here is a far cry from its light-hearted representation in *Ranma 1/2,* suggesting that in the world of pornography the notion of any continuum between the sexes is simply unimaginable. Part of the difference here is of course due to the different genres being discussed, pornography versus romantic comedy, but it is also worth underlining the difference in the generations depicted as well. Pornography is an "adult" genre centering on characters who have presumably finished changing because they have grown up. Sexuality is threatening enough without having to introduce the even more threatening notion of change to it. But sexuality also cannot be escaped. In pornography it becomes an expression of rage and frustration, forcing the male and female into angry separate realms whose boundaries can only be crossed through sexual intercourse, usually in a brutally violent form. While the fantasy worlds of *Ranma 1/2* and pornography both privilege sexual demarcation, in *Ranma 1/2* it is a cause for humor whereas in pornography it is a cause, usually, for despair.

As a result it is perhaps not surprising that pornographic anime often takes place in a gothic context that is also essentially apocalyptic.

This is most obvious in *Wicked City* and *Twin Dolls,* the narratives of which clearly revolve around evil forces trying to take over the world, but it is interesting to note the preponderance of religious settings and literal "demons" in many other pornographic works as well, such as *La Blue Girl* and *Legend of the Overfiend* (see chapter 11). These religious references may also relate to the idea of the festival or *matsuri,* which is based on religious practices. Certainly the constant transformations and intensive sexuality may suggest a festival mode, although in this case the festival mode is a particularly dark one, reminiscent of Ian Buruma's description of the *matsuri* as the "primitive, obscene, and frequently violent side of Japanese culture."[24]

Finally, one may also find glimpses of the elegiac mode in certain pornographic anime in terms of the emphasis on traditional Japanese culture, seen in the pastoral landscape of *La Blue Girl* and the shrine setting of *Twin Dolls.* This privileging of a rapidly fading traditional society is fascinating in comparison to the "statelessness" of so much of anime. It may well be that depiction of gender relations in their most basic form accentuate a still-active nostalgia for an earlier, more understandable period in which male and female roles were more firmly fixed. If this is the case, then the pornographic in anime turns out to be a deeply conservative genre at heart, offering its male viewers visions of fantasy identities integrally linked to a lost traditional culture.

CHAPTER FIVE

GHOSTS AND MACHINES: THE TECHNOLOGICAL BODY

Man's insecurity stems from the advance of science. Never once has science, which never ceases to move forward, allowed us to pause. From walking to ricksha, from ricksha to carriage, from carriage to train, from train to automobile, from there on to the dirigible, further on to the airplane, and further on and on—no matter how far we may go, it won't let us take a breath.

—Natsume Sōseki, *The Wayfarer*

This picture—[of a transformer]—man mounted on machine, a joystick gripped in each hand, was and is the epitome of Japan's technological dream.

—Ron Tanner, "Mr. Atomic, Mr. Mercury, and Chime Trooper: Japan's Answer to the American Dream"

> Fusion with the technological . . . is tantamount to stepping into a
> suit of armor.
>
> —Claudia Springer, *Electronic Eros*

THE BODIES DISCUSSED in the previous chapters have all been
strongly linked with notions of identity, from the frighteningly
unstable to the rigidly fixed. The fixed masculine body types
displayed in pornography suggest a negative response to the transgressive potential that the female and adolescent body is shown to be
capable of. This yearning for a contained or armored body is not
limited to pornography, however. The world of hard science fiction
anime known as *mecha* revolves around a quest to contain the body,
this time quite literally in the form of some kind of technological
fusion. As with the phallic demon in pornography, this kind of
"containment" can also be read as "empowerment," perhaps even
more obviously than the demons, since the viewer sees the frail
human body literally becoming stronger as it fuses with its technological armor.[1] Usually huge, with rippling metallic "muscles" and
armed with a variety of weapons to the extent that it almost parodies
the male ideal,[2] the *mecha* body clearly plays to a wish-fulfilling
fantasy of power, authority, and technological competence.

However, this kind of empowerment can be a double-edged
sword. Although the most conventional *mecha*, along with certain
Western science fiction films such as *Terminator*, seem to privilege the
robotic or cyborg body, many other anime present the technologically
armored body with profound ambivalence. Not only do these anime
partake in the contradictory "double vision"[3] that science fiction scholar
J. P. Telotte ascribes to many Western science fiction films (the simultaneous celebration of technology through its privileged presence in the
narrative and an excoriation of its destructive and dehumanizing
potential), but many works in the *mecha* genre actually enact this double
vision on a more profound and darker level through insistently presenting the fusion of human and technology as one of ambiguous value. This
often negative view of technology may surprise audiences who tend to
think of the Japanese as masters of technological wizardry. However, it
is a view long held by many thoughtful Japanese, such as the writer
Natsume Sōseki quoted above, or more recent writers such as Abe Kōbō,
who vividly describe the human cost of technology in their novels.[4]

The *mecha* genre of anime carries on this tradition. Perhaps the most ubiquitous of all anime genres, *mecha*'s vision of what Alessandro Gomarasca terms the "technologized body" is one that has only increased in importance since 1963, when Japanese television premiered *Astro Boy* (*Tetsuwan Atomu*). This was not only the first Japanese animated television series, but the first of a long line of anime involving robots with human souls. In that same year the first "giant robot" series aired, *Iron Man # 28* (*Tetsujin 28 go*) based on the comic by Yokoyama Misuteru. *Iron Man # 28* already displayed characteristics important to the genre, the most significant being that, unlike *Astro Boy*, the robot was controlled by a separate human being. As the genre developed, human and robot often combined, with the human inside guiding the powerful robotic body.

While the imagery in *mecha* anime is strongly technological and is often specifically focused on the machinery of the armored body, the narratives themselves often focus to a surprising extent on the human inside the machinery. It is this contrast between the vulnerable, emotionally complex and often youthful human being inside the ominously faceless body armor or power suit[5] and the awesome power he/she wields vicariously that makes for the most important tension in many *mecha* dramas.

The three anime we will examine in this section, the two OVA series *Bubblegum Crisis* and its sequel *Bubblegum Crash* (*Baburugamu kuraishisu* and *Baburugamu kurashu*, 1987-1991), *Neon Genesis Evangelion* (*Shinseiki Ebuangerion*, 1997), and the video *Guyver: Out of Control* (*Kyōshoku soko gaiba*, 1986), all explore this ambiguous process of body-technofusion with varying degrees of skepticism toward the empowering nature of body armor. Although the three differ considerably from each other in tone and style and from other, more optimistic *mecha* works such as *Gundam* or *Orguss*, they all contain certain tropes common to the *mecha* genre that make their darker tone particularly interesting.

In contrast to the abjected feminine worlds of the gothic and the occult, which privileged women's bodies and their terrifying potential to engulf the male inside dark, organic spaces, the worlds of *mecha* might be seen as stereotypically masculine in their emphasis on hard-edged, thrusting, outward-oriented power, privileging what scholar Claudia Springer calls "the violently masculinist figure."[6] The futuristic settings of *mecha*, inevitably high-tech and/or urban, with immense skyscrapers, laboratories, elevators, space stations, and huge corporations permeated with robotic equipment, also evoke a hard-edged technological world, far removed from the traditional settings of gothic anime.

Also in contrast to the gothic and occult pornography, the narrative climaxes of *mecha*, while also fast-paced and often accompanied by throbbing music, are climaxes of combat rather than sex. Virtually any *mecha* narrative will build up to a lengthy climactic fight between huge and powerful machines engaged in combat involving crushing, dismemberment, and explosions. These climaxes evoke not so much fear as what Springer calls "technoeroticism," a euphoric state of power, excitement, and violence often associated with war. Indeed, Klaus Theweleit's discussion of the imagery and tropes employed by the German Freikorps (elite troops created in the aftermath of World War I), which resulted in an ideology in which each young man became a machine and this "machine" was both "one of war and sexuality,"[7] seems appropriate to the many intense confrontations in *mecha*.

From this point of view, it seems fitting to call the *mecha* a conservative genre, one that has links with such Western science fiction tech noir or even "technophobic" films as *Robocop, Teminator,* and *Total Recall.* These films, although more complex than some of their critics give them credit for, certainly seem to both privilege and problematize the robotic or cyborg body as a frightening form of the "technofascist celebration of invulnerability," to use Andrew Ross's evocative phrase.[8] The cyborg or robotic body is therefore simultaneously appealing and threatening, offering power and excitement at the expense of humanity.

Of the three works to be examined, two of them, *Guyver: Out of Control* and *Bubblegum Crash,* certainly have conservative and specifically technophobic aspects to them at the same time as they glory in the *mecha* on *mecha* confrontations that make up a large part of each work. The two series also clearly display a nostalgia for what might be called "Japanese family values" and the premodern pastoral world. *Evangelion* is harder to pigeonhole, refusing to give any easy solutions to the horrific world it presents. Although *Evangelion* clearly has both nostalgic aspects (as in an early episode when Shinji, the protagonist, runs off into the country) and technophobic ones, they take place within an acknowledgment of both the fragmentation and the complexity of the real world that the other film and series resist. Even more than most *mecha*, the *Evangelion* series problematizes human interaction with technology from the simplest to the most complex level.

THE ARMORED BODY:
GUYVER, BUBBLEGUM CRASH, AND EVANGELION

> By what means is a young boy made a soldier? . . . How does body armor attain its final form, what are its functions? How does the "whole" man who wears it function—and above all—what is the nature of his ego? . . .
>
> . . . This, I believe, is the ideal man of the conservative utopia: a man with machinelike periphery, whose interior has lost its meaning . . .
>
> —Klaus Theweleit, *Male Fantasies Vol. 2*

The quotation above, taken from Theweleit's book on the early twentieth century German Freikorps, gives a sense of some of the conventional ways Western critics have looked at the technologically armored body. In this view the armored body (be it robotic or cyborg) is spiritually empty, hypermasculine, implicitly associated with fascism, and conceived of only in terms of its ability to wreak violence. Or as Springer says of the armored creations in *Terminator* and *Robocop*, "What these cyborgs do best is kill."[9]

Springer and Theweleit are basing their conclusion on Western prototypes, but at first glance much of what they say seems to work well in relation to Japanese *mecha*. The *mecha* in all three works we are looking at are also excellent at killing. Indeed, many of *mecha* anime's narrative structures are built around at least one but often several long fight scenes of *mecha* on *mecha*, scenes that are not simply violent in terms of mechanical brutality but bloodily anthropomorphic as well. The fusion of human pilot inside armored machine leads to bizarre combinations of mechanical/organic violence in which huge machines combat each other in fantastic displays of mechanical agility while at the same time hinting at the organic bodies inside them with graphic glimpses of dismembered limbs flying around and blood seeping through mechanical armor. The power and exaltation of the augmented body noted by Springer and Theweleit[10] is clearly on display in *mecha* as well; indeed, it is the dominant trope around which *mecha* plots revolve.

The Japanese stories often reveal a much bleaker world view than such Western fantasies as *Star Wars* or even *Terminator*, in terms of how much an individual can actually accomplish. This is partly due to the greater emphasis on the interiority of the characters than would seem to be the case in most Western science fiction films. These characters are far more complicated than the action heroes privileged in conventional Western science fiction. Although many *mecha* series of course have relatively one-dimensional characters, the protagonists of the three works to be examined here show a notable amount of emotional complexity, from Sho's lonely suffering as the Guyver to Priss's attempt to change the world in *Bubblegum Crash* to the hypersensitivity of *Evangelion*'s antihero Shinji.

The very idea of "body armor," as opposed to the conventional robotic type of Western science fiction film, emphasizes the body instead of the armor. In much Western science fiction film even if there is a human body inside the machine, as in *Robocop*, the emphasis is much more on the protagonist's dehumanization by the alienating powers of technology. Likewise, the robotic hero of the *Terminator* series, while gradually appearing to develop some human emotion in the second film, is still seen largely in terms of a robot with only flashes of humanity, almost the opposite of the *mecha* protagonists who are first and foremost humans in robotic armor.[11] Contrary to Theweleit's and Springer's visions of the armored body as lacking interiority, therefore, the protagonists in *mecha* anime often have a surprising amount of interiority.

The first text, the 1986 video *Guyver: Out of Control* is based on a popular manga series by Takaya Yoshiki that also spawned an OVA series, although the single video is far darker than the series. Both works have similar plots concerning a young boy named Sho who, through a chance discovery, fuses with something called "bio-booster armor" to become a hideous cyborglike entity known as a "Guyver." He must protect himself from equally hideous agents of the evil Chronos corporation known as "Zoanoids" while attempting to protect/rescue his girlfriend and, in the OVA series, his father. While the

Guyver OVA episodes are a relatively uncomplicated series of fights between good Guyver and evil Zoanoids in which good triumphs over evil, the film *Guyver: Out of Control* has a far less triumphal tone, displaying, in certain scenes at least, a fundamental fear of and repulsion from technology. It is also a notably conservative work. It harks back, especially in its women characters, to a peaceful, pretechnological world in which a mother's welcoming breast explicitly contrasts with the dark and hard-edged technological nightmare into which the main character is plunged.

Guyver: Out of Control begins with a traditional pastoral scene: a rainy night in the mountains. Into this scene speeds an earthy truck driver who picks up a seedy looking man with a mysterious bag. When the truck driver attempts to question him about the bag the man only responds that it contains "spare parts," at which point the truck driver, incensed, kicks him out of the truck, keeping the bag. Seconds later a demonic face (bearing striking similarities to the monster in the Hollywood *Alien* series) appears in the windshield and two arms burst in to kill the driver and take the bag.

In this early scene technology seems both powerful and negative. The truck blasts through the bucolic landscape as the monster's hands blast through the windshield to pick up the "spare parts." Even the humans associated with technology, the coarse truck driver and his seedy passenger, are singularly unimpressive. In contrast, the next scene opens to a world of peace and order where Fukamachi Sho and his girlfriend Mizuki are walking home from school. Clearly the 97-pound weakling type, Sho is almost knocked over by a male classmate on a bicycle. Soon after, however, he and Mizuki find a mysterious mechanical object that, in classic male science fiction fashion, Sho decides is a "great discovery" while Mizuki just wants to leave it and go home. Too late.

Sho begins to transform into a grotesque monster while Mizuki screams helplessly. Soon a group of similarly revolting monsters try to abduct Mizuki but the now-transformed Sho kills them all (in various bloody scenes) and saves her. Although Sho then transforms back into human form, this is only temporary. Sho has unknowingly activated a Guyver, a top secret new kind of "bio-booster armor" that organically attaches itself to the body's musculature to give it tremendous strength and other powers such as the ability to fly.

Agents from the sinister Chronos Company try desperately to retrieve the Guyver. They kidnap Mizuki and follow Sho to his high school, where they murder all his friends. Now an outcast, Sho hides for a while but finally decides to change into Guyver form and rescue Mizuki. The rescue sequence involves an immensely destructive fight with a female Guyver named Valkyria, who is a former human like Sho but, unlike the innocent boy, an aggressively evil employee of the Chronos Company. Sho-as-Guyver destroys Valkyria and, in an impressive series of explosions and fires, the Chronos Company as well. Although he also rescues Mizuki, who recognizes him despite his Guyver armor, he realizes he can never return to normal life and sadly disappears (to return, of course, in a lengthy series).

Altogether bloodier, more violent, and containing much more nudity than an American superhero story, *Guyver: Out of Control* is still a recognizable version of the universal adolescent fantasy of a weakling's transformation into a superhero. This is a very dark fantasy however. The actual transformation sequences seem agonizing rather than empowering. Even more negatively, Sho's new powers only serve to bring about the death of his friends and isolate him from humanity permanently.

Unlike the female transformations we have discussed in the section on pornography, Sho's metamorphosis is seen as painful and alienating. In many ways it echoes, on a more simplistic level, Tetsuo's extraordinary metamorphosis scene in *Akira*. As in *Akira*, the transformation is intensely grotesque and the protagonists' agony comes across vividly. Unlike Tetsuo, however, Sho manifests no signs of exulting in his new strengths. The transformation scene itself is much shorter and quickly cuts to the fight scene with the female Guyver to which Sho seems more resigned than excited.

Furthermore, in radical contrast to Tetsuo, Sho remains vulnerably human both in his concern for his girlfriend and his memory of his mother. There is even a poignant scene in which Sho recalls himself as a child running to his mother and being cradled at her breasts. The contrast between the little Sho and the revolting monster he has become is something that would be quite unimaginable in an American tech noir film such as *The Terminator*. The final scene when Mizuki recognizes him through his Guyver armor is also significant. Rather than appreciate his muscles and strength, Mizuki sees and wants the "real" Sho.

Women are thus seen in their most traditional form as oases of comfort (the mother whose breasts enfold Sho) and spirituality (Mizuki, who is capable of seeing the "real" Sho through his armor). As is typical for this kind of conservative fantasy, untraditional women come across as threatening and evil. Although the Chronos corporation contains various greedy old men, it is significant that Sho's final Guyver enemy, Valkyria, is a woman.

Even before she becomes a Guyver, Valkyria is consistently associated with technology. The viewer first encounters her in a weight room, where she is seen molding her voluptuous body with the use of various steely machines. This linkage of sexuality and machinery is even more pronounced in the scene where she metamorphoses into a Guyver. Unlike Sho, who retains his clothes during transformation, the Guyver's tentacles are seen entwining around her nude body in a clearly phallic fashion. When her final transformation into Guyver form is completed, however, the only real difference between her shape and that of Sho are her pointed, armor-plated breasts.

Distinctly different from the fluid and engulfing female body of anime pornography, Valkyria's Guyver form is a rejecting and resisting entity, confronting rather than inviting the male protagonist. In the high tech world of *mecha*, both male hero and female enemy confront each other in armored isolation with no hope even for the sexual union achieved by Taki and Makie in *Wicked City*. Interestingly, Sho does not actually kill the female Guyver, as he did with the male monsters early on. Instead, her "control meter" is damaged and she falls apart, moaning horribly and ultimately dissolving into a pinkish puddle-like entity, a final form that of course has more feminine connotations.

It is only in that final fluid image that Valkyria seems to reassert a feminine presence, but her dissolving body is horrifying rather than welcoming. In both forms, therefore, Valkyria's body is seen as essentially hideous. Sho is briefly able to turn for relief to the recumbent form of Mizuki, who is clad in her traditional school uniform. But this relief is attained only through the violent subjugation of the technologically empowered female Guyver and can only provide a transient respite from a violent and frightening world. In the long run the body offers neither comfort (since his union with Mizuki is temporary) nor protection (since Sho's own armored body is simply a means of torment).

As Springer says of the (often misogynistic) violence endemic in American cyborg films, "Violent, forceful cyborg imagery participates in contemporary discourses that cling to nineteenth-century notions about technology, sexual difference and gender roles in order to resist the transformations brought about by the new postmodern social order."[12] Whether *Guyver's* notions about technology are strictly "nineteenth-century" is perhaps questionable, but clearly its values are traditional ones and the film resists any notion of a technologically wrought utopia. In its relentlessly bleak vision, *Guyver: Out of Control* seems very far from Ron Tanner's description of Japan's postwar culture as having "been built on the unflagging belief in the benefit of all things high tech."[13]

A somewhat more complex vision of technology—and of women in technology in particular—may be found in the popular 1980s series *Bubblegum Crisis* and its sequel *Bubblegum Crash*. Set in a high-tech near future where machines known as "boomers" do most of the work for humanity, the series features a group of attractive young women who occasionally leave their normal working lives to become the "Knight Sabers" a technologically armored paramilitary group who help out when the (also armored) police are unable to cope with various forms of high-tech banditry inevitably wrought by perpetrators in equally heavy *mecha* armor (or else the armored machines themselves). Although the series contains many scenes of *mecha* mayhem, the emphasis is not entirely on action. The series contains a certain amount of psychological depth in its characters as well as some satirical flourishes that amusingly skewer the materialist society of contemporary Japan. In fact, *Bubblegum Crisis/Crash* seems to suggest that the women are more fulfilled inside their battle armor than when they return to "normal" materialistic life.

In *Bubblegum Crash* Episode 1 the Knight Sabers seem to be on the verge of breaking up. Priss, the most masculine one, appears poised to become a teen idol, while another colleague, Linna, has become a stockbroker and is euphorically making money. Only one of the characters seems disconsolate about the breakup of the group but is unable to circumvent her friends' yuppie-esque obsession with material success. Fortunately, for the future well-being of the group, a band of terrorists calling for a new world order threaten the city, and the Knight Sabers somewhat reluctantly reconstitute themselves.

However, once they don their heavily armored (but at the same time curvaceously feminine) mobile suits, they swing enthusiastically into battle and easily defeat the terrorists. At the end of this episode the two characters who seemed ready to quit the group now see the error of their ways. No longer obsessed by their shallow consumerist lifestyles, they are willing to dedicate themselves more fully to their careers as Knight Sabers.

Although the episode contains hints of female empowerment, with the women winning out over their enemies, it also shows a strongly conservative subtext. While hardly a paean to militarism, the series still implicitly positions the technological, armored world of the Knight Sabers and the police against the shallow yuppy lifestyles that two of the characters initially embraced. The communal, self-sacrificing spirit of the Knight Sabers, underlined by their ability to coordinate with and support each other once they get into attack formation, stands in obvious contrast to their giggling and back-biting while still in the throes of materialist consumer culture.

Bubblegum Crisis/Crash is far from being entirely protechnology, however. Machines without human guidance are consistently shown as ineffective and often dangerous. Or, as anime scholar Antonia Levi concludes in regards to the "boomer" machines in the series, "they are forever going on the rampage, shooting up innocent civilians and destroying urban areas. They are the whole reason for the existence of the Knight Sabers and the A. D. Police. Pure mecha equals pure menace."[14]

In *Bubblegum Crisis* Episode 3 both technology and modernity in general are shown as evil and destructive. In this episode Priss befriends a young boy whose working mother dreams of moving with her child to the country. The mother's dream is thwarted by the plans of the evil Genom corporation, which is taking over and destroying her housing area. Priss, in human form, tries to take on Genom's thugs but discovers, when she tries to hit one of them, that they are actually "boomer" machines disguised as men, and the demolition continues. The mother is killed under a collapsing building and Priss again takes on Genom's thugs in vengeful fury. This time, wearing her Knight Saber power suit and aided by the other Knight Sabers, she is triumphant. But the final tone of the episode is far from exultant. In the last scene the viewer sees a long shot of Priss delivering the now orphaned boy to what is clearly an institution of some sort while a moody rock song plays on the soundtrack.

The episode's final message is an ambiguous one. Technology and the huge modern corporations are destructive of both the land-scape and the land. Yet the only way the Knight Sabers can successfully attack is to fuse with technology themselves. This is most obvious in the scene where Priss, in nonaugmented form, attempts to take on the boomer thugs from Genom but is too weak. Once in her power suit, however, she and her friends easily deal with them.

Yet the overall theme of this episode seems to be one of nostalgia for a simpler world in which Knight Sabers, like some latter day band of *ronin*, can combat modernity with weaponry that is as much spiritual as it is technological. In a voiceover, Priss recalls the young boy's mother's desire to go to the country, and this seems to fuel her anger even further.[15] But unlike more simplistic *mecha* series, which might have ended with Priss and her friends' celebration after having avenged the boy's mother, the episode concludes on a deeply pessimistic note, one that emphasizes the powerlessness of the orphan boy in the face of institution. In the final analysis the individual can only do so much.

Both *Bubblegum Crisis/Crash* and *Guyver: Out of Control* limn worlds in which outside forces overwhelm individual action, especially on the part of young people. The only way they can resist these forces is to augment their bodies through technological means. This theme is taken to its greatest extreme in the ground-breaking television series *Neon Genesis Evangelion*. An extraordinarily complex work, and one that has spawned a small cottage industry of criticism about it, the immensely popular *Evangelion* can be seen as a deconstruction of the entire *mecha* genre. Although it showcases brilliant combat scenes of *mecha*-on-*mecha* confrontations, these scenes take place within a bleak context of seriously dysfunctional family, work, and sexual relationships that is permeated with a mystical and apocalyptic philosophy and interwoven with surreal graphic imagery.

In its basic plot outlines, *Evangelion* is classic *mecha*. Set in the near future after a catastrophe called the "Second Impact," the narrative follows the adventures of a young boy named Shinji who is summoned to NERV headquarters, a secret government organization in the city of Tokyo III, by his mysterious and coldly distant scientist father. In Episode 1 Shinji learns why he has been summoned—to pilot an enormous robotic weapon known as an "Evangelion" (EVA for short), which has been constructed to fight the "Shito" (translated as "angel" but actually meaning "apostle"), huge grotesque-looking creatures presumably from outer space that are stalking the planet. While adult scientists made the EVAs, only young adolescents (described with the English word "children") can actually "synchronize" with the EVAs well enough to pilot them. Although initially protesting his inability to pilot the EVA, Shinji finally complies, partly due to his glimpse of the only other EVA pilot available, a girl named Ayanami Rei. Rei has already been so exhausted by previous combat that she has to be wheeled into the control center on a stretcher. Despite his reluctance, Shinji synchronizes very well with the giant EVA ("49.9 percent synchronicity," a scientist crows), and, after some early problems when it appears he will be defeated, ultimately triumphs over what the viewer later learns is only the first of a series of "angels."

Recounted in this way, *Evangelion* would seem to adhere to all the most important *mecha* conventions, a near-future high-tech setting, a fast narrative pace, and above all a youthful hero who pilots his robotic machine to victory over an apparently evil and apparently mechanical enemy. The television series even has an inspiring pop theme song exhorting an unnamed youth to "become a legend." However, the series actually turns these conventions inside out to produce a text that is as fascinating or perhaps puzzling as it is almost unrelentingly grim.

This subversive tone is established early in the first and second episodes. Perhaps the most obvious difference that helps set the tone is Shinji's attitude toward his *mecha*. Unlike the Knight Sabers with their cheerful enthusiasm or even Sho, who grows more enthusiastic in his work once he realizes he can rescue his girlfriend (and in the television series actually shows some real zeal for transforming into his "biobooster armor"), Shinji looks on his augmented self with absolute loathing. His very first encounter with the EVA is instructive. Guided by his superior, Misato, he walks into the EVA holding pad to find it pitch black. When the lights are switched on he finds himself confronting an enormous robotic face, bigger than his entire body, a sight that makes him recoil in horror. Shinji's continuing sense of unease is clearly telegraphed by his disturbed expression as he is loaded into his EVA and propelled out to the fight with the Angel. He seems agonizingly reluctant, a far cry from the willing body-metal fusion on the part of more conventional protagonists.

The actual encounter with the Angel, while certainly exciting, is much more grimly presented than the usual slam-bang extravaganzas of typical mecha-on-mecha confrontations.[16] The soundtrack music is foreboding and the encounter itself is limned in a shadowy chiaroscuro, quite different from the brightly colored fight scenes of most *mecha*. Finally, the actual fight sequence ends up in a fascinatingly low-tech manner. Menaced by the seemingly victorious Angel, Shinji's EVA, which has suffered enormous damage, manages to right itself at the last moment to produce, not a high tech weapon, but a huge knifelike piece of metal. The scene becomes even more shadowy and the viewer sees the dark silhouette of Shinji's EVA savagely attacking the Angel with the metal piece.

No doubt, part of this grim tone is due to the apocalyptic nature of the text. With the fate of the world riding on Shinji's shoulders, it is hardly surprising that this is not a light-hearted fight scene. The apocalyptic aspects will be explored later but for the purpose of this chapter, it is enlightening to look at what these dark early episodes say about body and identity.

It is possible to see this opening encounter in more mythic and/or psychoanalytical terms as the beginning of Shinji's reluctant rite of passage into manhood, with the EVAs and the Angels as aspects of the Self and Other that Shinji needs to confront in order to form his own identity. Many critics have noted that the construction of the EVA has a feminine aspect, in that it encloses Shinji in a liquid-filled womblike space. It can be suggested that the machine has a masculine aspect as well, in that it is essentially an offensive weapon thrust out of NERV headquarters to take Shinji on his quest for selfhood.

The actual journey begins when Shinji enters the darkened room and, as the lights suddenly go on, sees the EVA for the first time. The scene of the small boy's face next to the gigantic face of the EVA is a memorable one. It is as if Shinji were looking into a distorting mirror and is horrified by the self that he finds there. Shinji is unable to escape from this repellent aspect of himself, however. In the next scene we see him, looking very frail and vulnerable, being enclosed by the mammoth machine while a clear liquid rises around him that, the technicians assure him, will make it easier for him to breathe. As the liquid covers him the EVA begins to move out to the launching pad, and, after a few more technical procedures, Shinji and the EVA are ejected out of NERV headquarters to fight with the Angel.

With its image of a small human encapsulated within a large liquid cylinder, Shinji's immersion (perhaps a more appropriate word than "fusion") in the EVA strongly suggests a birth scene. To make the message even clearer, the technicians are shown unlocking the so-called umbilical bridge (the English words are used) as the EVA moves out into battle. Thus the EVA has both aspects of the maternal—Shinji is inside its protective capsule—and the self—Shinji is "synchronizing" with it, fusing with it to make it act under his volition. In fact, the critic Kōtani Mari points out the increasing feminization of Shinji in later episodes, hinting at the affect that the EVA has on Shinji's personality.

Kōtani views the basic structure of the series—the combat between EVA and Angels—as one in which the patriarchal family, NERV, fights with the abjected feminine Other, the Angels.[17] Although I believe that this is an important and illuminating point, since NERV is indeed depicted in an explicitly patriarchal way and the angels have clear links with the abject, I would also suggest that, at least early in the series, the Angels could also be seen as father figures, whom Shinji must annihilate. Huge, brutishly grotesque, and coming down from above, they exhibit an authoritative presence. They are also explicitly associated with Shinji's real father, a man who seems to have rejected his own son in order to work on the mysteries of EVA and the Angels and who appears to be the only person to know the real meaning of the Angels. In this light, the savagery of Shinji's final response to the first Angel is highly suggestive. This is not simply one machine attacking another, but, as the surprisingly primitive knifelike weapon attests, a deeply primal and murderous confrontation. The phallic nature of the knife is also interesting, suggesting that Shinji is attempting to arrogate his father's masculine power.

It is important to realize, however, that just as the EVA is both mother and self, it is also possible to see the Angel as both father and self. After all, the closest equivalent to the gigantic, powerful, and grotesque Angel is the gigantic, powerful, and grotesque EVA with which Shinji is fused. In this light, Shinji's final victory over the Angel is reminiscent of George Lucas's science fiction epic *The*

Empire Strikes Back (1980), in particular the scene in which Luke Skywalker engages in a sword-wielding confrontation with Darth Vader, whom he is not aware is actually his father. In a scene of mythic and psychoanalytical resonance, Luke finally manages to cut off Vader's "head" (his helmet), only to discover that the head is actually his own.

In the case of most of the more conventional *mecha*, the triumphant resolution of a fight is a prelude to further victories that will explicitly or implicitly celebrate the growing competence of the youthful protagonist and his maturation into an adult form of identity. In *Evangelion*'s darker vision, however, such a celebratory coming-of-age fantasy is largely undermined. The sexual transgressiveness and ambiguity that mark both EVA and Angel are embodied in a more psychosocial way in the general dysfunctionality of the human protagonists. This is clear throughout the series as the focus turns at least as much to the bickerings, sexual angst, and family secrets of the three young *mecha* pilots and their mentors as to the *mecha* action. Also, as has been shown with Shinji, the characters' attitude toward their high-tech body armor is often ambivalent at best. Rather than empowering them, their huge EVAs leave them wracked with pain and deeply vulnerable. Far from bringing victory, body armor in this series only leads to physical and emotional damage.

Indeed, the EVAs can be seen as outward manifestations of the characters' own defenses, not only against the world but against each other. Instead of enabling them to feel protected and potentially more capable of human interaction, the EVAs only add to the characters' alienation from each other. Thus, while Shinji and his roommate and fellow EVA pilot, the striking Asuka Langley, might be expected to develop a romantic attraction for each other, their sexual tension, although clearly evident in some episodes of mutual fumbling, is usually subsumed under Asuka's intense competitiveness as to who gets to lead in combat with the Angels. As in *Ranma 1/2* this theme of competition can be seen as having links with the heavy pressures that Japanese society places on its citizens, but unlike *Ranma 1/2*, the competition here is apocalyptic rather than festive. Shielded in their EVA armor, Asuka, Shinji, and Rei are incapable of any meaningful interaction beyond competitiveness in combat and the occasional bleak foray into sexual experimentation.

The alienation of the characters, especially that of Shinji, is spectacularly apparent in the puzzling and genuinely subversive final episode, a grand finale in which, bizarrely for a work in the *mecha* genre, not a single *mecha* is shown. Episode 26 comes after a dizzying series of revelations concerning both family and institutional secrets interwoven in a highly technological framework in which, among many other things, the true function of NERV and the real identity of the first EVA pilot, Ayanami Rei (she is actually a clone of Shinji's dead mother), are revealed. In contrast to the technological revelations of the previous episodes, however, the final episode is fascinating and to many viewers disappointing in its virtual lack of any high-tech special effects or apocalyptic imagery.

Instead, the final episode is an almost classically psychoanalytic exploration of the personal identities of Shinji and his friends/colleagues at NERV, who, the viewer has by now discovered, are all deeply psychologically damaged. The surreal framework in which the exploration takes place is a series of questions flashed across the screen that Shinji and the others then try to answer, as if they were prisoners being interrogated. The question that occurs most often is "What do you fear?," and Shinji's answers have nothing to do with high-tech weaponry or Earth-threatening Angels and everything to do with his deeply dysfunctional family life and profoundly introverted personality.

In answer to "What do you fear?" Shinji first responds, "I fear the hatred of my father" and adds "My father abandoned me. He hates me." As the question continues to be pressed, however, Shinji expands his circle of fear to reveal that his deepest fear is "not being wanted [by anyone]." This leads him to confess, in answer to another question, that he pilots the EVA because his "life is pointless otherwise," and, "Without the EVA, I had no value." The others apparently have similar revelations concerning their own sense of worthlessness and their need for the EVA to give their lives meaning.

As the episode continues however, Shinji learns that all of this is taking place in his own mind and, as the outside voice repeatedly tells him, this is a vision of the world that he has come to through his own decisions. Continually being asked the question "What am I?" Shinji finally sees himself as utterly alone in a blank white world, a lonely cartoon figure floating in a perimeterless space.

Having come to the ultimate in identity deconstruction, Shinji then has a surreal vision of an alternate anime universe, a self-reflexive version of an animated high-school sex comedy that proves to him that there are many possible directions his anime life could go in. With this knowledge he appears ready to begin rebuilding his life and states "I see I can exist without being an EVA pilot." The series ends with Shinji thanking his father and saying goodbye to his mother.

Looking at this final episode unironically, Shinji's story is in a sense a coming-of-age drama as much as that of Luke Skywalker or the protagonists of more conventional *mecha*. Indeed, critic Endo Toru sees the final episode as an explicitly sexual coming of age in which Shinji, through the interrogation of the personas of his fellow female combatants in his mind (his anima, perhaps), ultimately is able to separate from his dead mother and move on to a more adult sexuality.[18] At one point in the episode, for example, he is told in Lacanian fashion that "the first person you see is your mother" and at the end of the episode, he says goodbye to his mother. Even if Shinji's "maturation" is perceived in a straightforward manner (and, given the dark tone of the series this would be rather problematic), it still seems to be highly ambiguous. Indeed, in the film *The End of Evangelion*, Shinji's sexual coming of age is shown in the bleakest of terms as the opening sequence reveals him masturbating miserably over the wounded body of Asuka. In contrast to Luke's learning to use the "Force" in the *Star Wars* series, it seems clear in both film and these final episodes that mastery of the EVAs leads only to alienation and despair.

The very ubiquitousness and popularity of the *mecha* genre makes *Evangelion* in general and this final episode in particular peculiarly jarring. Through Shinji's self-questioning, the viewer is insistently reminded of the fundamental worthlessness of the power derived from the mechanical armor, thus undermining the whole basis of the *mecha* genre. The final scenes in which the unarmored Shinji floats gently in a world without directions, boundaries, or human contact are in striking contrast to the scenes of armored bodies in combat that ended many of the previous episodes. In the solipsistic world of *Evangelion*, *mecha* are finally unimportant except as a means to know the self. Even the human body is less important than the mind that creates its own reality.

CHAPTER SIX

DOLL PARTS: TECHNOLOGY AND THE BODY IN *GHOST IN THE SHELL*

Unlike the hopes of Frankenstein's monster, the cyborg does not
expect its father to save it through a restoration of the garden.
[T]he cyborg would not recognize the Garden of Eden.

—Donna Haraway

I am doll parts.

—Hole

By the very act of denying the existence of the ghost in the
machine—of mind dependent on, but also responsible for, the

actions of the body—we incur the risk of turning it into a very
nasty, malevolent ghost.

—Arthur Koestler

SIMILAR TO *EVANGELION*, which seems to deconstruct or even to
repudiate the technological instrumentalities of the *mecha* genre that
concentrates on the complex and vulnerable psychology of its human
protagonist, the final work to be discussed in this section, Oshii
Mamoru's 1995 film *Ghost in the Shell* (*Kōkaku Kidōtai,* although the
English title is used as well) also turns inward in its exploration of the
possibilities of transcending corporeal and individual identity. Less
popular in Japan than *Akira, Neon Genesis Evangelion,* or the films of
Miyazaki, *Ghost in the Shell* was a critical and cult success in the United
States. It remains a favorite of many Western anime fans because of its
combination of technically sophisticated (and extremely beautiful)
computer animation and its complex and philosophically sophisticated story line.

The plot revolves around a search for the apparently sinister
entity known as the Puppet Master (*ningyōzukai*) that can hack into
top-secret computers and high level cyborg brains. Responsibility for
the search is given to a top-secret government agency known as
Section 9 whose best operative is Major Kusanagi Motoko of the
Kōkakukidōtai (Shell Mobile Force), a superbly effective cyborg
assassin. Although part of the *mecha* genre, the film manipulates
traditional *mecha* tropes such as the cyborg and urban high-tech
settings to explore more inward states of consciousness. Rather than
using *Neon Genesis Evangelion's* psychoanalytic lens, however, the
framework for this exploration is based on the complex relationship
between body and spirit. In addition, *Evangelion* (Shinseiki Ebuangerion, 1997) is more of a psychoanalytic examination of adolescent
identity in which technology acts as one more instrument of alienation. *Ghost in the Shell* is a genuinely metaphysical work that is
concerned less with individual identity in society than with such
philosophical questions as whether one can possess a soul in an
increasingly technological age. Furthermore, while the television
series of *Evangelion* privileges loneliness and emotional disconnection,
Ghost in the Shell explores the possibility of psychic connection
through technological means.

Its choice of vehicle for this exploration is not a human body but a cyborg one, the beautiful female body of Kusanagi. As its use of a cyborg heroine may hint, *Ghost in the Shell* is one of the least technophobic of any of the works discussed in this section. Instead, it raises the possibility of technology's positive potential, not only in terms of the physical and mental augmentation offered by the cyborg but also in terms of the possibility of spiritual development offered by an artificial intelligence known as the Puppet Master. This Puppet Master offers Kusanagi the possibility of transcending her cyborg body and becoming part of the "net," a reference not only to cyberspace but to a kind of non-material Overmind. *Ghost in the Shell* is a unique text in that it presents the viewer with two kinds of technological futures, artificial intelligence and the cyborg body, as it attempts to reconcile them through a structure that has clearly theological underpinnings. As we will see, however, what it does not offer is much hope for the organic human body, which is seen as essentially a puppet or a doll (the Japanese word "*ningyō*" means both "doll" and "puppet") to be manipulated or transformed by outside sources.

In its exploration of such profound issues as the relations between soul, body, and technology, *Ghost in the Shell* owes as much to American science fiction, such as Ridley Scott's landmark 1982 science fiction film *Blade Runner*[1] or William Gibson's classic 1980 cyberpunk novel *Neuromancer* as it does to any specific *mecha* anime. *Blade Runner*'s influence, both in terms of metaphysics and in terms of the film's memorably textured dark mise-en-scène, is very obvious.[2] *Ghost in the Shell*'s dystopian vision of an alienated, near-future world, shadowy government agencies and a dark, urban setting of rain-lashed skyscrapers all evoke *Blade Runner*, while its image of a tough weapon-toting heroine dealing with sinister computer hackers is evocative of *Neuromancer* and other cyberpunk works. At the same time, the film's superb animation, rhythmic pacing, and dark, metaphysical story line give it an extraordinary and unique lyricism all its own. Rather than categorizing *Ghost in the Shell* purely as a *mecha* film, therefore, it might be at least as accurate to call it a "cyberpunk-noir film" with elegiac, gothic, and even apocalyptic overtones. As we saw in our discussion of pornography, the gothic is usually seen as a female mode and it is possible to suggest that *Ghost in the Shell,* in contrast to the other *mecha* works, has a strongly "female" sensibility in terms of the traditional female links with the irrational and the uncanny and the interior and the reflective.

While the film's basic narrative is strongly redolent of cyberpunk, it is balanced by a lyrical and reflective emotional framework and an often surprisingly slow narrative pace. The film is far less action-driven than most Western cyberpunk or *mecha* anime. For example, many slow, hauntingly beautiful scenes, often involving water (another obvious link to the feminine since in East Asian culture the female principle of *yin* is associated with water), in which the film explores Kusanagi's essential loneliness, counterbalance its brilliant scenes of technological combat (including one tour de force sequence involving the pursuit of an invisible man wearing "thermo-optic camouflage").

In addition, an implicit lament for a lost (or perhaps never really existing) world of human connection is one of the film's more distinctive elegiac aspects. The lyrical scene in which Kusanagi is shown riding a boat down an urban canal, quietly watching the city dwellers moving through the rain clearly conveys this point. Through her eyes, the viewer focuses through the rain on lonely individuals backlit by the urban neon, including a presumably human woman who appears to be a double of Kusanagi herself. At the end of the scene the viewer sees a brightly lit department store window whose shadowy, armless mannequins not only reflect Kusanagi's own nonhuman state but also underline the film's powerful sense of the corrosive loneliness of the human condition. Another distinctive aspect of the film is the figure of Kusanagi herself. Unlike the other "heroes" of the *mecha* works profiled in this book such as Shinji, Sho, or Priss, or the protagonists of *Blade Runner* and *Neuromancer,* Kusanagi is not a human or a human enmeshed in body armor but a cyborg, who, while possessing human features, is actually a technological creation. Her "birth" is shown in a sequence under the opening credits and her non-human quality is underlined by one of the film's catch phrases, "She was born in the net."[3]

In some ways Kusanagi fits comfortably into scholar Donna Haraway's vision of the cyborg as a creature without human limitations. For Haraway, the cyborg is a liberating entity "not afraid of [its] joint kinship with animals and machines,"[4] "a creature in a post gender world."[5] Thus the birth scene shows Kusanagi as both organically and technologically constructed but totally free of human origins. The viewer first sees her as a series of computerized digits glowing across the screen and then as a mechanical body frame in which her head is opened up to allow for various technological implants. The viewer watches her gradually take human shape as her now flesh-covered body floats in a fetal position immersed in a vat of liquid prior to her final ejection into the real world. This ejection gives no sense of any human agency being involved. Furthermore, although Kusanagi is hardly genderless (she has a very female figure), she is characterized more clearly by her profession of assassin and is never shown with a sexual partner or in any form of sexual association, as if to render her innately free of any basic human ties.[6]

Haraway also points out that "Unlike the hopes of Frankenstein's monster, the cyborg does not expect its father to save it through a restoration of the garden [of Eden]"[7] and therefore has no concern with its father or mother. As is clear from her birth scene, Kusanagi has no past or any associations with parent or parentlike figures. This is in striking contrast to Shinji's obsession with his parents in Evangelion, and is also significantly unlike the "replicants" of Blade Runner, who collect old photographs and bond together in a pseudo kinship group. Kusanagi, on the other hand, seems explicitly uninterested in origins or history. A subplot reminiscent of the 1990 film Total Recall deals with the implanting of fake memories in an innocent pawn of the Puppet Master, and Kusanagi seems outwardly unfazed by the cruelty of the procedure.

However, Kusanagi is not completely comfortable in her cyborg identity and she does not totally fit Haraway's paradigm of self-satisfied autonomy. The real "action" of the film is not so much the hunt for evil perpetrators or even the Puppet Master but is rather a quest for her spiritual identity. Although outwardly unconcerned with origins, Kusanagi is profoundly concerned about whether she possesses something that she and the film call her "ghost," the spirit or soul that animates her being. Although she often discusses her ghost with herself and her colleagues in dialogue that is striking in its philosophic overtones, it is Kusanagi's cyborg body rather than her mind that becomes the vehicle for this quest. For it is her body, standing at the nexus between the technological and the human, that can best interrogate the issues of the spirit. This is made clear in the narrative structure of the film, which arranges itself around the theme of the fall, both literally and figuratively. Oshii visually represents Kusanagi's complex and contradictory search in a variety of dazzling sequences that track Kusanagi's body and mind through a series of "falls." In these falls, which clearly have a theological subtext, Kusanagi's body is seen as both vulnerable and powerful, as both object and subject. Furthermore, in the final fall she comes to the point of leaving her body behind.

The first fall privileges the body. It occurs in the opening scene of the film, a sequence occurring before the credits that begins with the words "in the near future corporate networks reach out to the stars[;] electrons and light flow throughout the universe," and is followed by the potentially ominous statement that "the advance of computerization, however, has not yet wiped out nations and ethnic groups" (this introduction is a shortened version of the one that appears in the manga). The view then opens out to focus on Kusanagi standing on the roof of a high building, the wind slightly ruffling her hair, trying to make voice contact through circuits implanted in her brain with her colleagues in Section 9. When one of her colleagues, Batou, complains about "there being a lot of noise in your brain today," she answers flippantly, "It's that time of the month." Unzipping her clothes, she stands on the building's ledge, her slim, apparently nude figure managing to appear both sexual (although in a relatively androgynous way, compared to the typical hypersexualized female body in most anime) and vulnerable at the same time. She proceeds to jump into the darkness and fall downwards, in what seems to be an agonizingly slow process, only to be caught by a strong cable that breaks her fall just outside a window where a meeting is going on.

The scene shifts inside the building to an angry meeting of high-level government officials who are attempting to prevent the defection of an artificial intelligence operative to a hostile country. As the meeting breaks down, the representative of the hostile nation declares angrily, "our country is a peace-loving state." From outside the office window a female voice is heard saying sardonically, "Oh, really?" and gunfire erupts through the window, killing the official.

This scene reveals a number of contradictory elements encompassed in Kusanagi's mind and body. Although she looks "human," she is not really human, a fact that is highlighted by her sarcastic reference to menstruation while she is connecting a radio implant into her head. She is also both powerful and vulnerable. The viewer is impressed by her physical prowess and fearlessness (her ability to leap off tall buildings) and also by her toughness (her cynical assessment of peace-loving assertions). At the same time, however, the body is also shown as potentially vulnerable. Because the viewer is at first not privy to the fact that this is a carefully arranged assassination, his or her first reaction to Kusanagi's fall is one of unease. She is apparently nude, prey to the currents of the air, and falling. It is only the single cable that is able to suspend her, marionette-like in the air. Furthermore her body encapsulates both presence and absence, signified first by her disem-bodied voice outside the window, and then by the next scene in which after the successful assassination, we see her become invisible, thanks to her thermo-optic camouflage, allowing the viewer to suddenly see, through the disappearing outlines of her body, the vast electronic high-tech city toward which she falls.

Kusanagi's initial fall is metonymically associated with her birth as the film segues into the aforementioned birth sequence. Although both the technological and organic imagery is redolent of science fiction tropes of monster-making, the sequence itself is lyrical, quiet, and rhythmically paced. Unlike Shinji's "birth scene" we are given no sense of horror or fear for there is no emotion shown on Kusanagi's face. Instead the mood is mystical, enhanced by otherworldly music and slow pacing.

In some ways however, this "birth scene" is not totally dissimilar to the one in *Evangelion* in that in both cases the entities being "born" are at the mercy of powerful outside forces. In Shinji's case these forces are focused in his sinister father, giving him an obvious target to resist. Kusanagi's world, however, is fatherless. She is a product of the immense "corporate networks" mentioned in the film's introduction, dependent on them for her career and her identity. In this regard, the slender cable that suspends her as she falls can be seen as having both umbilical associations and associations with a corporate, or at least governmental, form of Puppet Mastery; the institutions literally bind her to her work as an assassin.

Although Kusanagi seems to have no explicit interest in origins or parents, it is interesting that her next "fall" occurs after the scene in which she and Batou observe an unfortunate victim of the Puppet

Master who has been told that all his memories of family life are artificial implants and he really lives alone in a small room. Although apparently unmoved by this vision of mental deconstruction, the next scene shows Kusanagi risking death by diving deep into the rusty waters of the urban harbor. As she comes to the surface, Batou first scolds her for her recklessness and then asks her what she sees deep in the water. She responds with a series of emotions rather than facts: "fear, anxiety . . . maybe even hope." Here Kusanagi seems to be attempting to discover a core self, one that is accessible through the technological apparatus of her diving gear but is encased within the organic womb of the sea. With surprising abruptness, the film then interjects another element that underlines even more emphatically the notion that this is a quest for identity. Kusanagi, still sitting on the boat, suddenly quotes from The Book of Corinthians in the Bible the lines, "For although I see through a glass darkly soon I shall see face to face."

Although the film later reveals that this is the Puppet Master speaking through Kusanagi, it is clear throughout *Ghost in the Shell* that Kusanagi herself is looking through a glass darkly, searching for some fuller image of herself, one that may go beyond her lonely individuality. She seems to achieve this in her final "fall," this time a metaphorical one, a "dive" into the mind of the Puppet Master, whom she has finally located in temporary possession of another beautiful, female cyborg body. The scene where she dives in is a memorable one: By this point in the film both Kusanagi and the Puppet Master's host body have been ripped apart by gunfire so that only their armless upper torsos are left. Placed side by side on the floor of a cavernous hall, supposedly based on London's nineteenth-century Crystal Palace Exhibition Hall,[8] they strongly resemble the armless mannequins Kusanagi gazed at previously in department store windows. Then, as Kusanagi "dives in," the Puppet Master begins to speak through the mouth of her own body in a male voice, inviting Kusanagi to fuse with him in a world beyond the body. Invoking Plato, the Puppet Master begs her to come out of the cave and into the light.

This scene questions the notion of body and identity in a variety of vivid and disturbing ways. The two armless female torsos at first look utterly helpless, torn fragments of femininity left in an echoing, empty building. Yet the viewer also knows that these are cyborgs, not "real" human beings. Are they then simply broken machinery ready to become the scrap metal of the postmodern state?[9]

In fact, the film firmly resists any postmodern celebration of fragmentation. We have been coached by Kusanagi's own ruminations to believe that she, at least, has a "ghost" within her machinery, which means that she will live beyond her fragmented body. However, her "dive" into the Puppet Master's mind, and his appropriation of her vocal chords is as disconcerting as it is replete with boundary transgressions. After the dive, Oshii shifts the point of view to the Puppet Master's eyes as we are allowed to look up at the cavernous hallway from the torso's place on the floor. This viewpoint shot achieves a kind of double identification: The viewer is identifying with Kusanagi who is now "identifying" with the eyes of the Puppet Master. Then, when Kusanagi begins to speak in the Puppet Master's voice, a further dislocation occurs because we now see Kusanagi's body as permeable as well. Kusanagi's fall has allowed her finally to leave her body and to begin to move toward a larger, more encompassing entity.

The film ends with one final vivid and genuinely surprising boundary transgression. Rescued by Batou just after the military has devastated the hall and is about to destroy the final fragments of her body, Kusanagi appears in a new body, one scavenged in desperation by Batou. This is the body of a young girl.[10] For the viewer this final image is perhaps the most disorienting one of all. Kusanagi's head remains but her body is no longer that of the sleek, hardened, female super agent. Instead she sprawls in schoolgirl uniform in a large chair, looking like an abandoned puppet. She even speaks initially in a little girl voice, underlining her loss of power and identity.

Although the original manga had Batou scavenging a *male* body for Kusanagi, the film's insistent privileging of the female body is an important addition. While Kusanagi is never shown in a sexual situation, her uncertainty as to her identity, her dependence on outside forces, and the scene in which she becomes a fragmented torso all suggest some underlying issues that could perhaps be read through a feminist lens. Ultimately, Kusanagi's strength and agility seem hollow, underlined by the many dependent, vulnerable, and damaged modes in which the viewer sees her. Furthermore, the fact that the supposedly sexless Puppet Master speaks in a somewhat masculine voice and essentially invites Kusanagi to perform a kind of "wedding" with him seems to emphasize Kusanagi's dependent feminine status.

But it is also possible to argue that, rather than making Kusanagi a feminist icon, Oshii is instead using her vulnerable female body and the "feminine" lyrical mode of the film itself to underline the vulnerability of all human beings in a world that is increasingly governed by oppressive and incomprehensible outside forces. The film's solution to this vulnerability is a surprising one, however. At the film's end it becomes clear that Kusanagi has fused with the Puppet Master. Righting herself and regaining her original voice, she marches out of Batou's apartment and looks down at the city spread out below in an echo of the film's opening scene. This time she does not fall but simply stands, asking herself, "So where do I go from here?" The final line of the film is Kusanagi's reflection to herself that "the net is wide and infinite." In contrast to the opening sequence, this final scene ends on a transcendent note as she looks up at the sky and implicitly at the "net."

This final embrace of a technological world is a unique one in comparison with the previous texts profiled in this book or with the American tech noir works we have alluded to. As a number of critics have pointed out, the replicants in *Blade Runner* can be compared with fallen angels, mentally and physically superior creatures who "fall" to Earth in search of their creator, the mysterious head of the Tyrell Corporation, in hopes of prolonging their four-year life spans.[11] Kusanagi, of course, is already earthbound and her falls are more connected with a search for identity than for a desire for life. In both films, however, this notion of the fall brings up complex questions of what it is to be human in an increasingly technological world where the gods seem to have disappeared and the human soul seems more and more vulnerable to technological and institutional exploitation. Both films highlight hunts or quests that are both physical and spiritual—in *Blade Runner*'s case the hunt by the detective Deckard to find the replicants and "retire" them is played in counterpoint to the quest by the replicants to find their creator and prolong their lives, their "humanity," as it were.[12] *Ghost in the Shell* also features two forms of hunts, that of Kusanagi for the Puppet Master and, implicitly, her quest for her "ghost." In Kusanagi's case the two quests fuse as she finds the Puppet Master and he offers her the opportunity to combine her ghost with his into a more satisfying form of identity and a new version of "life."

Although both Kusanagi and the replicants may therefore be seen as engaging in broadly spiritual quests, their ultimate aims are significantly different. The replicants want to be "human" in the most organic sense of the word, to live as long as possible and experience as much as possible. *Blade Runner's* emphasis on eyes and seeing underlines the deeply physical aspect of their hunger. In contrast, Kusanagi wants to escape the physical, be it technological or organic, to fuse into a nonmaterial world where her ghost can roam free. In a sense the two films are opposites of each other. While the replicants "fall" into humanness and life in all its heart-breaking transience, Kusanagi takes leave of the human for a chance at bodiless immortality. Both films contain clearly Christian references, such as the dove that Batty, the chief replicant, holds at the end of his life in *Blade Runner* and the Puppet Master's quotations from the Bible in *Ghost in the Shell*. The Puppet Master himself has certain godlike aspects in his vision of creating a new world.[13] But Kusanagi is obviously not searching for a Christian notion of transcendence. Instead, *Ghost's* other influences may well be both Shinto and Buddhist. For example, while acknowledging the obvious Christian references in the script, Oshii and his screenwriter Ito Kazunori also argue that Kusanagi's final "wedding" with the Puppet Master is evocative of the sun goddess Amaterasu's decision to take part in the world of the gods.[14] In the myth the sun goddess is lured out of a rock cave by seeing her image in a mirror, perhaps the "dark glass" that the Puppet Master has Kusanagi invoke. The film's haunting theme song is also clearly inspired by Shinto liturgy,[15] in its invocation to the gods to come and dance with the human. In fact, Oshii states that the "net" can be equated with the myriad gods of the Shinto religion,[16] underlining the notion that Kusanagi's fusion with the Puppet Master has strongly theological overtones. I might also suggest that the notion of a bodiless union with an amorphous greater entity has clear evocations of the Buddhist concept of nirvana, where the self is said to become like a single drop in a vast ocean.

Rather than trying to emphasize one religious influence or another in *Ghost in the Shell,* it seems safe to say that the issues the film raises are ones that religion and philosophy have struggled with from ancient times. What is exceptional about the film is its welding of these age-old issues within an extraordinarily contemporary package that manages to be both elegiac and cutting-edge at the same time. *Ghost* may lament the loss of the individual soul epitomized in Kusanagi's forlorn beauty, but it also accepts the new technological world and the possibility of different kinds of spiritual connections.

Unlike films like *Blade Runner* or *Robocop*, which J. P. Telotte says "offer . . . a path back to the private self,"[17] *Ghost in the Shell* turns in a different direction to offer a path out of the self. While the American films seem to privilege a kind of individual humanism as a last resort against the encroaching forces of technology and capitalism, *Ghost* simply repudiates the constraints of the contemporary industrialized world to suggest that a union of technology and the spirit can ultimately succeed. In the world of the film, human bonding, human aspirations, even human memories are finally repudiated, just as the Crystal Palace-like structure, with its nineteenth-century associations, is blown to bits.

It is possible that there may be cultural differences at the heart of these two visions of technology and the soul. As mentioned before, there are Buddhist and Shinto associations with the "net," and it is a truism that a willingness to give up the self into a larger entity has been an important element in Japanese communal morality for centuries. However, Kusanagi's dive into the Puppet Master's mind may also be seen as a form of defiance against the government and the corporations that first made her their tool, a "marionette" whose identity was fixed as an assassin. It is important to remember, moreover, that the notion of a bodiless supermind is one that has been a staple of Western science fiction as well, since at least the 1950s when Arthur C. Clark's classic novel *Childhood's End* envisaged future children linking together into a transcendent greater entity.

Whatever image Kusanagi finally finds through the mirror, it is surely one that will question not only the fixed categories of the machine and the soul but also the basic notion of what it is to be "normal" at the end of the twentieth century. Indeed, all the works mentioned in this section implicitly problematize what it is to be a "normal" human being, offering an incredible variety of alternatives that play with the notion of a fixed identity. Not all of these alternatives are accepted, however. Ranma searches desperately for a return to normality, *Wicked City* denies the promise/threat of the transforming female body and forces the female back into maternal mode, and the heroes of most of the *mecha* films show ambivalent feelings toward their augmented powers. Even the films that seem to embrace alterity also show its potential for threat. Thus Tetsuo's "birth" into a new universe is seen as accompanied by agonizing pain and Kusanagi must destroy her own body before she can join the net.

Other differences may just be due to the directors' or writers' personal choices. *Ghost in the Shell*'s use of a female protagonist may be related to the fact that Shirow Masamune, the author of the manga on which the film is based, has a predilection for tough, active heroines. Whatever the cause, Kusanagi's obvious femininity may be one reason the film seems imbued with a more ethereal quality than either the typical cyberpunk or *mecha* film. It goes well beyond the typical science fiction privileging of the mechanical and the logical, the world typically associated with "masculine" discourse. Although it gives us an indubitably cyberpunk world replete with cyborgs, computers, robots, and other *mecha* tropes, at the same time it is a world clearly imbued with a sense of otherness that seems remarkably feminine.

In fact, *Ghost in the Shell* shares with other works discussed in the previous chapters a fundamental concern or even unease with the body and thus, implicitly, with identity itself. *Ghost in the Shell, Akira,* and *Evangelion* all seem to be showing attempts to escape the body and thus the constraints of human identity. The new identity that these characters appear to be seeking is one that transcends the categorizing nature of society, especially that of traditional Japanese society. Perhaps the most memorable vision from the last episode of *Evangelion* is the scene in which Shinji's body floats free in a completely empty white space, underlining his need to go beyond the expectation of others. In Tetsuo's case he frees himself from society in a scene that also contains a vision of white blankness as he metamorphoses into an isolated eye. But this transformation is enacted through apocalyptic violence, the physical correlative of Shinji's mental anguish. Kusanagi, in contrast, seems serenely content to leave her body behind, although her transformation is in some ways an apocalyptic one as well, implying the jettisoning of the entire organic world.

Whether these boundaryless figures are regarded as icons of liberation from a constricting society or as sinister harbingers of an inhuman future, they all suggest that identity in anime, even in the most basic form of the body, cannot be taken for granted. The metamorphic process lying at the heart of the animated medium ensures that both characters and viewers can explore the rewarding, though sometimes oppressive, possibilities of creating and encapsulating worlds.

*

PART THREE

MAGICAL GIRLS AND FANTASY WORLDS

THE ANIME DISCUSSED IN THE PREVIOUS SECTION deal with the increasingly problematic issue of identity in the contemporary world, emblematized by the ubiquitous trope of the metamorphosing body. The body was inscribed in various forms and in relation to various problems, including questions of gender identification and relations between the sexes, which in this section are issues of particular interest.

Saito Minako has suggested in her book *Kōitenron* that anime can generally be divided into two categories, the "country of boys" and the "country of girls," implying a very strong gender demarcation in the creation, targeting, narratives, and imagery of anime. Her analysis goes beyond traditional assumptions that *mecha* series and films were more apt to be viewed by males and romances with girl protagonists more likely to have female viewers. She brings up interesting distinctions, such as the fact that while both male and female series may involve transformation (*henshin*) sequences, the male transformation usually is in terms of body armor (such as Sho in the *Guyver*) while female characters usually change clothes and makeup.[1]

In practice, however, many anime blur these distinctions, perhaps increasingly. Scenes of introspection and psychological interaction balanced *Neon Genesis Evangelion*'s action sequences. In addition, although Shinji transforms with the help of EVA body armor, so do his female collaborators. In the end the real "transformations" in the series are internal ones, as the characters begin to understand more about themselves and their relations with the opposite sex. Even the violent and hard-edged *mecha* anime *Ghost in the Shell* was deeply imbued with a dreamy ethereality that could well be called feminine. Going further back to the 1980s, *Ranma 1/2* delighted in showing a highly explicit form of gender confusion, crossing comically back and forth between "boys' country" and "girls' country." At their most interesting, therefore, anime texts seem to be exploring both the complex relations between the sexes and the problematics of gender identification itself.

These problems of gender demarcation and issues between the sexes are not exclusive to Japan of course, but it is important to note that Japanese society has developed strategies of containment that are quite distinctive. One of the most interesting of these strategies has been the notion of "*shōjo* culture." *Shōjo* literally means "little female" and originally referred to girls around the ages of 12 and 13. Over the last couple of decades, however, the term has become a shorthand for a certain kind of liminal identity between child and adult, characterized by a supposedly innocent eroticism based on sexual immaturity, a consumer culture of buying "cute" (*kawaii*) material goods, and a wistful privileging of a recent past or free-floating form of nostalgia.[2] This nostalgia, as summed up by John Treat on the subject of the famous *shōjo* writer, Yoshimoto Banana, tends to be "focused precisely where Japanese 'everyday life' is its most destabilized and fragile,"[3] in particular, the increasing absence of the traditional family.

In the worlds of manga and anime, *shōjo* are everywhere. Whereas in the 1980s they were often hidden away and had a mysterious or even uncanny quality (like the secretive young vampire Miyu of *Vampire Princess Miyu* who combined occult powers with a little girl giggle and a hair ribbon[4]), more recent anime represent *shōjo* as extremely outwardly active. They range from the adorable but vulnerable Saber Marionettes, who help guard an alternative historical Japanese world, to the adorable, fluffy-headed but superpowered Serena of the hugely popular *Sailor Moon* series. Popular among male and female viewers (and readers) the dreamy and charming world of the *shōjo* stands in attractive counterpoint to the darker and more violent texts of much science fiction anime.[5]

Although the *shōjo* genre used to be a popular genre confined to manga and anime (especially in manga, which has been producing a wide variety of *shōjo* comics for decades), the *shōjo* phenomenon now seems to permeate contemporary Japanese culture. As Tamae Prindle says:

> Surely the nation's gaze is more and more focused on girls. Girls occupy a distinctive place in Japan's mass media, including films and literature. What fascinates the Japanese is that the *shōjo* nestle in a shallow lacuna between adulthood and childhood, power and powerlessness, awareness and innocence as well as masculinity and femininity.[6]

In contemporary Japanese society, girls, with their seemingly still-amorphous identities, seem to embody the potential for unfettered change and excitement that is far less available to Japanese males, who are caught in the network of demanding workforce responsibilities. It is not surprising, therefore, that it is the female Kusanagi in *Ghost in the Shell* who melds with the Puppet Master, or that it is Ranma's transformation into a girl that gives the series its narrative pleasure. Even in pornography, it is clear that it is the female's ability to transform that adds excitement to sometimes conventional narratives, although this transformative power is always ultimately contained.

The next two chapters focus on the topos of the *shōjo* in anime, although I should stress that *shōjo* is an extremely elastic term; it is ambiguous at what point on the continuum that the *shōjo* ends and the more adult female begins. Thus film director Miyazaki Hayao's young female characters are indubitably *shōjo* in terms of their age and general innocence but some of them are moving out of their liminal state toward a sense of identity as mature human beings. Conversely, the "magical girls" in chapter 8 are older and in some ways more independent and more erotically delineated than the quintessential *shōjo,* but they still exist in a clearly liminal state in which adult concerns and responsibilities play no part.

What does seem certain is that many Japanese are able to project issues of identity construction onto the attractive and unthreatening figure of the *shōjo.* Indeed, in the case of Miyazaki's works the *shōjo* offer blueprints for a better identity that seems to combine both the nurturing aspects of the feminine and the strength and independence associated with the masculine. Even in the more conservative world of romantic comedy, the magical young girls display contradictory powers of aggression and nurturance. In contrast to the armored *mecha* body, the *shōjo* exhibits strength *plus* vulnerability in a way that is intriguingly feminine.

CHAPTER SEVEN

THE ENCHANTMENT OF ESTRANGEMENT: THE *SHŌJO* IN THE WORLD OF MIYAZAKI HAYAO

Dear Mr. Miyazaki:

I am a girl in middle school. I am a big fan of yours. I think "Conan" is wonderful. I really enjoy watching it on television.

But there is one thing I was wondering about. Your girl characters aren't real at all and seem strange to me and my friends of the same age. I can't believe that those kinds of girls really exist.

—Murase Hiromi, *Pop Culture Critique*

I don't try to create according to a particular model of the world . . .
my world is one part of a larger world.
　　　　—Miyazaki Hayao in an interview with Yamaguchi Izumi,
　　　　　　　　　　　　Eureka, Special Issue on Miyazaki

[*My Neighbor Totoro*] is not nostalgia; it is an appeal to know what
we have lost.
　　　　　　　　　　　—*Eureka, Special Issue on Miyazaki*

AS JAPAN'S MOST FAMOUS ANIMATED FILM DIRECTOR, Miyazaki Hayao
has played a vital role in creating *shōjo* in anime. It should be stressed
at the outset, however, that Miyazaki's *shōjo* are of a very distinctive
type, often quite assertive and independent, attributes that are consonant with the fact that Miyazaki's animated worlds are also highly
distinctive. In fact, Miyazaki is perhaps best known for two particular
elements in his works, his richly realized fantasy worlds and his
memorable female characters. Although they vary, sometimes substan-
tially, from film to film, both his fantasy worlds and his female
characters are always recognizable Miyazaki creations. His intensely
colored animated worldscapes filled with his trademark images of
flying machines, soaring clouds, and supernatural creatures take on a
breathtaking life of their own while his brave, inquisitive, and risk-
taking young female characters are far removed from the identity
confusion that characterizes many *shōjo* characters.[1]

Miyazaki takes anime's basic propensity to defamiliarize consen-
sus reality in a direction that allows him to develop his own agenda,
one that incorporates an ethical and aesthetic universe that is both
exotic and yet at some level familiar. As Yamaguchi points out in the
interview quoted above, "This is not realism at the level of daily life
but rather the expression of an independent imaginative universe."[2]
Although Miyazaki's worlds are indeed "independent," their careful
mixture of realistic and fantastic details makes them able to exist
comfortably inside a larger realm that could legitimately include our
own universe as well, as Miyazaki suggests in the same interview. This
heightens the fantasy world's "believability." The viewer finds in each
film a topography that is exotic (or even totally alien, like *Nausicaä of
the Valley of the Wind*'s future world), but at the same time so richly
realized down to minute details that it seems at least potentially

contiguous to our own world. Judging by Miyazaki's tremendous popularity in Japan and his increasingly high reputation abroad, most viewers must enjoy the richness of his films' overall vision.

What is Miyazaki's vision? It is one that incorporates an ethical (some critics would say moralistic) agenda that is expressed not only in terms of narrative and characters but also through his extraordinary animation. More than any other animator dealt with in this book, Miyazaki has the most potential for didacticism. However, the exceptional beauty of his imagery creates an "Other" world of immense appeal that transcends a specific agenda, and softens the more didactic elements of his vision. This vision is not only of "what is lost," as the quotation above suggests, but also, perhaps most importantly, of *what could be.*

"What is lost" includes a world in which nature is not yet dominated by humanity and exists as a powerful force in itself, strong in its identity as the nonhuman Other. This vision is seen most clearly in Miyazaki's privileging of forests and trees in prewar or even premodern settings in works such as *My Neighbor Totoro, Princess Mononoke,* and *Laputa.* Concurrently in these works and others, especially *Nausicaä,* he highlights images of postindustrial (or even postapocalyptic) barrenness and devastation. But what is lost is not restricted only to the natural. In his marvelous renderings of a defamiliarized Europe that is both fantastic and yet believable (*Porco Rosso, Kiki's Delivery Service*), Miyazaki evokes a world of serene architectural and natural beauty and civilized, harmonious urban life, "a Europe in which war had never happened" as *Eureka* describes it.[3]

Often there is a strong element of the apocalyptic in Miyazaki's works not only explicitly as in *Laputa, Nausicaä,* and *Princess Mononoke,* but also implicitly in the animator's refusal to use contemporary Japan as a setting. As critic Shimizu Yoshiyuki sums it up,

> . . . [m]ost of Miyazaki's works take place in worlds where the systematizing structures and rationalizing processes of the modern world have been destroyed and a condition of disorder has overturned everything, future worlds such as *Nausicaä,* or *Conan,* or worlds before the process of modernization has been finalized (*Laputa, Porco Rosso*). In other words, modern Japan as a narrative

site is consistently avoided. It is as if his narrative can only exist before modernization or after modernity has been destroyed.[4]

"What could be" is of course the other side of "what is lost," worlds in which nature still exerts independent power, embodied in the scene in *Princess Mononoke* of the great woodland god, the *shishigami*, extending its neck in the moonlit forest. Other possible worlds include a collective vision of hope and renewal, as presented in the final scene in *Nausicaä*, or simply the power of love, as evidenced in Sheeta's and Pazu's willingness to die together for the sake of the world in *Laputa*. Frequently this theme of possibility is expressed through the many images of flight that pervade virtually all of Miyazaki's works (with the exception of *Princess Mononoke*). In these soaring images, from gliders and warplanes to the flying island of Laputa to Nausicaä's climactic walk through the sky, Miyazaki's vision reaches its most magical heights, suggesting the possibility of freedom, change, and redemption.

Besides Miyazaki's fantasy worldscapes, the other key element of his independent imaginative universe is his deployment of female characters, in whom he provides a crucial potential for change, growth, and compassionate empowerment. Precisely because they are indeed not "real" at the "level of daily life," his heroines are the conduits through which the promise of Miyazaki's magical alternative realities are mediated or idealized guides helping the viewer understand and imaginatively participate in Miyazaki's distinctive and defamiliarizing vision of the real.

Although Miyazaki's works include some impressive older female characters (see chapter 10), Miyazaki's favorite type of female character is the *shōjo*. Fascination with *shōjo* identity began in the 1980s, the period in which Miyazaki created some of his greatest films, all of which highlighted young female characters. Although his *shōjo* incorporate the elements of the wider *shōjo* identity described above, it is important to emphasize how much they also differ from the accepted ideal. Unlike the classic *shōjo*, who is usually characterized by an ultrafemininity that is often passive or dreamy (or perhaps ditzy, as in the case of, say, Serena in *Sailor Moon*), Miyazaki's girl characters are notably independent and active, courageously confronting the variety of obstacles before them in a manner that might well be described as stereotypically masculine.

Indeed, the journal *Eureka* characterizes Miyazaki's young female characters as simply "youths wearing *shōjo* masks."[5] While this statement may be considered too broad, since his female characters also possess qualities of nurturance, compassion, and, perhaps, an innocent eroticism that are more typically feminine, *Eureka* is correct in highlighting what might be called their "unfeminine" elements, because these are what make Miyazaki heroines so remarkable. A few of the many possible examples of Miyazaki's *shōjo*'s unfeminine behavior include the shocking scene in *Nausicaä* in which the protagonist kills with a sword the men who murdered her father, the confrontation between Sheeta and the evil Muska in *Laputa* in which Sheeta steadfastly refuses to give him her magic stone, the opening scene of *Kiki's Delivery Service* when the 13-year-old Kiki leaves home wavering on her broomstick to begin a new life alone in a strange city, and virtually all the actions of *Princess Mononoke*'s female protagonist, San, whose decidedly "unfeminine" behavior consists of attacking and attempting to destroy as many members of the human race as possible.

The distinctiveness of these characterizations cannot be overemphasized. While many anime heroines such as Cutey Honey or the "knights" in *Bubblegum Crisis* are clearly constructed as "action heroes" (albeit extremely sexy action heroes), they are usually adult women, and their actions tend to be essentially one note, consisting of various forms of violent retribution toward evildoers. Furthermore, these more typical heroines tend to be part of a larger group (crime fighters, space patrollers, etc.), while Miyazaki's heroines are normally on their own. The opening scenes of *Nausicaä, Laputa,* and *Kiki's Delivery Service* all show the heroine alone and literally in flight. Even the two very young girls in *My Neighbor Totoro* explore their supposedly haunted house by themselves. Traditional to mythic and fairy tale conventions, the girls are often orphaned (San, Sheeta), or with absent mothers (Nausicaä, Mei, Satsuki), or without parental support (Kiki), but their active independence is unusual for most fairy tales, particularly in Japan, where active protagonists are almost exclusively male.

Playing on traditional conventions with a contemporary twist, Miyazaki is clearly not only attempting to break down the conventional image of femininity but also to break down the viewer's conventional notion of the world in general. He is forcing us to become estranged from what we take for granted and to open up to new possibilities of what the world could be. By highlighting his female characters and making them steadfast, empowered, and independent, Miyazaki throws these attributes into sharp relief, forcing the viewer to be aware of these qualities at a level of perception that a more conventional male protagonist would be unlikely to stimulate. It is not surprising that virtually all his *shōjo* characters are strongly associated with flight because it is in images of flying that the possibilities of escape (from the past, from tradition) are most clearly realized.

This chapter examines Miyazaki's use of the *shōjo* in three of his major films: *My Neighbor Totoro* (*Tonari no Totoro*, 1988), *Kiki's Delivery Service* (*Majo no takkyūbin*, 1989), and *Nausicaä* (*Kaze no tani no Nausicaä*, 1984), both in the context of the *shōjo* image and in terms of the films' relation to the alternate realities they illuminate. In contrast to the critic Murase Hiromi's critique, written by her childhood self, quoted at the beginning of this chapter, I would argue that Miyazaki's female characters are indeed "real" and richly believable *within the confines of the narrative*. As Phillip Brophy says of the world of the Warner Brothers cartoons, "these cartoons (along with their Disney counterparts) are unavoidably and alone, material. Their *own* material, with their own dynamic energy and textual life."[6] While Murase, as a junior high school student, insisted that "peaceful, quiet, nature-loving girls just don't exist," in the alternate realities created by Miyazaki, these girls can and do exist, inspiring many viewers to identify with them as role models if not as surrogate identities.[7]

MY NEIGHBOR TOTORO: THE USES OF ENCHANTMENT

In developing both his heroines and his fantasy worlds, Miyazaki draws on a huge variety of sources including myth, ancient Japanese court tales, Japanese history, science fiction, and fairy tales. Although very different in style and content, his films also share two important commonalities. One is that each narrative stems from an extreme situation, the dissolution of a world.[8] While *Nausicaä of the Valley of the Wind's* situation is the most obviously apocalyptic (the narrative takes place after a series of horrific wars have engulfed the earth), both *My Neighbor Totoro* and *Kiki's Delivery Service* contain psychological parallels involving the loss of the family. *Totoro*'s plot begins with a move from city to country due to the grave illness of the mother of the family, while *Kiki*'s narrative begins with her leaving home at the age of 13 to spend a year on her own in a strange city. The other commonality is that each narrative is defamiliarized through the use of the *shōjo* characters, whose curious, assertive, but still feminine personalities add fresh notes to classic stories.

Turning to *My Neighbor Totoro* first, we find that although its two heroines are very young children they still convey a notable degree of three-dimensionality. This is particularly true of little Mei, whose stubborn steadfastness is utterly believable, adding a realistic note to a story of fantasy.

In fact, *Totoro* stands as a clear example of a genre that the literary critic Tzvetan Todorov labels as the fantastic, a surprisingly limited genre characterized by the reader/viewer's response to a seemingly strange event that could be interpreted as either supernatural (i.e., fantasy) *or* real (for example, the fantastic occurrence actually turns out to be a hallucination or dream). The true genre of the fantastic, according to Todorov, contains works in which the moment of hesitation remains unresolved, leaving the viewer/reader in a state of uncertainty. This is essentially what happens in *Totoro*, where the fantastic world that the children discover could be either supernatural or an expression of their own imaginations.

Although interesting from the point of view of genre discussion, *Totoro*'s membership in the genre of the fantastic is even more intriguing from the point of view of how this ambiguity relates to Miyazaki's depiction of his *shōjo* characters. One of the film's implicit points is that the fantastic allows even very young children to take care of themselves psychologically in times of stress or disturbance. Furthermore, whether the viewer believes in a natural or supernatural explanation, the characters' ability to connect with the Other, be it the unconscious or the supernatural, is clearly coded as a sign of inner strength and mental health. Mei and her older sister Satsuki face bravely such major disturbances as a move and a parent's illness, epitomizing the dynamic spirit typical of the Miyazaki heroine.

The two girls' literal and metaphorical "childishness" works particularly well with the small scale and intimate quality of the film, while the film's focalization through their eyes is especially appropriate for its quasi-fairy-tale narrative. Set in Japan in roughly the 1950s, *Totoro* encompasses a world where nature and the rural scene not only play a significant role in people's lives but are also a bridge to the world of the supernatural and the enchanting. As anime scholar Helen McCarthy says of the film, "the deliberate reduction of scale from the epic to the everyday makes one of the major points of the film—that importance and impact are relative to viewpoint, that the tiniest trivia have huge impact on those earliest years and how they shape us."[9] The importance of viewpoint in relation to a child's focalization is remarkably close to a Japanese scholar's encapsulation of the *shōjo* ideal: "Because shōjo are not adults, they can perceive things that those in control of society cannot; because they are not young men they see things that those who will someday rule society cannot see."[10]

A young girl's fresh and clear-eyed perception of the world is the key to *Totoro*. The simple story follows the adventures of the two little girls, especially the youngest, Mei, as they begin a new life in an old house in the country while their mother is in the hospital. Although the girls live with their kind, anthropologist father, he and the handful of other adults in the film are peripheral to the girls' discovery of the magic literally in their own backyard. This magic begins with Mei's discovery of the seemingly supernatural "dustbunnies" (*kurosuke*), tiny shimmering points of blackness that infest the supposedly haunted house but disappear when the light is turned on. These "spirits," critic Hirashima Natsuko suggests,[11] are really symbols of the little girls' anxiety over moving into a new house and fear at the possibility of losing their mother, emotions more effectively conveyed through images rather than words. More positive representations of the supernatural include a giant camphor tree outside the house, whose ancient presence the family finds both comforting and mysterious. The magical aspect of the film is best epitomized, however, by the creature known as a "totoro," a large furry beast incorporating both the cuddly aspects of a panda and the mysterious aspects of a cat. It is Mei who is the main conduit to the *totoro*, and the scene of her first encounter with it captures her growing sense of excitement and awareness in a way that, as Japanese critics have noted, is not unlike Alice's discovery of the white rabbit in *Alice in Wonderland*, another fantasy focused through the innocent eyes of a young girl.

Left alone while her father works in his study and Satsuki is off to school, Mei wanders idly until she happens to pick up a bucket and peers through a hole in it. Through the hole she sees first a shimmering in the grass, then an acorn, then the acorn gatherer, a strange little creature (actually a miniature *totoro*) whom she follows with clearly mounting excitement. Another, slightly larger one soon accompanies the creature. After crawling through a long tunnel of tree roots and emerging at the base of the giant camphor tree, Mei falls down a crevice in the tree to find a giant *totoro* sleeping placidly on its back. Unafraid, she crawls on top of its stomach and asks the creature its name. In a gesture that could be terrifying, it opens its enormous red mouth complete with large white teeth only to emit a sound that she takes to be its name, "to-to-ro."[12] Satisfied that the creature is harmless, Mei falls asleep on the *totoro*'s massive furry stomach. While soft music plays, shots of other peaceful moments follow: A butterfly plays around the sleepers, a snail crawls up a leaf, and ripples form quietly on a pond.

The scenes of Mei's first encounter with the *totoro* effectively create a low-key sense of the enchantment lurking in daily life, epitomized by the broken old bucket that Mei peers through to see her first fantastic creature. Although the similarities with *Alice in Wonderland* (even including Mei's tumbling down a hole) are significant, it is more worthwhile to consider the important differences between the two works. The world of *Alice in Wonderland,* although indubitably magical, is also inherently absurd and even threatening. Unlike the *totoro,* the rabbit whom Alice follows is confused, selfish, and petty, as are virtually all the other characters in the text. Furthermore, the beautiful garden that Alice longs to enter—and finally does at the end of the book—turns out to be an ominous place of nonsense games, inedible feasts, and shouts of "off with her head." In contrast, Mei's encounter with the various *totoro,* although initially slightly disorienting because they change in size, shape, and quantity and potentially frightening because the final *totoro* is so huge with such a large mouth,[13] is actually one of serenity and comfort, surrounded by images of harmony and beauty.

The following scene when Mei wakes up and tells her family about the *totoro* is also intriguingly different from *Alice.* Rather than accepting the experience as a dream, Mei insists that it was real and gets angry when her father and sister laugh at her. They soon take her seriously, however, and her father tells her that she must have met "the king of the forest" and takes the two girls to bow down in front of the giant camphor tree. Her family's willingness to take Mei seriously is a crucial element in the narrative's incorporation of the fantastic in the mundane.[14] In contrast to *Alice's* compartmentalization of "Wonderland" from the real world, *Totoro* insists on a porous membrane between fantasy (or the imagination) and reality. Furthermore, that the father acknowledges Mei's vision is a vital factor in contributing to her own feeling of security, a feeling clearly threatened by the move and her mother's illness and absence.

In an analysis of *Totoro,* Shimizu argues that the *totoro* fantasy is simply a product of the children's imagination, an instrument of comfort devised by Mei, permitted by the father, and ultimately participated in by the older sister Satsuki as well. Pointing to the essentially forlorn situation of the girls, uncertain as to whether their mother will ever recover and come home, Shimizu comments on the comforting quality of the *totoro,* especially the creature's tendency to appear at particularly lonely moments. Examples are the first encounter, when Mei is left to her own devices, or the first time Satsuki actually sees the *totoro* when the two girls are waiting in the rain at a lonely bus stop looking for their father to come home. Instead, the *totoro* appears and Satsuki lends it an umbrella, "almost as if she were lending it to her father." Even more than fatherhood, however, the *totoro* evokes a warm and embracing mother, not only in its own comfortable, furry body but in the "cat bus" it summons on two occasions in the film, another furry creature that in the climactic scene literally opens up to enfold the girls "in an embrace that gives the impression of a mother's warm, tactile connections."[15]

Totoro can thus be seen as a classic fantasy of compensation but one that is more or less controlled by the girls themselves, since the fantasy stems from their own imaginations. In one particularly beautiful scene, for example, the two girls awaken one night to watch as the *totoro,* accompanied by two miniature *totoros,* performs a ritual dance to help fertilize the "magic" seeds the creature gave the girls as a present. Impelled to join in, the girls are soon caught up in the dance and then literally caught up in the *totoro* itself as, mimicking the actions of the two miniature *totoros* (their fantasy alter egos perhaps) they attach themselves to the *totoro*'s body as it whirls in the air, taking them on a moonlit flight above sleeping forests, rice paddies, and houses. Flying scenes are crucial in Miyazaki's oeuvre, but this one is particularly important. Not only does their soaring flight above the mundane world suggest "the child's sense of omnipotence,"[16] but in this case it also hints very specifically at the two girls' ability to transcend their most frightening anxieties and fears, emotions that occur most intensely at nighttime.

At the film's climax, however, this ability becomes temporarily problematic when the girls discover that their mother, who was supposed to come home to visit them that weekend, has caught a cold and must stay in the hospital. Their excitement turns to despair and each girl regresses: Mei becomes stubbornly whiny while Satsuki loses her temper with her. Angry and miserable, Mei runs away, apparently to seek her mother in the hospital, while Satsuki descends into hysterical action, running futilely through the paddy fields in a vain search for her sister. Almost giving up hope, Satsuki finally calls on the *totoro* to help her and once again it appears, this time to summon the magical "cat bus" that will take her first to Mei and then to the hospital. As Hirashima points out, it is only when Mei disappears that Satsuki gets directly in touch with the *totoro*.[17] This suggests that at the moment of crisis the older Satsuki must connect with her more childlike elements (i.e., her own imaginative resources) rather than relying on adults for guidance.

Whether or not the final scene, in which the children watch their parents while happily ensconced in the branches of the tree outside of the hospital, is simply a product of the children's wishful imagination, is far less important than the overall sense of joy and harmony that the film's ending evokes. Indeed, if the scene is only a product of their imagination, this underscores the girls' ability to take care of themselves psychologically at a time of great stress and need. That magic (or the power of the human imagination) can exist in the world in alliance with the mystery of nature is part of *Totoro*'s fundamental message. But perhaps the more important part of the message is that, in order to connect with that power, there is a need not only for bravery, endurance, and imagination, but also for a willingness to admit need, a vulnerability that is perhaps best epitomized in the figure of a young girl. In expressing this message Miyazaki uses his own superb visual imagination coupled with a subtle evocation of the psychology and perceptions of two children to give the viewer a brief encounter with a world that is perhaps not so much estranged from reality as it is an enchanting enhancement of it.

KIKI'S DELIVERY SERVICE:
FEAR OF FLYING

In its evocation of the Japanese landscape, complete with farmhouses, paddy fields, and Shinto shrines, *Totoro* is the most self-consciously "Japanese" of the three works discussed in this chapter. In contrast, 1989's *Kiki's Delivery Service,* the next film to be discussed, takes place in an amorphous but clearly European-looking world and deploys such Western fairy-tale archetypes as witches and black cats. But *Kiki* also deals with the same issues of imagination, bravery, and belief in oneself that were played out in *Totoro,* although on a somewhat more adult level. McCarthy sums up the film's special appeal: "Not many films allow a child—and in particular a girl—to deal with the problems of selfhood, self-reliance, personal adequacy, creativity and love, and not many struggles take place in so beautifully executed a setting."[18] The story follows a young witch named Kiki, who at the age of 13, in accordance with tradition, must make her way alone for a year. Bidding a fond but rather casual farewell to her parents, Kiki settles in a beautiful, vaguely Mediterranean-looking city where she opens her own delivery service.

Kiki is very much the Miyazaki heroine in terms of her stalwart resolution, liveliness, and charm. Like Mei and Satsuki she encounters and vanquishes obstacles all on her own, but they are of a somewhat different type than those in *Totoro.* Some of them are simply the physical problems of finding a new home and getting established, not to mention learning to fly her broom properly, but none are earth-shattering issues on the level of a parent's potential death. What is remarkable, however, is the fact that Kiki is a girl. The idea of a girl leaving home and setting up her own business would be surprising in any culture but particularly so in Japan. In Kiki's happy independence we see Miyazaki's technique of defamiliarization working most effectively. Traits that might have been taken for granted had the protagonist been a boy—autonomy, competence, and ability to plan—are freshly highlighted through Kiki's femininity to create a memorable coming-of-age story.

Kiki is not always competent, of course, and much of the film's gentle pleasure comes from watching her deal with an occasional misadventure, such as the time when, flying hurriedly on a delivery, she drops a child's treasured toy deep into the forest below. The accident ends happily, however, as it leads her to an encounter with another independent young woman, an artist named Ursula who seems in many ways a more grown-up version of Kiki. Happily surviving on her own, Ursula offers Kiki the role model of a woman deeply satisfied in her work. In this and in her other encounters with the kindly townsfolk and with a young boy named Tombo, Kiki is given models of friendly, thoughtful interaction that help her in her own growth toward maturity.

Kiki does have one serious crisis in her personal development, however. She loses her ability to fly and this crisis operates as the film's emotional climax. Her sudden loss might initially seem surprising, given that the viewer would probably assume that flying is an innate witch talent. As the film makes clear, however, flying is based on both confidence and competence, and Kiki's self-doubt destroys her powers. Or, as scholar Ishihara Ikuko explains Kiki's problem, "witch's power is not something you inherit naturally, you must nurture it in yourself in order to acquire it."[19] What might be taken for granted in a traditional fairy tale, such as supernatural powers, is problematized in such a manner that the audience sees it anew.

The film is thus an allegory of maturation in which belief in the self is the key to genuine development. In the film's action climax Kiki's powers are restored to her at the moment she needs them most, when trying to rescue her young friend Tombo, who is clinging to a rope dangling from a damaged airship. No longer thinking of herself and her own worries, Kiki is free to call on her old powers. The film ends on a note of satisfaction as Kiki writes home to her parents saying how much she likes life in her new community.

Although the film does not emphasize this, it is interesting that Kiki's loss of power/confidence occurs during puberty, a period when many young girls question their innate competence. Even though Kiki's sexuality is kept deliberately low-key, it is significant that the return of her powers comes about through her involvement with a boy.

In a reversal of the conventional male coming-of-age tale, which might end with the young man rescuing a damsel in distress, it is Kiki who rescues Tombo, solidifying her passage on the road to genuine independence. Liberated from her own worries by her concern for someone else and capable of fast and efficient action, it is hardly surprising that Kiki's story ends on a note of quiet triumph.

Unlike most of Miyazaki's other films, which are usually based on narratives of his own devising, *Kiki's Delivery Service* is based on a popular children's story of the same name. There are a few major differences between the original and the film. Of these, two of the most important are the film's more explicit incorporation of a money economy within the narrative and, perhaps most significantly, that the book contains no scene of Kiki's losing her ability to fly.[20]

As opposed to the original work, in which Kiki usually bartered her services in a friendly fashion, it is clear in the film that money and survival are strongly linked, a contrast not only to the book but also to virtually all of Miyazaki's other films, which seem to take place in either pre- or post-capitalist societies. *Kiki's Delivery Service* includes not only many scenes where Kiki is directly paid for her services but also scenes of Kiki shopping, worrying that she will not be able to afford what she needs, and fearing that she will have to survive on pancakes for the rest of her time alone.

These scenes are interesting for two reasons. First, they take the narrative, which, with its mise-en-scène of idealized Mediterranean architecture and luscious green and blue landscapes could easily slip into purely fairy-tale format, and ground it firmly in a recognizable framework of the "real." Consequently, despite its clearly fantasy elements of witches and flying, *Kiki* is one of the few Miyazaki films closely connected to the nitty-gritty of real life. Second, this emphasis on the money economy makes Kiki remarkably real, as witches go. Her desire to work hard and to prove herself are unpretentious goals, even though she does fly on a broom in order to accomplish them. Thus, Miyazaki uses two forms of defamiliarization here: first, as we have already noted, by having a heroine who is independent and active, and second by making her a witch whose fantastic powers are prosaically anchored in the need to survive in a modern money economy. By balancing fantasy with the real, the film's message of empowerment becomes far more effective.

The film's second plot addition of Kiki's loss of her powers is another element that strengthens the film's message. This loss has nothing to do with fantasy (e.g., another witch's curse or growing too old to use her witch's powers) and everything to do with psychological realism. Kiki's loss and subsequent recovery of her powers at the film's climax provide scenes that are visually exciting (the scene when Kiki and her broom almost fall straight to the ground is thrillingly conceived) but emotionally satisfying as well, a mixture of fantasy and action movie techniques that creates a psychologically realistic allegory of self-discovery. As with *Totoro*, the film's portrait of a young girl coping with the world is a fantasized and idealized one, and yet it rings true on the deepest of psychological levels.

THE FLYING WOMAN:
NAUSICAÄ OF THE VALLEY OF THE WINDS

While *My Neighbor Totoro* and *Kiki's Delivery Service* are both rather subtle portraits of female empowerment, *Nausicaä of the Valley of the Wind* is a flamboyant paean to an ideal of femininity that is both remarkably contemporary and yet at the same time epic in its scope. Just as *Totoro* takes another look at children's fantasy and *Kiki's Delivery Service* defamiliarizes the conventional coming-of-age story, *Nausicaä* takes the traditional epic and makes it new and fresh through the character of its eponymous heroine. Omnicompetent, blessed with special powers, and potentially even a messiah figure, she is perhaps the single Miyazaki heroine who genuinely warrants Murase's criticism of being "not real at all." And yet it must be reiterated that within the confines of the narrative, Nausicaä is indeed "real." She is a genuine hero in a narrative of epic proportions. Through the complex figure of Nausicaä, who is simultaneously enchanting, lethal, brilliant, and compassionate, Miyazaki takes what might have been a conventional postapocalyptic science fiction story and creates a unique masterpiece of hope and redemption.

Nausicaä's larger-than-life quality is obvious from the beginning of the film when the viewer first encounters her. The film opens with a fearsome vision of the postapocalyptic wasteland and segues into a shot of an ancient tapestry unscrolling to reveal its final image, which is that of a winged figure in blue. The scene changes abruptly to a vision of the open sky and a long shot of a little glider soaring through the air as the film's theme music swells around it. Underscored by the music, this flying sequence evokes a sense of power, freedom, and limitless possibility encapsulated in the small figure of the glider's pilot. The focus shifts to show that the pilot is a female in blue.

It is only after the glider has landed that the viewer gets a glimpse of its pilot from the front as she marches into the forest, and even then she is still wearing a mask that covers much of her face. Thus, Nausicaä is first presented as a mysterious, perhaps even androgynous, figure appropriate to the bizarre landscape she inhabits and as metonymically associated with the supernatural figure on the tapestry. The impression of an enigmatic but competent presence is deepened by her subsequent actions as she puts plant specimens into a test tube and finds the shell of an Omu, a species of enormous insect that populate this postapocalyptic world.

A new note to her personality is interjected at this point, however, as she cries out in excitement at the shell and reveals a cute *shōjo*-esque voice. This distinctive combination of adult, even professional competence and lyrical *shōjo* charm is continued through the rest of the scene, which shows her first efficiently detaching the shell through the use of gunpowder and carving tools and then whirling around joyously with the now detached shell in her arms. Sitting dreamily among the softly falling spores, she murmurs "*kiree*" (beautiful) as she seemingly falls into a reverie, only to be awakened by the sound of a distant explosion. Although reverting to warrior mode—running toward her glider with a weapon in her hands—she also utters a quick "sorry" to the insects she disturbs with her running. Taking to the air again, she locates the source of the explosions, rescues a beleaguered human cowering behind a shelter, and ultimately sends a giant invading insect back to the forest.

This opening sequence offers a fresh take on the generic science fiction trope of a lone survivor in the postapocalyptic wasteland. Through his use of a *shōjo* character who is at the same time efficient with weaponry and yet joyously aware of the beauty of the strange but dangerous world she inhabits and his employment of extraordinarily beautiful visuals and music, Miyazaki defamiliarizes what could be a stock science fiction scene of a human character venturing into an unearthly world. The strangeness of the setting, when filtered through the eyes of the distinctive character of Nausicaä, leaves a powerful impression on the viewer. She is a unique personality whose combination of "feminine" qualities (aesthetic delight, compassion, and nurturance) and "masculine" qualities (mechanical and scientific ability and fighting prowess) create a memorable figure. Nausicaä's almost intimidating omnicompetence is leavened by her clearly feminine voice and actions, such as her whirling with the insect shell and her instinctive apology as she runs through the forest. This combination is constantly underlined throughout the film, climaxing at its end when Nausicaä's "masculine" bravery is matched only by her "feminine" willingness to sacrifice her life for the sake of world harmony.

Perhaps the most surprising display of these mixed qualities comes in one of the few really shocking scenes in any of Miyazaki's films. This sequence occurs after Nausicaä returns to her homeland in the Valley of the Wind. Upon returning to her family's castle she finds that her father has been murdered by an advance guard of the invading Torumekian army. Wild with grief and fury, Nausicaä attacks with her sword and succeeds in killing every one of the soldiers who had slain her father. While the scene is a brief one with little overt bloodshed, the fact that it is the normally controlled, compassionate Nausicaä who kills is deeply shocking and seemingly out of place in a narrative that largely positions her as a heroic, almost perfect figure.[21] In fact, Nausicaä's justifiable fury and bloodshed may well be considered appropriate for a male epic hero but the fact that it is a girl who performs these feats makes the sequence particularly startling. As *Eureka* says of Miyazaki's older women characters, many of whom are warriors as well, "the last means to prove men's superiority to women is violence."[22] By making his women characters violent or even more violent than his men, Miyazaki defamiliarizes yet another popular stereotype.

Following the scene of murderous revenge, Nausicaä acknowledges her own contrition at what she has done. Crying out to her mentor, Master Yupa, that "I'm even frightened of myself," she goes on to admit that "I lost my temper and killed. I don't want to kill anyone else." This scene is as important as the killing scene, since it allows the viewer to see Nausicaä as vulnerable for the first and only time in the film. In marked contrast to Satsuki, Mei, or Kiki, who were character-

ized by a simultaneous combination of fortitude and vulnerability
(Satsuki's and Mei's half-excited, half-frightened exploration of their
new house; the beginning of Kiki's adventure as she wavers clumsily
on her broom), Nausicaä seems totally in control throughout the film.
By presenting her in a small but intense moment of violence followed
by equally intense contrition, Miyazaki humanizes her, making her an
even more complex creation. Perhaps even more important, he problematizes the notion of violence in a genre (the apocalyptic) that is
often saturated with it.

In the final scene of the film Nausicaä sacrifices herself only to
be reborn as the possible savior of the world. This is less ambiguous
and more appropriate to the film's epic character than was the killing
spree. Nausicaä's willingness to sacrifice herself for the world combines both her heroic and her nurturing aspects. Her final apotheosis,
seen in a long shot of her small figure walking among the golden
feelers of the Omu insects, high above the heads of her fellow humans,
is reminiscent of her first appearance at the film's beginning. Small but
stalwart and linked to a world above the earth, she remains a powerful
symbol of the possibility of redemption after unimaginable loss.

The importance of flying in Miyazaki's films has been mentioned
before. While it is not always only the young girls who fly (see *Porco
Rosso* and *Laputa*) it is clear that flying is a major symbol of
empowerment for his *shōjo* characters. In flight the girls transcend the
strictures of the real, be they the expectations of society or simply the
limitations of the body itself. Flying also adds a carnival or festival
element to the narrative, as these sequences give an impression of
exhilaration and excitement (and sometimes, as in *Kiki,* of the comic),
an obvious escape from the ordered, earthbound world.[23] Most
importantly, however, the image of the flying girl sends a message of
boundless possibility in which emotions, imagination, and sometimes
even technology (for example, Nausicaä's soaring glider) combine to
offer hope of a potentially attainable alternative world that transcends
our own.

CHAPTER EIGHT

CARNIVAL AND CONSERVATISM IN ROMANTIC COMEDY

Enacting ideologies of naturalization, women in [Japanese] TV families defer to their husbands, serve them tea, and clean up after them . . . women's subordination to men . . . is promoted in politics, in theory, and on television as eternal features of the national landscape.
—Andrew A. Painter, "The Telepresentation of Gender"

FANTASTIC ROMANCE IS ONE OF THE MOST POPULAR GENRES in recent Japanese animation. It is usually presented in episodic situation comedy format, distinctive for its high-spirited tone and broad, often slapstick, humor and revolves around what are usually known as "magical girlfriends."[1] These magical girlfriends have genuinely magic powers and are somewhat older than the *shōjo* characters in Miyazaki's works. Furthermore, in contrast to the rather androgynous Miyazaki heroines, they are sexualized figures who engage in a wide continuum of erotic play with their decidedly unmagical human boyfriends. However, in contrast to the totally sexualized female characters in pornography, these "girls" still project a strongly innocent quality, closer to the still immature *shōjo* than to an adult woman.

In this regard they, like Miyazaki's characters, seem to occupy a pleasantly fantastic space, far removed from any strictures of history or reality in general. Each series adheres to the standard boy-meets-girl paradigm of romantic comedy, but in these anime, the "girl" is usually a literally otherworldly female, ranging all the way from Scandinavian goddess to video-generated fantasy. Interwoven with bizarre imagery and events, the material seems to offer perfect escapist fantasy. Frequently festivalesque in the amount of anarchic craziness that their narratives engender, each series may be analyzed for the inventiveness of its story lines and its imaginative and sometimes poignant imagery.

Furthermore, romantic comedy anime, not unlike its American television counterpart, is fruitful material for examining a variety of social dynamics, including neighborhood, family, and male-female interactions, at the end of the twentieth century. While Miyazaki's works were carefully structured calls to activism in an attempt to change the world, these works, with their copious fantasy elements, wild plot twists, and absurd exaggerations of character, act as transforming mirrors of certain prevalent currents in modern Japanese society. Sometimes, as in the case of *Video Girl Ai* and *Oh My Goddess,* the works also play a compensatory role as well, allowing the male characters to enact wish-fulfilling fantasies, but in all cases, the exaggerations help to highlight issues of concern that might be contained or swept away in a more realistic drama. As scholar Lynn Spigel says of the suburban sitcom during the 1960s in America, "the fantastic sit-com provided a cultural space in which anxieties about everyday life could be addressed, albeit through a series of displacements and distortions."[2]

In anime these "displacements and distortions" include such crucial issues as the growing independence of women, the changing role of the family, and the increasing importance of technology. The changing status of women in particular has had repercussions throughout society as women became more critical of the conventional Japanese lifestyle that, in the words of one Japanese woman, "emphasizes efficiency, order and harmony and . . . makes no effort to respect lifestyles [ikikata] which stray from the norm,"[3] In contrast to this statement, the anime romantic comedies not only overturn the ideals of "efficiency, order, and harmony" but also appear to privilege, superficially at least, "lifestyles which stray from the norm." However, far from being radical statements of feminine independence, these alternative visions are usually undermined by a fundamentally conservative narrative structure in which the female continues sacrificing herself for the sake of the male. In the end they seem to resemble the supposedly more "realistic" home dramas[4] discussed by Andrew Painter in the epigraph to this chapter.

Examining three series over a roughly ten year period from the early 1980s (Urusei Yatsura) to the mid 1990s (Oh My Goddess [Aa! Megamisama] and Video Girl Ai [Denei shōjo Ai]) we find a trajectory that encompasses the complexities of contemporary society in which significant social changes occur concurrently with conservative desires for a restoration of traditional order. Thus, while the comedies present a world in which the nuclear family is fragmenting, women are growing increasingly independent, and technology is becoming omnipresent, the fundamental gender division between the supportive woman and the libidinous male seems to remain miraculously intact. On the other hand, the fact that the women in these comedies are endowed with magical powers brings an important destabilizing influence into each comic world that defamiliarizes conventions of hierarchy, place, and status, subtextually underlining the changing currents of Japanese society over the last two decades. In the fantastic and clearly wish-fulfilling world of the anime sitcoms, however, this process of destabilization is ultimately contained by the abiding love of the magical females for their all-too-human mates.

As mentioned earlier, the medium of animation itself works effectively to create anarchic visions of uncertainty and confusion. In this case these chaotic circumstances are engendered by the magical girls' use of their powers. The tension between the fantastic chaos put in motion by the women's magical powers and the idealized stability of the "realistic" male-female dynamic is an important source of creative energy throughout each of the series.

This is clearly demonstrated in the early 1980s classic sci-fi comedy series *Urusei Yatsura* (several films were later based on this series, including *Urusei Yatsura Beautiful Dreamer,* discussed in chapter 12), which is about a high school student, an alien girl, and the chaotic effects their relationship has on family, friends, neighbors, and sometimes the entire world. Based on the best-selling manga by Takahashi Rumiko, *Urusei Yatsura* was created before her other series, *Ranma 1/2* (discussed in chapter 3), but the text already shows such Takahashi trademark features as dazzling inventiveness, zany but strangely appealing characters, and comedy that includes everything from physical humor and clever puns and word play to parodies of the Japanese literary and folkloric canon. In its ability to defamiliarize the "normal" world of high school, family, and neighborhood, *Urusei Yatsura* is truly carnivalesque, upending the conventions that support society's basic structures.[5]

Urusei Yatsura is also a pioneering work in the magical girlfriend genre.[6] In *Urusei Yatsura's* case the magical girlfriend is Lum, a beautiful female *oni* (a creature out of Japanese folklore translated variously as "ogre" or "demon") complete with fangs who, in a science fiction twist, comes from a planet far from Earth. Through a series of mishaps, Lum ends up living with Ataru, perhaps the most lecherous youth on the planet, and his long-suffering parents, the Moroboshis.

Convinced that Ataru ultimately wants to marry her, Lum settles in for an apparently permanent stay, getting to know Ataru's high school chums and dealing with the many other female rivals whom Ataru inevitably lusts after. These include not only his high school girlfriend Shinobu but also a bevy of otherworldly females, ranging from a sexy *miko* (shrine sorceress) known as Sakura to a "sleeping beauty," the Princess Kurama Tengu, who is awakened by Ataru's slurping kisses and who tries but fails to make him an appropriate consort for her. The other female constant in Ataru's life is his increasingly jaundiced mother, whose most frequent utterance is the sigh "If only I had never born him," and who, as if in retaliation for both her son's idiocies and her husband's indifference, tends to fall for whatever handsome or appealing alien male that Lum's antics happen to bring home.

It is Lum, however, who is the most important female protagonist in the series. With her long, flowing, blue-black hair, her voluptuous figure scantily clad in a tiger skin bikini (*oni* in folklore wear tiger skins), and her tendency to beg Ataru to sleep with her, she appears to be the embodiment of every boy's fantasies. In fact, however, her aggressive possessiveness grates on Ataru almost immediately, as do the electric shocks that she can administer to him when they touch. Simultaneously attractive and repellent, she constantly follows Ataru, impeding his associations with other girls and wailing at his infidelity. Furthermore, her magical associations and friends from outer space often get both Ataru and his friends and family into serious trouble. It is hardly surprising that although there are moments when Ataru seems to appreciate Lum, his more common stance throughout the series is a desire to be rid of her and to be a "free man."

Lum's aggressiveness, the fact that she can drive a space ship, and her relative independence from her *oni* family, not to mention her ability to give electric shocks, might suggest a liberated form of female identity. Indeed, she is certainly far from being the passive female vessel of tradition who typically provides the "still point in the turning world,"[7] as Japanese women are said to have done in the films of the immediate postwar period. Lum's profoundly destabilizing influence is apparent in an early episode when Ataru's friends' infatuation with Lum lead them to summon a "space taxi," the fare of which turns out to be all of Earth's oil reserves. Furthermore, in crucial contrast to American fantastic sitcoms such as *Bewitched* or *I Dream of Jeannie,* where the chaos created by the magical female character is harmoniously resolved at the end of each episode, almost every *Urusei Yatsura* episode ends on a carnivalesque image of a world permanently out of control. Examples from just the first half-dozen episodes include: the Moroboshi house exploding in a mushroom cloud while the family, dressed like war refugees, looks on; giant swallows growing huge by eating Lum's magic candy and terrorizing Tokyo in a Godzilla-like fashion; dinosaurs, brought back accidentally through a "time slip" activated by Lum, cavorting through the neighborhood; and an amusing parody of the tenth-century classic *The Tale of Genji,* in which the denizens of the Heian era are brought into the twentieth century through the workings of a misplaced time bomb and end up fighting in the streets with a group of twenty-first-century *oni*. Sometimes these chaotic invasions seep into succeeding episodes, but, more frequently, the next episode opens ready for a new kind of confusion, already imbued with a sense of *Urusei Yatsura's* world as a roller coaster ride that never ends.[8]

Clearly, Lum is far from being a tranquil oasis in a troubled world, as has so often been the assigned role for women in modernizing societies, not only in film but in literature as well. In other respects, however, she does retain some strongly traditional features, most notably her total absorption in her man. Although she may sometimes use her fantastic powers for her own minor pleasure, most of the time these powers are used in some way involving Ataru. Consequently, although the problems her powers create are almost never resolved, they still are subsumed within the framework of her love and need for a man. As the craziness she unwittingly engenders swirls around her and Ataru, her unceasing devotion and his (often exasperated) acknowledgment of it are never actually affected.

Stripped of its fantastic trappings, Lum and Ataru's relationship often seems like a humorously exaggerated parody of a common Japanese husband and wife dynamic, that of the jealous but long-suffering wife and the active libidinous male. This dynamic, while in flux now that women are becoming more independent, is supported by both traditional Confucian culture in which women were confined to the home and the twentieth-century bar and entertainment culture that implicitly allows men to go outside the home to fraternize with bar hostesses or prostitutes or maintain mistresses while the wife takes care of the family.[9] Although Lum certainly does not stay at home and suffer silently, she almost never seriously considers separating herself from Ataru, and, while she often gets angry with Ataru, she always forgives him.

Episode 10 is particularly illustrative of this dynamic. The opening scenes show Ataru's friends, who have become increasingly fed up with his treatment of Lum, plotting to humiliate him in front of both Lum and his schoolmates. They arrange for a beautiful girl to meet Ataru in a coffee shop and then for her to make him look like a fool. The schoolmates, also at the coffee shop, happily anticipate Ataru's downfall. Unfortunately for them, Lum finds out about the plan and, although initially furious at his infidelity, decides that she cannot let her "Darling" (she uses the English term) be made a fool of in public. Dressing up as Ataru's new date, she enters the coffee shop, heaps affection on Ataru, and escorts him out under the puzzled gaze of his would-be punishers. For once, Ataru is moved by her ministrations and treats her affectionately. The episode ends on an unusual note of restored harmony.

While Ataru's behavior in this episode remains typical of his innately lecherous character, that of Lum is more thoughtful than usual. In much of the series she seems to act on instinct, but here she is given a moment to reflect on and to be hurt by Ataru's concupiscence; despite this she still decides not to go along with the scheme to punish him. Indeed, she essentially sacrifices herself since, by dressing up as Ataru's "date" and not allowing him to be humiliated, she makes Ataru's friends believe that it is once again she herself who is being humiliated by Ataru's egregious behavior. Through this sacrifice, however, she is finally "rewarded," if only briefly, by Ataru's moment of consideration for her.

Another interesting aspect of this episode is that Lum's fantastic powers are hardly used, as if to suggest that this particular dynamic between Ataru and Lum (sacrifice rewarded by consideration) does not need fantasy to bolster it. In addition, Lum metes out no punishment to Ataru whatsoever. In other episodes Ataru is often punished by the other women he chases or simply by the chaos Lum engenders (chaos that is usually blamed on him), but Lum herself is ultimately all-forgiving, treating her "Darling" as if he were an addled but basically endearing child.[10] In this too, their relationship echoes the traditional paradigm of the wife who performs a mothering function that puts the husband in a condition Joyce Lebra calls "childlike dependence."[11]

Underlying the chaotic world of *Urusei Yatsura* are certain basic dynamics of reassurance: that Ataru may be badly affected but ultimately will be forgiven or that the world may be overrun with monsters at the end of every episode but will itself continue. It is worthwhile to look at these dynamics of reassurance more closely, both in terms of the narrative structure of the series and in terms of their relationship to 1980s Japanese society.

In the narrative it is clear that the openendedness of each episode helps to support the zany, festivalesque atmosphere of the series, while the nature of the medium (series television) is itself fundamentally reassuring. If the chaos unleashed at the beginning of an episode *were* to be solved by the end, the fundamental character of the series—what I have called its roller-coaster ride aspect—would be lost. At the same time the distancing nature inherent in the television format and the fact that Lum and company return unscathed episode after episode allows for an overall framework of reassurance. Viewers have the chance to experience the pleasure of being out of control, yet any danger is contained within the safe space of television fantasy.

For Japanese viewers during the 1980s this joyful but safe frolicking with chaos may have had particular resonance. In a society where the ideals of "efficiency, order, and harmony" (not to mention conformity) are heavily emphasized, the free-for-all atmosphere of *Urusei Yatsura* must have presented a welcome respite. Japanese high schools emphasize rote learning in preparation for nationwide exams, which tends to stifle all but the mildest expressions of creativity and freedom and leads to anti-social manifestations of stress like bullying and suicide. It is hardly surprising, therefore, that the manga version of *Urusei Yatsura* had its greatest popularity among 15-year-old males to whom the vision of high school anarchy must have been particularly appealing.

However, *Urusei Yatsura* does not exist simply as an escapist antidote to social tensions. It also defamiliarizes and underscores some of the complex stresses affecting Japanese society in the early eighties, while at the same time ultimately containing them through comforting contrivances. One of the most important of these stresses was the changing status of women. From the 1970s on, women had become an increasingly important part of the Japanese work force. Feminist thought, although never reaching the degree of influence that it exercised in Western society, penetrated Japanese society to an unprecedented extent. Not only were women going to work in greater numbers, but they were also putting off marriage and childbearing to such an extent that the government actually issued white papers on the "problem." Although, as Kathleen Uno points out, "the vast majority of women lacked the educational attainments or personality traits required for career-track employment and, rather than regarding the family as a source of oppression, viewed it as a wellspring of personal satisfaction,"[12] it is also true that more women were "expressing dissatisfaction with their roles in the workplace and the home."[13]

In some ways Lum embodies these contradictory images. Her determination and aggressiveness seem removed from the traditional image of the submissive female while at the same time she seems significantly less hostile than the traditional *oni* of folklore. Most importantly, her destabilizing powers are iconic in a modern sense, not of a particular female type but rather of the overall unsettling effect of women's increasing independence. The chaotic world that Lum often unwittingly creates is an amusing one when confined to the theater of fantasy, but the subtext has a threatening quality to it, suggesting that in the real world women are increasingly uncontrollable as well.

The inherent threat of Lum's powers, as previously mentioned, is ultimately mitigated by the essentially traditional relationship she has with Ataru. Lum's (women's) destabilizing power is contained through her total commitment to her man, suggesting that, no matter how independent and aggressive she may become, she is still profoundly tied to a traditional male-female dynamic. The impressive powers that Lum possesses—such as her ability to fly,[14] her magical electrical shocks, and her connections to a galaxy beyond the earth—would seem to make her superior to Ataru. However, her emotional subordination to him ultimately guarantees that she will occupy the traditional (i.e., comforting) female subject position.

Lum's reassuring commitment to Ataru stands in significant contrast to the other female characters of the series, almost all of whom embody some of the more threatening aspects of women's independence. They are an intensely independent and assertive group that includes Ataru's previous girlfriend (Shinobu) and princesses, goddesses, and shamanesses, whose otherworldly stature suggests once again an implicit female exceptionalism and even superiority. While Ataru lusts after them, they almost always end up putting him in his place, from his experience with the shamanness Sakura, who uses him to exorcise her own health problems, to the rigorous discipline Princess Kurama inflicts on him when she tries to make him worthy of being her consort. If the comedy of *Urusei Yatsura* consisted only of Ataru's encounters with these belligerent women, the atmosphere of threatening femininity might be overpowering, but, within the consoling framework of Lum's devotion these other female characters come across as comic rather than disturbing.

Perhaps the most surprising female character is Ataru's mother, who is not only unsupportive of Ataru but is often actively hostile toward him. She frequently expresses her wish that she had never given birth to him, and she constantly criticizes him for all the misery he has brought into the household through his association with Lum. In one deadpan sequence, Ataru's father comes home and, sensing another typically chaotic day in the household, asks his wife, "So, Ataru—is he still alive?" His wife replies despondently, "Yes, I guess human beings just don't die that easily." Ataru's mother is also shown constantly seeking solace from various male alien creatures, ranging from Lum's handsome former boyfriend to a small blue demon who is accidentally conjured up by magic.

The mother's openness to infidelity may be less a comment on the increasing sexual independence of wives (although it may be that as well) than a veiled displacement of the growing uncertainty about a mother's role in contemporary Japanese society, or about the stability of the Japanese family itself. In contrast to earlier animated mother characters, such as the popular Sazaesan, who served as a pillar of the middle class family, Ataru's mother exists in attack mode, criticizing her disappointing son, ignoring her husband, and flirting shamelessly with alien visitors. Her willingness to criticize her only son is particularly interesting when we remember that the mother-son bond is perhaps the single most valorized family relationship in Japanese society. While this reversal is clearly for the sake of comedy, it is still suggestive. Ataru's mother can be seen as embodying certain masculine fears about the changing role of the mother, from being a well of limitless support who lives for her children to being someone with desires of her own upon which she might even someday act.

In the end Ataru's mother does not strike out on her own. Contained within the comic format, her hostility never goes beyond the humorous. Furthermore, she also participates in the dynamics of reassurance in at least one respect, her cooking. Indeed, her single motherly trait seems to be her willingness to continue placing food on the table, no matter what happens or how put upon she is. Since cooking seems to be the one attribute in romantic comedy that is always gender defined, this is not an unimportant gesture. In the world of *Urusei Yatsura,* the nuclear family may be rocked, but certain fundamental aspects of conventional life are maintained.

Urusei Yatsura also defamiliarizes other aspects of conventional social life, especially relations with the neighbors, which are represented as uniformly acrimonious. Indeed, at various moments in the series the neighbors, incensed at the latest disaster, start putting together a lynch mob against Ataru. Moreover, Ataru returns their hostility. In one episode (episode 7) Ataru learns (from Lum, of course) how to make voodoo dolls and immediately starts making effigies of all his neighbors, who he gleefully proceeds to torment. While these scenes are often humorous, like the aggressive women, they suggest a world that is increasingly different from that of the harmonious social ideal maintained in traditional Japanese culture.

Of the three anime series profiled in this chapter, Urusei Yatsura has the widest social canvas; family, friends, neighbors, and even the government play a part in the dynamics of the anarchic narrative. In the two works from the 1990s, Video Girl Ai (Denei shōjo Ai) and Oh My Goddess (Aa! Megamisama), we see that the focus is narrower and that society and the family are of much less importance.[15] At the same time, while the "magical girls" certainly bring confusion into the male protagonists' lives, there is much less of the euphoric zaniness that characterizes Urusei Yatsura. This conservativeness is true not only of the narrative structure but also thematically and in terms of values. For example, the "magical girlfriends" are presented as less aggressive than Lum, and the emotional depths of the relationship between boy and girlfriend are highlighted far more often.

These changes are, of course, partly due to the individual taste of the manga and anime creators but they also suggest some of the cultural and social changes that occurred during the decade after Urusei Yatsura. The narrowness of the social canvas, for example, may be a reflection of the increased fragmentation of Japanese society brought about by not only women's independence and economic prosperity but also the proliferation of technology itself, from the spread of home computers to a television set for each member of the family. As if to emphasize this familial fragmentation, mothers are absent in these series, a difference that may be comparable to similar changes that took place in American television in the 1960s. These shows introduced new kinds of families in which the absence of parents (usually written in as dead) was a veiled reference to divorce, although in the Japanese case it may also be an implicit acknowledgment of the rising number of working mothers.

On the other hand, the more conservative nature of *Video Girl Ai* and *Oh My Goddess,* especially in their representation of women, may not be a reflection of but a reaction to the increasingly assertive voices of the Japanese female. When these shows aired in the early nineties, the divorce rate in Japan, though still very low compared to America, was beginning to creep up. At the same time many younger women began to see the single life as an equally attractive alternative to getting married. The media, of course, took notice of this and began depicting unmarried affluent women as "self-centered and indulgent," even terming them the *Hanakozoku,* the name of a popular upscale women's magazine.[16] Perhaps the most famous media controversy concerning these "new" versions of women was the so-called yellow cab phenomenon of the late 1980s. The "yellow cab" was a term used to describe "wealthy and leisured young Japanese women who travel to exotic locales to pursue . . . sexual liaisons." The shock value of this phenomenon was not just from the sexually assertive behavior of the Japanese woman but from the fact that these liaisons were specifically not with Japanese men, which constituted a "coherent, although indirect, critique of Japanese patriarchy."[17] In fact, this critique was also at times extremely direct. An article in *Fujin kōron,* which purported to explain why Japanese women rejected Japanese men for foreigners, quoted young Japanese women as saying that Japanese men "have a bad attitude toward women," "they are bad-mannered," "they can't take care of themselves," and "they can't do housework."[18]

Although the actual numbers of women who were part of the *Hanakozoku* or who participated in "yellow cab" behavior were probably minuscule, it is not difficult to imagine that the huge media play given to these new types of womanhood must have been extremely unsettling to the Japanese male. It is against this background that the conservative "magical girlfriends" and, to some extent, the narrowness of focus of *Video Girl Ai* and *Oh my Goddess* make sense. The girls profiled in both series are almost literally "dreams come true" (in radical contrast to *Urusei Yatsura*'s Lum, whom Ataru sometimes treats as his worst nightmare), existing only for the sake of the male protagonist and innocent of any wider connections to society and the world. This narrow focus places more emphasis on the relationship between the male and female characters, making for a more concentrated narrative, but at the expense of a broader social comedy and commentary. Furthermore, although the girls' fantastic presence does create comic confusion, their "dream come true" characterization adds a more romantic, or perhaps compensatory, twist to both narratives that contributes to a bittersweet tone quite foreign to *Urusei Yatsura's* festive zaniness.

The confusion they create is a much more minimal kind than that engendered by Lum, and their consoling role is far more obvious than in *Urusei Yatsura*. In *Oh My Goddess* we see this difference function clearly in the first episode, "Moonlight and Cherry Blossoms." Keichi, a bored and hungry young college student left alone by his thuggish upperclassmen, phones for take-out only to be magically connected with a "Goddess Service." It sends him a beautiful young goddess named Belldandy (named for the Norse goddess Verdandi), who promises to grant him one wish. Taken aback, Keichi wishes simply for "a girl like her to be by his side forever." Belldandy grants him the wish by staying with him herself, but her now-constant presence causes a problem in the dorm and the two are asked to leave. Initially refused wherever they go, they are finally guided by magic forces to an old temple just as Keichi collapses from fever. Belldandy restores the temple to its former beauty and nurses Keichi through his sickness. In the episode's festive ending the upperclassmen from Keichi's dorm come to party with them, and, while Keichi is annoyed at not having more time to be alone with Belldandy, he is consoled in the final scene when she puts her hand on his shoulder and they gaze together at cherry blossoms in the moonlight.

This opening episode differs markedly from the typical *Urusei Yatsura* episode in terms of its ultimate sense of containment. While the beginning highlights confusion and uncertainty (the unexpected appearance of the goddess to Keichi and their subsequent expulsion from the dorm), the ending suggests a welcome restoration of order and the promise of peace and happiness. While Belldandy's caring for Keichi during his illness suggests motherly nurturance, the final scene in the moonlight evokes delicate erotic connotations, and the party going on inside suggests a wedding celebration. Not only is Keichi restored to health and the good graces of his friends, but the temple (a symbol of tradition) has also been restored through Belldandy's magic powers.

Of course such visions of peace and harmony cannot sustain an essentially comic series, and the next four episodes (there are only five in the initial OVA series) work to create more narrative tension. The second episode introduces Belldandy's older sister Urd, an explicitly eroticized character who aggressively sows confusion in Keichi's and Belldandy's lives. Urd fills a trickster role similar to Lum's, though without her loving devotion, which becomes purely the domain of Belldandy. The narrative also provides dramatic tension in the final two episodes, in which it sets up the premise that the love between human and goddess has opened a fissure between worlds that invites demonic "bugs" into the human world and causes explosions whenever Keichi and Belldandy come close to each other. In the poignant final episode it appears that despite their best efforts Belldandy must return to heaven, but at the very last moment (typically) it seems that their love will be maintained through Belldandy's discovery that she and Keichi knew each other in a shadowy childhood moment. The series ends with the implication that their relationship will be maintained, although only by destroying Keichi's memory of their initial encounter.

Oh My Goddess therefore ends on a note of positive closure with the themes of self-sacrifice and all-conquering love privileged over the complexities (comic or otherwise) of human-goddess relationships. In certain ways it is the most clearly "escapist" of the three series discussed here since Belldandy is almost a perfect dream of feminine nurturance—caring for her sick sweetheart, cooking him delicious meals, and speaking in an adorable little girl voice. The fact that she is a goddess out of Norse mythology in flowing robes rather than a fanged, tiger skin–wearing *oni* also underlines her soothing and escapist function. Furthermore, unlike Lum she never scolds or tries to put her desires first. As she herself declares at one point "I am here for Keichi's sake" (*Keichi no tame ni iru*).

Video Girl Ai deals more intensively with the complexities of love between an alien and a human, although ultimately in a context that is more poignant than comic. The title of the opening episode, "Let Me Console You" (Nagusamete ageru), sets the emotional tone of the series. In this episode Yota, a high school boy, frustrated in his love for Moemi, a pretty fellow student, rents a video with the risqué title of "Let Me Console You." To his surprise the beautiful girl in the video

A scene from *Speed Racer*

The Space Battleship Yamato *(Star Blazers)*

Tetsuo rides Kaneda's motorcycle through Neo Tokyo *(Akira)*

Kaneda marvels at the final transformation of Tetsuo *(Akira)*

A fight between Ranma and his father in panda-form *(Ranma 1/2)*

Ranma and Akane *(Ranma 1/2)*

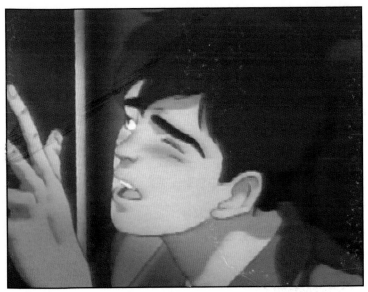

A voyeur in *Legend of the Overfiend*

A scene from within a women's locker room *(Legend of the Overfiend)*

A demon leering at a human girl *(Twin Dolls)*

A fight scene from *Twin Dolls*

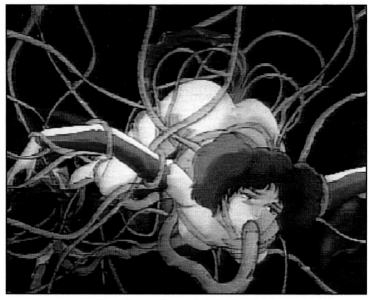

Tentacle sex *(Legend of the Overfiend)*

Cutey Honey from *Cutey Honey*

Sho in his guyver suit embraces his girlfriend Mizuki *(The Guyver)*

A fight scene from *The Guyver*

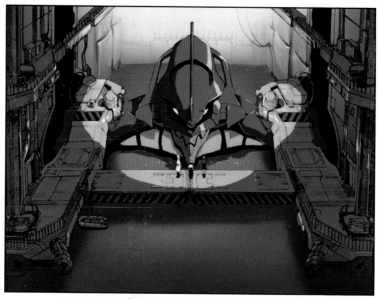

An EVA in its hangar at NERV *(Neon Genesis Evangelion)*

A fight scene from *Neon Genesis Evangelion*

Kusanagi shoots a laser rifle *(Ghost in the Shell)*

Kusanagi raises her visor *(Ghost in the Shell)*

Mei asleep on the totoro's stomach *(My Neighbor Totoro)*

Mei, Satsuki, and the totoro perform a dance *(My Neighbor Totoro)*

Kiki rescues her friend Tombo *(Kiki's Delivery Service)*

Kiki looks out over the moonlit town *(Kiki's Delivery Service)*

Nausicaä walks through the Sea of Corruption
(Nausicaä of the Valley of the Wind)

Nausicaä and Teto fly on a mehve *(Nausicaä of the Valley of the Wind)*

Belldandy and Keichi *(Oh My Goddess)*

Child caught in Hiroshima's atomic blast *(Barefoot Gen)*

Seita and his sister Setsuko play in the bath *(Grave of the Fireflies)*

Seita catches a firefly for his sister *(Grave of the Fireflies)*

San fights Lady Eboshi *(Princess Mononoke)*

San cares for the ailing Ashitaka *(Princess Mononoke)*

Taeko walks with friends *(Only Yesterday)*

Taeko takes a break from planting rice *(Only Yesterday)*

suddenly comes through the screen and materializes in front of him. Far from immediately "consoling" him, Ai ("love" in Japanese) unsettles him by first shrieking at him angrily (his malfunctioning video machine has caused her breasts to shrink), then cooking terrible-tasting food, and finally acting seductively (but still confusingly) by stripping in front of him in the bath and insisting on giving him a backrub. At the end of the episode, however, they curl up to sleep together and, knowing about his frustrated love for Moemi, she whispers "cheer up."

This first episode incorporates a number of seemingly disparate themes and tropes in a formulation subversive of the "magical girlfriend" genre. The episode undermines expectations set up both by the suggestive title of the episode, which evokes easy sexual submissiveness, and by Ai's identification as a "video girl," a term that connotes a voluptuous fantasy female cavorting for the male gaze. The first of the "magical girls" to be explicitly associated with technology, Ai's fantasy "video girl" premise is immediately undermined by the fact that she comes out of a malfunctioning video. In contrast to both the salacious expectations of her video-generated sexuality and the expectations of technology working efficiently to create a perfect two-dimensional video puppet, Ai comes across as a relatively complex creation who, although she does ultimately offer some consolation, has her own desires, demands, and disappointments. Her mercurial characterization—from screaming anger at the beginning to flirtatious appeal in the bath scene to, finally, her whispered encouragement—may seem exaggeratedly "feminine," but it is certainly far from the one-note sexuality the title of the series implies. Her fresh-faced, short-haired attractiveness also subverts her sexy "video girl" persona, while the trope of her shrinking breasts metaphorically suggests both Yota's shrinking expectations of her and also the narrative's insistence on not letting her be pigeonholed into a formulaic "anime babe" characterization.

The series is also unusual in its characterization of Yota, who comes across as surprisingly thoughtful and even generous. In marked distinction to Ataru's one-note lechery or even to Keichi's unquestioning enjoyment of his goddess's presence, Yota appears as a complex figure, torn between his apparently hopeless love for Moemi and his increasing appreciation of Ai. In a number of episodes he surprises her by his thoughtfulness, at one point buying her a dress and in another episode by eating the dinner she had hidden away when she discovered that Moemi planned to cook him dinner instead. Although these are gestures that might not be considered very liberated from a feminist standpoint, they are still remarkable for this genre of comedy.

Other episodes highlight a more disturbing element—the increasing uncontrollability of technology. In the series' most carnivalesque episode, "Psycho Girl Ai," the malfunctioning tape causes their first date together to go out of control as Ai's personality fluctuates radically. More threateningly, the fact that the tape can only play for three months means that their time together is limited. Here, in contrast to *Oh My Goddess*, it is technology rather than magic that is uncertain.

Also unusual is the series' poignant ending. In episode 4, "Electric Currents of Love," a malfunction in Ai's original tape causes their already prescribed time together to grow even shorter, just as she acknowledges that she is falling in love with Yota, something that "video girls" are supposedly not allowed to do. She becomes increasingly wracked by electric currents and in a disturbing scene reminiscent of the violent pornographic genre, she is shown lying in an alley with her skirt up and panties exposed, being observed by a sinister male stranger. At the moment Yota and Ai begin to admit their true feelings for each other, Ai is spirited back into the video world by the sinister stranger. In a surreal sequence embellished with eerie images of clocks ticking and chasms opening, Yota follows her into the video. He first finds himself alone in an empty desert space, and then he is confronted by Moemi, who appears out of nowhere to finally say she loves him. Yota realizes he can no longer lust after two women at once (in marked contrast to Ataru, needless to say) and tells Moemi to go away. He then stands before a stunning, immense glass staircase. In a striking sequence he begins to climb the staircase hand over hand while the glass cuts into him and the staircase starts to disintegrate. Growing increasingly bloody, Yota still continues his climb, reflecting that "this is the pain of love." When he finally reaches the top he finds Ai naked, roped into what appears to be a torture chair. Ai simply tells him that he can leave because she "now believes in love." The final image of the series is that of a ticking clock.

Video Girl Ai's mysterious and downbeat ending puts some of the most intriguing aspects of the fantastic romance into sharp relief.

While it is perhaps the most realistic of the three—in that it allows for both characters to become more generous and develop self-knowledge—the surreal imagery of the final episode underlines the explicitly fantastic nature of the genre. In addition, the scenes of Ai wracked by electric currents and the final image of her in the torture chair suggest not only the pain of love (expressed poignantly in the explosions generated between Keichi and Belldandy and more humorously in Lum's electric shocks) but also a possible link with anime pornography.

In certain ways the fantastic romance genre is a kind of flip side to the pornographic genre profiled in chapter 4. While the pornographic genre privileges images of powerful, frightening, otherworldly women who must be sexually controlled or violently subjugated by men, the romantic genre focuses on powerful otherworldly women whose potentially frightening qualities are contained by their love for their men. Although Ai and Yota cannot be together, he knows that she will always love him. In an almost Pygmalionesque fashion, he has created in her the ability to love, and nothing, not even the implicit threat of out-of-control technology, can affect that. The romantic genre thus acts out the implicit anxieties of the male viewer by presenting some confusion and uncertainty only to show at the end that the established social order of a dominant male and a submissive, devoted woman still prevails.

In this regard, the trope of cooking is an important one. During the 1970s a Japanese television ad (criticized by some feminist groups) showed a fresh-faced mother-daughter team merrily announcing "I am the person who cooks!" (*Watashi tsukuru hito!*) to which a boy responds "I am the person who eats!" (*Boku taberu hito!*). This blatant vision of gender demarcation, although increasingly unlikely in real life, remains as a fundamental ideal in all of the series discussed here. Belldandy's exquisite cooking is constantly commented on by the other characters while Yota at one point states simply that "The shape of a girl who's cooking is really good." Even *Urusei Yatsura,* which defamiliarizes the normal more than any of the other series, still contains many images of Ataru's mother cooking while anarchy breaks out all around her (although Lum herself is a terrible cook). The underlying message seems to be that even in a frighteningly changeable world, women cooking suggests a fundamentally stable social order.

In addition, cooking is clearly coded as an expression of the women's love for their men, which highlights the role of love and romance in this genre. Surprising to those who stereotype anime as sexual and violent, the "romance" in this genre is genuinely crucial. In contrast to the pornographic genre, sexuality is hinted at but is never explicit, while the pains and tribulations of love are thoroughly explored. Beneath the surface insanity and humor, the notions of loving and caring for someone, ideas that are not necessarily currents in American television, are strongly emphasized here.

Annalee Newitz has speculated about the popularity of romantic fantasy anime in America and states that "Americans who consume anime values are also responding to—and perhaps attempting to escape—the hypersexuality of their own media culture by reimagining romance as a relationship that goes beyond the purely sexual."[19] My own research bears this out to a degree (see the appendix) and I would suspect that this assertion is even more valid for Japanese viewers. However, it appears that it is not just "hypersexuality" that they are escaping but also a perceived loss of the woman as traditional nurturer and comforter.[20]

This would seem particularly true for the male viewer, for, although these fantastic romances certainly appeal across gender boundaries, in comparison to conventional female-oriented romances like the Harlequin romance novels (popular in both Japan and the West), these narratives are essentially from the *male* point of view. In a world where women (and life in general) seem increasingly out of control, the notion that certain truths about love and relationships in which the male identity remains stable and the male ego is restored rather than destroyed may have more appeal than ever. It is surely no accident that the "magical girlfriends" depicted in these series are not only magical but also alien—an implicit recognition that such marvelous fulfillments of male dreams now exist only in an alien world far from reality.

*

PART FOUR

REMAKING MASTER NARRATIVES: ANIME CONFRONTS HISTORY

THE ANIME TEXTS DISCUSSED have tended to focus on the construction of social and individual identity, usually in an ahistorical context. The following two chapters move away from individual identity to anime texts that deal instead with Japanese history and the question of constructing a Japanese national identity. Although anime texts dealing with history are less common than those of the science fiction or fantasy genres, they are still an important part of the anime mainstream. Indeed, some of the "historical" anime, such as the comedy *Saber Marionettes*, actually incorporate fantasy or even science fiction elements to create imaginative visions of Japanese history, indicating that national identity is no longer a fixed construction.

Throughout the twentieth century, cinema in general has been one of the main vehicles for constructing a sense of national identity. This has been the case particularly for the historical film. Although all filmic texts are inevitably linked at some level with the culture that engenders them, the historical film must deal with history at a highly conscious level by selecting, rejecting, and shaping the materials of a nation's past. Not only do they help to reflect a nation's or a culture's sense of self, but the completed film will also help to further shape that sense of self. As Ella Shohat and Robert Stam put it, "narrative models in films are not simply reflective microcosms of historical processes; they are also experiential grids or templates through which history can be written and national identity created."[1]

Japanese live-action cinema has been nearly synonymous with Japanese national identity during the postwar period, especially in its many brilliant recreations of a premodern past. Epics such as Kurosawa Akira's *Seven Samurai* and ghost stories such as Mizoguchi Kenji's *Ugetsu* have given both domestic and international viewers a sense of a premodern Japanese world. The fact that these "worlds" are idiosyncratic and ideologically charged creations of the past does not take away from the strength and staying power of their imagery. These are worlds that are based on "an understanding of the past that depends less upon data than what we might call vision . . . [T]he historical film is history as vision."[2]

Japan, despite being a country fascinated by history, has remained extremely ambiguous about some of its own most significant historical moments. The most important has been World War II, a period that many Japanese tend to remember in notably selective ways—concentrating on the period from 1941-1945 and ignoring the long war in China—in order to privilege individual reminiscence over a sense of national responsibility. Japan's attitude toward its premodern past has been selective as well. Just as America's mythic past has been dominated by the shadow of the cowboy and frontier culture, Japanese culture, both popular and elite, has tended to concentrate on samurai heroes and a romantic vision of medieval warfare, especially in the so-called *chambara* or samurai films. These films celebrate martial spirit and impressive combat without necessarily taking much account of wider historical events.

Historical anime share these cultural tendencies but add some elements of their own. As with live-action film, historical anime often dwell lovingly on the quintessential elements of traditional Japanese culture, such as the soaring roofs of a farm house or the glittering horizontals of wet rice paddies. In works such as the 1990s OVA and television series *Rurōni Kenshin* set in the Meiji period, the designs use intense jewel-like colors that resemble modern woodblock prints to recreate a premodern Japanese world in all its exquisite materiality. These rich renderings almost take on a life of their own, evoking a hyperreal alternative past that is cleaner, tidier, and more beautiful than what actually might have existed.

In terms of narrative, animated films set in the premodern past usually revolve around samurai, but often with a strongly fantastic twist. For example *Ninja Scroll* (Jubei ninpocho, 1993), pits "good" ninjas (masters of the secret martial arts) against supernatural monstrous "evil" ninjas led by a demonic samurai who has risen from the dead to destroy the Tokugawa shogunate and supplant it with his own dystopian realm. He loses, of course, but not before some horrific and fantastic battle scenes. This emphasis on fantasy elements is not only a feature of anime, however. The historical dramas of the kabuki theater (as well as classic live-action films like *Ugetsu* or *Rashomon*) often contain supernatural plot elements such as wizards, magical protagonists, and ghosts from the historical past and famous legends. However, anime adds its signature style of fast-paced narrative movement, marvelous, sometimes stomach-churning metamorphosis sequences, and powerful images of wide-scale destruction, such as the finale in *Ninja Scroll*, in which the evil ninja lord's boat is burned in an arresting sequence. Even the more sober works contain striking images of violence, such as the atomic bombing of Hiroshima in *Barefoot Gen* and the bloody fighting scenes in *Princess Mononoke*. It should also be remembered that some of the best of these works, such as *Rurōni Kenshin*, *Grave of Fireflies*, and *Princess Mononoke*, also contain countertendencies toward the elegiac and the lyric that enable them to speak for the past in a lower key, with memorable and individual voices.

The following two chapters concentrate on three historical anime—the bleak depictions of World War II contained in *Grave of Fireflies* and *Barefoot Gen* and the complex vision of the fourteenth century expressed in Miyazaki Hayao's blockbuster hit *Princess Mononoke*. None of these is necessarily historically accurate. Instead, in their own way, they present "history as vision"—visions that are both selective and even ideological but that still contain universal images of great power and resonance.

CHAPTER NINE

NO MORE WORDS: *BAREFOOT GEN, GRAVE OF THE FIREFLIES,* AND "VICTIM'S HISTORY"

"Oh look there's an enemy plane coming." . . . Thereafter there were no more words.

—Hiroshima survivor Kijima Katsumi,
quoted in John Treat, *Writing Ground Zero*

THE TWO MOST FAMOUS ANIME DRAMAS concerning World War II, Mori Masaki's *Barefoot Gen* (*Hadashi no gen*, 1983) and Takahata Isao's *Grave of the Fireflies* (*Hotaru no haka*, 1988), share in the collectivity of the Japanese memory as well as individual autobiographical accounts of personal suffering. In this regard, they attempt to "speak for history" in a personal voice that, through the power of vivid images of suffering, destruction, and renewal, becomes a collective voice of the Japanese people. They are both essentially family dramas seen through the eyes of children, and, although there are scenes of horrifying violence and devastation (especially in *Barefoot Gen*), the films contain many powerful scenes of human-scale interaction that are subdued and imbued with a childlike, innocent tone.

The reasons behind this subdued treatment of the war are complex but quite understandable and common to other media depictions as well. As many scholars have pointed out, the Japanese version of World War II may generally be described as a "victim's history,"[1] in which the Japanese people were seen as helpless victims of a corrupt and evil conspiracy between their government and military. This "victim's history" is partly due to the collaborative American-Japanese efforts under the Occupation to create an image of a postwar democratic Japan that would free the Japanese from an inescapable fascist and militarist past. By shifting the burden of responsibility for a devastating war onto the military and the government, it was felt that the slate could be wiped clean and Japan could undertake the task of rebuilding, liberated from the dark shadows of war guilt and recrimination. Consequently, both official and cultural versions of the war have played down citizens' involvement with the actual machinery of combat and aggression to the point that they ignore or elide Japan's aggression against China, which began in 1931.[2] Instead, official vehicles, such as textbooks and government ceremonies as well as popular and elite culture, emphasize the period from Pearl Harbor to Hiroshima, which, in Carol Gluck's neat phrase, "set a balanced moral calculus" essentially allowing the atomic bombing to cancel out responsibility for Pearl Harbor and simply glossing over the colonization of Korea and the previous ten years of aggression against China.

Cultural works allied with this victim's history are numerous. They include writings by atomic bomb survivors and live-action antiwar films such as *Harp of Burma* or *Fires on the Plain,* all of which share strong anti-war sentiment but show little inclination to delve into issues of guilt or responsibility. These traits are shared by *Grave of the Fireflies* and *Barefoot Gen*. Centered on the 1940s, the two films fit into victims' history in certain obvious ways. First, the films evoke an unproblematic response of heartfelt sympathy on the part of the viewers by focusing on innocent children devastated by war's destruction. As two anime critics sum up the film's impact: "It is frankly impossible to watch this production [*Grave of the Fireflies*] without being drained emotionally."[3] The use of generally realist conventions (*Grave of the Fireflies* in particular has an organic, naturalistic look, and both films work effectively to create a wartime period feel in their depictions of architecture and traditional dress) and a straightforward narrative structure also help the viewer identify with the heartwrenching stories on screen.

Within the category of victim's history, however, the two employ very different dynamics. In *Grave of the Fireflies* both text and subtext embody an endless nightmarish vision of passivity and despair, while *Barefoot Gen* has at its core an indomitable spirit of resistance and renewal, despite the scenes of almost unimaginable horror that it depicts.

Grave of the Fireflies has a pervasive tone of powerlessness from the very beginning of the film. The first scene shows an emaciated and disheveled young boy slumped against a pillar in a vast train station while a voice-over intones, "September 21, 1945 was the night I died." As other passersby look on with a mixture of contempt and horror, he slumps further and ends up lying on the ground. A maintenance man takes his pulse and pronounces, "he's a goner." Another man looks through his possessions and finds a small candy tin. Throwing it away, it clatters on the ground and opens up to disgorge a few small white objects. Later on the viewer discovers that these are the cremated bones of the boy's sister.

The opening scene—its action composed of a series of downward movements—sets the despairing tone of the film. The boy's posture of helplessness only intensifies as he goes from slumping to prone. No one extends any aid to him, and instead the passersby move away from his dying figure while maintenance men crouch to paw his possessions. In a further downward movement they throw to the floor the box, which opens to show only symbols of death that also scatter in a downward arc.

The narrative structure of the film follows a similar downward trajectory. Based on an autobiographical story by the novelist Nosaka Akiyuki, most of the action takes place in the coastal city of Kobe toward the end of the war when Allied aerial bombing began to intensify, leading to enormous numbers of civilian casualties. A boy, Seita, and his sister, Setsuko, lose their mother (their father is a commander in the Navy) and are forced to live with an unsympathetic aunt whose coldness and hectoring at the boy's unwillingness to work eventually drive them to make a home of their own in an abandoned bomb shelter. Their time in the bomb shelter allows for a few poignant scenes of childish happiness, especially for Setsuko, who loves the fireflies that her big brother catches for her. But she is sad that the fireflies die so quickly and ends up making a "grave" for the firefly corpses that litter their shelter. In the end the two children are unable to survive on their own. Setsuko dies from malnutrition, and the final scene shows Seita collecting her ashes.

The film contains moments of beauty and even happiness, especially in its signature image of the fireflies illuminating the faces of the two children laughing together in the darkness of the bomb shelter. However, the image that most dominates *Grave of the Fireflies* is that of the bomber planes that appear throughout the film at consistently recurring intervals. The action of the narrative actually begins with planes fire-bombing the street where the children live and turning it into flames while, later in the film, a joyous day at the seaside ends with planes sweeping above the beach and the children running for shelter. Another aerial image occurs in one of the film's quietest and most effective moments. Returning to the shelter to help his sister (whom he will find dying), Seita sees a single spectral plane fly silently overhead and vanish into the distance, the true sign that the war is finally over.

The recurring image of planes flying above the heads of children evokes a world that can never be safe—a world where ultimate horror rains down from the innocent sky. Rather than using language, the film uses simple repeated visuals to capture this overwhelming sense of vulnerability. These visuals include the horizontal movement of planes sweeping across the sky, an image that is initially counterbalanced by the small, defiant verticals of the children. The balance shifts when the bombs (or bullets) begin to rain down, and the screen is enveloped in an overwhelming downward movement, symbolically evoking the hopelessness of the children's situation.

In many ways the almost static narrative of *Grave of the Fireflies* evokes Harootunian's description of postwar Japan as existing in an "endless present, more spatial than temporal," while its autobiographical memoir style privileges what he describes as "the authority of the inner."[4] There is no discussion of the causes of the war (and consequently no broader explanation for the children's suffering), and no sense of hope or of a new turning point at the war's end. Instead there is a dreamlike, strongly elegiac quality to *Fireflies* that suggests a history that can never be escaped or transcended but that must be continually experienced as harrowing, painful, and relentlessly oppressive. Dialogue is minimal, underlining the point that words are useless; only the searing parade of images of destruction from the sky (Harootunian's "spatial present") has any final meaning, and it is one that shuts out the possibility for action.

In contrast, *Barefoot Gen* is obsessed with action and with the temporal, particularly with two temporal moments, the period of time leading up to the bombing of Hiroshima and the period immediately following it. This is not surprising given the nature of the events that the film describes. The awareness of time (signified by the pages of a calendar and at one point by the hands of a clock) imbues the scenes before the bombing with a taught suspense. What is surprising, however, is that the overall tone of this film, while still surrounded by an aura of suffering, is very far from the mood of passivity and powerlessness that pervades *Grave of the Fireflies*. Although the film in certain ways fits into the "victims' history" model, it is actually a far more complex version than *Grave of the Fireflies* and in many aspects is a more powerful antiwar film with a strongly activist subtext.

This activism is due to the nature of the event that *Barefoot Gen* attempts to represent, the world's first atomic bombing. Unlike *Grave of the Fireflies,* the temporal continuum of which is an endless present punctuated by scenes of bombardment that numb the characters into miserable passivity, the atomic bombing of Hiroshima is a single event that changed the world. This is not to minimize the suffering depicted in Takahata's film, but it is important to recognize just how unique and overwhelming the atomic bomb was. In Japan the initial reaction to the bomb was largely one of silence, guilt, and even repression on the part of the survivors (and on the part of the horrified nation as well). Even while official censorship was in place, however, popular culture dealt with the bomb, although in the displaced form of horrific monsters from outer space or from the lower depths, immortalized in the live-action series of *Godzilla* films introduced in 1953 (this displacement is clearly still influential in anime from *Akira* to *Neon Genesis Evangelion*). Furthermore, a few survivors and activists refused to accept this repression and began to write in an attempt not only to memorialize the destruction but also, through their literary voices, to work against further atomic destruction.

All of these writers, novelists, poets, and essayists confronted the problem of how to "convey the unconveyable,"[5] especially through words, which to some seemed weak instruments to represent such devastation. As John Treat explains, "In fact, when seeking the words to express what they wish to say, it is nearly rote for atomic bomb writers to tell us they despair of ever finding those words."[6] One solution to this problem of words came in 1968 with the publication of Nakazawa Keiji's manga, *Kuroi ame ni utarete* (pelted by black rain), which was followed in 1973 with his manga, *Hadashi no Gen* (Barefoot Gen), an autobiographical series describing the destruction of Hiroshima and a young boy's response. The anime version of the manga was released in 1983. Initially, a manga or animated version of the nuclear destruction of a city might seem in bad taste. Indeed, some *hibakusha* (atom bomb survivors) are said to have questioned its appropriateness. However, in the wake of Art Spiegelman's *Maus*, a graphic novel depiction of the Holocaust, not to mention the growing acceptance of comics and animation as art forms in their own right, such criticisms seem misdirected.

In fact, it is precisely the graphics of manga or anime that can help to "convey the unconveyable" of the bomb's horror. The stunning visuals employed in the film to represent the bombing and its aftermath are hideous, painful to look at, and unforgettable. While *Grave of the Fireflies* uses the elegiac mode and realistic graphics to show a slowly dying world, *Barefoot Gen* indulges in the apocalyptic mode with a grotesque and frenzied graphic style to show a world paradoxically dynamic in its own destruction. Scenes that even with contemporary special effects and contemporary values would be difficult to present and watch in live-action film become, in the nonrealistic space of animation, enduring evocations of a genuine hell on earth. Furthermore, the distancing involved in watching animation allows the viewer to process these scenes and then return to the narrative action, something that might not be possible to do with a live-action film. On one level, animation's simplified representation allows for easier identification on the part of the viewer. On the other hand, the fact that these are not "real" humans or "real" destruction being depicted provides a kind of psychological buffer zone to keep the viewer from being too affected by the traumatic events depicted.

The vitality of the animated images also supports the film's dynamic pacing, which contrasts with the emphasis on passivity and victimhood in *Grave of the Fireflies*. Admittedly, there are elements in *Barefoot Gen* that support a "victims" interpretation. The film begins with a brief shot of the attack on Pearl Harbor, ignoring the previous ten years of warfare in China. Furthermore, while the English language version specifically mentions the "attack on Pearl Harbor," the Japanese version merely gives the date, "December 8, 1941" and explains that Japan "plunged into" war with the Americans and the English. This opening image is followed by the names of exclusively Japanese cities written in stark white characters ending with the ominous name "Hiroshima." This simple but powerful opening sequence underlines the sense of Japan and the Japanese as targets. Horrific scenes of the bombing and its ghastly aftermath reinforce the image of powerless victims terrorized from the sky.

Despite these examples, the film's narrative, pacing, and imagery refuse to uphold such a one-note interpretation. In stark contrast to *Grave of the Fireflies*, *Barefoot Gen* interweaves moments of hope and triumph within its dark tapestry of devastation and despair. The film begins with an image of vibrant life, a scene in which Gen, the young protagonist, goes out to look at the wheat fields with his father and little brother, Shinji. The boys laugh when their father delivers an evidently well-worn homily on the virtues of wheat, praising its strength and its endurance, but both the sermon and the boys' laughter are effective counterpoints to the grimness of the wartime setting. The sense of hopefulness in adversity is underlined by the fact that the first thirty minutes of the film are devoted to Gen's family life *before* the bombing.

The narrative momentum in these early scenes is of resistance rather than acquiescence. In one scene Gen and Shinji attempt to help out their family, particularly their pregnant mother, by stealing a carp from a temple pond. Like the wheat, the carp is identified with hope and resistance as it struggles against capture.[7] The carp's fierce struggles and frantic jumps from water into air also provide a visual trope of upward momentum that parallels the boys' psychological unwillingness to be beaten down.

The boys capture the carp but are caught themselves by one of the priests in the temple. This is a scene similar to one in *Grave of the Fireflies* in which Seita tries to steal vegetables for his starving sister. Food in war films often "becomes a signifier for struggle,"[8] not just for physical sustenance but for humanity as well. In both cases the boys are attempting to feed more than just themselves—they are attempting to maintain the human connection in the face of overwhelming outside forces. Despite their similarities, the two scenes end quite differently. While Seita apologizes profusely, head bowed to the ground, and eventually winds up in the police station, Gen and Shinji confront the priest and ultimately persuade him to give them the carp.

In another, more explicitly political scene of resistance, Gen's father heatedly criticizes the conduct of the war, telling his sons that the government is in the hands of "madmen" and pointing out to them that "Sometimes it takes a lot more courage not to fight than to fight." Although it seems unlikely that such sentiments (no doubt shared by some) would have been expressed publicly during the war period, the father's words help to maintain a critical outlook toward the military involvement that led to the bombing while demonstrating his unwillingness to be crushed by higher authorities.

This tone of dynamic resistance early in the film is consequently contrasted with the scenes of the atomic bombing itself. While the first part of the film is shot in a realistic style, the actual bombing of Hiroshima is an extraordinarily rendered sequence of surreal horror. The day of the bombing is indicated by shots of a calendar while scenes of a ticking clock add to the feeling that time and other forces are no longer under the control of the family. The narrative builds in suspense by having the family initially take shelter during an air raid only to appear on the street again in relief that it was a false alarm. Although these actions are based on historical events, they also serve within the diegesis to heighten the feeling of ominousness as Gen then goes out on the street to play. Intermittently cutting to scenes of the Americans in the cockpit of the Enola Gay, the viewer looks through Gen's eyes as he bends down to pick up a coin (thus presumably shielding himself from the blast) at the very moment the atomic bomb is dropped.

In a scene that could only have been rendered effectively in animation (because of its spectacular quality and the necessary distancing that the animated image provides), we see the architecture and the people of Hiroshima turning black and white, lit by an uncanny radiance.[9] This is followed immediately by scenes of transmogrification. Most memorable is the image of the little girl with whom Gen had been playing, as she turns instantaneously from a "realistic" cartoon character into a damned soul from Buddhist mythology, a "walking ghost," hair on fire, eyes popping out, and fingers melting into hideously extended tendrils. In other brief shots we see a dog transforming into a flaming creature and, in a series of neon-colored images (contrasting both with the black and white of the initial moment of the bomb and with the conventional pastels of the first part of the film), the viewer sees the architecture of authority—Hiroshima Castle and the Hiroshima Prefectural Industrial Promotion Hall—dissolving into an incandescent nightmare of fragmenting ruins.

Barefoot Gen's depiction of the atomic bombing is powerful and horrifying, yet the narrative and visual structure of the film resists overwhelming the viewer with this scene or the ghastly aftermath of the bombing. Although the film continues to show many scenes of postbombing horror, it intersperses these with scenes and images of effort and hope. For example, shortly after the bombing Gen runs home to look for his parents. He finds that his father, sister, and little brother are all trapped under a burning beam and can discover no way to save them. However, this scene (perhaps the most affecting in the entire film) refuses to wallow in tragedy. Between the agonizing cries of his brother and sister, his father admonishes him to "take care of his mother," insisting that Gen is now the head of his family.

This pattern of tragedy, intercut with moments of resolution and hope for the future, continues throughout the rest of the film. Gen delivers his baby sister without any medical help and even manages to get a job that will allow him to buy milk for her (though he is too late; she dies of malnutrition). Whereas the sister's death in *Grave of the Fireflies* signaled the climactic moment in a downward spiral, Gen and his mother manage to regroup themselves for the sake of each other. They even take on the care of an orphan boy, Ryutaro, a Shinji look-alike who clearly stands for the ability of the family to reconstitute itself, revitalize, and endure. In the film's final scene the image of the wheat returns as Gen and Ryutaro walk through a barren wasteland, speculating whether grass will ever grow there again. Through Gen's downward gaze, the viewer sees the grass shooting up at the same time as Gen discovers that his hair, which had fallen out due to the bombing, is also growing again. *Barefoot Gen* ends with soaring music and this final movement of upward momentum.

The overall impact of *Barefoot Gen* is radically different from that of *Grave of the Fireflies*. This is demonstrated in some of the more archetypal structures in the two films, most notably the way masculinity is positioned in each one. As Marie Morimoto points out, "Perhaps the most conspicuous metaphors of war are those of masculinism."[10] Both films privilege the masculine as the dominant force in the family structure by showing two young boys taking care of their respective female relatives. The two films differ sharply, however, in how this masculine role is carried out. In *Grave of the Fireflies* Seita is seen as nurturing and sensitive (in one affecting scene, as the two wait for news of their badly burned mother, he performs gymnastic feats on playground equipment in an attempt to distract the unhappy Setsuko) but he is ultimately unable to play a dynamic role in taking care of either his mother or sister. He runs away from his unsympathetic aunt rather than confronting her, and apologizes to the angry farmer rather than stand up to him when he is caught stealing vegetables. Although he finally does withdraw all the family's life savings to take care of Setsuko, it is too late to help her. This passive behavior contrasts significantly with Gen who, if anything, seems energized by adversity. Thus, in the scene with the carp, Gen does not back down and emerges with the priest's respect and friendship.

The two films also differ in relation to their depiction of the father and of authority in general. Seita's absent father is in the navy and seems aligned with an unproblematic vision of authority. While Seita is shown as preferring to live outside the system because of his aunt's cruelty, the system itself is never criticized, and he and his sister wait hopefully for the day their father will sail triumphantly home. In one scene Seita is shown nostalgically remembering a naval regatta in which he sees white uniformed figures (presumably including his father) lined up on the bridge of a naval destroyer while military music plays. Other male authority figures also fare well. One of the few characters in the film who is actively kind to Seita is an elderly policeman, who offers him a glass of water after his humiliation by the farmer. Gen's father, in contrast, is clearly aligned against the authorities. A day laborer who wears a simple undershirt and loudly criticizes the "madmen" who run the government, Gen's father is as down to earth and "present" as Seita's father is ethereal and absent. It is clearly his father's influence, from his exhortations to "look after your mother" to his homilies about the wheat, that inspires and sustains Gen throughout the film.

However, the two films are alike in implicitly presenting the death of the father, an important symbolic mode that has dominated much of Japanese postwar culture. Scholars argue that Japanese culture now exists in a demasculinized state, overwhelmed by feminine "cuteness" but still haunted by images of a dead, absent, or inadequate father and a problematic masculinity.[11] The reasons for this loss of the father are clearly spelled out in the historical realities of the postwar period. Not only did many Japanese actually lose their fathers due to military service or allied bombings, but they also lost the cult of the emperor, who was represented in prewar propaganda as the symbolic head of the Japanese nation-as-family. Although the Allied occupation attempted to "replace" the emperor-as-father with the larger-than-life figure of MacArthur, such a substitution was uneasy at best, and profoundly disturbing at worst.[12] Characteristically, the anti-authority *Barefoot Gen* ends with an invocation to a still symbolically present individualistic father, while *Grave of the Fireflies* portrays its central character as a literal and spiritual orphan, abandoned by his naval officer father and rejected by a society in which the father is literally and symbolically dead.

While the two films show important contrasts in their depiction of the role of the father, the performance of the feminine, in terms of both motherhood and the role of little sister, is similar in both works. Although female characters remain an oasis of security, comfort, and strength in most prewar film and literature and in many popular early postwar films as well (as in the famous *hahamono* or "mother matters" genre), the female figures in both these films of the 1980s appear notably weak and tenuous. Although the mother in *Barefoot Gen* is a comforting and reassuring presence, after the bombing she becomes helpless, simply another victim to be taken care of by the stalwart Gen.

In fact, she is even shown in moments of near madness, as when, immediately after the bombing, she confronts the horror of her family's demise, her hair wildly undone and her face ravaged by screams, or when she responds to the death of her baby with a fixed glazed stare. Seita's mother is also seen in terms of victimhood. She is first shown heading to the shelter before her children, because of a weak heart. The next view is of fragmented shots of her body swathed in bandages, and the last glimpse is of her body being loaded onto a truck.

Both of the sister figures in the films also exist as the embodiment of victimhood. Gen's sister is born the night of the bombing, survives a few days, crying helplessly, and leaves only silence (the mother's mad stare) at her death. The figure of Seita's sister is even more pitifully constituted. She is shown as adorably helpless, riding on her brother's back, taking food from his hands, and ultimately sinking into a pathetic daze of starvation and illness. Even her one "positive" action, her construction of the grave of fireflies, is linked with evanescence and death.

Given the importance of female characters in their relation to traditional Japanese culture, it is possible to read these helpless/dying/ mad female victims as expressions of a fundamental unease on the part of the films as to any real possibility of cultural survival. While Gen and his adopted little brother jumping in excitement and hope at the end of the film may be read as a brave attempt to suggest the possibility of human survival in the most devastating conditions, the absence of an equivalent strong female presence hints that such endurance (at least of traditional Japanese culture) may be problematic. *Grave of the Fireflies* is even less ambiguous. The fireflies that are metonymically and metaphorically linked to the little sister also have a long symbolic tradition in Japanese culture. The downward spiral of their evanescent life, which ends in the little hollowed-out grave, only serves to illuminate the equally transient life of the sister, the image of whose little white bones haunts the entire film.

In her discussion of postwar Japanese films, scholar Patricia Masters points out how in postwar Japan the "national metaphors of self" became essentially "trans-sexual," both "feminized" and "virilized."[13] In the case of the anime discussed here, it is clear, especially in *Grave of the Fireflies*, that Japanese identity is almost completely "feminized," not only in terms of the dominating image of the dying younger sister, but also in the character of Seita himself, who is "demasculinized" from the film's very beginning. This feminization, however, leads only to despair and nostalgia for a dying culture. *Grave of the Fireflies* is thus an elegy for a lost past that can never be reconstituted.

In contrast, the narrative tension that animates *Barefoot Gen* is a resistance to "feminization" (coded not simply as weak but as irrational, even mad in the figure of the mother) and a privileging of a resurgent masculinity, metonymically troped in the growing blades of wheat and Gen's growing strands of hair. *Barefoot Gen's* insistent method of uplift and inspiration may strike some viewers as too pat, too ideologically grounded, or too dangerously unbalanced a picture of Japanese culture, although this simplicity may have to do with the fact that the film is consistently shown in elementary schools for its antiwar message. Yet it may also be that the cataclysmic nature of the event itself may summon forth simplified images of uplift and renewal in response. Scholar Carole Cavanaugh has suggested that Hiroshima calls for "remembrance and repression." *Barefoot Gen* remembers Hiroshima and refuses to repress the horror, but it may also repress a realistically grounded awareness of the bleak complexities confronting a nation's attempt to renew itself for the sake of a message of reassurance.

Writing on Holocaust literature, Holocaust scholar Lawrence Langer suggests that, "Among the leading ideas we are forced to surrender as we read through these pages is the comforting notion that suffering has meaning," and that "the anguish of the victims can be neither soothed nor diminished by a vocabulary of consolation."[14] Confronted by their own version of hell on earth, Japanese writers and artists still clearly search for meaning, if not consolation, in working through images of suffering. *Grave of the Fireflies* attempts to construct an elegiac ideology of victimhood and loss that allows for a national identity in which the loss of the war gives depth to the Japanese soul. *Barefoot Gen* acknowledges suffering but resists victimhood, offering instead a new model of human resurgence and consolation. Compared to some of the most complex Holocaust literature (or the literature of the *hibakusha*), such treatment may seem naive, but these animated visions of loss, beauty, and (in the case of *Barefoot Gen*) hope, allow a defeated nation, and those who died for it, a transitory moment of dignity.

CHAPTER TEN

PRINCESS MONONOKE: FANTASY, THE FEMININE, AND THE MYTH OF "PROGRESS"

IN HIS INTRODUCTION to *Movies and Mass Culture,* John Belton asserts that "movies assist audiences in negotiating major changes in identity; they carry them across difficult periods of cultural transition in such a way that a more or less coherent national identity remains in place, spanning the gaps and fissures that threaten to disrupt its movement and to expose its essential disjointedness."[1] This is an ambitious statement, but it seems an appropriate one in many cases. Despite their use of traditional tropes of endurance and nobility, the final vision of both *Grave of the Fireflies* and *Barefoot Gen* is that of a fragmented national identity, a major characteristic of which is a deep sense of loss of a structured, patriarchal past. In the case of these two films the fragmentation is implicit, but in the next film to be considered, Miyazaki Hayao's 1997 epic *Princess Mononoke* (*Mononokehime*) the sense of a broken heterogeneous world is stridently manifest. *Princess Mononoke* problematizes archetypes and icons, ranging from the notion of the emperor's untouchability to the traditional iconization of the feminine, to create a genuinely new vision of a Japan at the crossroads of history. The film also emphasizes loss, even privileges it. In contrast to *Grave of the Fireflies* and *Barefoot Gen,* however, Miyazaki's work deals with the loss of a Japan that existed before the patriarchal system, a Japan in which nature, rather than humans, ruled. In some ways one might characterize the film as a violent, indeed apocalyptic, elegy for a lost Japan at the same time that it offers an alternative, heterogeneous, and female-centered vision of Japanese identity for the future.

Although *Princess Mononoke* is not based on an actual historical event, it belongs properly in a section on animation and history because, in its distinctive way, it is a meditation on Japanese history that provides a counternarrative to some pivotal myths of Japanese culture and society. These include such crucial notions as "top down history" (history as belonging only to the court and the samurai warrior aristocracy) and the idealized concepts of the premodern Japanese as a homogeneous race living in harmony with nature.

Princess Mononoke is the highest-grossing Japanese film (not just anime) of all time. Its appeal seems to extend to all parts of Japanese society, going beyond the typical family base of most Miyazaki films, despite its complex, ambiguous, and often dark text that calls into question many long-held notions of Japanese identity. What is it about *Princess Mononoke* that strikes such a chord with the Japanese audience? And what does it say about Japanese identity at the end of the twentieth century that a film set in the medieval period actively subverts some of the major myths of the Japanese past?[2] In contrast to idealized myths of harmony, progress, and an unproblematic, homogenous "people" (*minzoku*) ruled by a patriarchal elite,[3] the film offers a vision of cultural dissonance, spiritual loss, and environmental apocalypse. If *Princess Mononoke* is indeed negotiating changes in identity for its Japanese audience, what kind of new identity is taking form?

To answer these questions it is first useful to see the ways in which *Princess Mononoke* undermines the myths of traditional Japanese identity while offering a counternarrative in their place. Although this counternarrative is not original (it builds on much recent scholarship from the last decade), *Princess Mononoke* reenvisions the conventions of Japanese history through a variety of distinctive and effective strategies. Perhaps the most important is one of subversion and defamiliarization. The film defamiliarizes two important icons in Japanese culture, the myth of the feminine as long-suffering and supportive and the myth of the Japanese as living in harmony with nature, often expressed through a union of the feminine with the natural.

Furthermore the film defamiliarizes conventional notions of Japanese history through Miyazaki's decision to set the film during the fourteenth-century Muromachi period and his subsequent subversion of conventional expectations concerning what a film set in that era should be "about." The period is usually considered to be an apex of Japanese high culture, when well-known cultural products like the tea ceremony, Noh theater, and Zen-inspired landscape gardens reached their most brilliant form. It was also an era of relative peace, when the ruling samurai class grew increasingly literate and refined as they settled in the Muromachi section of the capital city of Kyoto, where they rubbed shoulders with the court aristocracy.[4] *Princess Mononoke,* however, takes place in a mythical space deeply removed from the capital, both literally and symbolically. As Miyazaki states in his introduction to a book about the film, "Contrary to the usual period film [*jidaigeki*], this is a movie in which few samurai, peasants, or feudal lords appear. This is a film in which the main protagonists are those who usually do not appear on the stage of history. Instead, this is the story of the marginals of history."[5]

The film's "marginals" comprise a diverse and unusual group that includes women, outcasts, and non-*Yamato* (nonethnic Japanese) tribes, but perhaps the most unusual inclusion is that of the *kami*, the ancient gods of the Japanese people who either embody or are closely linked to the forces of nature. It is these *kami*, who range from sentient beasts to supernatural spirits, whose war against the humans provides the narrative impetus of the film. Or perhaps it would be equally accurate to say that it is the war of the humans (or perhaps more appropriately, the war of the humans against the *kami*) that is one of the main drives of the film. As Komatsu Kazuhiko explains, "The motif that runs at the foundation of the story is that of the 'extermination of ghosts' [*bakemono taiji*]."[6]

The term "ghosts" (*bakemono*) can be equated with *kami*, but it also encompasses a more negative range of natural and supernatural forces. They represent the nonrational, nonhuman world, a world that by the fourteenth century was seriously threatened by the increasing dominance of human collectivities. In the film, the *kami/bakemono* exist in opposition to the human realm. The marginals, in particular the female characters linked with the *kami/bakemono*, represent the abjected Other, the untamable supernatural outsider haunting the boundaries of the increasingly "civilized" world of Japan dominated by the imperial court, the shogun, and the samurai.

From the film's very beginning it subverts what might be called the "samurai ethic" of traditional period cinema (although it should be noted that the "samurai ethic" has also been resisted in such "high culture" films as Kurosawa's *Seven Samurai* and *Yojimbo*). Rather than opening with a scene of samurai battle or courageous peasants resisting warlords, *Princess Mononoke* starts squarely in the realm of the nonhuman. It begins with a wide-angle shot of mist-laden mountains, over which are superimposed the words, "Long ago, this country was covered by deep forests in which, from ancient times, there lived the gods." Although the time frame soon becomes more identifiable, this opening vista immediately places the audience in a liminal, mythic space. This space does not exist as mystical refuge, however. Instead, it is figured as a site of resistance, and even of attack.

As the focus narrows in on the forest, the hitherto serene natural space is rent by a series of plunging assaultive movements. The forest's pristine interior is ravaged by the sudden grating movement of trees falling, which cuts jagged horizontals across the screen. The trees are not being felled by humans but by a *tatarigami*, a kind of violent god that has taken over the body of an injured wild boar. The boar's injury is from an iron ball lodged in its body, which enrages it. The plunging movements of the maddened boar seem to fill the screen as it rushes through the forest. Finally it escapes from the forest to attack the world of humans, in this case a clan in eastern Japan known as the Emishi (equated in notes to the film with the non-Japanese Ainu race), whose young lord, Ashitaka, ultimately manages to kill the boar.[7]

The boar's deadly encounter with the humans subverts audience expectations. Rather than the tidy disposal of a wild animal, the boar's death becomes the impetus for the film's subsequent narrative. As it dies, the boar places a curse on Ashitaka, represented visually by a tentacular stain on his right arm. Knowing that he will die if he cannot rid himself of the curse, Ashitaka leaves his people and journeys west toward the central land of the Yamato kingdom, the area where the Japanese court held most sway during that period. The boy, however, ends up finding two places that are very far from court or samurai culture. The first is an immense forest that is ruled by a fantastic deerlike presence known as the *shishigami* and contains supernatural creatures such as the doll-like forest spirits known as the *kodama* and clans of sentient animals such as wolves, monkeys, and boars. The second is the fortress of Tatara, where the iron ball that originally injured the boar was produced. Ashitaka discovers that Tatara is essentially a weapons manufacturing factory where they mine iron ore to make armaments. In another example of subversion, guns, rather than swords, play a major part in this supposedly medieval setting. Tatara is informally allied with the Yamato court since they are both united against a common enemy, the gods of the forest. Consequently, the important battles of the film are not between samurai or even between samurai and peasants but between various human factions and the beasts and spirits of the forest. Or, as Miyazaki titles his introduction to *The Art of Mononokehime*, "This is a story of battle between humanity and the wild gods."[8]

In another undermining of traditional conventions, Tatara is not governed by a man but by a woman, Lady Eboshi, who has constructed Tatara as a utopian refuge for outcast women and people with incurable illnesses like leprosy. Eboshi is pitted not only against the forest creatures but also against another female human, a young girl named San who is the "*mononokehime*" or "possessed princess" of the title. Although "*mononoke*" traditionally means possession by a human spirit, San is clearly possessed by the fearsome spirits of nature. Raised by a female wolf known as Moro, San detests all things human and lives only to destroy human civilization, represented by

Tatara. Eboshi in turn is determined to take over the forest, a victory that would involve killing the *shishigami.*

In the film's apocalyptic climax, Eboshi, along with samurai and priests from the court, battles against all the creatures of the forest and succeeds in cutting off the head of the *shishigami.* This action sets off the destruction of the entire forest, shown through images of the earth turning brown and cracking open and the forest spirits dying, while the immense *shishigami,* barely alive, searches helplessly for its head. Eboshi has promised the head to representatives from the Yamato court, who intend to take it back to the emperor, but, in the film's climactic scene, San and Ashitaka unite to seize the head and return it to the *shishigami.*

The film ends with the apparent restoration of nature and harmony as the world turns green again, but ambiguous currents remain beneath the surface. Although Ashitaka is freed from his curse and decides to stay in Tatara to work with the now penitent Eboshi, he cannot convince San to live with him. She insists that she cannot forgive humans and laments the death of the *shishigami.* Ashitaka in turn maintains that the *shishigami* is still alive, but she remains unpersuaded. The last lines that the two speak have them agreeing to "visit each other sometimes."

Princess Mononoke is a powerful and moving work but also a disturbing one. Unlike previous Miyazaki films, which end on an unambiguous note of hope and reassurance even if they present visions of destruction and horror, *Princess Mononoke's* "message" fits much more appropriately into what can be termed the cinema of "de-assurance." As anime critic Helen McCarthy points out, this is a film about love in its many aspects—love of nature, love of family, love between the sexes—but it is also, as she says, a film about "the extent to which love involves loss of many kinds."[9] It is a wake-up call to human beings in a time of environmental and spiritual crisis that attempts to provoke its audience into realizing how much they have already lost and how much more they stand to lose.

This power of the film depends on Miyazaki's strategies of subversion that problematize many of the accepted myths of Japanese culture. In keeping with Miyazaki's striking ability to blend the "real" with the fantastic, *Princess Mononoke* creates a world that appears to have some kind of historical basis but then consistently destabilizes audience expectations of how that world should be. One example of the pervasiveness of this destabilization is in the choice of historical setting. This is an important change from his previous works, virtually all of which have been set in what might be called "international fantasy space," fantastic nonplaces characterized by vaguely European-style architecture and Western-looking characters. The only exception to this is *Totoro,* which is set in a rural suburb of Tokyo in an idealized near-past corresponding roughly to the 1950s. *Totoro's* beautiful fantasy spaces work to create a sense of escape, pleasure, and hope. The film is also deeply nostalgic, a quest for an imagined personal past.

In contrast, *Princess Mononoke* refuses to sentimentalize the medieval history it highlights, preferring to problematize the past and, implicitly, the attitudes toward it. Furthermore, although his depiction contains important fantasy elements, Miyazaki's decision to use a specific historical period is for reasons of education rather than escapism. In Miyazaki's view, the fourteenth century is a period of significant historical transition from a world that was still in close contact with both natural and supernatural forces to a world that would become increasingly oriented toward the human. As he says, "It was in this period that people changed their value system from gods to money." Since the period is one of transition, its variability also holds great attractions for him as a time when "life and death were sharply delineated. People lied, loved, hated, worked, and died. Life was not ambiguous. Even in the midst of hatred and slaughter there were still things that made life worth living. Marvelous encounters and beautiful things could still exist."[10] It is this complex and dangerous world that *Princess Mononoke* attempts to evoke, and, although permeated by historical allusions, it is also very much Miyazaki's own world, his own "history as vision." As Komatsu says, "This is not a work based on historical faithfulness . . . [T]his is fantasy dressed as historical fiction with a variety of facts and fictions gathered together."[11]

The way in which the film mixes "facts and fiction" is an important element in its destabilizing effect. Two of the most important aspects of this destabilization are the film's defamiliarizing of conventional female characterization and its "supernaturalization" of nature. Turning to his female characters, it is evident that in *Princess Mononoke* Miyazaki not only undermines a plethora of female stereotypes from conventional Japanese culture and from the anime world itself but also moves away from his own previous female creations. Animation scholar Paul Wells says that earlier Miyazaki films "operate in ways which re-negotiate narrative paradigms accentuating masculine power and authority,"[12] and this is especially true for *Princess Mononoke*. As critic Murase Hiromi points out, there are three important female characters in the film: Eboshi, the leader of Tatara; San, the human girl who has joined wild nature; and Moro, San's adoptive wolf mother. Female characters have traditionally been of great importance throughout Miyazaki's oeuvre, but these three characters depart from his more typical heroines in a variety of intriguing ways. While virtually all of his female protagonists, from the stalwart Nausicaä to the inquisitive little girls of *Totoro*, are impressively independent and self-possessed creations, they still tend to have conventionally female gendered aspects like sweetness and cuteness, which, as has been shown, are typical of the *shōjo*. Since cuteness is such an important part of contemporary Japanese culture, it is not surprising that Miyazaki's female protagonists participate in this cultural construction, and it makes its absence in the three female characters of *Princess Mononoke* all the more remarkable.

Overall, the female characters possess a gender-neutral, or at least deeply ambiguous, characterization compared to traditional female stereotypes, and they remain completely outside the misogynistic patriarchal collectivity that rapidly became the foundation of premodern Japan. Eboshi is a leader who cares for the sick and the outcast but is equally concerned with military matters and the destruction of the *shishigami*. Moro appears to be a wise and brave mother, but she is also a ferocious killer. Most intriguing of all, San, the "heroine" of the film, is shown as a ruthless figure of virtually unrelenting violence. Although she has moments of softness, as when she takes care of the injured Ashitaka in the forest, the viewer is most likely to remember her first appearance in the film, clad in a costume of fur and bone, her face bloody from sucking out blood from a wound in Moro's side.

This initial appearance is worth examining, especially since it is this depiction of San that appeared frequently in promotional material for the film. Her blood-smeared face, fierce demeanor, and fur clothing obviously connect San with both violence and nature, but there is also a strong hint of the sexual primordial female as well. The blood around San's mouth, metonymically reinforced by two red slashes of paint on her cheeks suggests menstrual blood and also an aggressive sexuality that is confrontational rather than alluring. The fur around San's neck, visually reinforced by Moro's furry coat, may also suggest genitalia, but it is an explicit picture of female sexuality that is more ominous than erotic. San's body is thus inscribed with wildness and primordial sexuality, making her Otherness not simply female but bestial as well.

This reading is supported by her subsequent appearances in the film, beginning with her attack on Tatara. The viewer first sees her from a distance, running with her two wolf "siblings" in a horizontal streak of assaultive lightning. Horizontals switch to verticals as she leaps, rolls, and plunges from rooftop to rooftop, knife in hand. Overwhelming all resistance from the outmatched denizens of Tatara and far more frightening than her wolf companions, she appears as terrifyingly Other, a creature of supernatural forces totally outside the realm of the human.

San's "mother," Moro, is also a destabilizing mixture of characteristics.[13] Although clearly sentient and intelligent, she is a far cry from the cuddly anthropomorphic creations that viewers of family animation have traditionally come to expect. She does have nurturing qualities (for example, at one point San buries her face against Moro's fur, creating a rather unsettling picture of mother-child bonding), and she gives wise advice to both her real offspring and to San. However, she is also a relentless fighter, as the scene in which she dies, her teeth still firmly clenched in Eboshi's arm, clearly demonstrates.

Eboshi is the most ambiguous character of the three. Without any apparent family ties or hint of male support, she rules Tatara independently. Even more than Moro, she is characterized by an odd amalgamation of the nurturing and the ferocious. She is clearly protective of her diseased and outcast citizens, but at the same time she is fanatically determined to destroy the *shishigami* and, by extension, the natural world of the forest. Even more than Moro or San, she seems removed from any historical context. While there is a tradition of isolated utopian communities throughout Japanese history and the references to iron ore manufacturing are apparently accurate, the notion that such a community would have been led by a woman, and one who was both a military commander and a fiercely determined fighter, seems clearly fictional. She too is a kind of Other, but, in direct contrast to San and Moro, Eboshi aligns totally with technology and culture.

In her provocative essay, Murase Hiromi sees the three females as occupying significantly different positions in relation to the nature/culture dichotomy that exists as one of the main pivots of the film. For Murase, San and Moro exist as a mother-daughter coalition aligned with nature and in opposition to the "civilization" of Tatara over which Eboshi rules. Eboshi in turn may be seen as a kind of artificial mother to the collectivity of Tatara. In the death of Moro at the film's end, Murase sees nature being overwhelmed by culture and perceives a hint of the transition from the flesh-and-blood ties that characterized premodern Japan to the kind of suprapersonal relationships that characterized the industrial collectivity of contemporary Japan.[14]

Murase also suggests that Miyazaki may be covertly playing with gender boundaries behind the screen of the nature/culture dichotomy. It is certainly true that all three female protagonists possess characteristics traditionally coded as male, and that, with the important exception of Ashitaka, there are no male "heroes" in the film. It is also possible to suggest that the use of females in conventionally male-coded roles is another link within the film's overall strategy of destabilization. In each of the three cases, the use of a female character defamiliarizes what might otherwise have been a fairly hackneyed film role. This is even true in the case of Moro who, at first glance, could just as easily have been made into a male wolf. By making her both female and a mother but refusing to allow her any conventionally maternal characteristics (such as those of the lioness mother in *The Lion King*), the film once again destabilizes the audience, who are not permitted the reassurance of finding the beast nonthreatening. Moro remains an unrepentant threat to the humans until her own death, which itself is portrayed totally without sentimentality.

Even more defamiliarizing is Eboshi. While most standard historical dramas use the main female character as a "vehicle for tradition,"[15] Eboshi's character subverts the conventional notion of the traditional female role. Furthermore, had Eboshi been a *male* leader in charge of making armaments, governing a collectivity, and leading her troops into battle against the denizens of the forest, the audience would likely have found her far less interesting and might have seen the character as another typical representation of the evil human male pitting his draconian technology against helpless nature. By making the character a woman, and one who can both destroy and rebuild, the film problematizes facile stereotyping of technology, armaments, and industrialized culture as evil. In the film's presentation, Eboshi is in some ways a tragic figure, but her tragedy is that she is not actually evil. Instead, she is coerced into her destructive attack by her natural desire to protect a utopian collectivity.

Eboshi's character thus defamiliarizes both our notions of femininity and of culture, showing a more complex face of the feminine. San's character also defamiliarizes the feminine, but, more importantly, she also defamiliarizes the conventional view of the feminine and the natural as a form of sanctified Japanese harmony (*wa*). Even today, modern Japan places a strong emphasis on the woman and nature as emblems of traditional Japanese aesthetics. Upscale fashion magazines such as *Katei gahō* make a point of featuring only Japanese models, usually kimono clad, performing some seasonal activity to promote the magazine's image of traditional harmony: "together with nature, something Japanese."[16] Obviously, San's connection with nature is in significant contrast to this mystically aesthetic ideal. The "nature" that San seems to epitomize suggests associations with assault, destruction, and profound, unstoppable rage. Again, while this concatenation of negative elements might be surprising or disturbing in a male "wild child" character, in an attractive young female it is far more destabilizing.

Manga critic Natsume Fukanosuke has noted the important connection between young girls and myth in Miyazaki's work,[17] but San's character seems to spring from the myths of early Shinto, unlike his previous female protagonists. In Shinto's animistic beliefs individuals as well as natural products and forces such as animals, rocks, and mountains could become *kami*. These *kami* were gods not because of any moral attributes (as is the case in the Buddhist pantheon, a later addition to Japan) but because of their literally awesome powers. While perhaps not quite a *kami*, San possesses clearly supernatural powers, both in her extraordinary fighting capability and in her ability to speak telepathically with Moro and the other beasts. In many ways her ability to bond with the nonhuman is reminiscent of Nausicaä, but, in important contrast to Nausicaä, she shows very little capacity to bond with the human.

Despite her human origins, San is clearly a liminal figure, closer to the animal and other *kami* characters, who are at least as important in the film as the human protagonists. It is this use of the fantastic and the uncanny aligned with nonhuman actants and nature that is the second major destabilizing strategy in the film. While critic Robin Wood in discussing fantasy film has stated that fantasy "can be used in two ways, as a means of escaping from contemporary reality or as a means of illuminating it,"[18] *Princess Mononoke*'s use of fantasy is clearly to disturb or problematize our notions of reality.

The center of the film's fantasy space is, of course, the forest that stands in uncanny opposition to the civilization of Tatara. In terms of Freud's definition of the uncanny as something that is both unfamiliar yet eerily familiar (*unheimlich* in the original German), the forest fits appropriately. For Miyazaki, the great forest exists as a buried archetypal memory. According to critic Komatsu Kazuhiko, *Princess Mononoke*'s forest is based on Miyazaki's reading in historical ecology, in particular the writings of Nakao Sasuke, who wrote about the origins of agriculture in Japan. For Miyazaki, reading these works was almost a spiritual revelation. As Miyazaki himself puts it,

> Upon reading [Nakao], I felt my eyes being drawn to a distant height. A wind blew over me. The framework of the nation state *[kokka]* the wall emblemized by the word "racial people" *[minzoku]*, the heavy weight of history, all fled away from me and the breath of life from the evergreen forests flowed into me. Everything was woven together in this book—the forests of the Meiji shrine where I liked to stroll, theories about farming in Shinshū during the Jomon period, the tales of everyday life in Yamanashi that my story telling mother liked to relate—and it taught me what I was the descendant of.[19]

It is Miyazaki's notion that he and presumably other Japanese are the spiritual descendants of the "glossy leafed forests" that Nakao theorizes once covered Japan before the country became dominated by rice culture. Once rice paddy culture arrived, wet rice cultivation began to destroy the wilder kind of nature, and by the twentieth century it had almost completely disappeared from contemporary Japan.[20] Miyazaki believes that these vanished forests still exert a spiritual pull on the average urban dweller, and it was this that he attempted to dramatize in his creation of the forest of the *shishigami*. He explains "If you opened a map of Japan and asked where is the forest of the *shishigami* that Ashitaka went to, I couldn't tell you, but I do believe that somehow traces of that kind of place still exist inside one's soul."[21]

In this interpretation, the forest of the *shishigami* is a place of magical and spiritual renewal. Its construction draws together Nakao's historical research, archetypal Shinto beliefs, and Miyazaki's own imagination. The forest's magical qualities come across expressively in the film's brilliant animation and exceptional use of color. In contrast to the pastel palette of many of the director's films, *Princess Mononoke*'s forest is designed in deep greens and browns, with the occasional radiant shafts of light penetrating the depths of quiet forest pools. Night scenes are even more remarkable, especially the moonlit vision of the *shishigami* as it metamorphoses into the *detarabochi,* an immense phantom of the night that is its alter ego. These scenes might suggest that the forest in *Princess Mononoke* is a classic example of the traditional Japanese valorization of nature. Indeed, in its depth, power, and beauty the forest does suggest some of the spirit of premodern Japanese poetry, particularly the lengthy Shinto-inspired celebrations of nature in the tenth-century poetry collection, the *Manyōshu*. It is crucial to point out, however, that Miyazaki radically defamiliarizes any conventional stereotyping. Despite its beauty, the forest has little in common with the traditional Japanese landscaping that reached its apogee during the Muromachi period. Influenced by the Zen priest-hood, the Muromachi landscape was an enclosed one, the carefully cultivated and safe framework of the Zen garden. In significant contrast, the forest of the *shishigami* is a wild and threatening place, consistently avoided by the human characters in the film. Rather than a refuge it is a locus of revenge.

The motif of revenge begins with the terrifying vision of the wounded boar bursting out of the forest, who, as it dies, intones a message of eternal hatred against all humans. A sense of anger and desire for human blood animates virtually all the other animals in the film (with the exception of Ashitaka's domesticated steed, Yakurtu), from the monkeys (whose refrain is, "We will eat humans!") to the pitiless Moro and her children. Even the *shishigami,* despite its gentle demeanor and deerlike characteristics, is clearly not a sentimentally benevolent deity. Although it does save Ashitaka when he is wounded in the initial battle with San, this could be a result of San's intercession or, as Ashitaka guesses, a means of prolonging his life so that the boar's curse may legitimately destroy him. In either case, the *shishigami* itself is unconcerned with any larger moral implications, wishing only to protect its forests and the forest's denizens. Once again, a comparison with *The Lion King* might be apt here. Unlike the approachable and all-wise father lion, the *shishigami* is characterized in a deliberately mystical way, speechless, enigmatic, and, in its *detarabochi* transformation, truly godlike.

Miyazaki's "supernaturalization" of the natural is a deliberate defamiliarization strategy offering an alternative vision to the conventional Japanese view of nature, which, while acknowledging the wildness of nature, prefers to view it as something that can be tamed and cultivated.[22] In the film nature is beautiful, sacred, and awesome, but it is also vengeful and brutally frightening. Embodied in the spiritually remote *shishigami,* it exists in the eyes of Eboshi and the Yamato court as yet another vision of the Other, an object to be repudiated and ultimately destroyed. Modernist

The theme of repudiation and destruction returns to the notion of the abjected Other touched upon at the beginning of this chapter. Certainly one of Miyazaki's major strategies in *Princess Mononoke* is to privilege a vision in which the abject revenge themselves. This is not an entirely original vision (another version appears in *Akira*). It is rather one that has lingered on the boundaries of twentieth-century Japanese culture and has undermined the dominant discourse of modernity and progress through the presentation of alternative visions that privilege the irrational, the supernatural, and the apocalyptic. Often these visions have been linked with women.[23] Throughout much of the twentieth century, women in modernizing Japan have been seen as sites of what literary scholar Nina Cornyetz calls "the nostalgic uncanny."[24] Cornyetz suggests that the modern tendency to associate women with the nostalgic uncanny is actually a form of abjection, a process in which the "culturally repulsive aspects of the premodern and the undifferentiated maternal body"[25] are repudiated and jettisoned from the dominant collectivity. Abjecting the Other (female, supernatural, premodern, etc.) allowed the modern male Japanese subject to develop.

In *Princess Mononoke* there are two different and almost contradictory processes at work. First, the revenge of the abjected is encapsulated in the wild and assaultive body of San. The second is a provocative acknowledgment of the brutal complexities of "progress," dramatized through the character of Eboshi. Turning to the question of abjection first, there are many examples of this process in both film and literature, from the savage and seductive female ghost in Mizoguchi's film *Ugetsu* to the forest-dwelling enchantress of Izumi Kyōka's story *Kōya hijiri* (the holy man of Mount Kōya). While San is delineated in essentially asexual terms, her association with blood and with spirit possession links her to premodern archetypes of ferocious femininity—the shamanesses, mountain witches, and other demonic women who are the opposite trope of the all-enduring, all-supportive mother figure. Read in this light, San's femininity is aligned with the uncanny and the "supernatural natural" embodied by Moro in resistance to modernity. However, unlike the females in *Kōya* or *Ugetsu*, who are defeated by the world of the Symbolic (the written word of the Buddhist scriptures), San is shown as able and willing to strike back against "civilization."

Ultimately, although San and Moro do not exactly triumph, they are also not entirely defeated. The supernatural forces with which they are connected are strong enough to threaten an apocalyptic end to the environment, which temporarily defeats the monks and samurai, and forces the material civilization of Tatara to rethink its position vis-à-vis the forest. San's refusal to live with Ashitaka and her decision to stay in the forest ensure that a sense of loss or absence inevitably permeates the film's conclusion. As a result, the ending of *Princess Mononoke* is a kind of draw, with neither side triumphant and the abject still not entirely repudiated.

However, looking at the ending with the long gaze of twentieth-century hindsight, it is clear that the forest of the *shishigami* no longer exists except, perhaps, as an archetypal shadow on the contemporary unconscious. In this regard, the complex, intriguing, and enigmatic character of Eboshi and her association with the proto-industrial Tatara take on pivotal importance. In the film's refusal to destroy Eboshi or Tatara we see an implicit acknowledgment of the inevitability of "progress."[26] *Princess Mononoke*'s abjected Others function as an all-out confrontation with the notion of modernity as progress, but the film is too sophisticated to offer only a simple antiprogress/antimodernity message. By acknowledging Eboshi's "humanity" (in both senses of the term) the film forces the viewer out of any complacent cultural position where technology and industry can be dismissed as simply wrong. It is worth reemphasizing that Eboshi's femininity, especially her nurturing capacity, ensures that the viewer cannot slip so easily into a simplistic moral equation of industrial equals evil. Miyazaki problematizes the issue even further by making Tatara not just a site of industrial production but a site of *weapons* manufacturing. In addition, one of the weapons it produces, the iron ball that lodged in the *tatarigami* [boar], has engendered a lasting curse on humanity. However, it is these weapons that give employment to Tatara's outcast citizenry, who surely have as much right to survival as the denizens of the forest.

In contrast to a vision of a fundamentally approachable world in which conventions may be destabilized but never totally undermined, *Princess Mononoke* subverts the traditional history, aesthetics, and gender relationships of Japanese society. In opposition to elitist and masculinist versions of Japanese history, the emperor and the court are seen as struggling with powers potentially beyond their control, while the only authoritative guidance comes from a female wolf and the female leader of a weapons manufacturing community. Most shockingly, in contrast to the dysfunctional but still archetypally feminine women of *Grave of the Fireflies* and *Barefoot Gen* or the sexually attractive, nurturing women of the romantic comedies, *Princess Mononoke* uses female characters who exist in their own right, independent of any male interlocutor. Furthermore, these independent females are not domesticated by marriage or a happy ending but are instead interested in living separate but presumably fulfilling lives, San with her companions in the natural world, Eboshi with her industrializing community.

In contrast to the traditional tropes of homogeneity and harmony, the film offers a vision of what might be called a Japanese form of multiculturalism. This observation is supported by a striking essay by critic Saeki Junko in which she compares *Princess Mononoke* to director Ridley Scott's 1982 film *Blade Runner.* Although acknowledging the obvious difference between an American science fiction film set in the twenty-first century and a Japanese historical fantasy set in the fourteenth century, Saeki points out that the films possess a significant commonality in their mutual fascination with the problem of Otherness. In her eyes, both films are highly conscious of such questions as "How do we accept the existence of the Other or reach a mutual understanding [in a society] in which different worlds cannot fuse together but will eternally maintain their separate territories?" Saeki's conclusion is that both *Blade Runner* and *Princess Mononoke* answer this question by promoting a willingness to accept difference as an essential part of life, an acknowledgment that she sees as a product of globalization. Ultimately, she suggests that both *Blade Runner* and *Princess Mononoke* are narratives that relate a "dialogue with the Other" as an attempt at some kind of "global standard in a period of . . . 'internationalization' in which countries continue to maintain their identity while accepting the inevitable need for exchange with the Other."[27]

Saeki's vision of what I have called *Princess Mononoke*'s "multiculturalism" is intriguing not only in relation to *Blade Runner* but also in regards to a more recent work, the 1999 animated Disney film version of *Tarzan*, released two years after *Princess Mononoke*. Both films feature primordial natural settings and human protagonists raised by animals, and both privilege to an extent a fantasy of revenge by the natural world upon human technology. However, the narrative strategies and imagery they employ are significantly different, as are their ultimate ideological messages. While *Princess Mononoke* insists on difference, the Disney film attempts to erase it. Thus, despite its jungle setting and an ending that seems to suggest the autonomous power and appeal of the natural world, *Tarzan*'s underlying message privileges an anthropocentric view of the world, emphasized by the film's final scene, in which Tarzan, Jane, and her father are seen frolicking with the anthropomorphically rendered apes in a paradisial jungle. In a sense this is a vision of a Garden of Eden, in which all species live together in contentment. It is also a vision that ignores the steady march of history, technology, and progress that ultimately destroy any hope of such an Eden in the contemporary world. In contrast, *Princess Mononoke*'s world is one in which nature, emblematized by the inhuman *shishigami,* remains beautiful but threateningly and insistently Other. This is also a world in which technology cannot be erased or ignored but rather must be dealt with as an unpleasant but permanent fact of life. While *Tarzan* uses fantasy to gloss over the inconvenient facts of historical change and cultural complexity, *Princess Mononoke* employs the fantastic to reveal how plurality and otherness are a basic feature of human life.

In contrast to the melting-pot vision of American cultural hegemony, Japanese society remains deeply aware of plurality and otherness. Miyazaki's earlier films reflect this awareness in an upbeat way, offering enchanting visions of other worlds and identities in a nonthreatening, even empowering, manner. *Princess Mononoke* takes a darker and more complex look at this issue. In Ashitaka's and San's agreement to live apart but still visit each other (the opposite of the inclusionary ending of the Disney work), the film suggests the pain involved in choosing identities in a world in which such choices are increasingly offered. Although set in a historical past, *Princess Mononoke* reflects the extraordinary array of pluralities that suggest the ever more complex world of the twenty-first century.[28]

CHAPTER ELEVEN

WAITING FOR
THE END OF THE WORLD:
APOCALYPTIC IDENTITY

PRINCESS MONONOKE'S VISION OF NATURAL DISASTER is a distinctive one, but its emphasis on apocalypse is certainly not unique in Japanese animation. Indeed, perhaps one of the most striking features of anime is its fascination with the theme of apocalypse. From *Akira's* unforgettable vision of the mammoth black crater that was once Tokyo to *Neon Genesis Evangelion's* bleak rendering of social and psychological disintegration, images of mass destruction suffuse contemporary anime. While some, such as *Princess Mononoke,* hold out a promise of potential betterment alongside their vision of collapse, many others tend to dwell on destruction and loss. Destructive or hopeful, these anime seem to strike a responsive chord in the Japanese audience. In fact, it might be suggested that the apocalyptic mode, often combined with the elegiac or even the festival, is not simply a major part of anime but is also deeply ingrained within the contemporary Japanese national identity.

Depending on one's viewpoint, this assertion might appear either natural or surprising. If apocalyptic imagery and themes tend to increase at times of social change and widespread uncertainty, then present day Japan, shadowed by memories of the atomic bomb and oppressed by a more than decade-long recession that closed off an era of explosive economic growth may seem an obvious candidate for having visions of the end.[1] Furthermore, given the enormous changes that Japan has experienced in the century and a half since modernization, an "apocalyptic identity" might be one easily understood, perhaps even embraced, by its citizens.

It should be noted, of course, that Japan is not alone in being affected by apocalyptic thinking. Critic Rita Felski cites "[a]n existing repertoire of fin-de-siècle tropes of decadence, apocalypse and sexual crisis"[2] in contemporary Western culture as well. Perhaps the twentieth century itself, with its mammoth social and political upheavals and its incredible rate of technological change, is the chief culprit behind the enormous range of apocalyptic visions that exist in the world today. Apocalyptic awareness exists in Europe but is particularly strong in the United States, where the constant resurgence of doomsday cults, from the nineteenth century Shakers to the followers of David Koresh in Waco, gives strong support to John W. Nelson's assertion that "[a]pocalyptic is as American as the hot dog."[3] What sets Europe and America apart from Japan, however, is that they share the common tradition of the biblical Book of Revelation the themes and imagery of which have become the fundamental version of the apocalyptic narrative: a final battle between the forces of the righteous and the forces of Satan, the wholesale destruction of the world with the evil side being cast into hell, and the ultimate happy ending with the evildoers condemned and the righteous believers ascending to the kingdom of heaven.

Traditional Japanese culture has never shared in this vision. Neither traditional Buddhism nor Shinto envisions anything like the final battle between good and evil of Revelation. Furthermore, the notion of the punishment of nonbelievers and the ascent into heaven of the believing few is notably absent from both religious traditions. In spite of these facts, however, both high and popular culture in Japan are inundated with apocalyptic visions. The 1973 novel by the Nobel prize laureate Ōe Kenzaburō, *The Floodwaters Have Come Unto My Soul* (*Kyōzui wa wagatamashi ni oyobitamau hi*), contains visions of both an apocalyptic flood *and* a nuclear holocaust. Among younger writers, one of the major works of the best-selling "post-postwar" writer Murakami Haruki is his 1985 *Hard-Boiled Wonderland and the End of the World* (*Sekai no owari to hado boirudo wandarando*), which presents a solipsistic vision of the end of the world contained within the mind of a single character. Murakami has also written *Underground* (*Andahguroundo*, 1997), a nonfiction look at the survivors of the 1995 gas bombing by the religious cult Aum Shinrikyō.

As the Aum Shinrikyō episode shows, not just Japanese culture but Japanese society as a whole has been concretely influenced by notions of the end of the world.[4] Indeed, a number of "millenarian" cults have risen in Japan since the beginning of the nineteenth century[5] and are flourishing today. In 1999 even Aum apparently had a recrudescence among believers. As mentioned earlier in the book, both Aum followers and Asahara Shōkō, the leader of the sect, were reported to be interested in apocalyptic manga and anime. Indeed, Asahara was known to be "a fervent reader of *Nausicaä of the Valley of the Winds*."[6]

The connection between fictional apocalypse in anime and manga and real world actions is of course an amorphous one, but it is certainly true that the media in which images of apocalypse hold most sway are anime and manga. Some of the most popular genres of anime, specifically science fiction, fantasy, and horror may even be said to be dominated by apocalyptic visions.[7] Ranging across an impressive variety of imaginative possibilities, these visions include the horrific "Ceramic Wars" that produce the toxic wasteland in *Nausicaä of the Valley of the Winds*, the sinister robotic creatures that stalk the earth of *Evangelion*, the post-nuclear junkyards of *Appleseed* and *Gray*, the telekinetic holocaust in *Akira*, and the bizarre pornographic apocalypse of the Overfiend in *Legend of the Overfiend* (*Urotsukidōji*).[8]

This chapter examines these visions of apocalypse in contemporary Japanese animation against the broader canvas of apocalypse in medieval and twentieth-century Japanese culture. As a first step, however, it is important to clarify the meaning of "apocalypse." The most common understanding of apocalypse is as something on the order of global destruction. But its original meaning is actually "revelation" or "uncovering," as of secrets or the fundamental nature of things. The confusion arises from the use of the Greek *apokalypsis* that, as the original title of Revelation, describes a final, world-destroying conflict between good and evil. Despite this, the original sense remains important, even though it is lost to conscious usage, because so many of our images, ideas, and stories about the end of the world continue to contain elements of revelation. Furthermore, the anticipation of the revelation of "secrets" or "mysteries" is an important narrative technique in all the apocalyptic texts examined in this chapter. In many works of anime, much of the narrative tension is not from "waiting for the end of the world" but from the revelation of how and why the world should end.

Given the distance between Japanese religious tradition and Christianity, it is fascinating that present-day Japanese notions of the end of the world echo much in Revelation. These notions encompass not only the subtext of revelation and images of mass destruction but also such deeper archetypal structures as an obsession with a "grotesquely exaggerated vision of death and desire,"[9] messianic figures who deliver the powerless from terror or oppression often in a form of revenge fantasy, and an ambivalent or negative attitude toward history and temporality in general. Of course these commonalities are essentially coincidental, but they do suggest that at a fundamental level visions of the end of the world are significantly similar.

Traditional Japanese culture, recent history, certain aspects of contemporary Japanese society, and the art of animation itself may all be considered influential in developing a distinctively Japanese notion of apocalypse. Turning to history first, we see that, while Buddhist and Shinto scriptures do not contain visions of good fighting evil at the end of the world, the Buddhist doctrine of *mappō* or "the latter days of the Law," does revolve around the notion of a fallen world saved by a religious figure. In this account, thousands of years after the Buddha's death, the world will fall into degeneracy and decadence, as his teachings lose their power. The day will be saved by the Maitreya Buddha, who will appear at this hour of need to usher in a new age of Buddhist enlightenment. An influence in both the high and mass culture of medieval Japan, the doctrine of *mappō* became widespread in the eleventh century (coincidentally, close to the time that millenarianism swept the West). A grass-roots revivalist movement, it featured intense religious meetings where followers chanted the nenbutsu prayer in a frenzied search for salvation. Although the question of whether the Maitreya Buddha is a messianic figure or not remains problematic, certain popular permutations of the doctrine suggest a utopian, salvatory aspect not unlike the image of the savior and the heavenly kingdom in Revelation.

It is even possible that the medieval notion of *mono no aware* (the sadness of things), an aesthetic philosophy emphasizing the transient and sad nature of life, may still have a subtle influence on the way contemporary Japanese look at the world and its possibilities. Certainly various geographical and climactic factors peculiar to the Japanese archipelago have supported a philosophy based on transience and the imminence of destruction. The archipelago's devastating earthquakes and volcanic eruptions, its vulnerability to typhoons and tidal waves, along with the frequent fires that used to sweep premodern urban areas all combine to create a people acutely aware of the fragility of human civilization.

Of course, the atomic bombings of Hiroshima and Nagasaki are the most obvious catalysts to apocalyptic thought.[10] As of today, Japan is still the only country in the world to have suffered the devastation of atomic destruction. Although the bomb itself is not always specifically delineated, it stalks through a notable amount of postwar Japanese culture in a variety of displaced versions, from the immediate postwar hit *Godzilla* (1953) and its many descendants to the aforementioned works of writers like Ōe or Abe Kōbō. It is not surprising, therefore, that the popular culture iconography of apocalypse is suffused with images of catastrophic explosions, world-threatening monstrosities, and social chaos. In fact, in her article on *Akira* Freda Freiberg argues that Japan, even more than the West, has been gripped by a notion of what she calls the "post nuclear sublime." She suggests that in *Akira*'s case "the national experience of nuclear disaster animates and propels the film in an exhilarating mixture of dread and desire."[11] This "exhilarating mixture" occurs, although in different degrees, in all the anime we will be examining in this chapter, since it is one of the basic paradoxes of apocalyptic destruction that, in its very magnitude of catastrophic intensity, it is both feared and welcomed.

This is particularly true in contemporary society, where the notion of spectacle increasingly holds sway. That "crisis is institutionalized as commodified spectacle"[12] in American films is perhaps even more true of anime, in which the "visual excess of catastrophe[13] becomes a kind of aesthetic end in itself. The protean quality of the animation medium, with its emphasis on image, speed, and fluctuation is perfect for depicting this. The most obvious case of this "excess of catastrophe" is captured in the extraordinary imagery of *Akira's* postmodern apogee of metamorphosis and self-destruction. Even the more traditionally constructed *Nausicaä* contains some memorable representations of mass destruction, most notably the so-called God Warriors (*kyōshinpei*), bioengineered, humanoid weapons whose pulsating, giant warhead-shaped torsos rimmed by licking flames powerfully suggest the menace of annihilation. Indeed, it is undeniable that one of the pleasures of watching any of the works discussed in this chapter is the incredible variety and range of catastrophic imagery that literally animates the screen and provides at least some viewers with an exhilarating form of catharsis and of the festival. Freed from the restraints of language and live-action cinema, the abstract visual medium of animation works brilliantly to "convey the unconveyable."

This is not to say that apocalyptic anime consist *only* of spectacle. In fact, appropriate to the basic ideology of apocalypse, most works, even the apparently nihilistic *Akira*, include such elements as an explicit criticism of the society undergoing apocalypse and an explicit or implicit warning as to why this society should be encountering such a fate. These reasons are almost always related to human transgression, most often the misuse of technology, but they are also frequently linked with the destruction of traditional social values, most obviously embodied by the family. Whereas the nuclear family was a crucially important trope in the two World War II films discussed earlier, it is virtually absent in anime such as *Akira* and *Appleseed* (replaced by a kind of peer group bonding in both works) and completely dysfunctional in works such as *Legend of the Overfiend* or *Evangelion*. This vision of the dysfunctional family contrasts with the recent American apocalyptic film *Armageddon* (1998), in which the family, initially threatened, is successfully reinscribed through the world-saving sacrifice of the father and the traditional church wedding of his daughter to another one of the heroes. In Japanese animation it is most frequently the children who are sacrificed in a world where traditional society seems increasingly absent or meaningless.

One further element in the Japanese vision of apocalypse that is perhaps distinctively Japanese is the sense of the elegiac. In postwar Japan this takes the form of an awareness that the extraordinary economic growth and the old-fashioned values of hard work and self-sacrifice that helped to bring it about are not trends that can last forever. While Japan, in the year 2000, is a long way from the devastation of 1945, an awareness of deep-seated vulnerability to awesome outside power is one that can never be entirely uprooted for many older Japanese. Japan is not a country where prosperity is taken for granted. The national soul-searching that has followed the economic malaise of the 1990s attests to this. It is perhaps not coincidental, therefore, that the second rise in apocalyptic themes (after the initial spate in the immediate postwar period) occurred in the 1970s, just when Japan had to confront the economic decline of the 1973 oil shock.

A live-action example from this period is the 1974 film *Japan Sinks* (*Nippon Chinbotsu*). Although the film, a narrative of Japan literally sinking beneath the ocean due to a chain reaction of earthquakes and tidal waves, was tremendously popular with Japanese audiences, it never made much impact overseas. This was probably because its vision of the end of the world was so culturally specific. Although the film contains a fair number of typical disaster scenes of volcanoes erupting and crowds panicking, the dominant tone is softly elegiac, a kind of popular culture version of *mono no aware*. In the film's last scene the audience sees a high-altitude shot of an empty blue ocean. The shot is held for a long time while the audience sees, superimposed on the ocean, the names of the great Japanese cities, Tokyo, Osaka, Kyoto, Sapporo, all now sunk forever beneath the waves.

The animated visions of apocalypse current in the 1980s and 1990s seem remote from such elegiac visions. The end of the world is often imagined in fast-paced, dizzying flurries of images. However, even the most overtly postmodern ones show a bitter awareness of a lost past, usually signified by images of parental abandonment or a yearning for a world of pastoral harmony. Apocalypse in Japan seems both personal and suprapersonal, a disaster visited upon both the individual and the collective, often metaphorically expressed in the disintegration or even the transgression of the family. Four of the most fully realized visions of apocalyptic disaster in Japanese animation are *Nausicaä of the Valley of the Winds* (*Kaze no tani no Nausicaä,* 1984), *Akira* (1988), *Legend of the Overfiend* (*Urotsukidōji,* 1987-1991), and *Neon Genesis Evangelion* (*Shinseiki Ebuangerion,* 1997). *Akira, Evangelion,* and *Nausicaä* have been discussed earlier but this chapter will examine them from the point of view of their intriguing similarities and dissimilarities within the apocalyptic mode.

The OVA series *Legend of the Overfiend* is a hardcore sadistic pornographic horror fantasy, with none of the character development or depth of the other three works. The series does have, however, a genuinely intriguing narrative that makes it fascinating to compare with *Akira, Nausicaä,* and *Evangelion.* Furthermore, in its invocation of apocalypse on a largely sexual plane, the film demonstrates perhaps one more underlying reason behind the contemporary Japanese obsession with apocalypse, the demise of male patriarchal privilege in the decades since World War II. *Legend of the Overfiend*'s intensely sexual imagery also makes clear what the other films only hint at, the connection between apocalypse and sexuality, most notably the orgasmic subtext to the apocalyptic spectacle, which theorist Robert Lifton describes as "the orgiastic excitement of the wild forces let loose— destroying everything in order to feel alive."[14]

The four works contain a number of important commonalties. All of them focus on a chaotic post-holocaust world in which the authority and the values of the old order are either vanishing or nonexistent. All four do a memorable job of animating their respective apocalyptic worlds, creating stunning images of bleak and devastated landscapes. However, each one manifests a radically different approach to apocalypse.

Their similarities are clear from the opening scenes of each anime. *Nausicaä* opens with a long shot of what seems to be a bleak desert with howling winds, reminiscent of the blasted postnuclear holocaust landscapes of the Australian *Mad Max* film series. Slowly, a hooded rider appears on the horizon. There is no music, only the hiss of the wind. The rider enters a dilapidated house and picks up a doll, only to have it crumble in his hands. He mutters "Another village lost" and rides off. Words superimposed on the desert scene explain that "centuries in the future" the world has never recovered from the poisons emitted in "the Ceramic Wars."

Akira opens in silence: The shot travels down what seems to be an ordinary city street with the date July 18, 1989 superimposed on the scene. Suddenly, the screen fills with an immense white radiance, sinister booming music begins, and the next shot is of an enormous black crater upon which are superimposed the words, "Neo Tokyo A.D. 2019 . . . 31 years after World War III." The scene shifts abruptly to a chaotic view of downtown Neo Tokyo where a gang of young bikers zooms through the streets, ending up at the looming dark crater, apparently the site of the former "Old Tokyo."

Legend of the Overfiend opens with eerie music and a vision of flames with the tale of the Overfiend superimposed on the screen in an unfurling scroll style. The introductory words chronicle the creation of three worlds, the demonic, the manbeast, and the human, that now await the Overfiend, who appears once every 3,000 years to "eternally unite" the three realms. (Why he has to appear every 3,000 years if he can eternally unite them is but one of the many inconsistencies in the series.) The introduction also belittles those "arrogant humans" who believe that they are the "supreme rulers" of the world and who will shortly be proven wrong. As if to underline this threatening tone, the scene shifts to a vision of a grotesque orgy in which demons penetrate human women moaning in agony.

Evangelion begins with a scene of yet another Neo Tokyo, this one a technopolis that has been built following a mysterious catastrophe known as the "Second Impact." In this arresting opening the viewer catches a glimpse of an enormous grotesque creature slipping through empty city streets. Over the sound of a buzzing cicada (a symbol of evanescence used often in classical Japanese poetry), a loudspeaker gives an announcement to evacuate as we see shots of massed tanks preparing for battle. The scene shifts abruptly to a young boy, the protagonist Ikari Shinji, waiting at a telephone booth. The scene then changes to some kind of military command headquarters, in which a bearded man (later revealed to be Shinji's father) announces ominously to some military personnel, "It's the Angels."

All four works begin with a menacing tone appropriate to the apocalyptic genre. *Akira* is perhaps the most impersonal. Its opening image of a blinding radiance evokes what Freiberg and others call the "nuclear sublime." Freiberg contrasts this white silence to the "hysterical sound and imagery" of most of the film and suggests that "these bright white frames, at the beginning and end of the film, represent the sublimity of nuclear destruction."[15] *Legend of the Overfiend*'s intense sexual imagery of rape and torture and the introductory words' implicit obsession with dominance and control clearly evoke what film scholar Frank Burke describes as "male hysteria—an excessive, often violent, reaction to the loss of [patriarchal] privilege."[16] At the same time the text attempts to transpose this kind of apocalyptic rage onto a mystical plane in the form of traditional, almost incantatory language and invocations of other, nonhuman realms. *Nausicaä*, with its image of the crumbling doll, brings the destruction down to a human, implicitly personal level, while Shinji's evident loneliness and confusion in *Evangelion* also add an explicitly personal and emotional tone to the sense of overall impending disaster.

All four narratives position themselves around a world-destroying event. The reasons behind these events are varied. In *Nausicaä* the destruction is seen as the result of the misuse of technology (very typical of Western films of this type), while the reason for *Akira*'s destructive event is ambiguous, although events ultimately reveal that the destruction was caused by both technological and psychic forces. It is only in *Legend of the Overfiend* that the reason is explicitly religious, implicating not one but two supernatural realms and hinting at punishment for human "arrogance." *Evangelion* begins and remains deeply mysterious for much of the series about the reasons behind the Second Impact. It hints at a religious explanation in its use of the Christian term *shito* (which literally means "apostles," although it is translated in the series as "angels") to refer to the terrifying creatures menacing Tokyo and in its reference to predictions embedded in the Dead Sea Scrolls. However, as the movie version of *Evangelion* reveals, the Second Impact is also explicitly connected with the misuse of technology.

Nausicaä introduces some potentially religious imagery during its opening as well—a figure in blue who appears in an ancient tapestry. As the viewer learns later, this figure is a messiah, expected to save his people from destruction. The male messiah figure is implicitly equated with Nausicaä, who appears immediately after, clad in blue

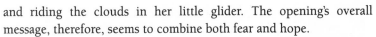

and riding the clouds in her little glider. The opening's overall message, therefore, seems to combine both fear and hope.

The tone of each film's opening sequence is maintained throughout their respective narratives. *Nausicaä's* story is clearly the most optimistic and adheres most closely to the structure of the Book of Revelation's apocalyptic framework. The film's apocalyptic tropes are numerous. Nausicaä, the young princess of the Valley of the Winds, has to save her kingdom and humanity in general from not one but three world-threatening phenomena. The first is the poisonous toxins, produced by the Ceramic Wars, which cover most of the earth. In various scenes the film shows Nausicaä using her impressive scientific prowess to work on this problem, and there are strong hints that she may reach at least a partial solution. The second threat is the God Warriors, enormous robotic weapons that were used by a previous civilization to utterly destroy their enemies. Nausicaä succeeds in dissuading at least some of the other kingdoms from using this weapon and thus saves the world from an almost certain technological holocaust. Her coping with the final threat, an attack of giant insects known as Ohmu, has a more supernatural aspect to it. Nausicaä quells them through her miraculous ability to mentally bond with them rather than through violence.

Typical of classic apocalyptic narratives, *Nausicaä* ends with a sequence of death and rebirth. A herd of Ohmu enraged by humans' treatment of them, run over Nausicaä, whose body is then borne aloft in the insects' huge golden feelers. Like her own people, the Ohmu also seem to love and appreciate Nausicaä for her gentleness and compassion. While sweet music plays, Nausicaä revives and begins to walk among the golden antennae, an image that echoes that of the blue-clad messiah figure shown in the tapestry at the film's beginning who is said to walk in a field of gold. Placed gently back on the ground, she watches as the Ohmu head home in peace. The people of the Valley of the Winds surge around her ecstatically as the music swells in a triumphant finale. With such a traditional ending, the film may be described as an example of "conservative apocalypse," because its narrative supports the values of a conservative collectivity in which authority and order are ultimately restored. In this traditional vision of apocalypse, it is appropriate that Nausicaä should be a princess, deeply attached to her father the king, and profoundly beloved by her people.

As with Revelation, the film balances images of horrifying danger (the Ohmu, the God Warriors, poisoned air) with serene visions of beauty and harmony (Nausicaä's pastoral Valley of the Winds, the tapestry's depiction of the field of gold, the constant motif of flight). And, although the future of humanity is still uncertain at the end of the film, the resurrection of Nausicaä and the taming of the Ohmu suggest a coming era of peace.

At the same time certain aspects of *Nausicaä* veer significantly away from the traditional. Most obvious of these is Nausicaä herself, who, unlike conventional messiah figures, is an active female. While quite feminine and clearly nurturing, Nausicaä displays virtually no overt sexuality. In fact, the critic Kamata Tōji has suggested that, given her association with the male figure in the tapestry, Nausicaä is an essentially androgynous figure, perhaps even equivalent to a Bodhisattva, a disciple of Buddha who combines compassion with active salvatory works.[17] Nausicaä's combination of androgynous and activist elements seems also very contemporary, however, making her a particularly appealing modern heroine. *Nausicaä*'s subtext is also much less punitive than the traditional Christian version of apocalypse. Although evil doers exist in the film, the film's final message is not a simplistic advocation of punishment and reward.

Instead the final scene seems to imply that, with kindness and intelligence, all varieties of humans (and even insects) can learn to live together. The film's ultimate vision is of a reaffirmed collectivity that extends beyond humans to embrace nature in general. Although *Princess Mononoke* problematizes such an optimistic solution, this earlier vision of apocalypse allows for a shared sense of hope and redemption.

Akira takes a much different approach: It is in many ways a postmodern celebration of apocalypse. *Akira*'s postmodern aspects include four major elements: the film's rapid narrative pace (reinforced by its soundtrack); its fascination with fluctuating identity, as evidenced in Tetsuo's metamorphoses; its use of pastiche both in relation to Japanese history and cinematic styles; and its ambivalent attitude toward history. This last element is embodied both in its negative treatment of parents, who are seen as having abandoned their children, and in its powerful final sequence, in which a climactic fight scene takes place at the rebuilt Yoyogi Stadium, the site of the 1964 Tokyo

Olympics and a symbol of Japan's resurgence from the devastation of World War II. In the destruction of the stadium and the vision of the dark crater of Old Tokyo, *Akira* literally deconstructs Japan's recent past by blowing it away.

However, *Akira's* postmodern aspects should not obscure some other aspects of its structure and themes that hark back to the ancient Greek genre of the menippean satire and the Japanese festival. Rediscovered by critics such as Northrup Frye and Mikhail Bakhtin, the menippean genre is essentially carnivalesque including, among other aspects, a distinctive comic or parodic element, a "bold and unrestrained use of the fantastic and adventure," "an organic combination of . . . the free fantastic with a crude slum naturalism" and a "representation of the unusual, abnormal moral and psychic states of man with an emphasis on phenomena such as dreams, scenes of scandal and eccentric and unusual behavior."[18]

Although the apocalyptic aspects of the film certainly place it in the same tradition as *Nausicaä*, *Akira* is far removed from the essentially optimistic and conservative structure of the earlier film. Instead, it uses the structures and themes of the menippea, such as the emphasis on strangeness, "experimental fantasy" and crudity, to create a world enveloped by disorder and chaos. Indeed, reality itself is challenged in *Akira's* ambiguous ending, its frequent visual and sometimes subtextual references to hallucinogenic drugs,[19] and its many surreal, even nightmarish sequences, including a scene where Tetsuo lying on a hospital bed, is assaulted by gigantic toys (actually psychic manifestations of the mutant children). This scene combines the menippea's parodic sensibility with its privileging of fantastic elements to create an eerie vision in which the grotesque toys undermine such established Japanese conventions as the sweetness of children and the culture of cuteness (*kawaii*) in general. The scene also implicitly questions the authority figures who run the hospital and whose reckless experiments have caused the safe world of childhood to run amok.

Akira's world may be also be connected with the festival or carnival in its surrealism and sense of incipient chaos. Indeed, the film's biker gangs (Tetsuo and Kaneda's gang and their enemies, a group called, perhaps significantly, "The Clowns") seem to echo the important role that young men perform in actual festivals. During the *matsuri* (festival) it is the local young men's group (only recently infiltrated by women) who travel through the streets in a religious state of drunkenness and ecstasy carrying the festival shrine, in which the shrine's god is believed to temporarily reside, on their shoulders. In many ways the frenzied wanderings of the bikers, reaching toward a state of speed-induced pleasure that Ikuya Sato calls "flow," are *Akira*'s secular equivalent of this festival state. It is even possible that the mysterious "Akira" himself (at one time an actual human child but now existing only in test-tube form) is similar to the Shinto deity inside the shrine, a being that is essentially a free-floating signifier onto whom believers project their own dreams and nightmares.

The European notion of carnival and the menippea expresses itself through other important ways in *Akira,* such as in its overall structure, which does not merely shake the conventions of society but actually overturns them. While "the Japanese *matsuri* seek an equality or leveling within society rather than a reversal,"[20] *Akira*'s narrative climax is clearly based on total reversal. This is apparent in the final scene, in which Tetsuo intones "I am Tetsuo," suggesting a new world order. In the manga version this is even more obvious since Tetsuo actually becomes a ruler on earth, a blatant reversal of his previously marginal status. Tetsuo's final sequence of horrifying mutations also suggests the menippea. In significant contrast to Nausicaä's level-headed intelligence and compassion, Tetsuo is a walking compendium of "unusual, abnormal moral and psychic states,"[21] and his bizarre physical metamorphoses act as visual validations of the turmoil within. Thus, his final mutations and presumed apotheosis may be experienced as liberating, although only on a totally selfish level, since he breaks through every social boundary that initially constrained him. In contrast, Nausicaä's rebirth is a return to even greater responsibility as the protector/savior of the world.

One commonality between *Akira* and *Nausicaä* is the messianic and supernatural attributes of their protagonists, although their respective messianism comes across very differently. In the film we see that Tetsuo is conflated with Akira, the most powerful and most threatening of the psychic mutants, whose coming is eagerly awaited by various cults active in Neo Tokyo.[22] However, as a messiah Tetsuo is largely negative and solipsistic, since he engages in all-out destruction and then creates a world that appears to have little relevance to the rest of humanity. Nausicaä's superhuman attributes are purely constructive, enabling her to communicate with the Ohmu and to inspire them to compassion toward the human race. Moreover, Nausicaä sacrifices herself in a truly messianic way.

Both films also rely on the fundamental imagery of apocalypse—destruction. The visually exciting scenes of explosions and violence allow many viewers to find a paradoxical exhilaration in their vision of catastrophe, which enables them to achieve a kind of catharsis. According to biblical scholar Tina Pippin, cathartic destruction, often related to revenge fantasies, is the most basic element of traditional apocalypse, allowing the viewer/reader the pleasure of watching the end of evil or danger and experiencing its final transcendence in surrogate fashion.[23] This is evident in the climax of Nausicaä when the rage and the hostility of the charging Ohmu literally fade before the viewer's eyes when the Ohmu's eye color changes from raging red to pacific blue as they stop their stampede and retreat into the forest.

In contemporary texts the destruction of evil is less important than simply destruction itself, the "pleasures of making a mess," as Susan Sontag describes it.[24] Akira's devastating ending leaves us finally with the ultimate contemporary spectacle, the "obscene ecstasy of alienation," to use cultural theorist Jean Baudrillard's phrase.[25] Yet it seems legitimate that contemporary viewers experience catharsis as much with Akira as with the more traditional Nausicaä, although it does not allow for a carnivalesque overthrow of authority and hierarchy: As Bakhtin says, "carnival is the festival of all annihilating and all renewing time . . . the joyful relativity of all structure and order of all authority and hierarchical position."[26] Akira's narrative both embodies and celebrates this relativity of structure.

While Nausicaä's scenes of destruction are recontained by the framework of renewal and rebirth and Akira's destructiveness by its carnivalesque quality, our next work to be discussed, Legend of the Overfiend, takes destruction to a much more disturbing level, where the devastation seems oppressive rather than cathartic. The dark tone of the opening scene, in which demons rape human women while a sepulchral voice warns "arrogant humanity," is echoed and amplified throughout the rest of the film and its many OVA installments.

Legend of the Overfiend's plot revolves around the search for and eventual identification of the terrifying supernatural entity known as the Overfiend but the real focus of the narrative is on the inevitable destruction and horror that the Overfiend wreaks. All of this takes place in a narrative heavily laced with truly horrifying scenes of sexual depravity, torture, and mutilation. Although *Legend of the Overfiend* might easily be dismissed as pornography, it is important to recognize that a dense and complex narrative, which, in many ways corresponds even more closely to the apocalyptic structure than either *Akira* or *Nausicaä*, frames the scenes of degradation and violence. Indeed, *Legend of the Overfiend* shows some fascinating commonalities with Revelations in three major areas: its obsession with transgression and punishment, the importance of sexual themes and imagery in the film (the evil Whore of Babylon is one of the most important figures in Revelation), and a focus on the basic meaning of apocalypse, "to reveal" or "uncover." These three elements figure prominently in a memorable episode from the fourth series of *Legend of the Overfiend,* entitled "Inferno Road." This episode follows a band of outcasts who are trying to survive in the twenty-first century wasteland brought about by the destructive powers of the Overfiend. The most important of the outcasts include Buju, a half-demon, and Himi, a little girl with immense telekinetic powers whom Buju is supposed to protect.

While bringing Himi to Osaka, the group discovers an enormous crater shrouded in mist that turns out to contain an apparently uninhabited ruined city. The group soon encounters an adolescent girl and boy named Yumi and Ken, who are desperately fleeing a group of strange children. The children recapture Yumi and Ken and invite Buju, Himi, and the others to a banquet that evening presided over by a mysterious little boy whose name appears to be "Phallus."

The evening's entertainment begins with an orgy on the part of all the adult citizens of the city. At a signal from Phallus, the adults begin to have sex with each other in a vast arena while the city's children watch with expressions of bemused impassivity. What follows is even more explicit. In a horrifyingly graphic sequence, Ken is humiliated and tortured while Yumi is raped by demonic creatures. Apparently, this is their punishment for having reached puberty and the reason for their attempted escape. In the eyes of the city's children, sexual maturity is seen as a transgression meriting the most hideous form of punishment.

Further secrets are revealed. The adults are kept around by the children only in order to bear more demonic children. When any child reaches puberty he or she is either destroyed or forced to become a breeding machine. Phallus murdered his own parents when he was very little and keeps his twin brother's corpse with him as a kind of alter ego.

While images of sexual degradation set in a supernatural wasteland dominate most of "Inferno Road," the film actually reaches some positive form of closure. Horrified by the depravity around her and intent on escape, Himi wreaks furious destruction on the city. In an arresting final sequence, we see Phallus's memories of his parents and their murder, his own death, and the deaths of the other children of the city. Finally the dead children are reunited with the spirits of their parents in a soft blue sky, the pastel shades of which contrast vividly with the gray wasteland that dominates most of the film. Even Ken and Yumi are allowed a "happy" ending. They are finally able to escape and die—happily—when they are unable to breathe the clean air beyond the city.

By interweaving the archetypal elements of apocalyptic literature of destruction, transgression, punishment, and revelation, "Inferno Road" offers its audience a surprisingly complex version of the apocalyptic vision that is quite different from that of *Akira* or *Nausicaä*. While all three works contain brilliantly evoked imagery of a devastated world standard to works in this genre, only *Legend of the Overfiend* links this destruction explicitly to sexual transgression. Not only does sex itself become a metaphor for destruction, as is clear in the many scenes of brutal and violent sex interspersed throughout the series, but the "revelation" of sexuality itself, or at least of "adult" sexuality, is seen as the ultimate transgressive act. A telling scene is one in which the children watch as the adults copulate on the floor. In striking contrast to conventional pornographic animation in Japan, where scenes of enthusiastic and participatory voyeurism are almost a staple of the genre, the children in "Inferno Road" gaze at the sexual activity with expressions hovering between impassivity, disgust, and amusement.[27] For a pornographic film the lack of pleasure on the part of the onlookers is thought-provoking. The reaction of the children is left as another uncovered secret in a series of increasingly horrifi revelations. These eventually lead to the final revelation that sexual adulthood, and even civilization itself are all worthless and must be punished and destroyed by apocalyptic means.

To examine the consolidated sequence of revelations in more detail: the chain of events begins with the discovery that the crater contains a city hidden in the mist.[28] While the city in traditional Revelation lore can be either evil or good (Babylon vs. Jerusalem), the city in "Inferno Road" is clearly evil. The city is also associated with adulthood, since adults built the city. The next revelation involves the orgy scene, in which the outsiders discover that adults are forced to have sex only in order to create legions of demonic children. Adult sex is cast as unappealing, something necessary only to create the next generation. A further realization is that Ken and Yumi must be punished because they dared to grow up and attempted to escape (i.e., achieve an autonomous adult identity). The final revelation is that Phallus murdered his parents.

This sequence of revelations highlights the fact that *Legend of the Overfiend* is finally not so much about sexuality as it is about the transgressive nature of growing up and the iniquity of the parental generation. Although women are clearly viewed as suspicious and deserving of punishment since they are always the ones who are objects of sexual torture, adults in general are seen as evil. In the world of the Overfiend, becoming an independent, socialized adult is a transgression that must be stopped by total annihilation. In the final scene, in which the dead children are united with their dead parents, there might be a sense of catharsis as the hellish vision of the city is replaced by imagery of sky and life, but this catharsis, based on violent and sadistic intragenerational strife, seems a spurious one at best.

The last work to be considered, *Neon Genesis Evangelion* also takes issue with a positive view of adulthood. The work's disturbing vision of dysfunctional adults and victimized children links it with both *Legend of the Overfiend* and *Akira* much more than with the fundamentally hopeful world of the family-oriented *Nausicaä*. Like *Overfiend*, *Evangelion* also focuses on the motif of hidden revelations, although these secrets are of a largely personal (and often pathological), rather than a public, nature. Indeed, *Evangelion's* fascination with revelations and origins makes critic Kōtani Mari's description of it as a "family romance"[29] particularly appropriate.

The tone of darkness and mystery is set from the initial episode. Shinji, left unevacuated in Neo Tokyo, is finally picked up by Misato Katsuragi, a beautiful young woman from the secret organization known as NERV. The top scientist of NERV is Shinji's father, and he has arranged for Shinji to join a group of three 14-year-olds who alone can "synchronize" with the robotic machines known as Evangelions (EVAs) that NERV has developed to combat the "Angels."

Questions are raised in this first episode: What are the Angels? What is NERV's real purpose? Some of the questions are answered in revelatory moments interspersed throughout the series while many are also addressed in the subsequent film, but it must be said that *Evangelion* is the most opaque of all the works discussed here. Even when its secrets are revealed, they often lead to more perplexing questions. *Evangelion* is also the most purely apocalyptic of the four works, both in terms of its fascination with secrets and sexual transgression, and in its unremitting emphasis on destruction, not simply of the material world, but also of the inner world of the human spirit, which is shown as vulnerable, fragmented, and ultimately broken under the extraordinary weight of late-twentieth-century alienation.

One of the most notable aspects of *Evangelion* is its tone of psychological discordance. Unlike the other three works discussed previously, there is virtually no sense of catharsis. Instead, the television series and film both end on a note of dark ambiguity, with the characters still trapped in a world of awesome and enigmatic outside forces that permit no real hope of resolution.

Contrary to more typical action-oriented works, therefore, much of the real action in *Evangelion* is psychological. Thus, despite the requisite and truly chilling scenes of combat with the Angels, the series also contains a greater number of scenes in which the characters bicker and insult each other or else engage in intense brooding about their angst-ridden childhoods and their equally dysfunctional and disappointing parents. Far from being potential young heroes, each character is burdened by the memory of such transgressive episodes as parental abandonment and sexual betrayal. As critic Arai Hiroyuki summarizes, they are "all traumatized, lacking, hypersensitive individuals."[30] This psychological discordance is revealed through various elements in the series. Critics have noted the unusual use of *non-*

movement in the series to convey a wealth of psychological subtleties. For example, Takanaka Shimotsuki discusses a scene in episode three in which the two annoyed characters, Ayanami Rei and Asuka Langley, neither move nor speak in an elevator for about 50 seconds (an astonishingly long time in anime and even in television in general), and the passage of time is conveyed by the noise of the elevator rather than any mechanical movement. As Shimotsuki explains, "This stillness is almost unthinkable in typical anime, but the sense of psychological tension flowing between the averted glances of Asuka and Rei creates an almost suffocatingly dense space."[31] Even when there is action, it is often there to amplify the clever, mordant dialogue. Thus, one scene shows Miyagi Ritsuko, one of the top scientists of NERV, attempting to fix a computer "brain" while reminiscing about her mother (whose brain has literally become part of the computer she is fixing). While Ritsuko penetrates the brain with an evil-looking needle, she coolly comments "I never did like my mother."

When more conventional action does occur, it takes a notably violent form, such as when Shinji literally pounds the enemy Angel to death or when Asuka is spiritually violated by the Angel she is fighting. The film, unconstrained by television censorship, is even more brutal and also contains a more overt sexual subtext than the series. It is also, in contrast to the ending of the television series, blindingly and almost incoherently apocalyptic, filled with scenes of destruction, death, and potential rebirth on an enormous scale.

The most important element of destruction raised in the film is the advent of the "Third Impact," a mystical apocalyptic moment that will destroy humanity. This event is promoted by yet another secret organization known as SEELE (the German word for "soul"). NERV tries to work against them, but SEELE has created its own group of nine EVAs to lay waste to NERV, destroy the three children, and set off the Third Impact.

The importance of the Third Impact is that it is not a deus ex machina from the sky but something engendered by human beings against other human beings. Thus, much of the film's action centers around the human heroism and tragedy of the bloody destruction of NERV by SEELE's soldiers, culminating in the death of Katsuragi Misato, Shinji's beautiful mentor, as she tries to protect him from them. Other moments of individual heroism include the attempts by Asuka to destroy all nine of SEELE's EVAs by herself. Although she rises to an unparalleled pitch of violence, stabbing, beheading, and mutilating the enemy EVAs in a variety of ways, she is ultimately unable to destroy them, and with her own power gone, she is set upon and eaten by the triumphant EVAs in one of the movie's most appalling scenes.

At the end of the film, Shinji (who has been unable to do much more than cower as destruction reigns around him) finally gets into to his own EVA suit to confront the Angels, but he is too feeble to stop them as well. The Third Impact begins as the nine EVAs take off glittering into the sky and form the shape of an enormous tree known as the Tree of Life. Explosions rock the world and in the midst of destruction a gigantic Ayanami Rei appears, apparently welcoming the souls of dying humanity who rise to meet her in the form of fiery crosses. Only Shinji's EVA is unable to be absorbed by her and is left floating in space. Shinji himself wakes up to an empty earth with only a reborn Asuka as his companion. He starts to strangle her but she stops him and he cries. The movie ends with Asuka's despairing words "*Kimochi warui!*" (I feel sick!).

Despite its many incongruities and incomprehensibilities, the ending of the film version of *Evangelion* is a fascinating tapestry of a dense and incredibly complex apocalyptic vision. Indeed, the movie is overstuffed with images of apocalyptic destruction, even in comparison with the three films discussed previously. In contrast, *Evangelion* both enlarges and narrows the vision of apocalypse. On the broader front, its images range across an extraordinary continuum of death, destruction, and even rebirth. Although the work shares with *Akira* and *Overfiend* the visuals of urban apocalypse, such as buildings crumbling and crowds scurrying, it tends to dwell more on the hard-edged spaces of the high tech world of NERV headquarters, as the forces outside begin to breach its defenses. *Evangelion* also goes well beyond the other three in envisioning the fiery destruction of the earth. Finally, the film insists on a supernatural and spiritual dimension beyond the messianism of Nausicaä or Tetsuo and the powers of the Overfiend, in its dramatic imagery of the awesome white Ayanami Rei absorbing the myriads of human souls into herself.

But *Evangelion* also narrows the apocalyptic scope through the profoundly personal nature of its apocalyptic vision.[32] Partly because it was a television series, as well as a film, and partly because of its overall psychological emphasis, the viewer knows and resonates with the characters on a much deeper level than the other three anime. Many fans of *Evangelion* strongly identify with Shinji and care deeply about the fates of the other characters as well. Thus, scenes such as Misato's bloody death, Asuka being eaten alive in the body of her EVA, and Shinji's powerless, miserable fate clearly carry an emotional impact deeper than any of the other films.

Shinji's powerlessness is also interesting to examine in comparison to the protagonists of the other films. Nausicaä, Tetsuo, and Himi are all capable of action on both a physical and psychological level, emblematized by their psychic abilities. In marked contrast, Shinji's overwhelming solipsism hinders all his attempts at action, from getting to know his colleagues to piloting the EVA. His impotency is metonymically portrayed in the opening scene of the film, in which Shinji, sitting by Asuka's hospital bed, suddenly discovers that she is naked. His only reaction to this revelation is to furtively masturbate with a miserable expression on his face. In the movie's final scene he attempts to kill Asuka, but that too is unsuccessful, and her final words are those of total rejection, "I feel sick."

Ultimately the real apocalypse of *Evangelion* is on a personal level, the bleak vision of Shinji's total alienation from others. While the narrative pays lip service to a potential new form of humanity as the result of the Third Impact, its clear emphasis is on the tragic quality of the human condition. This is evident not only in the case of Shinji but also in many of the film's other revelations, from the dysfunctional and often transgressive backgrounds that haunt each of the main characters to the revelation that humanity itself is the eighteenth Angel. This revelation, embodying the potential for human menace, is further underlined by the vicious hand-to-hand fighting between NERV and SEELE which prompts one character to lament "But aren't we all human beings?" (*onaji ningen na no ni*). The ghastly outside forces that beset the characters are thus essentially their own dark sides rising to overwhelm them.

THE APOCALYPTIC CONTINUUM

Using the four films, it is possible to trace a continuum of apocalyptic visions in which the destruction of the world changes from an event to be mourned in *Nausicaä* to one to be celebrated as a cathartic experience necessary for a new world in *Akira,* to the even more nihilistic visions of *Legend of the Overfiend* and *Neon Genesis Evangelion.* In *Overfiend* the end of the world is ontologically necessary precisely because there will be no worlds to replace it (i.e., maturation must be prevented at all costs), a shuddering vision of cultural despair. This vision of is embraced in *Evangelion* as well but is also united with a solipsistic one of personal despair ("I feel sick").

All the films are linked by a notion of human transgression that is perhaps both a universal aspect of late-twentieth-century society and a culturally specific element of modern Japan. Nausicaä's apocalyptic story revolves around a vision common to any nineteenth- and twentieth-century apocalyptic works, the transgression of nature through human technology.[33] Not only are the God Warriors products of human design, but the Sea of Corruption surrounding Nausicaä's country and the giant insects that roam her world are also a clear result of toxins released by war and over industrialization. *Nausicaä* resolves the issue of transgression through its heroine's willingness to sacrifice herself for the good of the world. The final apocalyptic destruction is averted by humanity's reinscription into the natural community. There is no need for a kingdom of heaven now that there is a possibility of utopia on earth.

Akira is also based on the notion of human transgression of interference with nature. As with the Ohmu and the God Warriors, both World War III and the mutant children are the result of science gone awry. However, unlike in *Nausicaä,* the grotesque products of scientific experimentation are humans themselves. *Akira* thus plays on the more recent notion of apocalyptic destruction as something wrought by figures who possess both demonic and human qualities. Also, rather than reinscribing its protagonist back into natural harmony, the film suggests a totally new world at its end, one in which humanity (in the form of Tetsuo) seems to be rejecting the old order in its entirety.

It has been suggested here that Tetsuo's metamorphoses limned Japan's struggles to create a new identity back in the 1980s.[34] This new identity was based on power and change, consonant with Japan's newly recognized role as a global economic superpower. Tetsuo's transformations suggest a far more contemporary world than *Nausi-*

caä's traditional status as princess, but her independence and empowerment also bring to mind some of the changes that Japan went through in the 1980s, especially in regards to the changing status of women. In both cases apocalyptic destruction brings about change and some form of growth in the characters.

In stark contrast, *Legend of the Overfiend*'s attitude toward change and power is extremely punitive while that of *Evangelion* is simply despairing. In her brilliant analysis of *Evangelion,* critic Kōtani Mari suggests that the "Second Impact" is actually equitable with the beginning of modernization in Japanese history, a process that "impacted" Japanese culture and society profoundly and permanently.[35] In her view this process of technologization and modernization is linked to the patriarchal structure. In the series both technology and the patriarchy are seen as negative but also crucial as Kōtani demonstrates in her analysis of episode 3 in which all the electrical power, which she sees as symbolizing modernization under the patriarchal system, is lost from the archipelago.[36]

These negative attitudes are in intriguing contrast with the other two films. While *Nausicaä* privileges positive changes in the human spirit and *Akira*'s carnivalesque structure seems to celebrate transformation for the excitement of it, both *Legend of the Overfiend* and *Evangelion* appear to suggest a basic shift in values that may well be connected with the events that occurred in Japan in the 1990s. The last decade has seen Japan fall into what seems to many to be an endless recession, which has shown the developments and values of the boom years to be empty shams. Most significantly, the vaunted structures of Japanese authority, specifically the government, big business, and bureaucracy, a triad hailed by commentators both at home and abroad as the key to Japan's successes in the seventies and eighties, were shown to be corrupt, inefficient, and brutally unmindful of the general citizenry.

Therefore it seems natural that *Overfiend*'s narrative is based on the destruction of "arrogant humanity," which is punished for its prideful ignorance, while *Evangelion*'s "Third Impact" is the result of factional warfare between NERV and SEELE. Nor is it a coincidence that both films are structured around a series of revelations. For the last decade Japanese society has been inundated by revelations of corruption, betrayal and ignorance on the part of its leaders, which has led to a pervasive sense of cynicism on the part of the Japanese public.

This decade is in marked contrast to the overall postwar period, which, while tempered by nostalgia and uncertainty, exhibited a strong faith in a united middle class and a hope for an increasingly bright future. It is not surprising therefore that the protagonists of the 1985 *Nausicaä* (made by someone who was born during the war and grew up during what is often called the "phoenix from the ashes" stage of Japan's industrial development) welcomed the chance for positive change and development as a way to correct some of the incipient problems of industrialization. It is also easy to understand the speed and change that *Akira's* postmodern exhilaration celebrates, even if it contains an underlying fear of change gone too far. The decade of *Overfiend* and *Evangelion*, however, sees only the skull beneath the skin of economic development, modernization, and societal change. *Overfiend* explores this dark vision through the metaphor of sexual transgression. Indeed, the film's orgy sequences may hint at the financial orgies engaged in by Japan's newly rich at the height of the bubble economy.[37]

In many ways *Evangelion* has the harshest critique of contemporary Japanese society. *Evangelion's* world, in which youth are forced by uncaring adults into armor that cuts them off from the rest of the world while they perform tasks that they often loathe and fear, is perhaps only a minor defamiliarization of the real world of contemporary Japan. In this world, history does not teach but is seen as a mysterious and uncontrollable outside force, as in the Second Impact, hinting at technological and postindustrial breakdown, or else in bleakly personal terms as familial dysfunction. Indeed, many of the revelations of *Evangelion's* script have to do with the iniquities of parents. The world with all its secrets revealed is still a disappointing, even sickening one. The almost incomprehensible devastation that ends the film version of *Evangelion* suggests the most virulent form of revenge fantasy, another fundamental feature of apocalyptic thought. But the final revenge may ultimately be on the characters themselves, left alone and without hope in a world in which even cathartic apocalypse is no longer an option.

In a sense the apocalyptic mode is the opposite of Harootunian's characterization of postwar history as an endless dreamlike continuum. In contrast, the apocalyptic allows for, indeed is predicated upon, the sense of an ending. Caught in a postwar world in which the dream of consumer abundance is less and less able to conceal a corrosive emptiness, the apocalyptic mode may seem to be the only sure means of escape.

CHAPTER TWELVE

ELEGIES

This is the use of memory:
For liberation—not less of love but expanding
Of love beyond desire, and so liberation
From the future as well as the past . . .
                                    —T. S. Eliot, "Little Gidding"

Memories aren't a way of escape.
                                    —*Magnetic Rose*

THE APOCALYPTIC AND THE FESTIVAL are perhaps obvious modes for anime. After all, animation in general, and anime in particular, is a medium that privileges presence in terms of the visible, the active, and the highly colored. In contrast, the elegiac mode suggests loss, absence, and unfulfilled desire. However, as pointed out earlier, the elegiac mode is a vitally important one in anime. In works ranging from *Video Girl Ai* to *Ghost in the Shell,* notes of isolation, sadness, and powerful grief subtextually express a world of far deeper emotional resonance than one might expect from the medium's stereotype of fast-paced moving images. Often it is the relative lack of movement, such as Yota's slow blood-soaked climb up the glass staircase in *Video Girl* or the *detarabochi,* the night version of the *shishigami,* gradually rising above the shimmering moonlit forest in *Princess Mononoke,* that best expresses the sense of exquisite transience that connects with the elegiac.

This mode of quiet intensity, usually aligned with feelings of nostalgia, is not exclusive to anime. As many commentators have noted, Japanese film and television directors frequently create works known as much for their lyrical "mood" as for their narrative structure. More importantly, as was suggested in the introduction to this book, the lyric and elegiac have long been a part of Japanese culture, providing an emotional underpinning to poetry, Kabuki theater, and many other forms of Japanese high culture. In addition, this elegiac sense only deepened as the Japanese nation shifted into modernity. Contemporary Japan has developed into a culture that on the one hand is on the cutting edge of consumerist and capitalist development while on the other hand is imbued with a tendency for "thematizing loss," as anthropologist Marilyn Ivy puts it. What is lost is sometimes amorphous, thematized through an obsession with a personal and usually problematic past, as is exemplified by the writings of the tremendously popular Yoshimoto Banana and a number of works by the equally popular Murakami Haruki. Both writers are often excoriated by older critics for what they see as a kind of free-floating, trivial nostalgia often tinged with narcissism.[1] For many other Japanese, however, it is the broader past of the nation itself that is lost and must be reclaimed.

Ivy describes a process in which "representative survivals" (such as the *matsuri* [festival], other traditional rituals, and cultural objects such as tea ceremony bowls or even chopsticks) become "refigured as elegiac resources."[2] In Ivy's view, this increasing need for elegiac resources stems from "a feeling of isolation which haunts many in Japan," despite, or perhaps due to, the nation's increasing involvement in global culture, which in turn she links to "a certain crucial nexus of unease about culture itself and its transmission and stability."[3] This anxiety indicates a troubling lack of success at the very interior of national self-fashioning, a recurrent motif in thinking about the instabilities of what is often depicted as uncannily stable.

While contemporary Japan is perhaps particularly adept at thematizing loss in a way that is almost ritualistic, it should be emphasized that an ambivalent relationship with history and a tendency toward the nostalgic is an element common to all contemporary cultures. As the 1943 quotation from Eliot at the beginning of this chapter suggests, a concatenation of emotionally charged elements—loss, change, renewal, and escape from a history that can be sometimes overwhelming, sometimes inspiring—is something that may be a basic part of the twentieth-century human condition.

Some critics see this ambivalence toward history as more specifically postmodern. In an important essay written in 1983, Fredric Jameson deplored what he saw as a reductively nostalgic tendency in postmodern film, suggesting that it stemmed from an inability today "to focus on our own present, as though we have become incapable of achieving aesthetic representation of our current experience."[4] Although other commentators, such as Linda Hutcheon, disagree, emphasizing instead that "postmodern film is, if anything, obsessed with history and with how we can know the past today,"[5] it seems that, at least in Japan's case these arguments are two sides of the same coin. Precisely because of the "instabilities" that Ivy pinpoints, contemporary society both desires to seek refuge in its past but at the same time shrinks from the reality of that past, preferring instead to "nostalgify it" or simply to escape it.

What is so impressive about anime is what might be called its aesthetic and narrative acknowledgment of both instability and ambivalence. Cultural instabilities are explored, even celebrated, on the animated screen in virtually every text examined so far, from the gender confusion of *Ranma 1/2* or apocalyptic excesses of *Akira* to *Princess Mononoke*'s courageous exploration of historical (and implicitly contemporary) otherness. Ambivalence toward the past also finds a place in such genres as the occult, the dystopian, or the apocalyptic.

This chapter examines texts that contain a different approach, not simply to the past but to loss in general. Rather than celebrating or exploring loss, the three anime to be discussed—*Magnetic Rose* (*Kanojo no omoide*, 1995), *Only Yesterday* (*Omoide poroporo*, 1991), and *Beautiful Dreamer* (*Urusei Yatsora*, 1983)—are at least initially about the attempt to contain, transcend, or even deny loss. In two cases (*Magnetic Rose* and *Only Yesterday*) this is carried out through an evocation of the past and a privileging of memory, while in *Beautiful Dreamer,* an arguably almost perfectly postmodern text, there is an attempt to transcend the passage of time to create an eternal present, liberated from history or memory.

THE RENEWAL OF THE SELF:
ONLY YESTERDAY

Turning first to the most clearly "nostalgic" work of the three, Takahata Isao's *Only Yesterday* is a text that contains a definite agenda both in terms of the present and the past. The story of a young woman from Tokyo who finds both happiness and a husband in the rural prefecture of Yamagata, the film is a paean to a disappearing way of life. Although produced by Miyazaki's Studio Ghibli, the film conveys absolutely no impression of the wild, threatening nature that dominated *Nausicaä* and *Princess Mononoke*. Instead, it is a perfect example of what anime scholar Taiitsu Kitano calls "Takahata's idealized vision of the village."[6]

The film's heroine, Taeko, is an office worker in Tokyo who is living what appears to be a normal city life, but she has always yearned for the countryside. In a revealing early scene, she announces to her boss that she is going to take off work for a country holiday and he comments in surprise "What is it? A broken heart?" (*Shitsuren de mo shita no,* literally, Did you lose your love?). In fact, the film's entire narrative is imbued with a sense of lost love, although not for any specific individual but rather for a world of tradition, community, and harmony with nature. The narrative posits this world as still in existence but discoverable in only remote rural areas. The film is structured between a series of flashbacks to Taeko's fifth-grade year, a period that haunts the grown-up Taeko, and her present enjoyment of farm life. The reasons behind Taeko's inability to let go of her past are varied, but the most likely is because this particular year was one of not only physiological development (there are a number of references to menstruation) but of emotional development as well. In one delicately drawn vignette, a boy whom she secretly likes and who secretly likes her confronts Taeko. When they discover a mutual liking for cloudy days, they are both thrilled and unable to speak. He throws his baseball triumphantly in the air, and she is overwhelmed by a vision of herself flying in the clouds. Through this simple, basically dialogue-free scene, Takahata is able to evoke the pangs of early love in a way that makes the viewer resonate with the intensity of a childhood left behind.

Another important reason why her fifth-grade year shadows Taeko is the fact that it was the time when she became aware of a longing for the country. There is an early scene in which the child Taeko comes home from school to ask her family why they aren't going to the country (*inaka*) for the summer, as all her classmates do. Her mother coolly responds that their family doesn't have an *inaka* to go to and ships the young girl off for a quick vacation at a hot springs resort, where the labyrinthine interiors of the baths are the exact opposite of the open countryside that Taeko craves. The film also shows the rest of Taeko's lonely summer upon her return to Tokyo, where she repeatedly exercises to music from a tape player by herself in an empty park. Other childhood flashbacks range from the positive, such as the enchanting scene of first love previously mentioned, to the upsetting, as when her father slaps Taeko for "selfish" behavior or when he refuses to let her take part in an adult theater group while she is still a child.

In contrast to these complex and realistic memories, the adult Taeko's gradual immersion into country life is presented in broad strokes that mix ideology with wish-fulfilling fantasy in a way that leaves little room for ambivalence or ambiguity. On her arrival in the country, a strapping young man who plays Hungarian peasant music and quotes Basho, Japan's most beloved haiku poet, meets Taeko at the station. He drives her around the countryside, which is presented in a palette of luminous greens and blues. At one point he stops to expound on how the scenery is actually a product of "farmers and nature working together," implying a connection between humans and place that is essentially primordial. As if in response to this evocation of a topological collective unconscious, Taeko exclaims that it must be the reason why she finds the landscape so "*natsukashii*" (nostalgic), as if it were her own "*furusato*" (native place).

The use of two such ideologically and emotionally charged words as *natsukashii* and *furusato*, both of which are seen by most

Japanese as untranslatable, quintessentially Japanese terms,[7] is not surprising given *Only Yesterday*'s clear agenda of privileging the traditional. In this regard, the entire countryside becomes a kind of elegiac resource for emotionally starved urban dwellers. Continuing in this same vein throughout the film, Takeo engages in a variety of rural tropes such as milking a cow, weaving wild grasses, and, most importantly, harvesting the *benibana,* or safflowers, which are used to make a red dye long used in a variety of traditional Japanese arts. The harvesting of the safflowers places Taeko in contact with centuries-old rituals, traditions, and legends. The film shows the farm work as arduous but also satisfying. Furthermore, this manual labor outdoors stands in contrast to Taeko's neon-lit office world of paperwork and computers.

Despite the privileging of rural life, this is not the most striking aspect of the film. Instead, Taeko's attempts to come to terms with her childhood memories form the most interesting elements of the film. Without them, the film would be an emotionally satisfying but otherwise conventional, romanticized narrative of a young woman's rediscovery of country life. More intriguing is the contrast between Taeko's individual memories of a sometimes happy, sometimes disappointing but always very self-absorbed or even "selfish" childhood with the broader archetypal memories that the film's farming segments attempt to evoke.[8] These include the young farmer's speech about the age-old connection between farmers and nature and the legends and rituals concerning the *benibana,* all of which privilege a wider world of collective history and tradition that has the potential to allow Taeko an escape from perhaps crippling personal memories. This provides the film with far more depth than a simple romance between an urban girl and a farmer would have allowed.

Only Yesterday therefore implicitly contrasts two forms of nostalgic memory: nostalgia for a personal past, a year of emotional and sexual growth in particular, with a nostalgia for a communal past that allows the individual to take part in the wider rhythms of nature and history. When Taeko returns to the country at the end of the film, she vows not to bring her fifth-grade self with her. This can be read as a desire to be liberated from the "selfish" individual self, and become part of a richer communal fabric. However, it is the film's inclusion of these brilliantly presented childhood memories that is *Only Yesterday*'s greatest strength, by suggesting the richness of personal memory that lives within every human. As opposed to the obvious tropes of farmers planting in the field and milking cows, the delicate psychological moments encapsulated in personal memory resonate deeply, and it is the combination of the two that gives the film its particular power. In Eliot's words, Taeko's self is both "renewed" and "transfigured" within a vision of the past that has been, in Ivy's words, "refigured" as an object of urban longing.

LIBERATION FROM THE FUTURE
AS WELL AS THE PAST: *MAGNETIC ROSE*

Magnetic Rose (*Kanojo no omoide,* literally "her memories") evokes a very different past from the childhood remembrances of Taeko and the collective history of the Japanese countryside. Directed by Morimoto Koji from a three-part manga anthology by Otomo Katsuhiro (writer, director, and producer of *Akira*), the film contains certain commonalities with *Akira*, although it confronts rather different issues. Like *Only Yesterday*, the film is structured around a woman's memories and her inability to let go of them, but like *Akira* the film prefers to challenge the past rather than celebrate it. The film suggests that the only "past" left for contemporary human beings is a rather dubious simulacrum, a lost world that tempts us to look for comfort within it but ultimately disappoints and thrusts us out once again into loneliness and emptiness.

The film is set within a claustrophobic spaceship in which an international group of salvagers roam through abandoned space lanes to find objects worth taking home. They hope to get back to Earth, but are tempted by an eerie distress call, the sound of an aria from *Madama Butterfly* emanating from what appears to be an abandoned space station. However, as the use of an opera suggests, this apparently generic sci-fi world is permeated by visions of other more traditional and historic worlds. In fact, the crew itself is unable to "focus on [their] own present."[9] Rather than dwell on their current dangerous and uncomfortable lifestyle, the crew prefers to dream of "houses in California" that they will buy when they find the ultimate salvage prize. In other attempts to escape reality, Aoshima, the Japanese member of the crew, croons over a collection of pinup girls while

Heinz, a German, carries a photograph of his 10-year-old daughter Emily and hopes to return to her soon.

Lost in dreams of a fantasized future (and fantasized femininity), the crewmembers are ill-prepared to deal with the bizarre and ultimately fatal environment that awaits them on the abandoned space station. The interior of the space station consists of a lovingly detailed recreation of a prewar European world. It houses an enormous manor, complete with huge chandeliers, statues, and portraits, as well as a hologram version of the European landscape, including green fields and a rose garden. The station has only one inhabitant, a woman in a red dress who turns out to be the hologramatic legacy of a famous diva named Eva Friel. After losing her voice and murdering her husband, she retreated alone to the space station to dwell in her happiest memories of the time when she was still successful and her husband still loved her. While it is revealed in the end that Eva is actually dead, her presence lives on in both her eerily lifelike and clearly evil hologram and the elaborate details of her residence.

While there are obvious echoes of Charles Dickens's Miss Havisham, the work's science fiction setting helps to defamiliarize and freshen what could be a stale story line. The vast emptiness of space and the scrap-metal quality of much of the space station's exterior contrast sharply with the museumlike world within, although it is a world that can turn dusty and abandoned-looking at the whim of the machines maintaining its appearance. This simulated European ambiance initially entrances the travel-weary crew, especially Miguel, a Spaniard who warms both to the house and to Eva's young and beautiful hologram appearance. Even after spitting out wine and declaring everything "fake," he remains enchanted by Eva's fantasy image and willingly succumbs to becoming part of her memories.

The fate of the stronger-willed Heinz is more tragic. Unlike Miguel, he resists being drawn into Eva's memories and asks her why she cannot accept reality. In response, Eva sets a trap for him, baiting it with his own memories. Heinz becomes lost in a flashback/dream about his family and his little girl Emily in particular. These memories turn dark, however, as Eva's machines create a simulated Emily who pursues him into the space station, crying, "Now I can be with you forever, Papa." Although touched by the simulacrum's sweetness and his own nostalgia for family life, Heinz wrenches away from "Emily" and declares to Eva that "memories aren't a way of escape." Heinz can no longer escape from Eva, however. Even though he shoots her hologram, it is too late for him to get away from the space station. His own crew, caught in a magnetic field, is unable to rescue him and must destroy the space station in order to save themselves. The space station collapses around Heinz and Eva to the strains of *Madama Butterfly*. Eva goes to her "death" intoning "welcome home, dear" (*okaeri nasai*) to emphasize the fact that Heinz will die trapped in her memories. In the film's final, lyrical shot, the viewer sees the dying Heinz drifting in space surrounded by rose petals.

Although structured in a relatively conventional sci-fi/horror format, *Magnetic Rose* raises a number of intriguing issues surrounding contemporary attitudes (and perhaps specifically Japanese ones) toward the past. Eva's obsession with the past is characterized as clearly unhealthy, signified not only by her own evil character but by the fact that the "house" itself sometimes transmogrifies from a museum-quality residence to a cobweb-ridden house. Miguel's declaration that everything in the residence is "fake" stresses that attempts to simulate a lost dream are pointless. However, Miguel's eventual entrapment by Eva's memories suggests the deep appeal that even the most obvious simulacrum carries. The fact that he is Mediterranean suggests that not only his personal but cultural identity is attracted by the elaborate construction of a European world. In contrast, Heinz stolidly retains his own identity only to be caught off guard by his daughter's simulacrum, suggesting that even positive memories can undermine the present.

Overall, the film's approach to the past seems ambivalent at best. The salvage crew serves essentially as collectors of memories, but memories that have been left behind as junk. The members do not seem interested in what they collect for its intrinsic quality but rather for the "houses in California" that it might buy them in the future. Confronted with the grandeur of Eva's space station, they are initially interested in it for its commercial possibilities as salvage. Lost in the "eternal present" of space, the crew seems to be free from the past and only amorphously drawn to the future. On the other hand, the film shows that personal memory, at least, is too strong a force to be denied. Miguel succumbs to Eva's past dreams while Heinz is temporarily overwhelmed by a favorite part of his own past. The fact that Eva dies while reciting "welcome home" also hints at a strong, if problematic, desire to have a home to return to.

However, in sharp contrast to *Only Yesterday,* the film shows nostalgia as fundamentally dangerous and denies all possibility of ever coming "home." In some ways the dark, claustrophobic salvage ship may serve the same function as Taeko's office in *Only Yesterday,* as a trope for the ugly, technology-ridden modern world that inevitably inspires dreams of escape to another, more welcoming life. Despite this similarity, the overall message of *Magnetic Rose* stands apart, taking a deeply pessimistic view of this desire. The strains of *Madama Butterfly* that initially lure the crew to the space station evoke a past world of beauty, elegance, and culture for which anyone might be nostalgic. But as the final shots of Eva's decomposing skeleton and Heinz's rose petal–covered body make clear, this is a nostalgia that kills rather than inspires.

Although very different from each other in style and overall message, *Only Yesterday* and *Magnetic Rose* both attempt to deal with "the whole issue of how to handle the aesthetic qualities of space and time in a postmodern world of monochromatic fragmentation and ephemerality."[10] *Only Yesterday* challenges this world by positing an Other world, spatially located next to the urban centers of modernity and postmodernity but linked to a primordial and archetypal temporal dimension that is coherent, composed, and untouched by either modern or postmodern trends. *Magnetic Rose* cynically offers a simulacrum of the past, located safely in outer space but still possessing enough imagistic force to affect both personal and cultural identity. *Only Yesterday* ends with the triumph of that Other world, suggesting that there is still a past and a place that contemporary humans can escape to. *Magnetic Rose* exposes the impossibility of such yearnings, ending with what might be called a darkly lyric celebration of fragmentation and collapse.

APOCALYPSE, FESTIVAL, AND ELEGY: *BEAUTIFUL DREAMER* AND THE POETICS OF STASIS

In addition to their explorations of nostalgia, *Only Yesterday* and *Magnetic Rose* also share another important element: their privileging of the feminine memory as the repository of the past. Although Taeko and Eva possess very different characteristics, they are both women and both are haunted by a personal past. While the male characters in each work also show some interest in the past, it is clearly the female who is coded as most deeply associated with personal memory, perhaps because in the world of the elegiac, the strongest voice is often an intimate, implicitly female one. This importance of feminine voice, dreams, and memory reaches its apogee in the film *Urusei Yatsura: Beautiful Dreamer,* directed by Oshii Mamoru and based on the manga and anime by Takahashi Rumiko.

In *Beautiful Dreamer,* a variety of dreams, or themes, are intensified by the pairing of these two artists. While *Beautiful Dreamer* retains the festive spirit of the original *Urusei Yatsura* television series, it combines this with the chilly sense of order captured in Oshii's *Ghost in the Shell* to produce a work that is both beautiful and unique. To Takahashi's festival spirit, Oshii adds a powerful but quiet apocalyptic tone, and her celebration of friendship and community is given a deeply elegiac quality by the film's poetic narrative structure. Like *Only Yesterday,* this structure suggests a refuge from "that schizophrenic rush of time . . . so central to postmodern living"[11] through the privileging of communal ties, but, like *Magnetic Rose,* the film also problematizes the possibility of such a refuge actually existing.

Beautiful Dreamer begins with a sequence of discordant images. It opens with a seagull lazily circling a mound of desiccated earth on a summer day as haunting music plays in the background. The focus shifts to an army tank partially submerged in water. As the tank begins to move, the seagull flies off to circle an old-fashioned clock tower. While the seagull suggests a classic summer vision, the devastated earth and the threatening image of the tank, clearly out of place, hint at something gone wrong. That these discordant images are somehow related to time is emphasized by the image of the clock tower.

The next series of images revolves around preparations for the annual Tomobiki High School Festival. While frantic announcements play over the school's loudspeaker concerning the need for order, the importance of maintaining a speed limit, and the prohibition of costume-wearing, the film shows characters breaking each of those rules. The sense of disorder is heightened when the tank breaks the school windows and crashes through the floor. Both threatening and funny, the image of the tank intrudes on a world that is already disordered by the joyful craziness of the festival and hints at a more ominous level of disorder to come.

The subsequent scenes grow increasingly fantastic and subtly menacing as the protagonists Ataru, Lum, and their friends attempt to return home from the school. One by one they find that they are unable to reach their own homes. Each wanders through a dark and strangely deserted city in which the only movement is the occasional glimpse of a young girl in an old-fashioned hat and a group of *chindonya*—traditionally dressed performers who advertise the openings of new stores. One of their teachers discovers the truth of what is going on when he manages to return to his apartment. He finds it covered with mushrooms and dust, but when he returns to the high school, the festival preparations are still going on. From this he determines that at the high school it is still yesterday, while in his apartment time has suddenly speeded up and many years have passed. He concludes that he is in a situation similar to the ancient tale of Urashima Taro, the fisherman who rides a gigantic tortoise down to the Palace of the Dragon King, only to find when he returns that his village has aged beyond recognition.

Other events allude to both traditional Japanese folklore and classic fantastic conventions. In a nod to fantasy and horror films, the school turns labyrinthine and also grows a fourth story while the water in the swimming pool begins to well up around it. Ataru becomes lost in a hall of mirrors and an "out of order" sign suddenly appears on the school clock tower. Realizing that both space and time are becoming twisted, the group tries to get away from the school by flying away in a private plane. However, as they soar away from Tomobiki, they see only blackness, and when they look down, they see that Tomobiki has been torn off from the rest of Earth and is being carried away on a giant tortoise—another evocation of the Urashima Taro tale. With nowhere else to go, the group ends up back at Ataru's house in Tomobiki, the only private residence that is now available to them, to begin a new life cut off from the rest of the world.

What follows is perhaps one of the more unusual and understated postapocalyptic visions in anime (or perhaps in any other medium) as Lum and her friends begin to explore the newly liminal space of Tomobiki. Instead of bemoaning their fate, the group largely acquiesce and even enjoy themselves. The film mixes classic postapocalyptic images such as abandoned cars, desiccated landscapes, and a deserted, fully-stocked convenience store with conventional images of leisurely summer pastimes. Lum, Ataru, and their friends dive in the water that is slowly submerging their high school, rollerskate over dried-out pathways, and set off fireworks at sunset over the ruined town. Meanwhile, their friend Mendou, one of the few characters who seems upset about what has happened, roams the town in the tank, dictating "the prehistory of Tomobikicho, 'The End of the World'" in an amusing parody of postapocalyptic survival stories.

Although the film contains many comic elements (such as the fact that Ataru's father Mr. Moroboshi's newspaper is delivered faithfully every morning by an unknown agency), it is ultimately a serious meditation on the relationship between reality and fantasy. It uses archetypal images from Japanese mythology in combination with farce and drama to provide a subtle exploration of the desire to deny loss and change. In *Beautiful Dreamer*'s drawn-out climax, Mendou discovers the secret of the new Tomobikicho, that it is all simply a dream. It is not hard to determine that the dream belongs to Lum, who states, "I want to live happily ever after with Darling [Ataru] and his mother and father and all his friends; that's my dream," earlier in the film. The creature responsible for making Lum's dream come true is a character from Japanese folklore known as Mujaki, the Dream Eater. Upon discovery, Mujaki explains how he met Lum at the aquarium (another liminal space) and, delighting in the "purity" of her dream, decides to grant it to her.

The humans summon Baku, the Eater of Nightmares, to eat up Lum's dream, supposedly liberating them back to reality. However, the viewer sees that fantasy, or perhaps the desire for fantasy, is not that easy to escape. Ataru goes through a series of dreams and awakenings, including one in a haremlike nightclub that he finds particularly pleasant, before finally confronting the mysterious little girl whose shadowy form he had glimpsed in the beginning of the film. The girl tells him that she is "Little Lum" and begs him to call out the "right name" in his final dive into reality. The "right name," of course, is "Lum," and he finally finds himself awake back in the "real world."

As mentioned earlier, it can be argued that *Beautiful Dreamer* is almost the perfect postmodern text for several reasons. The first is the film's brilliant use of pastiche, including everything from classic postapocalypse survival stories to the high-school romantic comedy that underlies the whole narrative. The film juggles these various genres brilliantly through the overall framework of the dream, a liminal space in which anything can happen and in this case frequently does. In keeping with its structure of pastiche, the movie is also postmodern in its disregard for fixed categories. The most obvious example is the lack of distinction between dreams and reality, which reaches almost hysterical proportions in the final sequences, in which Ataru keeps waking up from a dream only to fall into another one. It should be noted that this surreal device, while seemingly postmodern in its evocation of ambiguity, is actually a refiguring of a centuries-old Chinese philosophical anecdote in which the philosopher Chuang Tzu dreamed he was a butterfly, only to wake up and wonder if he might not be a butterfly dreaming it was Chuang Tzu. *Beautiful Dreamer* thus plays on both classic archetypes and postmodern visions to create its surreal atmosphere of narrative ambiguity. [12]

A perhaps more specifically postmodern element in the film is the crucial motif of fragmentation that permeates the narrative, from the anarchic prefestival sequences that threaten the order of Tomobiki High School to the physical fragmentation of Tomobiki from the rest of Japan and the world. Although this fragmentation is celebrated by most of the characters, there is also a subtextual note of fear and frustration that adds emotional complexity to the film. The motif of the festival itself is an ambiguous one, suggesting excitement and liberation and also the entry into a nighttime world. However, the fact that the festival is perpetually postponed (similar to the dinner in the film *The Discreet Charm of the Bourgeoisie* by Luis Buñuel) evokes a sense of unfulfillment, hinting that "redemption from time" may not always be satisfying.

Ultimately the film both celebrates and denies the dream of escaping time and its concomitant components of loss, grief, and absence. Essentially a elegy for a perfect summer and an adolescence that never ends, the film's beautiful images make Lum's desire for an endless present seem understandable. At the same time though, its use of eerie imagistic juxtapositions (the slowly submerging school, the rollerskates rolling over devastated earth) suggest the discordance at the heart of attempting to maintain a dream in a permanent stasis.

*

The three films discussed in this chapter vary greatly in tone and content but they all revolve around a desire to cling to a particularly beloved period of time. In the case of *Only Yesterday,* this desire is celebrated, as long as the object of desire is the collective, "traditional" past of the Japanese people. The personal past of the main character is treated with more ambivalence. In *Magnetic Rose* the desire to stay in a simulated personal past, a past that is palpably "fake" (its "fakeness" emphasized by the exaggerated, museumlike furnishings of Eva's space station), is held up as pathological. *Beautiful Dreamer* treats Lum's desire to deny the reality of anything beyond her own memories and desires quite sympathetically. The endless summer that Lum's self-absorbed wish creates is depicted as surreally appealing. But the fragmentation and alienation inherent in the dream make the viewer desire the final return to reality.

The three films can also be looked at in terms of Japan's changing position in the international setting. The world of *Only Yesterday* is quintessentially "Japanese," both in Taeko's memories of her stereo-typical Tokyo childhood and, even more so, in the traditional land-scapes of Yamagata. Its conservative narrative structure finds safety in the elegiac resources of ancient and native archetypes. In contrast *Magnetic Rose* occupies the global territory of science fiction and stresses this through its clearly European mise-en-scène (in itself perhaps a comment on contemporary Japan's fascination with "inter-nationalization")[13] to suggest that contemporary elegies can only be simulations that always end in fragmentation. *Beautiful Dreamer* partakes in global tropes from postapocalyptic science fiction, fantasy, and horror, but intersperses them with uniquely Japanese elements to create a work that is both distinctively Japanese and yet totally original, a elegy for a gossamer world of adolescent pleasure.

In certain ways *Beautiful Dreamer* can be compared to Murakami Haruki's 1985 novel, *Hard-Boiled Wonderland and the End of the World.* Both works privilege a solipsistic fantasy world created from the mind of the main character. In this regard they may be linked with what Harry Harootunian sees as the nation's tendency to dwell in an endless "postwar" period that "condenses the temporality of a duration into an endless spatial scape and present."[14] The works may also be linked to what some commentators see as an increasingly narcissistic tendency among Japanese youth to dwell in their own mental worlds of private emotion and memory. Both works accept the loss of a larger world for the pleasures of the interior self.

However, from another point of view, *Beautiful Dreamer* might also be seen as a self-reflexive celebration of the world of anime itself: festive, beautiful, and the product of someone else's dream. In its celebration of the liminal, the surreal, and the creative, the film evokes one of the most important pleasures of anime—the freedom to enter a world that is both Other and yet uncannily close to our own. The fact that this world is, inevitably, a temporary one only makes it all the more seductive.

A FRAGMENTED MIRROR

IT IS IMPOSSIBLE to try and sum up the world of Japanese animation. As this book has tried to show, the anime universe is an extraordinarily diverse one, and it would be futile to attempt to pigeonhole it into any single categorizing structure. Although certain tropes and themes, such as the dysfunctional family and the changing roles of women, as well as the overarching modes of apocalypse, elegy, and festival, reappear in many films and series, they are reworked with such variety and richness that it is absurd to suggest that there is one anime "take" on any particular issue. It is important to remember that the issues with which anime deals are universal ones, although some lend themselves more easily to the animated art form. In a discussion of very early American animation, Paul Wells describes the works of animator Winsor McCay as "revealing the deep-rooted fears of the Modernist era" in dealing with "anxieties about relationships, the status of the body, and advances in technology."[1] Over 80 years after

McCay began producing his works, these anxieties still remain in the forefront of much of Japanese animation.

There is perhaps one more, arguably postmodern, "anxiety" that could be added to the world of anime, however. This is the issue of cultural identity, a concern that has revealed itself, both implicitly and explicitly, in virtually every animated text discussed in this book. As this book has shown, anime offers an extremely heterogeneous kind of cultural self-representation, which is in fact one of its attractions. The "transformation and change" that the medium foregrounds resists any attempt at narrow cultural categorization. As a result, the Japanese national cultural identity put forward by anime is increasingly, and perhaps paradoxically, a *global* one. In this regard anime is perhaps the ideal aesthetic product for the contemporary period, at the forefront of creating an alternative cultural discourse that goes beyond the traditional categories of "native" or "international" to participate in what may well be a genuinely new form of global culture.

This is partly due to the distinctive properties of the animation medium itself, a medium that is genuinely unique. Animation, perhaps from its very inception, has existed as an alternative form of representation, a representation that privileges very different properties and conventions from that of live action. As Eric Smoodin suggests, "animated films [function] as an Other within a production practice dominated by live action films . . . embodying the irrational, the exotic, the hyperreal."[2] This very Otherness of the animation form, combined with the extraordinary creative properties of the medium itself, however, may be one of its major artistic strengths in the new transnational culture.

Anime offers an exhilarating vision of difference in which identity can be technological, mythological, or simply an ecstatic process of constant metamorphosis. To some viewers, such an array of possibilities can be threatening, but to others, they can be liberating sites of play. Ranma's transsexuality, San's affinity with the Otherness of the (super)natural, and even the demonic Overfiend all allow the viewer access to forms and positions that subvert the conventional at every turn. The wide range of identities, including nonhuman characters, that populate anime texts can suggest both the threatening possibility of dehumanization and the empowering possibility of going beyond any categorical notion of the human. Similarly, the blasted landscapes of apocalyptic anime or the lush beauty of Miyazaki's pastoral visions offer up worlds that exist as warnings or alternatives to the conformity of contemporary society.

The world and characters of anime are not simply representations of an idealized real world that is coherent and composed. Rather, they are uncanny evocations of a protean world of imagination that is both familiar and unfamiliar to the viewer, a world of simulations, possible states, and possible identities. What is visible through anime's technological mirror is an uncanny and fragmented collection of conditions and identities. For the Japanese viewer these fragments may have culturally specific resonance, but they are also fragments with which any twentieth-century viewer may empathize on a variety of levels.

The three anime modes on which this book focuses—the apocalyptic, the festival, and the elegiac—are all ones that implicitly or explicitly acknowledge fragmentation, loss, and possibility. The apocalyptic is based on the knife-edge between coherence and dissolution, often at the mercy of the forces of technology, while the festival celebrates the (temporary) dissolution of social boundaries and hierarchies. The elegiac naturally arises from an awareness of loss, but it also offers fragments—of hope, beauty, and even transient visions of coherence—to shore up the ruins that it so eloquently describes. These modes have powerful resonance within the Japan of the later twentieth century, but they offer no single overarching vision. Combined within the explicitly artificial space of animated technology, they provide flashing glimpses into the dreams and nightmares of a highly technological society beset by change yet still valuing a rapidly disappearing past. That these are not issues exclusive to Japan cannot be emphasized enough.

In *Modernity at Large,* Arjun Appadurai makes the argument that contemporary cultural flows belong to five different "landscapes": ethnoscapes, mediascapes, technoscapes, financescapes, and ideoscapes.[3] Anime takes part in all five of these landscapes, but it also exists in a sixth that could be called the "fantasyscape." This sixth landscape, which draws elements from each of the other five, has two key aspects, action and setting. The action is play, and the setting is a world constructed for entertainment, a world of simulacra. Unlike other, more ambiguous simulacra, however, anime makes no pretense of participating in the "real" except for what its viewers bring to it (which may be both very real and very serious). This is its ultimate attraction: The viewer may play in a liminal world of entertainment, free to take part in an infinitely transforming state of fantasy. Of course, this is what all cinema and video products do to some extent, but animation allows the play to take place to an even more liberating degree.

The traditional definition of animation is of something that "gives movement and life to inert materials." We have seen that anime gives movement and life to any and all fragments of identity in a world that is insistently unreal. Animation's shadow play is more explicitly artificial than that of the cinema, but that artificiality may allow the dance more creativity. While its technological basis points to society's increasing debt to the machine, its artistic virtuosity underlines the awesome powers of the human imagination. The fantasyscape that anime offers is one that at its best soars above the grimy surfaces of the real to allow entrance to the free play of the mind in all its liberating solitude.

APPENDIX

THE FIFTH LOOK: WESTERN AUDIENCES AND JAPANESE ANIMATION

For more and more cultural critics and historians, the absolutely crucial question has become not "what do texts mean?" but rather, "who are these meanings available to?" and, related to this, "how does meaning vary from audience to audience?"

—Eric Smoodin, *Disney Discourse*

ANIME IN GLOBAL CULTURE

I enjoy being part of a group that's not mainstream: i.e. that's slightly on the edge. I've always seemed to have followed my own

path . . . [S]o although many of my family members and acquain-
tances find my Anime devotion odd, it doesn't matter to me. My
interest has spawned many new experiences. I love learning about
the Japanese culture and I'm currently taking classes in the
Japanese language. I've met many interesting people, made new
friends, traveled to different cities, and developed a palate for
Japanese food. Anime has broadened my world.

—18-year-old female high school student

Anime is a serious art form.

—25-year-old male graphic designer

It's different.

—22-year-old male computer science major

THIS BOOK HAS LOOKED AT JAPANESE ANIMATION in both its local and
global context, though it has stressed the Japanese context more than
the international one. As a result, this appendix looks at anime from
another angle: its development as a cult phenomenon in the West,
particularly in the United States. Based on new research, it appears that
anime is attracting an increasingly diversified audience, expanding
from its original core of university students to include professionals in
high tech industries, finance, and law.

But what is it that draws Americans and other Westerners into
the world of amine? Is it the medium itself, its artistic and dramatic
effects, or is it because it is exotic and different? Is it because of its
often graphic depictions of sex and violence, which are usually
highlighted in discussions of anime?[1] Who are the fans of anime?
What relationship is there between anime and its Japanese origins in
terms of its attraction for Western viewers?

This appendix offers a few answers to these questions based on
preliminary research conducted from September 1998 to January 1999
using a questionnaire, interviews, and personal correspondence with
individual anime fans. Those surveyed include students in Copen-
hagen, California, New York City, and, most significantly in terms of
detailed statistical results, the University of Texas anime club. The
goals of the survey were:

Otaku Explanation

...op a profile of the anime fan, not only in terms of ...actors such as age, occupation, and interests, but ...relation both to other members of the world of ...in general and in relation to the "average Ameri-...ose habits and beliefs are tracked through the vast ...iterature already available;

• ...out what attracts them to anime;
• ...ver wh... *Stereotyping*... in anime had, if any, ...an inter...

In developing a profile of the fans, it was important to let the fans speak for themselves as much as possible, and they turned out to be a thoughtful, intelligent, and articulate group of people. Many fans are stereotyped, or even stereotype themselves, as *otaku*—"diehard fans who ignore everything else because they love anime so much," as one respondent defined it—but in general they are far more diverse and have far broader interests than this image suggests. It was also important to paint as detailed a picture of anime fandom as possible since the two major, if not only, English-language discussions about anime fans (Susan Pointon's "Transcultural Orgasm as Apocalypse: *Urotsukidōji:* The Legend of the Overfiend" and Annalee Newitz's "Anime Otaku: Japanese Animation Fans Outside Japan"), though containing many significant insights, tend to see fans in somewhat narrow terms. Both critics are correct to a degree when they suggest that a prime audience of young males often find a "fantasy escape and source of identification"[2] within anime's graphic violence, voluptuous female characters, and politically incorrect male-female relationships. However, both tend to see this as the main, or even the only, aspect of anime's attraction in the West. Pointon describes the medium entirely in terms of its "inordinately high content of sexual sado-masochism and graphic violence."[3] Given that Pointon is discussing *Legend of the Overfiend,* this description is hardly surprising, but it seems clear that anime's attraction for Westerners is far broader and more diverse than such an assessment conveys.

As for Newitz, she develops a somewhat contradictory theory that American anime fans, through their appropriation of a Japanese cultural product, are both exercising "a form of revenge on Japanese animation, so heavily influenced by Hollywood that it is itself already 'stolen' from American culture" as well as accustoming themselves to a subordinate position in relation to Japan, basing her argument on her theory that American fans "*are rejecting their national culture in favor of another national culture.*"[4] Newitz's assertion concerning how much anime has "stolen" from American culture is surprising when it seems that many of anime's themes (romance, war, the end of the world) are as universal as they are specifically American or Japanese. Furthermore, although there are inevitably Hollywood influences, there are far more distinctively Japanese elements, from narrative structure to social values, that make it hard to think of anime as a "stolen" form. Perhaps equally important in relation to her second assertion is that it seems increasingly hard to speak of purely national cultures in the current global world economy.

Rather than engaging in reverse cultural imperialism or in a particularly lurid form of spectatorship, anime fans are engaged in a relatively new form of spectatorship, that of the committed media fan. The fan's interaction with the cultural object is deeply engaged, transcending issues of national boundaries, content, style, or ideology, and it cannot be subsumed under any one-note description. The fact that anime is a Japanese, or at least non-American product, is certainly important but largely because this signifies that anime is a form of media entertainment outside the mainstream, something different."

In this way, anime fandom can be examined as a "fifth look," going beyond the three basic looks in cinema—the look between actors in the film, the camera's "look" at what it is filming, and the viewer's look at the screen. It also goes beyond John Ellis's notion of a "fourth look," the voyeuristic "look" in pornography in which the viewer is consciously aware of his looking at the screen and is also aware of the possibility of being "looked at" by others.[5] While watching anime is in no way equated with watching pornography, there is a heightened self-consciousness to watching anime. Indeed, this exists in any form of fan media spectatorship where the fans watching the work are looking at, and for, different elements than typical viewers do. This self-consciousness is heightened by three interlocking factors: the estranging or defamiliarizing aspect of the genres involved, the medium of animation versus that of live action

the way fans watch anime

(where it would seem easier to become part of the story), and the Japanese or non-American origin of the texts themselves.

THE DEVELOPMENT OF ANIME FANDOM IN AMERICA

Japanese animation in America has been around since at least the early 1970s (much earlier if we count *Astro Boy* in the 1960s), when animated television series such as *Speed Racer* became popular with young American audiences. Often they did not even realize that what they were watching was originally a Japanese cartoon. Although *Speed Racer* introduced a generation of American youth to the look and style of Japanese animation, the growth of anime clubs was a much more important development in setting the style of anime reception among American fans. Often a subset of science fiction conventions, anime fans would usually meet in hotel rooms for all-night viewings of Japanese imports. Although some fans knew Japanese and would shout out summaries and off-the-cuff translations to the rest of the viewers, many fans came simply for the unusual and sophisticated graphics, rapid pacing, and "adult" subject matter. Frequently, especially as the hour grew later, these imports had a strongly sexual and/or violent content that undoubtedly colored the way anime was first perceived by fans and by others only marginally aware of the phenomenon.

With the increasing accessibility of VCRs, other video technology, and the Internet, a distinctive anime subculture began to evolve, one related to, but in some ways different from, media fandom in general. Anime began to develop its own separate modes of fandom— its own hotel conventions and its own support network that now includes clubs, newsletters, Internet discussion groups, and general circulation journals such as *Animerica* or *Anime Fantastique.* Much of this development is similar to the fan culture of such iconic media phenomena as *Star Trek* and *Star Wars,* but there are some intriguing differences worth exploring.

Like all fan groups, anime fandom forms what media scholar Henry Jenkins calls "a cultural community, one which shares a common mode of reception, a common set of critical categories and practices, a tradition of aesthetic production and a set of social norms and expectations."[6] Often this community can function as a type of surrogate family, sometimes more supportive than the fan's real family or community. While this is true for such enormous fan groups as the fans of *Star Trek* (the granddaddy of media fandom), it may be even truer for anime devotees. Because the object of their interest is not an American pop culture icon, they may therefore feel more marginalized than fans of American cultural products.

The fan community functions as a place of retreat and revitalization. As one student who has attended anime conventions since high school explained, the "con" (convention) atmosphere "is one of unconditional acceptance and support—people feel like they have found a real family, a family that doesn't reject them for being 'geeky' or into weird things . . . Spending a weekend with people living, sleeping, eating in the same space with them (and going through sleep deprivation) and partying and watching lots of Anime creates that 'instant-family' feeling."

While conventions are the most high-profile form of community, anime clubs are "the backbone of American anime fandom," as Steve Pearl, the cofounder and current chairperson of the Anime Alliance, puts it.[7] The clubs range from small groups, such as the eight-person group founded by high school student Amber Weller, which "squeezes itself into the kid's section at the rear of the [Borders] bookstore" once a month, to the large university anime clubs (University of Texas has over 300 members), which usually meet weekly, maintain their own libraries, and often have sophisticated viewing facilities. According to Pearl, the largest areas of growth have been in university anime clubs, thanks not only to the facilities but also to the large "closed" community of students from which to draw members. However, this research indicates that the university clubs also draw members from outside of the student body (39.7 percent of the University of Texas club were not university students).

Like their counterparts in *Star Trek* or *Star Wars* fan clubs, anime fans show some ambivalence toward the outer, nonfan world. Fans feel that as anime receives greater media exposure, it runs the risk of diluting its special character. Most are pleased to have their favorite series or films shown on television channels such as the Sci-Fi Channel. At the same time, however, they worry that nonfans will not appreciate anime, and many particularly dislike the fact that anime is almost always dubbed before airing on American television. Anime clubs also try to maintain a distance from the burgeoning industry in anime product marketing, which includes everything from boxed sets of videotapes to the countless toys and gadgets based on popular children's series such as *Sailor Moon*. As Pearl puts it, "for the most part Fandom has always strived to be where the Industry isn't."[8] For example, anime fans take pride in not charging for copying tapes. Partly this has to do with copyright restrictions, but it is also clear that this is a way of differentiating themselves from the commercial enterprises that have sprung up around anime. Similarly, the subtitled videos often begin with the announcement "subtitled by fans for fans."

Anime fans are a proud and sometimes prickly group, intense about their own enthusiasm but wary of being misunderstood by others. In this regard, they resemble the larger world of *Star Trek* and *Star Wars* fans, whom Jenkins sees as "operating from a position of cultural marginality and social weakness,"[9] unable to do much to influence the giant industries that create the productions they love. However, there are significant differences between the fan groups. The most important difference is the simple fact that anime is not a Western product. While it is arguable how important anime's "Japanese-ness" is, the significance of not being typically American cannot be underestimated. Clearly one major (if not *the* major) attraction of anime is that it is "different."

The second major difference between anime fans and other media fans in America is the fact that anime is a medium, not a single television or film series, not even a single genre. Although within anime fandom there is a huge variety of different subgroups attached to particular anime series, films, or directors, it is clear that anime fans still see their overriding loyalty as being toward anime in general. Answers to survey questions that asked about anime preferences reveal the fans' interest in a variety of anime. Although some chose only one genre, the majority of fans chose at least two and usually three genres, ranging from romance/comedy to horror/occult. Furthermore, when asked to name their three favorite anime films or series, the answers cut across genres, suggesting that it is the overall anime experience that attracts people as much as any one particular film or series.

Another major difference between anime fans and more mainstream fans is gender. While *Star Trek* fans are generally female,[10] surveys have shown anime club membership to be predominantly male (approximately 76 percent in the University of Texas club).[11] This gender difference may translate into a different style of fandom. In discussing the largely male fan culture of the cult television series *Twin Peaks,* Jenkins suggests that the fans tended to translate "the confusions of human interactions" into a "technical problem requiring decoding." Comparing them to the *Star Trek* fans, whom Jenkins perceives as using the programs as a basis for sharing emotional experiences, he suggests that the *Twin Peaks* fans "hid behind the program, moving through a broad network of texts but revealing little of themselves in the process."[12] Some of this is certainly true for male fans of anime who often concentrate on technical/technological aspects of anime, such as the availability of laser disc or DVD versions of their favorite series or the quality of computer graphics in a particular episode.

However, the discussions are frequently far more wide-ranging. For example, the *Nausicaä* discussion group sometimes veers into philosophical questions inspired by Miyazaki Hayao's own concern with environmental and social issues. Virtually all the groups engage in the practice of what media critics call "cultural appropriation" (fan art and fan writing, the creation of graphics and stories involving the fans' favorite characters). While they may not reveal as much about themselves as *Star Trek* fans do, these are indications that anime fans are just as intensely and emotionally engaged as fans of *Star Trek*. However, the predominantly male viewership of anime may also account for the large number of violent and sexually explicit anime that are imported into America and, perhaps even more importantly, for the *perception* that anime is popular primarily because of this type of content.

THE PROFILE OF THE ANIME FAN

There are a few caveats regarding this section. First, most of the results are based on surveys from University of Texas fans and may not represent the full population of anime fans. Also, anime fandom is in a particularly fluid state as anime grows in popularity and shifts toward the mainstream, so the profile presented here is a snapshot of a body in transformation.

With those in mind, there are some general descriptions that seem clear. As stated earlier, most anime fans are male (76 to 85 percent). They also tend to be students, although a healthy number (15 to 20 percent) are already in the working world. A large number of the nonstudent respondents in New York were either artists or in some way connected to the animation industry. In Austin, a major center of high-tech industry, most of the nonstudent respondents were involved in computer programming or electrical engineering. In both cases, many of the professionals were engaged in jobs that made an interest in anime quite natural. Artists and animators are drawn in for aesthetic reasons. High-tech workers often come across anime in computer or video games, a popular form of recreation in the industry. In either case, it seems clear that anime's influence is spreading beyond the universities.

Of the respondents who were students, their majors varied across the spectrum to include English, art history, and pharmacy, but the largest percentages were in the sciences, specifically computer science and electrical engineering. Over 70 percent had a grade point average of 3.0 or higher, which is especially impressive when one considers the academic rigor of scientific fields. Surprisingly, few of them were Asian Studies or Japanese majors (in the case of Texas, only 1 out of 56) but 43 percent had taken a Japanese language course. Their ages varied from 14 to 48, with the average age around 22.

Although the relative youth of the fans and the high number of fans with interests in science and technology may not be surprising, other statistical findings were more unexpected. In terms of social, religious, and political values, responses varied widely, from radical to conservative. Thus, while 40 percent identified themselves as "liberal to very liberal," 34 percent saw themselves as "moderate to moderately conservative." In terms of religious beliefs, while only 5 percent saw the Bible as the "literal word of God," 31percent saw it as "the inspired word of God, although not everything in it should be taken literally." When asked to rate their feelings on a "Feeling Thermometer" from 0 to 100 (negative to positive) on the subject of the Religious Right, 39 percent gave a 0, and the majority (82 percent) rated their feelings for the Religious Right at 50 or below.

Attitudes toward homosexuality were similarly quite liberal. Results showed 45 percent rated their feelings at 50 or above, about the same level of positive feelings as they entertained for environmentalists (46 percent) or feminists (50 percent), although not nearly as high as the positive feeling for scientists or engineers (72 percent rated them at 50 or above). In answer to a question about same-sex relations, 46 percent maintained that such relations are "not wrong at all" and 47 percent believed that "being homosexual is something that people cannot change." While holding relatively liberal beliefs about homosexuality, respondents were quite conservative on the subject of marital fidelity. When asked their opinion of sex outside of marriage, 72 percent maintained that it was "always wrong" or "almost always wrong." This finding may suggest that the frantic and bizarre sexual activity exhibited in certain pornographic anime may serve less as an incitement to such activity than as a form of fantasy compensation to a relatively conservative lifestyle.

The answers to questions about their hobbies and interests outside anime also revealed a more complex figure than the stereotypical technologically obsessed "geek." While it is perhaps not surprising that 46.6 percent went to anime conventions, 20 percent of them enjoyed martial arts (although only 12 percent played other sports), or that 65.5 percent enjoyed video games, the most popular hobbies of all were reading (81 percent) and going to films (69 percent). Belying the image of anime fans as social outcasts who sit in their rooms all day, "attending plays, concerts, and other live events" was listed by 48.3 percent as their most popular hobby. The fact that a majority of respondents (46.4 percent versus 39.3 percent) preferred watching anime at an outside venue such as an anime club rather than at home also suggests that anime fans are quite socially inclined. The range of books and favorite films also went well beyond pure science fiction or cyberpunk. While the clearly favorite film was *Star Wars* (12.5 percent), other films mentioned included the contemporary fantasy *Sliding Doors* and even such classics as *To Catch a Thief*. Among favorite novels, science fiction and fantasy were the most popular, with the classic *Ender's Game* by Orson Scott Card being mentioned most frequently followed by J. R. R. Tolkien's *Lord of the Rings* trilogy. As with film, however, the literature choices covered a wide continuum ranging from *The Great Gatsby* to Woody Allen's *Without Feathers*.

While there is no doubt that certain aspects of the stereotype are correct (anime fans are predominantly young males involved in science or high tech), the broad range of responses suggests a far more complex group than the initial stereotype suggests. They entertain a wide spectrum of political and social beliefs and have a broad variety of interests and tastes.

WHAT ATTRACTS VIEWERS TO ANIME?

As far as what draws fans to anime, it is clear that, again contrary to the stereotype, graphic sex and violence are not nearly as important factors as certain others, the most important of these being the differences between anime and American animation, live-action films, and television series. Consistently throughout the responses anime was defined by what it was not. Thus, in answer to the multiple-choice question "What particularly attracts you to anime?" by far the most popular response (80 percent) was, "Its thematic complexity compared to other animation." In answer to an open-ended question on the same topic, many responses were remarkably similar. They included: "it's outside the mainstream"; "it's exotic, different, not American"; "its contrast to Western animation"; and "the fact that it's fundamentally different from US animation." Often the respondents specifically compared anime with Disney and other American cartoons, which they saw as being more child-oriented and less creative than anime. One respondent pointed out that "it is a highly developed art form and we need to get away from our candy coated Disney films." Another respondent went from critiquing Disney to a broad critique of American film in general, saying, "Unlike Disney which is geared toward young children, anime can be watched at any age. Most anime have plots and try to be different. Disney has become very repetitive, re-using ideas . . . I'm trying not to assume that everything Disney does is bad, but there is a repetitive commercialized quality in most American cartoons. This phenomena is rather like the stagnation of American blockbuster movies."

This perceived Otherness of anime is intriguing in contrast to *Star Trek* and *Star Wars,* both of which are seen as exemplifying "American" values. For the viewer of Japanese anime, the appeal is often seen in its very rejection or resistance to American cultural and production values. In terms of cultural values, it may well be its very lack of adherence to certain liberal democratic principles that is seen as attractive. As one respondent put it, anime is "not catering to kids only and therefore not PC all the time. There is a sense of freedom (of expression) which tends to lack in [the] American counterpart."

Annalee Newitz, whose work focuses particularly on romantic comedy that features female characters who are often distinctly "unliberated" in comparison to their American counterparts, noted this absence of political correctness. Writing about anime fans' fondness for romantic comedy, Newitz speculates that "the Americans who consume [anime values] are also responding to—and perhaps attempting to escape—the hypersexuality of their own media culture by reimagining romance as a relationship that goes beyond the purely sexual."[13]

To test this supposition, one question included in the survey asked specifically about whether male-female relations in certain romantic comedies were as close or closer to a romantic ideal than those traditionally found in American culture. Of the respondents who had seen these comedies, about 60 percent of the respondents were in general but not complete agreement. Of those who agreed, their answers suggested that the emotional aspect of many romantic comedies was indeed very appealing. As a sophomore in chemical engineering explained, "We all dream of having a deep understanding relationship of that sort. It's fun to watch." Another mentioned that "most women in American pop culture seem pretty shallow" (although he added that he personally thought that "anime girls" are "just too dangerous"). Another male student partially agreed, suggesting instead, "I would think that most American males are just happy to see well drawn female figures." Of those who disagreed, many pointed out that they watch that kind of anime for its humorous, rather than romantic, aspect. Sometimes the anime "world" in general is seen as a utopian alternative to the real world of the fans. As one female respondent expressed poignantly "Despite some of the content [presumably the violence], it reflects a more peaceful culture than the one we live in. It represents the fantasy of what that culture is (although I'm sure it's stifling in real life), and the 'exoticism' of it makes it more complete escapism."

While cultural values are clearly important to many fans, narrative and production values are equally significant. In terms of narrative values, many fans emphasized the interesting and complex plots available in anime, usually in contrast to the American offering. In fact, the third most popular response to the question, "What attracts you to anime?" was "[t]he imaginativeness of the narrative" (61.7 percent). While the critic Susan Pointon believes that most Americans would find the unusual plot elements, such as the lack of a satisfying resolution or the death of the heroine, "disturbing,"[14] many anime viewers seem to find this a major part of the appeal. As one respondent mentioned, "Western television seems geared to the average viewer and tries not to offend anyone by being unique, and each week another disembodied story is told—never building on past developing story plots."

Fans also mentioned the "more mature and interesting " characters in anime. Perhaps the most poignant response was from a female psychology student who wrote, "Disney animation is 'pretty,' but it lacks the emotion of anime. These characters are like us as we really are, not an idealized image of a hero 'bad-guy' etc. The good guys have bad qualities and the bad guys have good. The characters in anime are human." She also suggested that "the long series and movies [offer] better continuation and development to stories and characters." Another respondent said flatly that "anime are as good as feature films (or better) in my opinion." Others clearly identified with certain characters. One female respondent wrote about wanting to be "as adventurous as Lum." Two others mentioned that *Evangelion* was their favorite anime because they identified with the complex and tormented main character.

For many respondents, however, it is the aesthetic quality of anime that is the ultimate appeal. In answer to the question "What attracts you to anime?" the second most chosen answer (70 percent) was "the quality of the animation." One respondent called anime simply "a new form of art," while an art history student said that "seeing some anime was like going to a pop art exhibition." Others were more mystical. A 42-year-old jeweler wrote, "Anime possesses an aesthetic which is different to what is produced in the West—an aesthetic with an emphasis on a quality of beauty different from Western standards." Another suggested that "it's proof that artistic media like animation can be dramatic and intellectual, and all that stuff independent film is credited with." A chemistry major wrote simply, "watching anime reminds us of why we watch cartoons in the first place, a different world."

Up to this point, the reasons given for watching anime have been largely intellectual or aesthetic, quite different from the standard view that anime fans watch it mainly for its graphic sex and violence, but the issue of sex and violence cannot be ignored. As with many sensitive issues, this is difficult to explore in interviews and question-naires because questions on these subjects often make the respondent feel guilty if he/she responds with an answer supporting behavior frowned on by others. Two ways were used to get at this issue. The first was to ask directly if the erotic or violent nature of anime was one of the things that attracted the respondent to the medium. The second was to ask an open-ended "thought question" as to whether the respondent thought that *others* were attracted to anime because of the "adult" themes in anime. The first approach, as might be expected, produced limited results. In answer to whether they were attracted to the erotic content in anime, only 8 percent said yes. Of course, this may be an accurate assessment of this particular group, but given the popularity of "adult" anime films both in the anime club that was surveyed and in video rental shops in the area, it seems very unlikely.

Another question, which asked respondents to choose to what degree the sex or violence in anime was one of their reasons for watching, provided a more thorough response. It showed that 56.7 percent agreed that the violence was "exciting but not one of the main reasons for watching," and 50 percent felt similarly about the erotic content in anime. However, 8 percent did agree that the erotic content was "somewhat off-putting." As one (male) student put it, "It's often treated in such a ridiculous way that there's just nothing appealing about it, and I start to wish something else would happen." In both this section and in response to the thought question, there were a number of thoughtful and thought-provoking answers. A few respon-dents agreed that the adult content was a major reason behind anime's popularity. As one respondent, a 31-year-old male engineer com-mented, "there are many immature people who are incapable of being in an adult relationship. For them, 'adult anime' is a socially acceptable alternative to pornography."

Many other respondents agreed that "adult" themes were an important element in attracting the audience. As one respondent put it "Sure, some people start watching anime because they hear 'it's got naked chicks!'" but virtually no one suggested that these themes were the *only* attraction in watching anime. Furthermore, some respondents suggested that the sexual content of anime allowed for genuinely adult narratives. As a 48-year-old engineer explained, "good anime with 'adult' content is generally a well balanced dramatic presentation with a well–thought out script." Another writer suggested that, precisely because of the adult content, "more mature themes are broached, as opposed to ignored or avoided [as] in domestic animation."

Others strongly disagreed with the question. A 19-year-old chemical engineering student wrote, "No, I like [anime] and don't watch 'smut.' In fact I'm vehemently opposed to 'adult' material in general. People like animation for its music, violence, intricate stories, continuous series, Japanese culture. Some do like lewd content, though many more are like me." More practically oriented respondents pointed out that "if you're just interested in porn you can find it more easily on the Net," and a 28-year-old technician suggested that "A lot of anime appearing on the shelves have as much 'adult' content as the average sitcom or soap opera."

The question of the importance of the sexuality and violence in anime is hard to answer definitively. It may be that many fans are initially lured into the anime world because of its "adult content." But, as one respondent replied caustically, "if I just wanted porn I'd go to another section of the video store." Judging from the variety of thoughtful and detailed responses, it seems reasonable to suggest that the answer "I find the erotic content exciting though not one of the main reasons for watching" may well describe the majority of anime fans.

ANIME AND JAPAN

To explore the relationship between anime and an interest in Japanese culture the following questions were used: Is part of anime's attraction to you the possibility of learning about Japanese society? Have you taken a Japanese language class or been to Japan? Have you learned anything about Japanese culture and if so, give three specific examples? Can you define the Japanese word "*otaku*"?

The results were varied. For some, the Japanese connection was quite important, but for others, it barely mattered. While 86.7 percent felt that they had learned about Japanese culture from anime, only 45 percent said that it was one of their main reasons for watching anime. This figure complements the 41 percent who had taken or were taking a Japanese language course. Only 10 percent had visited Japan.

As for what respondents felt they had learned about Japanese society, the answers were interesting and often quite funny, although perhaps not always likely to gladden the hearts of academics involved in Japan. The answers were so varied that it is hard to group them, but a number of respondents mentioned improved language skills and vocabulary while some mentioned learning a variety of cultural practices. These ranged from sociocultural insights such as "everyone is really polite" or the "importance of the first kiss" to what might be considered examples of anime humor such as "an odd fascination with toilets." As the variety of these examples suggests, if the respondents based their knowledge of Japan solely on anime, such knowledge would tend toward the haphazard and the bizarre.

The answers regarding the definition of "*otaku*" were somewhat surprising. In Japan, the word is used derisively to describe anime fans, but in the West it has, to some extent, been adopted as a badge of honor among fans. Despite this, a full 30 percent surveyed had no idea what it meant (although there were some imaginative guesses, such as "shrimp dish"). This finding is intriguing because it would seem that such an exclusive term would appeal to the fan subculture by suggesting an intimate relationship with Japan, similar to the way martial arts students often like to choose Japanese terms for their practices. For a few respondents this was clearly the case, as several of them wrote the word in Japanese or gave long explanations of its Japanese origin. But many others showed little interest in the term beyond a basic definition while others obviously did not care.

The answers to all of these questions suggest that, on the whole, the issue of Japanese-ness is not the major attraction of anime for most of the respondents. In answers to the thought question "What appeals to you about Japanese animation?" only a handful even mentioned Japan, either explicitly or implicitly. Even when they did, it seemed clear that the real Japan was not seen as a Utopian Other. Thus, the respondent quoted above who found that anime "reflects a more peaceful culture than the one we live in" immediately acknowledged that this was probably just a "fantasy" and that "the reality is probably suffocating."

This relative lack of identification of anime with Japan is intriguing in comparison to other Japanese cultural products that have had followings in the West, such as the martial arts, Zen, or haiku. These products often seem to inspire mystical visions of Japan as an Orientalist utopia of sages and nature-worshipping monks. While a handful of respondents in the survey did seem to see anime in a slightly mystical fashion, they did not specifically identify this mysticism as Japanese.

Instead, it appears that it is the "Otherness" of anime rather than its specific "Japanese-ness" that is one of its fundamental appeals to the fans. As discussed earlier, respondents consistently mentioned how different anime was from American or Western products.[15]

Scholars have pointed out how text accumulates varied meanings through use, and it seems clear that anime has many different meanings for Americans. To some it is a means of mediating or enriching a relationship with Japan, while others see it as an aesthetic experience that contributes to their own artistic interests and knowledge. Some regard it as a chance to explore male-female relationships in a different culture, and for others the marginalized, antisocial protagonists strike a chord of recognition in the fan's own life.

Scholars Ella Shohat and Robert Stam describe media spectatorship as having the potential for becoming a "liminal space of dreams and self-fashioning . . . through its psychic chameleonism," pointing out that "the cinematic . . . fashions a plural "mutant" self, occupying a range of subject positions."[16] It seems clear that not only is the space of anime a liminal one (as is true of all artistic media), but also anime itself occupies a liminal space in the global economy, especially when looked at by non-Japanese fans. Neither specifically Japanese nor wholly influenced by the West, anime appeals to a generation of Americans who care much less about the national origins of a cultural product than they do about the quality of the product itself. Ultimately, anime is the remarkably appropriate medium for the contemporary era, at least for the most distinctive aspects, in which "Otherness" and the edginess of the nonmainstream are widely celebrated.

Anime thus stands in fascinating contrast to such "traditional" objects of fandom as *Star Trek* or *Star Wars*. According to media critics, such as John Tulloch or Henry Jenkins, these traditional series and films appeal precisely because the science fiction elements depicted in them are severely conservative instrumentalities. They allow the viewer to feel safe in the hands of a technologically competent elite who understand and control the more bizarre and fantastic manifestations of contemporary technology. In contrast to the psychological comfort offered by conventional science fiction shows, anime, along with other postmodern texts, offers a world of fluctuation, uncertainty, and excitement; respondents favorably mentioned the "chaotic" quality of anime while a number of others talked about its "intensity."

Media critics often point to fandom as a form of resistance to an unsatisfying outer world: "Fans, like all of us, inhabit a world where traditional forms of community life are disintegrating, the majority of marriages end in divorce, most social relations are temporary and superficial, and material values often dominate over emotional and social needs."[17] This is undoubtedly true for anime fans as well. The major difference between anime fans and fans of more traditional American texts is their willingness to embrace a form of disintegration or at least fragmentation within their favorite medium itself. The world of anime fandom may indeed offer a surrogate community. But anime itself, in both style and content, reminds the fan that at the beginning of the twenty-first century such wholeness is temporary at best, and most likely illusory. The spectatorship of the anime fan acknowledges a world that is inherently Other, but one that they can still make their own.

NOTES

CHAPTER ONE

1. John Treat, *Contemporary Japan and Popular Culture* (Honolulu: University of Hawaii Press, 1996), 12.
2. Ueno Toshiya, *Kurenai no metarusutsu: anime to iu senjō/Metal Suits: The Red Wars in Japanese Animation* (Tokyo: Kodansha, 1998), 9.
3. Annalee Newitz, "Anime Otaku: Japanese Animation Fans Outside Japan," *Bad Subjects* 13 (April 1994): 11.
4. In researching this book I could find no general agreement as to whether animation can properly be considered a "medium" or not. Cholodenko, for example, refers to it as a mode of film (Alan Cholodenko, ed. *The Illusion of Life* [Sydney, Australia: Power Institute of Fine Arts, 1991], 28), while Paul Wells, although not specifically defining it, contends that "animation as a film language and film art is a more sophisticated and flexible medium than live-action film" (Paul Wells, *Understanding Animation* [London: Routledge, 1998], 6). My own feeling is that animation, while obviously related to cinema, is indeed a medium in itself, one that privileges simulation over representation, and whose technological constraints and capabilities are significantly different from those of live-action film.
5. Richard Corliss, "Amazing Anime," *Time* 154 (22 November 1999): 94.
6. Ibid., 94.
7. See Sharon Kinsella, *Adult Manga* (Richmond, Surrey: Curzon Press, 2000), 131-133.
8. In fact, at a two-day symposium on anime hosted by the Japan Society of New York in January 1999, roughly a third of the focus was on the challenges of marketing anime in the West. Issues ranged from cultural differences such as different styles of humor and different attitudes toward nudity to nuts-and-bolts problems of packaging and distribution.
9. In fact, 1999 saw the publication by Giles Poitras of the book *The Anime Companion: What's Japanese in Japanese Animation?* (Berkeley: Stone Bridge Press), indicating the interest many Western fans have in the medium's Japanese origins.
10. Arjun Appadurai, *Modernity at Large* (Minneapolis: University of Minnesota Press, 1996), 12.

11. Susan Pointon, "Transcultural Orgasm as Apocalypse: *Urotsukidōji: The Legend of the Overfiend,*" *Wide Angle* 19, no. 3 (1997): 45.

12. In my own lectures on anime, this question comes up consistently and it is clearly a cross to bear for all Japanese animators abroad. In a discussion between anime director Oshii Mamoru and Ueno Toshiya, for example, Oshii mentions how American screenings of his philosophically complex film *Ghost in the Shell* were inevitably followed by questions focusing on the nudity in the work. Ueno responds to this complaint with the intriguing point that this is probably part of a general Western stereotype about Japanese culture ("Eiga to wa jitsu wa animēshon datta" [discussion between Oshii Mamoru, Ueno Toshiya, and Ito Kazunori] *Eureka* 28, no. 9, [August 1996]: 50-81). While this may be true as well, I would still suggest that the question most obviously springs from Western stereotypes about *animation.*

13. In discussing audiences' reactions to animation in general, Paul Wells suggests that "the very language of animation seems to carry with it an inherent innocence which has served to disguise and dilute the potency of some of its more daring imagery." (*Understanding Animation,* 19). This audience presumption of "inherent innocence," I would suggest, is a major reason why Western audiences, especially those new to the medium, tend to dwell so much on the so-called adult themes in anime despite the fact that, as many anime fans point out, the level of sexuality and certainly the level of violence is generally no higher than in most R-rated Western films. Clearly it is the fact that sexuality and violence are enacted within the context of a "cartoon" that strikes the Western audience as transgressive.

14. Trish Ledoux and Doug Ranney, *The Complete Anime Guide* (Issaquah, Washington: Tiger Mountain Press, 1997), 3.

15. In this regard I believe I am in agreement with most Japanese scholars who tend to analyze anime in terms of story rather than visuals. Minamida, for example, sees one of the key differences between "anime" and "animation" as the importance of narrative (*monogatari*) in the Japanese product (Minamida Misao, "Kindai animeshigairon," in *Nijūseikianimetaizen* [no editor] [Tokyo: Futabasha, 2000], 6).

16. J. P. Telotte, *Replications: A Robotic History of the Science Fiction Film* (Urbana and Chicago: University of Illinois Press, 1995), 170.

17. It is also perhaps not surprising that I was able to find a book on anime heroines (*Anime hiroingahō,* [B Media Books—no editor] [Tokyo: Takesho-bō, 1999]), with pictures, biographies, and commentary on literally hundreds of female protagonists but have not been able to find an equivalent one on anime heroes.

18. Wells, *Understanding Animation,* 15.

19. Mikhail Bakhtin, *Problems of Dostoevsky's Poetics* (Minneapolis: The University of Minnesota Press, 1984), 124.

20. For a detailed discussion of carnival in Bakhtin's thinking see ibid., 123-137.

CHAPTER TWO

1. Richard Corliss, "Amazing Anime," *Time* 154 (November 1999): 94.
2. For a discussion of the rise of the OVA market in relation to the development of anime pornography see Helen McCarthy and Jonathan Clements, *The Erotic Anime Movie Guide* (Woodstock, New York: The Overlook Press, 1999), 42.
3. For a summarized account of the evolution of Japanese animation up to the 1980s see Kinoshita Sayoko, "Japon: á côté de Goldorak . . . ," *Sommaire,* Special Issue, "Le Cinéma d'animation" (1993): 157-163.
4. For a discussion of *Astro Boy's* conception and development, see Fredrik Schodt, *Dreamland Japan: Writings on Modern Manga* (Berkeley, CA: Stonebridge Press, 1996), 244-248. Also see Trish Ledoux and Doug Ranney, *The Complete Anime Guide* (Issaquah, WA: Tiger Mountain Press, 1997), 9-10.
5. For a comprehensive history of animation in Japanese television, including an in-depth look at Tezuka Osamu's works, see Misono Makoto, *Zusetsu terebi anime zensho* (Tokyo: Harashobo, 1999).
6. Donald Richie, *Japanese Cinema: An Introduction* (New York: Oxford University Press, 1990), 80.
7. Minamida Misao, "Kindai animeshigairon," in *Nijuseikianimetaizen* (no editor) (Tokyo: Futabasha, 2000), 4.
8. Ibid., 7.
9. Stuart Galbraith, *Japanese Science Fiction, Fantasy, and Horror Films: A Critical Analysis* (Jefferson, NC: McFarland and Co., 1994), 15.
10. Schodt, *Dreamland Japan,* 20.
11. Luca Raffaeli, "Disney, Warner Bros., and Japanese Animation: Three World Views," in *A Reader in Animation Studies,* edited by Jayne Pilling (Sydney, Australia: John Libby & Co., 1997), 129.
12. This is not always the case, of course. Some anime texts are based on literature, such as *The Tale of Genji,* while others, including a number of the best products from Miyazaki's and Takahata's Studio Ghibli, are completely original. Recently, with the increasing tendencies in the manga industry to become more cautious, manga series are created at the same time as their anime tie-in (and tied in with other products as well, such as toys or games). An outstanding example of this new type of development is the popular *Sailor Moon* series that was the product of a "coordinated media offensive," (Schodt, *Dreamland Japan,* 93), in which the animated television series began at almost the same time as its first manga episode appeared.
13. Oshii Mamoru, in conversation, New York, January 1998.
14. For an exploration of the connections between literature and art in the Tokugawa period, see Howard Hibbett, *The Floating World in Japanese Fiction* (Tokyo: Tuttle Books, 1976).
15. This was also a period when the Japanese theatrical form of kabuki reached new heights of grotesquerie, especially in the savage dramas of Tsuruya Nanboku whose "gory scenes were designed to stimulate the senses of the audience" (Kato Shuichi, *Japan: Spirit and Form* [Rutland VT: Charles Tuttle Co., 1994], 197).

16. Melinda Takeuchi, "Kuniyoshi's Minamoto Raiko and the Earth Spider: Demons and Protests in Late Tokugawa Japan," in *Ars Orientalis* 17 (1997): 5. See also Kato Shuichi's description of the arts of this period in *Japan,* 195-201. Both Kato and Takeuchi see the rise of the monstrous as related to external sociocultural events. Kato suggests that it was a product of the "collective hysteria" (195) of the late Edo period as the culture began to fall apart from pressures at home and abroad. Takeuchi, on the other hand, sees them as expressing social satire, a form of veiled protest against the censorious Confucian government (12). Takeuchi also makes an important point that should be remembered when studying anime, that is, that the depiction of the supernatural was also a significant form of entertainment and enjoyment. As she says, "indeed monstrous or transformed creatures, including inanimate objects, are at the crux of the Japanese enjoyment of the supernatural" (10).

17. Susan Pointon, "Transcultural Orgasm as Apocalypse: Urotsukidōji: The Legend of the Overfiend," *Wide Angle* 19, no. 3 (1997): 44.

18. Ibid., 45.

19. In this regard, anime is in some ways a reflection of the present amorphous position of its country of origin. While for years discourse on Japan tended to focus on bipolar East/West distinctions, increasingly, commentators on Japan seem to be afflicted by what Marilyn Ivy terms a "profound categorical uneasiness." *Discourses of the Vanishing: Modernity, Phantasm, Japan* (Chicago: The University of Chicago Press, 1995). As Ueno Toshiya and many others point out, Japan is neither "Western" nor "Asian" but it is indubitably "modern," an aspect that echoes anime's position as well. Ueno Toshiya, *Kurenai no metarusuitsu: anime to iu senjō/Metal Suits: The Red Wars in Japanese Animation.* (Tokyo: Kodansha, 1998).

20. Yoshimoto Mitsuhiro, "Real Virtuality," in *Global/Local,* edited by Rob Wilson and Wimal Dissanayake (Durham, NC: Duke University Press, 1996), 107.

21. For a comprehensive discussion of the debate between Disney and the fans see Schodt, *Dreamland Japan,* 268-274.

22. In an interview with Rick Lyman of *The New York Times,* Lasseter states, "From a pure filmmaking standpoint, his staging, his cutting, his action scenes are some of the best ever put on film, whether animated or not . . . Watching one of his films is the best medicine when you have writer's block. When we at Pixar feel that we're beating our heads against the wall, we go in the screening room and put on a laser disc and watch one of his films and it's like, whoa look what he did." Rick Lyman "Darkly Mythic World arrives from Japan," *New York Times* (21 October 1999), sec. B, 1.

23. Ueno Toshiya also discusses the issue of *"mukokuseki"* and ties it to a colonialist perspective (*Kurenai* 141-144).

24. Oshii Mamoru, Ueno Toshiya, and Itō Kazunori, "Eiga to wa jitsu wa animēshon datta," *Eureka* 28, no. 9 (August 1996): 77. In the same article they also agree that there are exceptions to this *mukokuseki* aspect of anime, mentioning *Battleship Yamato* for its "Japaneseness," 78.

25. Oshii, Ueno, and Ito, "Eiga to wa jitsu wa," 80.

26. Ibid., 78.

27. Ueno Kōshi puts this same impulse more poetically suggesting that "Anime is a medium of desire, so animation creates an idealized non-Japanese world." "Tenkū no shiro Laputa: eiga no yume, jitsugen to sōshitsu," *Eureka* 29, no. 11 (1997): 159.

28. The issue of anime and Japanese popular culture as a potential form of Japanese cultural hegemony, especially in areas such as Taiwan, South Korea, the Philippines, and Southeast Asia, is a fascinating and problematic one, worthy of a book in itself. For the purposes of this book, it can be said, in the words of Leo Ching in his article "Imaginings in the Empires of the Sun," concerning Japanese mass culture in the rest of Asia, that Japan's cultural dominance in the area cannot simply be seen as a "generic form of cultural imperialism" since such an interpretation "ignore[s] the possibility of multiple readings of these cultural texts by the people and underestimate [s] their abilities to negotiate and construct meanings within their own particular cultural contexts." ("Imaginings in the Empires of the Sun: Japanese Mass Culture in Asia" in *Contemporary Japan and Popular Culture* [Richmond, Surrey: Curzon Press, 1999], 182). As will be seen in the Appendix on Western anime audiences, each viewer constructs his or her own meaning not only within "their own particular cultural contexts" but from their individual desires and experiences. Although the difference between a Western and non-Western (but still non-Japanese) context for viewing anime is an important one, the issue of viewer interaction in general (especially with the increasingly sophisticated forms of interaction available to global audiences) is not one that can be subsumed only into a vision of neocolonialist power relations.

29. Constance Penley's hypothesis concerning the increasing fascination with difference in science fiction and horror films seems appropriate both to anime and its reception in the West. Suggesting that the science fiction film genre "is now more hyperbolically concerned than ever with the question of *difference,* typically posed as that of the difference between human and nonhuman," she hypothesizes that "although science fiction has traditionally been concerned with this question [of difference], new pressures from feminism, the politics of race and sexual orientation, and the dramatic changes in the structure of the family and the workforce seem to have intensified the symptomatic wish to pose and re-pose the question of difference in a fictional form that could accommodate such an investigation." *Close Encounters: Film, Feminism, and Science Fiction* (Minneapolis: University of Minnesota Press, 1991), vii. Not only does anime deal with difference in its many narratives concerning humans and non-humans, it also implicitly embodies difference in its position as an "exotic" cultural product vis-à-vis the West.

30. As two Western scholars, David Morley and Kevin Robins, wrote in 1995: "if the future is technological, and if technology has become 'Japanized,' then the syllogism would suggest that the future is now Japanese, too. The postmodern era will be the Pacific era. Japan is the future, and it is a future that seems to be transcending Western modernity." (*Spaces of Identity*

[London and New York: Routledge, 1995], 149). With 2000 hindsight, "the Japanised future" seems less likely to be the dominating one, but it is still important to recognize the kind of assumptions and projections that both Westerners and Japanese had concerning Japanese society during the heady years of the seventies, eighties, and early nineties.

31. Ian Reader, "Japanese Religion Looks to the Millennium," (paper presented at the Symposium on Crisis and Change in Japan, University of Washington, 1995), 39.

32. Michael Ashkenazi, *Matsuri: Festivals of a Japanese Town* (Honolulu: University of Hawaii Press, 1993), 152.

33. Herbert Plutschow, *Matsuri: The Festivals of Japan* (Richmond, Surrey: Curzon Press, 1996), 45.

34. John Nelson, "Freedom of Expression: The Very Modern Practice of Visiting a Shinto Shrine," *Japanese Journal of Religious Studies* 23, no. 1-2 (1996): 141.

35. Ian Buruma, *Behind the Mask* (New York: Pantheon, 1984), 11.

36. Marilyn Ivy, *Discourses of the Vanishing* (Chicago: University of Chicago Press, 1995).

37. Douglas Kellner, *Media Culture* (London: Routledge, 1995), 110.

38. Robin Wood, "Papering the Cracks: Fantasy and Ideology in the Reagan Era," in *Movies and Mass Culture,* edited by John Belton (New Brunswick, NJ: Rutgers University Press, 1996), 206.

PART 2

1. J. P. Telotte, *Replications: A Robotic History of the Science Fiction Film* (Urbana and Chicago: University of Illinois Press, 1995), 51.

2. Paul Wells, *Understanding Animation* (London: Routledge, 1998), 69.

3. Ibid.

4. *Henshin* is of course not restricted to anime or manga. For an illuminating discussion of *henshin* in relation to Japanese culture in general and to the popular Takarazuka review in particular see Jennifer Robertson's chapter "Staging Androgyny" in her book *Takarazuka: Sexual Politics and Popular Culture in Modern Japan* (Berkeley: University of California Press, 1998), 47-88, passim.

5. Scott Bukatman, "X-Bodies," in *Uncontrollable Bodies: Testimonies of Identity and Culture,* edited by Rodney Sappington and Tyler Stallings (Seattle: Bay Press, 1994), 94.

6. Interestingly, there is very little tradition of the body, especially the nude body in Japanese art or literature. Woodblock prints highlighted an actor's poses or the sweep of a courtesan's robe, but the unclothed body never exercised the kind of fascination it has held in the West from at least the time of the Greeks. Even the ubiquitous and often very graphic *shunga,* or erotic, prints tended to morsellize the body into a courtesan's nipple or a customer's exaggeratedly large genitalia while covering most of the human figure in flowing and evocative robes. Besides costume itself, the accoutrements of

fashion or sex such as sashes, dildos, pipes, and swords were far more important than the actual human appendages. There is also little description of the nude in literature, at least until the twentieth century. The great medieval romance *The Tale of Genji*, for example, describes the hair, faces, and clothes of its characters at great length, but says nothing about their figures. *Genji's* creator, Murasaki Shikibu, does mention the nude body once in her diary, but in a highly uncomplimentary fashion: she describes a burglary at the palace, in which a robber stole the clothing of some of the women courtiers, and goes on to comment, "[B]ut I shall never forget the sight of them without their clothes. It was quite frightening and also rather amusing" (Richard Bowring *Murasaki Shikibu, Her Diary and Poetic Memoirs* [Princeton: Princeton University Press, 1982], 115). The fact that the greatest chronicler of romantic entanglements in Japanese literature should find the nude body "frightening" suggests an erotic aesthetic very different from that of the West. The arrival of Western art, Western morals, and Western technology at the end of the nineteenth century brought the body into focus in a variety of ways. Western-style painters began to paint the nude at the same time as authorities started closing down mixed public bathhouses, fearing Western censure. This disturbing clash of the aesthetic and the moral meant that the nude body, which had been taken for granted in premodern Japan, now became a problematic issue. This issue was brought even more to the fore with the importation of Western technology. Technology brought the still camera and the movie camera to focus on the body in new and provocative ways. Finally, the technology of animation, coming to the fore in the postwar period, brought something totally new, the animated body.

CHAPTER THREE

1. Marie Morimoto, "The 'Peace Dividend' in Japanese Cinema: Metaphors of a Demilitarized Nation," in *Colonial Nationalism in Asian Cinema,* edited by Wimal Dissanayake (Bloomington: Indiana University Press, 1994), 22.

2. See Susan Napier, *The Fantastic in Japanese Literature* (London: Routledge, 1996).

3. For more on the making of *Akira,* see Tony Rayns, "Apocalypse Nous," *Time Out,* 16 January 1991): 16. There is also a video documentary on the subject.

4. Jon Lewis, "The Road to Romance and Ruin: The Crisis of Authority in Francis Ford Coppola's *Rumble Fish,*" in *Crisis Cinema: The Apocalyptic Idea in Postmodern Narrative Film,* edited by Christopher Sharrett (Washington, DC: Maisonneuve Press, 1993), 144.

5. Tony Rayns, "Apocalypse Nous" 16.

6. Peter Boss, "Vile Bodies and Bad Medicine," *Screen* 27 (1986): 16.

7. For Kristeva's discussion of abjection see her *Powers of Horror* (New York: Columbia University Press, 1982).

8. Kelly Hurley, "Reading Like an Alien: Posthuman Identity in Ridley Scott's *Alien* and David Cronenburg's *Rabid,*" in *Posthuman Bodies,* edited by Judith

Halberstram and Ira Livingston (Bloomington: Indiana University Press, 1995), 203.

9. Ibid., 205.

10. In this regard it is instructive to compare Tetsuo's metamorphosis with the famous transformation scene at the end of Stanley Kubrick's 1968 film *2001*. Like Tetsuo, the protagonist in Kubrick's film goes through a visually stunning series of changes, ending with his metamorphosis into a giant embryo. Unlike *Akira*, however, the transformation scene, while overwhelming, is also quite beautiful, and the final image of the infant is a solemn one, underlining the film's technopositive message that humanity can evolve into a higher form. Another important difference is that Tetsuo speaks at *Akira*'s end, establishing his new identity and suggesting that he has finally entered into the Symbolic order of language, free from the maelstrom of the Imaginary that was his birth scene.

11. Tetsuo's loss of an arm may be compared to Luke Skywalker's similar loss in the 1980 film, *The Empire Strikes Back* (see Napier, "Panic Sites: The Japanese Imagination of Disaster from *Godzilla* to *Akira*, in *Contemporary Japan and Popular Culture*, ed. John Treat [Honolulu: University of Hawaii Press,1996], 250-251), the crucial difference being that Luke's arm grows back, albeit artificially, and he is once again inscribed into the normal collectivity.

12. Barbara Creed, *The Monstrous Feminine: Film, Feminism, Psychoanalysis* (London: Routledge, 1993), 58.

13. The themes of orphanhood of the body were important ones in the Japanese literature of the 1980s as well. Murakami Ryū's *Coin Locker Babies* (*Koiin rokka beebizu*, 1980) and Shimada Masahiko's *Dream Messenger* (*Yumetsukai*, 1989) both deal with orphaned boys deeply alienated from society, while Yoshimoto Banana's *Kitchen* (*Kichin*, 1987) treats the subject of an alienated orphaned girl in a slightly more gentle manner. (I am indebted to Sharalyn Orbaugh for pointing this out.) In all three of these works the absent mother is particularly important.

14. Scott Bukatman, "X-Bodies," in *Uncontrollable Bodies: Testimonies of Identity and Culture*, edited by Rodney Sappington and Tyler Stallings (Seattle: Bay Press, 1994), 119.

15. Philip Brophy, "Horrality—the Textuality of Contemporary Horror Films," *Screen* 27 (1986): 10.

16. Scott Bukatman, "X-Bodies," 116. Italics in original.

17. Sigmund Freud, *Totem and Taboo* (London: Routledge and Kegan Paul, 1983), 85.

18. Bukatman, "X-Bodies," 117.

19. It is worth mentioning here that Paul Wells sees *Akira* as also dealing with issues of gender, specifically masculinity, which he sees as "concerned with the survival of the fittest in the face of change and challenge" (*Understanding Animation* [London: Routledge,1998], 196). This assertion is also buttressed by Isolde Standish who interprets the gang groups in terms of traditional Confucian, even masculine, bonding ("*Akira*, Postmodernism and Resistance," in *The Worlds of Japanese Popular Culture*, edited by D. P. Martinez

[Cambridge: Cambridge University Press, 1998]). I think both these interpretations have value but I would still suggest that ultimately Tetsuo's desire to bond with an absent mother is of equal importance, and that both these aspects are ultimately subsumed in Tetsuo's final transcendence of both his gendered and bodily form.

20. Besides the inference of maternal abjection in Tetsuo's mutation scene, there is no doubt a straightforward sexual subtext to Tetsuo's transformations as well. Film scholar Andrew Tudor asserts that "sexual release has . . . always featured as a potential subtext in metamorphant movies" (*Monsters and Mad Scientists: A Cultural History of the Horror Movie* [Oxford: Basil Blackwell, 1989], 77). Certainly the frenzied nature of Tetsuo's metamorphosis, not to mention the sense on the viewer's part of looking at a taboo subject, suggests a potentially erotic element. James B. Twitchell goes even further in this regard, asserting that horror films are "fables of sexual identity" (*Dreadful Pleasures: An Anatomy of Modern Horror* [Oxford: Oxford University Press, 1985], 77) allowing the (typically adolescent) viewer to metaphorically explore such taboo subjects as incest or simply reproduction itself. It must be said, however, that the actual narrative of *Akira* is remarkably free of overt sexuality. Although Tetsuo has a girlfriend, she is shown almost exclusively in a nurturing role, rather than a sexual one.

21. Judith Butler, *Bodies that Matter* (London: Routledge, 1993), 126.

22. Commenting on pre-1960 female impersonator films, Rebecca Bell-Metereau asserts that "the cross-dressing in these films often functions as an expression of hostility and anxiety. By the end of the story it is clear that any haziness in sexual identity is unthinkable and must be purged from our imaginations by ridicule . . . By ridiculing the man who dresses as a woman, the closed film affirms the majority of the audience's supposedly normal status and confirms the sense of clearcut boundaries between genders" (*Hollywood Androgyny* [New York: Columbia University Press, 1993], 21). As we will see, *Ranma 1/2* is not quite so clear-cut in its enforcing of boundaries. At least during the fantastic space of the episode it allows for a certain amount of play across the boundaries. But it is true that in general each episode closes with a reinscription of the norms of a heterosexual and patriarchal society.

23. Elizabeth Grosz, *Volatile Bodies: Toward a Corporeal Feminism* (Bloomington: Indiana University Press, 1994), 75.

24. Ibid., emphasis added.

25. Bell-Metereau points out that "in early female impersonations, breasts were a focal point of the comedy (in American films)." (*Hollywood Androgyny*, 162) but as censorship laws became tighter, there was less focus on the breasts until the 1960s opened up treatment again, in works as varied as *Psycho* or *Myra Breckinridge*. It is important to note that Japanese censorship, while censoring the genitals, has consistently allowed depictions of the breasts, even in works aimed at young people, which certainly include *Ranma 1/2*.

26. Bell-Metereau, *Hollywood Androgyny*, 5.

27. Intriguingly, *Ranma 1/2*'s creator, Takahashi Rumiko insists that she had no interest in "enlightening male-dominated society" when she created *Ranma 1/2*. Asserting that "I'm not the type who thinks in terms of societal agendas," she states that "[i]t's just that I came up with something that might be a simple, fun idea" (*Anime Interviews*, edited by Trish Ledoux, [San Francisco: Cadence Books, 1997], 20). I see no reason to question Takahashi's statement but it is interesting to note that she writes in a style that she acknowledges as "*shōnen manga*" (boys' comic) and that she is a big fan of the Takarazuka theater (see Jennifer Robertson, *Takarazuka: Sexual Politics and Popular Culture in Modern Japan,* [Berkeley: University of California Press, 1998]) where women play men, both of which suggest that at some level at least she is interested in gender ambiguity.

28. For a discussion of the *bishōnen* comics, see Sandra Buckley's article "Penguin in Bondage: a Graphic Tale of Japanese Comic Books" in *Technoculture,* edited by Constance Penley and Andrew Ross (Minneapolis: University of Minnesota Press, 1991). The *bishōnen* comics are far more overtly sexual than *Ranma 1/2,* containing many graphic scenes of homosexual encounters. Buckley recounts, however, that even male students see these encounters in neither homosexual nor heterosexual terms but she argues that "this [is] a different kind of love" (180). She also suggests that "[t]he objective of the *bishōnen* narratives is not the transformation or naturalization of difference but the valorization of the imagined potentialities of alternative differentiations" (177). While *Ranma 1/2* does not go quite so far as to totally "valorize" these "imagined potentialities" it certainly allows the viewer the chance to indulge, if only temporarily, in an unthreatening fantasy landscape of sexual alternatives. For a discussion of the *Takarazuka* in relation to gender transgression see Robertson, *Takarazuka.*

29. It should be noted that, in the last couple of decades in particular, Hollywood movies have become far more explicit on the subject of gender transgression. Even Disney, as Bell-Metereau notes, has started re-figuring its characters, creating "stronger women and gentler men" (*Hollywood Androgyny,* xii). The most striking example of this is the cross-dressing warrior girl in the 1998 *Mulan.*

30. If we go even further back in Japanese cultural history to the 10th-century aristocratic culture of the Heian period, we will see an explicit willingness to play with alternate genders in literature. The 10th century fictional diary, *The Tosa Diary (Tosa Nikki),* for example, was written by a man (Ki no Tsurayuki) pretending to be a woman. (I am indebted to Lynn Miyake at Pomona for pointing this out.) Heian literature also contains two explicit cross-dressing romances (*monogatari*), *Torikayaba (If Only I Could Change Them)* and *Ariake no wakare (Partings at Dawn).*

31. For a discussion of the absent and/or inadequate father in postwar Japanese film see Satō Tadao, *Currents in Japanese Cinema* (Tokyo: Kodansha, 1982).

CHAPTER FOUR

1. For a discussion of the connections between horror and pornography, see Carol. J. Clover's "Her Body, Himself" in *Gender Language, and Myth: Essays on Popular Narrative,* edited by Glenwood Irons (Toronto: University of Toronto Press, 1992), in which she points out that "[h]orror and pornography are the only two genres specifically devoted to the arousal of bodily sensation" (255). It is surely no accident that three out of the four films discussed here can also be considered members of the horror genre.

2. Douglas Kellner, *Media Culture* (London: Routledge, 1995), 111.

3. Kinko Ito, "Sexism in Japanese Weekly Comic Magazines for Men," in *Asian Popular Culture,* edited by John Lent (Boulder, CO: Westview Press, 1995), 129.

4. Roger Fowler, *A Dictionary of Modern Critical Terms* (London: Routledge and Kegan Paul, 1987) 105.

5. The gothic is, of course, a very popular mode in contemporary America as well, and it is one that is both nostalgic in its use of traditional tropes of horror but also highly contemporary in terms of its fascination with boundary transgression. As the catalogue for a 1996 exhibition of contemporary Gothic art shown at Boston's Institute of Contemporary Art explains, "The old Gothic themes of the uncanny, the fantastic and the pathological, and the tension between the artificial and organic are infused in contemporary art with new potency as they address concerns about the body, disease, voyeurism and power."

6. As Rosemary Jackson points out, the gothic mode, while often "heavily misogynistic" drives toward a "'fantastic' realm, an imaginary area preceding the sexed identity of the subject and so introducing repressed female identities and absent unities." She goes on to note that "the center of the fantastic [or Gothic] text tries to break with repression." *Fantasy: The Literature of Subversion* (London: Routledge, 1981), 122. It seems to me that this is very much the process inscribed in the three most overtly pornographic and Gothic texts described above, in which the female protagonists actively try to "break with repression" (most memorably in the extraordinary visions of the female demonic in *Wicked City*) only to be constrained by the essentially conservative framework of the pornographic genre.

7. Barbara Creed, in her discussion of horror movies containing female monsters, points out the many sexual images of dissolution and castration, stating that "the vagina dentata is particularly relevant to the iconography of the horror film, which abounds with images that play on the fear of castration and dismemberment." *The Monstrous Feminine: Films, Fantasy, Psychoanalysis* (London: Routledge, 1993), 107.

8. See Susan Napier, *The Fantastic in Modern Japanese Literature* (London: Routledge, 1996), 23-25.

9. See Jackson, *Fantasy,* 15-43.

10. Creed, *The Monstrous Feminine,* 116.

11. For a discussion of the *yamamba* in folklore, drama, and literature, see Meera Viswanathan, "In Pursuit of the Yamamba: The Question of Female

Resistance" in *The Woman's Hand: Gender and Theory in Japanese Women's Writing*, edited by Paul Schalow and Janet Walker (Stanford: Stanford University Press, 1996).

12. This paradigm of the "bad girl" enjoying, even craving sex while the "good girl" resists it, is one that is not confined to Japan, needless to say. As Linda Williams points out in her analysis of American sadomasochistic pornography, the "good" female victim is allowed to survive and even receive (supposedly against her will) some sexual pleasure, although she cannot acknowledge it. Williams suggests that the survival of the good girls is dependent partly on the male viewer's bisexual identification with them as victims. The viewer can therefore enjoy the sadistic sex forced on the female victims while at the same time identifying with them in their victim and "good girl" status. She states, "But unlike the slasher film where the sexual 'bad' women do not survive as female victim-heroes with whom male viewers identify, in sadomasochistic pornography these identificatory victim-heroes *do* survive—though they are punished for their sexual pleasures." *Hardcore: Power, Pleasure, and the Frenzy of the Visible* (Berkeley: University of California Press, 1989), 209. *Twin Dolls* has both "good" and "bad" girls, thus allowing the male viewer to participate in an array of identifications without finally troubling his own sexual identity too strongly.

13. Helen McCarthy and Jonathan Clements, *The Erotic Anime Movie Guide* (Woodstock, NY: The Overlook Press, 1999), 54.

14. In fact, I was interested to learn from a young Japanese woman (in April 1997) that Cutey Honey was her "idol" when she was in junior high school, and the idol of her female friends as well. Less interested in the erotic nature of Honey's metamorphoses, the young Japanese girls were impressed by Honey's power and abilities.

15. Anne Allison, *Permitted and Prohibited Desires: Mothers, Comics, and Censorship in Japan* (Boulder CO: Westview Press, 1996), 33.

16. Ibid., 22.

17. The fascination with phallic substitutes is not limited to anime. Sandra Buckley in her work on what she calls "The graphics of representation through non-representation" ("'Penguin in Bondage': A Graphic Tale of Japanese Comic Books," in *Technoculture,* edited by Constance Penley and Andrew Ross [Minneapolis: University of Minnesota Press, 1997], 186), notes its roots in censorship but also reads the tendency as an attempted "reinsertion of phallic order" (187), an interpretation that seems to support my reading of pornographic anime as suggesting a fundamental lack of power on the part of the would-be sexual male.

18. Iwao sums up the problems that the Japanese male has dealing with the increasingly independent Japanese female in the following pessimistic manner: "The vigor with which the sex industry flourishes in Japan in several media (pornographic comics, telephone sex, videos, and other types of commercial voyeurism) and the large number of sex crimes against preadolescent female victims in recent years may suggest the stirrings of psychological problems engendered in men who are confused and unmanned by women who are aggressive, desire gratification of their own,

know their own minds, and can express themselves clearly" (*The Japanese Woman: Traditional Image and Changing Reality* [Cambridge, MA.: Harvard University Press, 1993], 269)

19. The relationship between social change and increasingly negative depictions of female sexuality is, of course, not limited to Japan. Andrew Tudor, noting the increasing conflation of sexuality and female vampirism in horror films since the 1970s suggests that "It is tempting to see in this remarkable development growing fears about predatory female sexuality. These were, after all, the years in which 'women's lib' . . . was much publicized and much maligned. Why should this not find devious expression in the vampire movie?" (*Monsters and Mad Scientists: A Cultural History of the Horror Movie* [Oxford: Basil Blackwell, 1989], 75).

20. The sublimation and displacement of male fear and anger through pornography is not restricted to Japan. Williams summarizes Alan Soble on this theme (in *Pornography: Marxism, Feminism, and the Future of Sexuality* [New Haven, CT: Yale University Press, 1986]), suggesting that "the contemporary increase in pornographic consumption can be accounted for by male loss of power in the wake of feminism and women's new unwillingness to accommodate their pleasures to those of men. Men who develop a dependence on pornography have . . . given up the struggle for power in reality. Recourse to pornography would be an escape into a nostalgic past where rape, ravishment and abuse of women was without censure" (*Hardcore* 163-164). Although I believe that Japanese pornography, particularly the excessively violent kind, also has roots in a more generalized sense of powerlessness within a conformist, highly structured, and highly pressured capitalist system, it seems logical to find connections between the specifically antifemale violence and the gradual empowerment of Japanese women over the last two decades.

21. Barbara Creed, for example, points to the muscular bodies of actors such as Sylvester Stallone and Arnold Schwarzenegger as examples of "performing the masculine," pointing out that the bodies of both actors resembled a "phallus with muscles." She goes on to suggest that "they are simulacra of an exaggerated masculinity, the original completely lost to sight, a casualty of the failure of the paternal signifier and the current crisis in master narratives" ("From Here to Modernity" in *Postmodern After-Images,* edited by Peter Brooker and Will Brooker [New York: St. Martin's Press, 1997], 52).

22. See Nina Cornyetz's discussion of the "dangerous man" trope in the writings of Nakagami Kenji for an analysis of how the male can occupy a site of abjection, in *Dangerous Women, Deadly Words: Phallic Fantasy and Modernity in Three Japanese Writers* (Stanford, CA: Stanford University Press, 1998), 159-225.

23. See Carol Clover's analysis of the role of the "final girl" in contemporary slasher films in her book *Men, Women, and Chain Saws: Gender in the Modern Horror Film* (Princeton, Princeton University Press, 1992).

24. Ian Buruma, *Behind the Mask,* New York: Pantheon, 1984.

CHAPTER FIVE

1. It is also true, as with pornography, that these bodily changes can have strongly erotic overtones. In the case of this "technoeroticism" (to use Springer's phrase) however, the erotic is usually not between male and female but between the human and the technological, as the body-armored human engages with his—or sometimes her—machine in what are usually intensely violent scenes of battle (Claudia Springer, *Electronic Eros: Bodies and Desire in the Postindustrial Age* [Austin TX: University of Texas Press, 1996], 4).

2. Although there are female transformer robots as well, the preferred machine woman in anime seems to me to be an android type such as Gally in *Battle Angel Alita* or Honey in *Cutey Honey,* whose mechanical bodies are, if anything, usually more beautiful and voluptuous than those of "real" women. As Springer suggests, "Cyberbodies, in fact, tend to appear masculine or feminine to an exaggerated degree." *Electronic Eros* (64) She suspects that this insistence on difference has to do with the fact that science fiction as a genre inherently questions human identity. She goes on to quote Janet Bergstrom's assertion that "[in science fiction] the representation of sexual identity carries a potentially heightened significance, because it can be used as the primary marker of difference in a world otherwise beyond our norms" (ibid., 67).

3. J. P. Telotte, *Replications: A Robotic History of the Science Fiction Film* (Urbana and Chicago: University of Illinois Press, 1995), 115.

4. See Abe Kōbō's 1980 fantasy *Secret Rendezvous* (Mikai) for an extraordinary depiction of sexuality's interconnection with technology.

5. Ron Tanner's article on Japanese robotic toys suggests some intriguing historical and cultural influences in their facial design, from Kabuki and Noh masks to the "[b]uglike facial features derived from the insect motifs of traditional Japanese art" ("Mr. Atomic, Mr. Mercury and ChimeTrooper: Japan's Answer to the American Dream," in *Asian Popular Culture,* edited by John Lent [Boulder, CO: Westview Press, 1995], 93).

6. Springer, *Electronic Eros,* 96.

7. Klaus Theweleit, *Male Fantasies* (Minneapolis: University of Minnesota Press, 1989), 154.

8. Constance Penley and Andrew Ross, "Cyborgs at Large: Interview with Donna Haraway," in *Technoculture,* edited by Constance Penley and Andrew Ross (Minneapolis: University of Minnesota Press, 1991), 7.

9. Springer, *Electronic Eros,* 96.

10. Both Springer and Theweleit stress the ecstatic, sexual subtext to the armored body. As Springer says, "significantly, muscle-bound cyborgs in films are informed by a tradition of muscular comic-book superheroes; their erotic appeal is in the promise of power they embody. Their heightened physicality culminates not in sexual climax but in acts of violence. Violence substitutes for sexual release" (*Electronic Eros,* 99). Or, Theweleit describes the Freikorps troop "machine" as being "one of both war and sexuality" (*Male Fantasies,* 154). He later goes on to quote Ernst Junger, a contempo-

rary commentator on the Freikorps, whose description strongly recalls scenes of *mecha* combat: "This was a whole new race, energy incarnate, charged with supreme energy . . . These were conquerors, men of steel tuned to the most grisly battle" (quoted in ibid., 159).

11. Ironically, perhaps the first example of a *mecha* series was Osamu Tezuka's early *Astro Boy* (*Tetsuwan Atomu*), in which the appealing eponymous protagonist really *was* a robot. In contrast to contemporary American comics in which the heroes, although "super," were always human, *Astro Boy* suggests that even in this early period Japanese animation and comics were willing to see the human within the technological.

12. Springer, *Electronic Eros,* 100.

13. Tanner, "Mr. Atomic," 90.

14. Antonia Levi, *Samurai from Outer Space: Understanding Japanese Animation* (Peru, IL: Open Court Publishing, 1997), 86.

15. In its privileging of an escape to the country, the episode recalls the cyberpunk masterpiece *Blade Runner,* which also pits spiritual and human values against the world of modern high-tech corporations and ends with its protagonists actually managing to escape into a bucolic landscape. This similarity is probably not entirely coincidental since both Priss and her rock band, The Replicants, have obviously been named in homage to *Blade Runner's* androids, one of the main characters of which is a replicant called Priss.

16. It is also interesting that the fight scene is not actually shown in the first episode. While the beginning of the encounter is shown in Episode 1, the episode actually ends with the fight's denouement still unclear. It is only in the second episode, which starts with Shinji in a hospital bed, that we are shown a *flashback* of his triumph against the Angel. This fracturing of the narrative structure confounds conventional anime-based expectations, in which a fight and victory would develop in linear form.

17. See Kōtani Mari, *Seibo Ebuangerion* (Tokyo: Magajin Hausu, 1997), 32-40.

18. Springer and Theweleit also see the fascination with technology as a means of escaping from sexuality. The Japanese critic Endō Toru, writing on *Evangelion,* also sees Shinji's story as an attempt to escape from both female sexuality and adult sexuality in general. Although, as Endō points out, it seems that Shinji simultaneously fears and desires a sexual relationship, until the final episode his desires are boundaried by the many quasimaternal relationships that he engages in, from the womblike body of the EVA itself to the quasimaternal ministrations of Katsuragi and even his ambiguous relationship with Rei. Only Asuka is allowed to seem explicitly sexual. Endō equates the sexual qualities Shinji discovers in Asuka in the final episode as being part of the "real world" that Shinji, by accepting the maternal ministrations of both the EVA and Katsuragi Misato, has been unable to escape ("Konna kitanai kirei na hi ni wa:fujori to iu sukui," *Pop Culture Critique* 0 [1997]: 92-93).

CHAPTER SIX

1. In conversation with Oshii I asked him about the significance of *Blade Runner* in his work. He responded that it was important not only to him but had undeniably influenced many Japanese animators (January 1999).

2. In the guide to the movie known as *The Analysis of Kōkakukidōtai*, which consists of a group of interviews with people involved in the production of *Ghost in the Shell,* the director explicitly acknowledges *Blade Runner*'s influence in relation to the film's gritty mise-en-scène. Oshii sets the film's action in a futurist city that most resembles Hong Kong, trying to create "a vision of the future that lies just beyond the landscape of reality." He explains that for him, Hong Kong was the equivalent of the Los Angeles of *Blade Runner.* Intriguingly, Oshii goes on to insist that once having found the right city (i.e., Hong Kong) the actual story didn't matter, underlining the importance of setting and atmosphere to the overall impact of the film. (Unfortunately the book contains no page numbers but these quotes are from the section "Concept Art Design: Comment 2" in *The Analysis of Kōkakukidōtai,* no editor, Tokyo: Kodansha Young Magazine, 1995.)

3. There are many definitions of the term "cyborg," usually revolving around whether the cyborg is purely a technological construct or something that is a combination of both the human (or at least the organic) and the technological. Telotte's description of the cyborg as a "humanoid robot" may be the most generally applicable (J. P. Telotte, *Replications: A Robotic History of the Science Fiction Film,* [Urbana and Chicago: University of Illinois Press, 1995], 4). In the case of Kusanagi, her humanity is, of course, somewhat ambiguous, since we see her clearly being "constructed" in the opening credits sequence. At the same time, however, this opening sequence also has hints of an organic birth scene. Furthermore, Kusanagi and her teammate Batou speak of being "alive" in a way that suggests that they certainly consider themselves to be human at some fundamental level.

4. Donna Haraway, *Simians, Cyborgs and Women: The Reinvention of Nature* (New York: Routledge, 1991), 154.

5. Ibid., 150.

6. This is in interesting contrast to the manga version of *Ghost in the Shell,* which not only shows Kusanagi in a relationship with a "boyfriend" but also contains an explicit sexual scene showing Kusanagi and some other female cyborg friends indulging in an artificially induced orgy. The American version of the manga, incidentally, deletes this scene.

7. Haraway, *Simians,* 151.

8. The use of the Victorian Crystal Palace, an exhibition hall designed to celebrate technology, as a base of design is intriguing. The action that takes place there is initially technologically based destruction, as the immense weapons of the military attempt to tear apart Kusanagi and the Puppet Master. This sequence, which results in the total fragmentation of the two bodies, seems to suggest a negative attitude toward the destructive quality of technology. The hall's mysterious beauty and the fact that this is the place where Kusanagi finally "dives" into the Puppet Master seem to hint at a

more spiritual side, however. In his commentary on designing the hall, the artist Watabe Takashi talks about trying to evoke Oshii's conception of a drowned world in which an archetypal feeling of pleasure can be found in the sense of submersion itself. (*The Analysis of Kōkakukidōtai,* "Landscape" section). This sense of pleasurable submersion is presumably what Kusanagi was seeking in her previous diving scene and what she has perhaps found in her immersion in the mind of the Puppet Master.

9. The vision of the two nude, fragmented female torsos is a potentially disturbing one, reminding us of Laura Mulvey's point that in cinema in general the woman's body is "fragmented by close-ups" ("Visual Pleasure and Narrative Cinema," in *The Sexual Subject: A Screen Reader on Sexuality* [London: Routledge, 1992], 30). *Ghost in the Shell* shows a literal fragmentation that, in this interpretation at least, can make the female seem particularly vulnerable. On the other hand it is possible to argue that the slow fragmentation of Kusanagi's body, which begins when she sits astride a tank attempting to wrest it open, an action that causes her back and shoulder muscles to begin to explode and ends with her armless torso on the floor, simply shows her progression from corporeal form to transcendent dweller in the Net. This scene is interesting in comparison with the final scene in *The Terminator* (1984) when the Terminator's artificial body begins to come apart. As Telotte describes it, "The Terminator's human *seeming* gradually disappears and . . . eventually the entire synthetic human covering burns off, leaving the underlying mechanical chassis to continue, relentlessly, with its deadly mission" (*Replications* 172). In contrast to *The Terminator,* Kusanagi's body does not grow more machinelike. Instead, it becomes increasingly insubstantial, even ghostly.

10. Intriguingly, the manga version of *Ghost in the Shell* has Batou scavenging the body of a *man* for Kusanagi. Given that she has presumably melded with the Puppet Master who speaks in a male voice, this form of boundary-crossing may seem more logical. The film's image of Kusanagi as a young girl is perhaps more interesting, however. Not only does the image of her sitting in the chair call up visions of discarded marionettes, but her childish figure suggests that she is a newborn, a still-undeveloped being about to enter a new world.

11. See, for example, David Desser, "*Blade Runner:* Science Fiction and Transcendence," *Literature/Film Quarterly* 13, no. 3, 1985), 175-183, in which he compares the film to Milton's *Paradise Lost.* Also see Rushing and Frentz, *Projecting the Shadow: The Cyborg Hero in American Film* (Chicago: University of Chicago Press, 1995), 155-156. It would appear that the notion of the fall and other Biblical implications is a paradoxically popular one in science fiction and meditations on science. Thus, Haraway implicitly rejects the notion of a fall in her discussion of the cyborg, when she insists that "the cyborg does not expect its father to save it by a restoration of the garden" (*Simians* 151). Vivian Sobchak briefly mentions the "fall" in *The Terminator* in her article "Child/Alien/Father: Patriarchal Crisis and Generic Exchange," in *Close Encounters: Film, Feminism, and Science Fiction* (Minneapolis: University of Minnesota Press, 1991).

Perhaps the most sustained vision of a fall is in William Gibson's cyperpunk novel *Neuromancer* in which Case, the novel's hacker antihero is forced out of the "net" by damage to his nervous system. As Gibson puts it, "[for Case] who'd lived the bodiless exultation of cyberspace, it was the fall. In the bars he'd frequented as a cowboy hotshot, the elite stance involved a certain relaxed contempt for the flesh. The body was meat. Case fell into the prison of his own flesh" (William Gibson, *Neuromancer* [New York: Ace Books, 1984], 6). Like Case, Kusanagi is also attempting to find the "bodiless exultation of cyberspace." Unlike Case, however, she apparently finds it through union with the Puppet Master.

12. In their book *Projecting the Shadow,* Rushing and Frentz suggest that the cyborg hero is actually a contemporary update of the archetypal hunter figure who stalks the American mythological landscape, weapon in hand. What Rushing and Frentz hypothesize, however, is that, with the stunning developments in technology over the postwar period, the "weapon" has actually become the hunter (the cyborg). As they put it, "the weapon eventually breaks free from [the hunter's] control, becomes technologically perfected, and, in a final profane reversal, turns against the very hand that used to wield it (5). Kusanagi, of course, is figured as a hunter from the opening scene, in which she carries out an assassination on her quest for the Puppet Master. Unlike the cyborg visions profiled in *Projecting the Shadow,* however, she is not seen as a dangerous monster but simply as a professional who happens to be a cyborg.

13. The Puppet Master is actually a very ambiguous creation, as its sinister-sounding name suggests. It is clearly uninterested in human morality or any "normal" human concerns, concentrating instead on transcending what is human in a single-minded way that is virtually monomaniacal. In this regard it resembles the clearly evil protagonists in two of Oshii's previous films, *Patlabor* (*Kido Keisatsu Patlabor,* 1989) and *Pat Labor 2* (*Kido Keisatsu Patlabor 2,* 1993), who are shown as totally self-obsessed and willing to wreak enormous damage on the world in order to get their way. The two earlier films differ from *Ghost* in one highly significant aspect, however. In the two *Pat Labor*s the Mobile Police fight against the agents of evil and each film ends with the collectivity saved by the triumphant police. This is, of course, very different from Kusanagi's resigned acceptance of the Puppet Master's ambiguous invitation.

14. Oshii Mamoru, Ueno Toshiya and Itō Kazunori, "Eiga to wa jitsu wa animēshon datta," *Eureka* 28, no. 9 (1996): 70.

15. According to Itō, he made up the words, which invoke a god coming down to dance with humans, from a variety of sources such as prayers and ancient poetry.

16. Oshii, Ueno, Itō, "Eiga to wa," 70.

17. Telotte, *Replications,* 164.

PART 3

1. Saito Minako, *Kōitenron* (Tokyo: Bireiji senta, 1998), 27.

2. For an illuminating discussion of the culture of *kawaii*, see Sharon Kinsella, "Cuties in Japan," in *Women, Media and Consumption in Japan*, edited by Brian Moran and Lise Skov (Richmond, Surrey: Curzon Press, 1995).

3. John Treat, "Yoshimoto Banana Writes Home: The Shōjo in Japanese Popular Culture," in *Contemporary Japan and Popular Culture*, edited by John Treat (Honolulu: University of Hawaii Press, 1996), 302. Treat's discussion of *shōjo* culture in this article is the most comprehensive in English that I am aware of. I would also recommend Ann Sherif's discussion of *shōjo*, once again in relation to Yoshimoto Banana in "Japanese Without Apology: Yoshimoto Banana and Healing," in *Oe and Beyond*, edited by Stephen Snyder and Philip Gabriel (Honolulu: University of Hawaii Press, 1999), 282–283.

4. For further discussion of *Vampire Princess Miyu* and the *shōjo* phenomenon in anime and manga, see Napier, "Vampires, Psychic Girls, Flying Women, and Sailor Scouts: Four Faces of the Young Female in Japanese Popular Culture," in *The Worlds of Japanese Popular Culture*, edited by D. P. Martinez, Cambridge: Cambridge University Press, 1998.

5. The popularity of female characters in anime is such that both general critical and fan literature in Japan tends to dwell on female anime protagonists far more than male characters. On the fan side one may find the lavishly illustrated book *Anime hiroingahō* (an illustrated history of anime heroines). On the critical side, Saito Tamaki has recently published *Sentō* *bishōjo no seishin bunseki* ([a character analysis of action beauties], Tokyo: Ota Shuppan, 2000), centering on the increasing number of strongly active and often sexually characterized young female characters in anime, whom she terms "phallic girls" (*fuarikku ga-ruzu*), and their fans both in Japan and in the West.

6. Tamae Prindle, "A Cocooned Identity: Japanese Girl Films: Nobuhiko Oobayashi's *Chizuko's Younger Sister* and Jun Ishikawa's *Tsugumi*," *Post Script* 15, no.1 (Fall, 1998): 35.

CHAPTER 7

1. See Tamae Prindle's discussion of the adolescent girl characters in the live-action films *Futari* (*Chizuko's Younger Sister*, 1990) and the 1990 film *Tsugumi*, based on a novel by the quintessentially *shōjo* novelist, Yoshimoto Banana ("The Cocooned Identity: Japanese Girl Films: Nobuhiko Ooba-yashi's *Chizuko's Younger Sister* and Jun Ishikawa's *Tsugumi*, in *Post Script* 15, no. 1, Fall, 1998). It is possible that literature and live-action films may tend to emphasize a more amorphous or identityless version of the *shōjo* while anime in particular tends to privilege a more action-oriented type.

2. Miyazaki Hayao in an interview with Yamaguchi Izumi, "Hikisakenagara ikiteiku sonzai no tame ni," in *Eureka*, Special Issue, "Miyazaki Hayao no sekai" 29, no. 11 (1997), 29.

3. "Panoramic Miyazaki" (no author), in *Eureka*, Special Issue, "Miyazaki Hayao no sekai," 29, no. 11 (1997): 1.

4. Shimizu Yoshiyuki, "Sukoyaka naru bōsō: *Tonari no totoro* no openu endingu o megutte," *Pop Culture Critique* 1 (1997): 93.
5. "Panoramic Miyazaki," *Eureka,* Special Issue, 2.
6. Philip Brophy, "Horrality—The Textuality of Contemporary Horror Films," *Screen* 27 (1986): 105.
7. This can be seen most obviously in the outpouring of letters concerning San, the heroine of *Princess Mononoke* in the book *Mononokehime o kaku kataru* (Tokyo: Comic Box 3, 1997). It is clear that many of the letter-writers consider both San and her male counterpart, Ashitaka, to be potential role models.
8. Shimizu, "Sukoyaka naru bōsō," 98-99.
9. Helen McCarthy, *The Anime Movie Guide* (Woodstock: New York: The Overlook Press, 1997), 78.
10. Quoted in Ann Sherif, "Japanese Without Apology: Yoshimoto Banana and Healing," in *Oe and Beyond,* edited by Stephen Snyder and Philip Gabriel (Honolulu: University of Hawaii Press, 1999), 282.
11. Hirashima Natsuko, "*Tonari no totoro:* fuantaji ga umareru kūkan," *Eureka* 29, no. 11 (1997): 166.
12. Shimizu and other Japanese scholars suggest that the word "totoro" is actually a corruption of "troll," a creature from European fairy tales, the "picture books" that Satsuki's dialogue refers to at one point. Mei's use of a pre-existing word for the supernatural creature she confronts, suggests Shimizu ("Sukoyaka naru bōsō," 95), is an indication that the totoro is entirely a product of Mei's imagination. If "totoro" is indeed derived from Western literary sources, it is also an interesting example of Miyazaki's facility in using Western influences, even in quintessentially Japanese settings.
13. The fact that the totoro does not speak is interesting as well. Compared to the important tradition of talking animals in Western fantasy (or for that matter the many talking creatures in Miyazawa Kenji's tales), the inarticulateness of the totoro may at first seem surprising. In fact, its relative silence (broken by the occasional soft roar) is actually more effective within the story's simple and subtle narrative. Because it is silent, Mei, and later on Satsuki, are able to project their own interpretations onto the creature, thus keeping control of the fantasy. This again is in major contrast to *Alice in Wonderland,* where words are an instrument of confusion and threat. For a discussion of talking animals in Western literature, see Ann Swinfen, *In Defense of Fantasy* (London: Routledge and Kegan Paul, 1984), 12-43.
14. It is interesting to compare the scene in which the family acknowledges Mei's vision to another famous English fantasy about a young girl's discovery of an other world, C.S. Lewis's *The Lion, the Witch and the Wardrobe.* In this work the perception of magic by the young heroine Lucy is clearly coded in Christian terms of faith and willingness to believe. Lucy's announcement that she has discovered the magic country of Narnia inside a wardrobe is initially met with scorn and even concern for her sanity by her brothers and sisters. As the narrative progresses, however, her siblings too eventually begin to "see" and thus "believe in" Narnia, a metaphor for the dawning of

faith in Christ. Miyazaki's work too has a moral agenda, in this case the acknowledgement of and respect for the mystery and beauty of nature. Unlike Lewis's novel, however, *Totoro* swiftly elides the tension between believer and nonbeliever, presenting to the viewer a world where any sensitive and intelligent person can accept, at least on some level, the possibility of enchantment.

15. Shimizu, "Sukoyaka naru bōsō," 97.
16. Hirashima, "*Tonari no totoro*," 169.
17. Ibid., 168.
18. McCarthy, *The Anime Movie Guide*, 102.
19. Ishihara Ikuko, "*Majo no takyūbin*: koko kara asoko e no aida no shōjo," *Eureka* 29, no. 11 (1997): 198.
20. Ishihara, "*Majo no takyūbin*," 193-199.
21. Japanese critics have also noted this scene. Chūjō Shōhei suggests that the scene shows the hidden powers of passion and cruelty lurking within her, and compares her to San in *Princess Mononoke* ("*Kaze no tani no Nausicaa*", *Eureka*, Special Issue, "Miyazaki Hayao no sekai" 29, no. 11 [1997]). As Chūjō points out, however, San is virtually all "passion and cruelty" (107), while Nausicaä is more balanced, uniting both love and hate. I would also suggest that the killing scene also suggests something of the far more psychologically complex portrait of Nausicaä in the manga. The manga's narrative is built even more overtly around the conflicting elements in Nausicaä's personality, highlighting both her extraordinary love and generosity, as in her "mothering" of the god warrior, and her darker side, as when she is tempted by the "nothingness" that the demons evoke in her.
22. "Panoramic Miyazaki," *Eureka*, Special Issue, 3.
23. It is interesting to contrast the images of flying in Miyazaki's film to the repeated images of falling in Oshii's *Ghost in the Shell*. In both cases these actions lead to empowerment, but perhaps very different kinds. Miyazaki's heroines always come back to earth, and their ability to fly can be seen as inspirational both to themselves and to the rest of earthbound humanity. Kusanagi in *Ghost* is essentially trying to leave the real world, and in her final "dive" she enters the world of the psyche, a potentially lonely world in which she and the Puppet Master are the only significant entities. *Ghost's* subtext is therefore one of solitary spiritual empowerment, while Miyazaki's works contain activistic messages that directly confront the real world.

CHAPTER 8

1. These fantastic romances may be usefully contrasted to earlier, more "realistic" animated comedies such as the immensely popular *Sazaesan*, an animated family comedy based on the equally popular newspaper comic strip that ran from 1946 to 1975. *Sazaesan's* eponymous main character was an appealing housewife who dealt with the everyday problems of running a household and looking after her children and slightly bumbling husband. As Frederik Schodt says of her, "Sazae . . . symbolized the new Japanese

woman: still family-oriented and respectful of tradition, but optimistic and independent minded" (*Manga! Manga! The World of Japanese Comics* [Tokyo: Kodansha International, 1983], 96). While the "magical girl-friends" may share some similar traits, the fantastic space in which they act and their own superhuman powers create a rather different overall effect.

2. Lynn Spigel, "From Domestic Space to Outer Space: The 1960s Fantastic Family Sitcom," in *Close Encounters: Film, Feminism and Science Fiction,* edited by Constance Penley, et al. (Minneapolis: University of Minnesota Press, 1991), 214.

3. Quoted in Karen Kelsky, "Flirting with the Foreign: Interracial Sex in Japan's 'International' Age," in *Global/Local,* edited by Rob Wilson and Wimal Dissanayake (Durham, NC: Duke University Press, 1996), 232.

4. Painter's discussion focuses on a popular home drama, *Yome, shuto, kekkon sodo* (wife, mother-in-law, and a complicated engagement), broadcast first in 1991 and rebroadcast in 1994. According to Painter's description, this drama initially seems to acknowledge some of the changes in women's roles over recent decades by presenting such characters as a mother who works and her daughter, a bride-to-be who is hesitant to marry an eldest son because she does not want to have to take care of her future mother in law (Andrew Painter, "The Telepresentation of Gender in Japan," in *Re-imagining Japanese Women,* edited by Anne Imamura [Berkeley: University of California Press, 1996]). By the series' end, however, these potentially unsettling elements have all been defused to provide a conservative, upbeat ending: the mother quits her job to care for her own mother-in-law, and the bride to be is so impressed by her mother's self-sacrifice that she joyfully decides to marry the eldest son. While as a live-action drama set in the contemporary period, this series comes across as perhaps more "realistic" than the anime discussed in this chapter, in fact it too presents a fantasy world in which women's movements toward independence are contained through their willingness to subsume their own desires and sacrifice themselves for others.

5. In fact, the Japanese critic Kitano Taiitsu, referring to the series' famous opening episode, in which a bikini clad Lum descends on the quiet world of Tomobikicho, describes *Urusei Yatsura* as a "complete *matsuri*" (*Niho-nanimeshigakukenkyūjosetsu* [Tokyo: Hachiman Shoten, 1998], 94).

6. See *Animerica* 7, no. 4 (1999), for its cover story, "Anime Dream Girls" (written by the *Animerica* Staff). The description "magical girlfriend" itself suggests the basic thrust of the genre toward an idealized fantasy vision of womanhood from the male point of view.

7. Thomas Keirstead and Deirdre Lynch, "*Eijanaika:* Japanese Modernization and the Carnival of Time," in *Revisioning History: Film and the Construction of a New Past,* edited by Robert Rosenstone (Princeton: Princeton University Press, 1995), 71.

8. The lack of conclusion to each episode may also be related to the fundamental openendedness in many Japanese literary forms, from the fifteenth century linked verse form known as *renga,* in which each verse followed the previous one in some fashion but did not need to create a

coherent whole, to the writings of Kawabata Yasunari, Japan's first winner of the Nobel Prize in literature, the ending of whose most important novel, *Snow Country* (Yukiguni), was famously added on to at various times over a number of years.

9. For a discussion of this traditional dichotomy in expectations concerning male/female behavior see Sumiko Iwao, *The Japanese Woman: Traditional Image and Changing Reality* (Cambridge, MA: Harvard University Press, 1993), 106.

10. Lum's total commitment to a life with Ataru is expressed most memorably (and eerily) in *Urusei Yatsura: Beautiful Dreamer,* the second film based on the series, in which she comments that her perfect dream would be to live forever with Ataru, his family, and her friends (see chapter 12). When her wish is granted, even at the cost of the rest of the world being destroyed, she is perfectly happy.

11. Quoted in Ogasawara Yuko, *Office Ladies and Salaried Men: Power, Gender, and Work in Japanese Companies* (Berkeley: University of California Press, 1998), 4.

12. Kathleen Uno, "The Death of Good Wife, Wise Mother?" in *Postwar Japan as History,* edited by Andrew Gordon (Berkeley: University of California Press, 1993), 316.

13. Nobuko Awaya and David Phillips, "Popular Reading: The Literary World of the Japanese Working Woman," in *Reimagining Japanese Women,* edited by Anne Imamura (Berkeley: University of California Press, 1996), 246.

14. For a discussion of the motif of flying as a metaphor for female independence in Japanese popular culture, see my "Vampires, Psychic Girls, and Flying Women: Four Faces of the Young Female in Japanese Popular Culture," in *The Worlds of Japanese Popular Culture,* edited by D. P. Martinez (Cambridge: Cambridge University Press, 1998).

15. In another popular "magical girlfriend" anime, *No Need for Tenchi,* the initial family consists of the protagonist Tenchi and his lecherous father and grandfather. Once again the mother is dead. As time goes on, however, and more and more "magical girls" come to live with them, the "family" becomes reconfigured on more horizontal lines as a kind of boarding house for young people, with the two authority figures (father and grandfather) typically incompetent and inadequate.

16. Awaya and Phillips, "Popular Reading," 264.

17. Kelskey, "Flirting with the Foreign," 174.

18. Ibid., 183.

19. Annalee Newitz, "Anime Otaku: Japanese Animation Fans Outside Japan," *Bad Subjects* 13 (April 1994): 6.

20. For a discussion of the change of women's status, from comforter to threat in fantasy literature, see Susan Napier, "Panic Sites: The Japanese Imagination of Disaster from *Godzilla* to *Akira,*" in *Contemporary Japan and Popular Culture,* edited by John Treat (Honolulu: University of Hawaii Press, 1996), 103.

PART 4

1. Ella Shohat and Robert Stam, "From the Imperial Family to the Transnational Imaginary: Media Spectatorship in the Age of Globalization," in *Global/ Local,* edited by Rob Wilson and Wimal Dissanayake (Durham, NC: Duke University Press, 1996), 154.

2. Robert Rosenstone, introduction to *Revisioning History: Film and the Construction of a New Past* (Princeton: Princeton University Press, 1995), 6.

CHAPTER NINE

1. See Carol Gluck, "The Past in the Present," in *Postwar Japan as History,* edited by Andrew Gordon (Berkeley: University of California Press, 1993), 83; also see John Treat, *Writing Ground Zero: Japanese Literature and the Atomic Bomb* (Chicago: University of Chicago Press, 1995), especially his discussion of Oe Kenzaburō, 229-258; and Reiko Tachibana, *Narrative as Counter-Memory: A Half-Century of Postwar Writings in Germany and Japan* (Albany, NY: State University of New York Press, 1998).

2. Even during the war, according to Patricia Lee Masters's summary of Tadao Sato's discussion of wartime films, "the concentration was on the human side of Japanese soldiers," with relatively few scenes of combat with the enemy ("Warring Bodies: Most Nationalistic Selves," in *Colonialism and Nationalism in Asian Cinema,* edited Wimal Dissanayake [Bloomington: Indiana University Press, 1994], 2). The humanization of war and the lack of engagement with the American Other is notable in both *Barefoot Gen* and *Grave of the Fireflies.*

3. Trish Ledoux and Doug Ranney, *The Complete Anime Guide* (Issaquah: Tiger Mountain Press, 1997), 6.

4. Harry Harootunian, "Persisting Memory/Forgetting History; The 'Postwar' *(sengo)* in Japanese Culture or the Hope that Won't Go Away," (paper presented at Association for Asian Studies Annual Conference, Washington, DC, March 1999), 4.

5. John Treat, *Writing Ground Zero,* 21.

6. Ibid., 30.

7. Interestingly, Imamura Shōhei also uses the image of the carp in his live-action version of the atomic bombing, the 1988 *Black Rain (Kuroi Ame).* Throughout this bleak and powerful film, the rumor of an elusive giant carp haunts a small group of stricken atomic bomb survivors. They occasionally gather by a pond in hopes of catching it, but it remains mythical. Just before the film's ambiguous but basically grim ending, however, two of the survivors, an uncle sick with radiation poisoning and his presumably dying niece, are afforded a glimpse of the massive carp as it makes huge leaps in the flashing sunlight. Although the overall tone of Imamura's film is more profoundly bleak than that of *Barefoot Gen,* we can assume that, as with *Gen,* the carp remains a (perhaps ironic in this case) symbol of hope and endurance in contrast to the evanescent fireflies of *Grave of the Fireflies.*

8. Masters, "Warring Bodies," 5.
9. One of the immediate imagistic consequences of the atomic blast was the creation of what are called "photo shadows." As Philip Brophy describes them, these were "projects of light energy so great that the human bodies caught unaware left their pulverized ash shadows frottaged onto surrounding concrete walls at the very moment their bodies were vaporized" (Philip Brophy, "Ocular Excess: A Semiotic Morphology of Cartoon Eyes," *Art and Design*, Profile 53 [1997]: 32). This process is brilliantly captured in the bombing sequence of *Barefoot Gen*.
10. Marie Morimoto, "The 'Peace Dividend' in Japanese Cinema: Metaphors of a Demilitarized Nation," in *Colonial Nationalism in Asian Cinema*, edited by Wimal Dissanayake (Bloomington: Indiana University Press, 1994), 19.
11. See Morimoto, "The 'Peace Dividend,'" 19.
12. This paralyzing unease is brilliantly depicted in "American Hijiki" ("Amerikan hijiki," 1967) available in translation in *Contemporary Japanese Literature*, edited by Howard Hibbett (New York: Alfred A. Knopf, 1997), which is another story by Nosaka Akiyuki, the author of the story on which *Grave of the Fireflies* is based. In "American Hijiki" certain subtexts only hinted at in *Grave*, such as the loss of masculine potency, are brought to the fore through the depiction of a middle-aged Japanese man's agonizing reminiscences about his passive role as a boy during the war. That this passivity is in a direct relationship with American military power is made clear by the fact that the man's reminiscences are inspired by a visiting middle-aged American whom the Japanese man attempts to provoke into acknowledgement of Japan's recrudescent power by taking him to a live sex show featuring "Japan's Number One Penis." Unfortunately, the show is a failure, and it is the Japanese who is forced to acknowledge his essential paralysis, realizing that "there will always be an American inside me like a ton of bricks" (467-468). The feared loss of masculinity that is subtextually limned in *Grave of the Fireflies* is given a typically more hopeful treatment in *Barefoot Gen;* in the final scene, as Gen triumphantly caresses the new hairs sprouting on his head, his adopted brother Ryūtaro looks hopefully inside his shorts for further signs of growth only to shake his head ruefully and announce, "Nothing there yet!" But this realization is met with laughter rather than despair.
13. Masters, "Warring Bodies," 15.
14. Lawrence Langer, *Art from the Ashes* (New York: Oxford University Press, 1995), 6.

CHAPTER TEN

1. John Belton, *Movies and Mass Culture* (New Brunswick, NJ: Rutgers University Press, 1996), 20.
2. Indeed the film has been explicitly viewed as a farewell to the legacy of *Seven Samurai*. In an article, film critic Kobayashi Kyūzo suggests that *Princess Mononoke* is a "reply" to the question of what was needed to create a new

vision of history, a history no longer based on simple humanism and righteousness but one that would have to have to take into account the collapse of the Cold War structure and a new period that puts ideas on trial and under examination. Kobayashi points out the darkness of *Mononoke-hime*'s vision but finds "one bit of hope" in Ashitaka's decision to keep fighting (Kobayashi Kyūzo, "*Shichinin no samurai* kara no ketsubetsu o kuwadate," *Mononokehime o kaku kataru,* Comic Box 3 [January 1998], 152-153).

3. As Thomas Keirstead and Deirdre Lynch point out, even the scholars of the so-called people's history still offer a vision of Japan as a homogenous "unitary collectivity" ("*Eijanaika:* Japanese Modernization and the Carnival of Time," in *Revisioning History: Film and the Construction of a New Past* [Princeton: Princeton University Press, 1995], 67).

4. Miyazaki Hayao, "Introduction" to *Princess Mononoke* (no author) (Tokyo: Tokuma Shoten, 1997), 8. Miyazaki's decision to use a historical Japanese context for *Princess Mononoke* may be usefully contrasted to the use of history and legend by Disney animators. Although Miyazaki can be fruitfully compared with Disney, since they both create wholesome, family-oriented movies of an often fantastic character, it is interesting to note how very differently they use cultural myth. As Scott Schaffer points out, Disney "utili[zes] stories from the past—from traditions, generally those of other countries—in such a way as to reinforce the values and cultural practices of America" ("Disney and the Imagineering of Histories," *Post-Modern Culture* 6, no. 3 [1996]): 5). By creating an artificial, foreign Other, Schaffer argues, Disney not only provides Americans with a touchstone of what they are not, but also creates a vision of the non-American world as a commodified bargain basement of exotic products and practices, onto which are grafted blatantly American values and lifestyles. The eponymous heroine of the 1998 film *Mulan* is an obvious example of this. While based on a traditional Chinese legend, the film version of Mulan depicts a plucky independent heroine who believes not only in filial piety but in individual rights as well. Perhaps not surprisingly, the film was not well received in contemporary China.

While previous Miyazaki films also "mined" Western culture, as in the *Gulliver's Travels*–inspired *Laputa* or the character and name of Nausicaä, who was partly based on a character in *The Odyssey,* they differed from Disney in that their deliberately international contexts were less an attempt to promote distinctively "Japanese" values than more universal ones such as humanity, courage, and respect for the environment. In the case of *Monon-okehime,* however, far from reinforcing the traditional Japanese identity, Miyazaki's decision to use a specific Japanese historical period seems to be a conscious attempt to problematize Japanese values and cultural myths.

5. Ibid.

6. Komatsu Kazuhiko, "Mori no kamikoroshi to sono noroi," *Eureka* 29, no. 11 (1997): 53.

7. This ground-based opening scene full of jagged lateral movement is in intriguing contrast to the openings of many, perhaps even most, other

Miyazaki films such as *Nausicaä, Kiki's Delivery Service,* and *Laputa,* all of which are visions of flying that privilege graceful vertical movements evoking an impression of freedom and escape from the travails on the ground. In contrast, perhaps unique in Miyazaki's Ghibli-period ouevre, *Princess Mononoke* has no scenes of flying, and its use of plunging lateral movements suggest a sense of entrapment and desperation.

8. Miyazaki Hayao, "Araburu kamigami to ningen no tatakai," Introduction to *The Art of Princess Mononoke* (Tokyo: Studio Ghibli, 1997), 12.

9. Helen McCarthy, *The Anime Movie Guide* (Woodstock, NY: The Overlook Press, 1997), 201.

10. Quoted in Komatsu, "Mori no kamikoroshi," 51.

11. Komatsu, "Mori no kamikoroshi," 51.

12. Paul Wells, "Hayao Miyazaki: Floating Worlds, Floating Signifiers," *Art and Design,* Profile no. 53 (1997): 23.

13. Intriguingly, in the Japanese language version of the film, Moro is voiced by a male actor, thus adding another layer of ambiguity to her characterization.

14. Murase Hiromi, "Kumorinaki sunda manako de mitsumeru 'sei no yami': Miyazaki anime no joseizō," *Pop Culture Critique* 1 (1997) 53-66.

15. Kierstead and Lynch, "*Eijanaika,*" 71.

16. Brian Moeran, "Reading Japanese in Katei Gahō: "The Art of Being an Upperclass Woman," in *Women, Media and Consumption in Japan,* edited by Lise Skov and Brian Moeran (Richmond, Surrey: Curzon Press, 1995), 121.

17. Natsume Fukanosuke, *Sensō to manga* (Tokyo: Kodansha, 1997), 134.

18. Robin Wood, "Papering the Cracks: Fantasy and Ideology in the Reagan Era," in *Movies and Mass Culture,* edited by John Belton (New Brunswick, NJ: Rutgers University Press, 1996), 223.

19. Quoted in Komatsu, "Mori no kamikoroshi," 49.

20. The forest in *Totoro,* with its magical denizens, may be considered a twentieth-century remnant of these wild forests.

21. Miyazaki Hayao, "Hikisakarenagara ikite iku sonzai no tame ni" (interview with Yamaguchi Izumi), *Eureka* 29, no. 11 (1997): 44.

22. Conrad Totman sums up the Japanese "love of nature" as being, paradoxically, an essentially urban sensibility. As he says, "The 'nature' of this sensibility is an aesthetic abstraction that has little relationship to the 'nature' of a real ecosystem. The sensibility associated with raising bonsai, viewing cherry blossoms, nurturing disciplined ornamental gardens, treasuring painted landscapes, and admiring chrysanthemums is an entirely different order of things from the concerns and feelings involved in policing woodlands and planting trees" (*The Green Archipelago: Forestry in Pre-Industrial Japan,* [Athens, OH: Ohio University Press, 1998], 179).

23. See Susan Napier, "Panic Sites: The Japanese Imagination of Disaster from *Godzilla to Akira,*" in *Contemporary Japan and Popular Culture,* edited by John Treat (Honolulu: University of Hawaii Press, 1996), chapters 2 and 3 for a discussion of supernatural female characters and their link to subverting conventional notions of progress and modernity. See also Carol Gluck's discussion of the "metanarrative of progress" as it underlies Japanese

modernization. ("The Past in the Present," in *Postwar Japan as History*, edited by Andrew Gordon [Berkeley: University of California Press, 1993]).

24. Nina Cornyetz, *Dangerous Women, Deadly Words: Phallic Fantasy and Modernity in Three Japanese Writers* (Stanford, CA: Stanford University Press, 1998), 33.

25. Ibid., 44.

26. In an interview shortly after *Princess Mononoke* came out, Miyazaki mentions being criticized for "letting Eboshi live" but defends himself by saying that, "I thought it was better to have her live in shame than to have her killed. I didn't want to put in death as some kind of punishment or catharsis," (Miyazaki Hayao, "Hikisakenagara," 31). The director's refusal to allow a sense of "catharsis" into *Princess Mononoke* underlines the film's differences from previous Miyazaki films.

27. Saeki Junko, "Nijūseiki no onnagami, saibogu=goddesu," in *Hayao Miyazaki (Filmmakers* 6), edited by Yoro Takeshi (Tokyo: Kinema Junpōsha, 1999), 143.

28. *Princess Mononoke*'s Japanese fans seem to have appreciated the film's resonances with contemporary life. In a book culled from the plethora of letters sent to Ghibli studios by fans of the film, one letter-writer states, "Even though it was supposed to be the Muromachi period, I felt that [the film] was showing our modern world. It went straight to my heart" (*Mononokehime o kaku kataru*, 21). Other fans were resigned and even sympathetic with the film's insistence on separation, with a 17-year-old girl pointing out that even though Ashitaka and San could never fully understand each other, "at least they could open their hearts to each other." It would be interesting to imagine what the reaction of American fans might be had Jane and Tarzan decided to separate at the end of the Disney movie.

CHAPTER ELEVEN

1. Susan Pointon finds parallels between the current sense of social anomie and the political chaos at the end of the premodern Edo period, which also privileged fantasy images of destruction. She says, "[A]s social unrest and foreign intervention increased, Hokusai and the equally venerated Utagawa Kuniyoshi infused their woodblocks with images of transgression, mutation, and catastrophe. Now similarly, in the years following the bombing of Hiroshima and Nagasaki and the subsequent evolution of the Japanese 'economic miracle,' anime and other Japanese artifacts from the fringes have progressively focused on narratives of technological oppression and premonitions of disaster" ("Transcultural Orgasm as Apocalypse: *Urotsukidoji:* The Legend of the Overfiend," *Wide Angle* 19, no. 3 [1997]: 50).

2. Rita Felski, "Fin de Siècle, Fin de Sex: Transsexuality, Postmodernism, and the Death of History," *New Literary History* 27, no. 2 (1996): 337.

3. John W. Nelson, "The Apocalyptic Vision in American Popular Culture," in *The Apocalyptic Vision in America,* edited by Lois Zamora (Bowling Green, OH: Bowling Green University Popular Press, 1982), 179.

4. For those interested in anime and manga, one of the most fascinating aspects of the Aum incident was the perceived link between it and apocalyptic animation and comics. The Japanese media, noting that many of Aum's believers were bright young people and avid consumers of science fiction and horror manga and anime, suggested that these works may have influenced the young believers' willingness to accept Aum's apocalyptic message. (See Helen Hardacre, "Aum Shinrikyō and the Japanese Media: The Pied Piper Meets the Lamb of God," [New York: Columbia University East Asian Institute, 1995], 27-30). If the media are correct (and no doubt at least some of their assumptions are rather exaggerated), then this is a very clear example of anime not simply reflecting society but affecting it as well.

5. For a discussion of the so-called newly risen religions (*shinkyō shūkyō*) and their apocalyptic and millenarian aspects, see Carmen Blacker, "Millenarian Aspects of the New Religions in Japan," in *Tradition and Modernization in Japanese Culture,* edited by Donald Shively (Princeton: Princeton University Press, 1971).

6. Inaga Shigemi, "*Nausicaa in the Valley of the Wind:* An Attempt at Interpretation," *Japan Review* 27 (1999): 120.

7. Japanese commentators have noticed this phenomenon as well. The February 1999 issue of the Japanese anime magazine *Animage* (228, no. 2), contains a special supplement entitled "Za Shūmatsu" (the end of the world) in which it traces notable apocalyptic moments in anime. Commenting on the virtual obsession with devastation evident in so many anime, Kasabe Jun offers the following tongue-in-cheek summary of anime destruction: "First, you have to 'destroy' something. This can be the 'Enemy' or it's okay if it's the 'thing which is almost as precious to the hero as his life' (sometimes it can be his actual life). Actually, sometimes it doesn't matter if it's something that has absolutely no relation to the hero at all . . . [T]hen once you've made the images as spectacular as possible and coordinated them, you make them weird and in their own way climactic." Kasabe goes on to complain that current anime contains "too many" of these "scenes of destruction" ("Mokushiroku e no shottai" in *Zenryaku Oshii Mamoru,* edited by Noda Makoto [Tokyo: Futtowaku 1998], 133).

8. Japanese live-action films also contain a variety of apocalyptic visions although the more "artistic ones" (as opposed to such popular culture displaced visions of the bomb as the *Godzilla* series) are usually centered specifically around the atomic bomb, such as Kurosawa's *Rhapsody in August* (1991) or his immediate postwar film *Record of a Living Being* (1955). American live-action cinema is also inundated with apocalyptic visions that often center around nuclear war. As Jerome F. Shapiro notes, "Between 1935 and 1991, approximately 600 films, both foreign and domestic, with images of nuclear weapons and related technologies have been released in U.S. theaters, and many more made since then." Shapiro, "Atomic Bomb Cinema: Illness, Suffering, and the Apocalyptic Narrative," *Literature and Medicine* 17.1 (1998): 126-148.

9. Tina Pippin, *Death and Desire: The Rhetoric of Gender in the Apocalypse of St. John* (Louisville, KY: Westminster Press, 1992), 58.

10. Even before the atomic bombings, the enormous stresses of Japan's modernization probably helped to give rise to the many new millenarian cults of the nineteenth and twentieth century. As Blacker puts it, "all three periods (of modern cult activity) were . . . ones of especially bewildering upheaval, insecurity and disrupted tradition" ("Millenarian Aspects, 571).

11. Freda Freiberg, "*Akira* and the Postnuclear Sublime" in *Hibakusha Cinema*, edited by Mick Broderick (London: Kegan Paul, 1996).

12. Catherine Russell, "The Spectacular Representation of Death," in *Crisis Cinema: The Apocalyptic Idea in Postmodern Narrative Film*, edited by Christopher Sharrett (Washington, DC: Maisonneuve Press, 1993), 179.

13. Ibid., 174.

14. Robert Lifton, "The Image of 'The End of the World': A Psychohistorical View," in *Visions of Apocalypse: End or Rebirth*, edited by Friedlander, Holton, Marx and Skolknikoff (New York: Holmes and Meier, 1985), 165.

15. Freiberg, "*Akira*," 95.

16. Frank Burke, "Fellini's *Casanova*: Male Histrionics and Phallocentricism," in *Crisis Cinema: The Apocalyptic Idea in Postmodern Narrative Film*, edited by Christopher Sharrett (Washington, DC: Maisonneuve Press, 1993), 153-154.

17. Kamata Tōji, *Ōdōron* (Tokyo: Shinyōsha, 1988), 140.

18. Mikhail Bakhtin, *Problems of Dostoevsky's Poetics* (Minneapolis: The University of Minnesota Press, 1984), 114-118.

19. Kawamoto Saburō and Itō Shunji, in a discussion on *Akira*, discuss at some length the film and manga's use of drugs both in terms of specific references to drugs and the works' hallucinatory imagery. Itō in particular invokes Timothy Leary to suggest that *Akira* is defining a new trajectory in its interweaving of drugs and technology ("*Akira*: Mirai toshi no arushibu," *Eureka* 20, no. 10, [1988], 89).

20. Herbert Plutschow, *Matsuri: The Festivals of Japan* (Richmond, Surrey: Curzon Press, 1996), 45.

21. Bakhtin, *Problems,* 116.

22. In fact, Tetsuo's messianic capabilities are an important plot strand throughout much of the manga version of *Akira*. In the long-running series, Tetsuo becomes head of his own empire, ultimately squaring off against Lady Miyako, another psychically empowered character who is shown in a more positive light than Tetsuo. As in the film, however, Tetsuo's inability to contain his powers is the dominant drive of the overall narrative. Two articles in a special issue of *Eureka* explicitly discuss the manga *Akira* as a religious text, although both writers (Kamata Tōji and Ōtsuka Eiji) dwell more on the problematic religious nature of the mysterious "Akira" than on the character of Tetsuo. See Ōtsuka Eiji, "Yugamaba yagate yonaoshi," and Kamata Tōji "'Nagare' to 'chikara' no hate ni," both in *Eureka* 20, no. 10 (1988): 54-67 and 68-73, respectively. The manga version of *Nausicaä* also shows her more clearly as messianic or Bhodisattva-esque (while simultaneously representing her in a much more complex and adult fashion than in the movie). In one scene in the manga, for example, she is given the chance to escape the world for a utopian oasis, but, in a traditionally Bhodisattva-

esque fashion, she chooses to remain on earth to help her suffering fellow creatures.

23. Pippin, *Death and Desire,* 28-43.

24. Susan Sontag, "The Imagination of Disaster," in *Film Theory and Criticism,* edited by Gerald Mast and Marshall Cohen (New York: Oxford University Press, 1985), 454.

25. Jean Baudrillard, "The Ecstasy of Communication," in *The Anti-Aesthetic: Essays on Postmodern Culture,* edited by Hal Foster (Port Townsend, WA: The Bay Press, 1983).

26. Bakhtin, *Problems,* 124. As was evident in chapter 10, *Nausicaä's* creator, Miyazaki Hayao, has offered a strong environmental message in many of his films, sometimes within an apocalyptic framework, as is clear in his 1997 blockbuster hit *Princess Mononoke.* This film contains a clearly Shinto-esque apocalyptic ending in which all of nature is threatened only to be saved at the last moment by the revival of the awesome nature god, the *shishigami.* On the other hand, as Inaga points out, Miyazaki is wary of imbuing Shinto and nature with too much ideological fervor, as is clear in his criticism of the conservative anthropologist Umehara Takeshi's work on animistic thinking. (See Inaga, "*Nausicaa,*" note 11, 125).

27. It should be noted that the adults also do not especially seem to be enjoying themselves. Rather than the sexual anarchy of the festival, *Legend of the Overfiend* offers a surprisingly circumscribed vision of sexual apocalypse.

28. As noted previously, the evil city is a basic trope of the biblical Revelations. It is even possible that the infernal city in *Legend of the Overfiend* may be a kind of demonic parody of the "conjured city" of the Lotus Sutra. In this parable the vision of a beautiful city is offered to a multitude of believers to give them rest on their arduous journey along the "bad road' to enlightenment. (See *Scriptures of the Lotus Blossom of the Fine Dharma* [New York: Columbia University Press], 130-155). In *Overfiend,* of course, the city is merely a gateway to increasingly horrifying revelations. I am indebted to Helen Hardacre for pointing out the possible connection with the Lotus Sutra.

29. Kōtani Mari, *Seibo Ebuangerion* (Tokyo: Magajin hausu, 1997), 19.

30. Arai Hiroyuki "Shinseiki Ebuangerion no baransu shiito," *Pop Culture Critique* 0 (1997): 70.

31. Shimotsuki Takanaka, "Anime yo anime! Omae wa dare da!?" *Pop Culture Critique* 0 (1997): 17.

32. A number of Japanese commentators have suggested that there is an autobiographical dimension to *Evangelion.* Certainly, much of the story is portrayed with exceptional realism, as Kitano Taiitsu points out, although he also maintains that the over-embellished ending betrays the series' initially realistic premise. *Nihon animeshigakukenkyū jōsetsu* (Tokyo: Hachiman Shoten, 1998), 145-148.

33. The theme of technological transgression is perhaps the single most common theme in Western apocalyptic works, at least from the beginning of the Industrial Revolution. Saul Friedlander, for example, discusses the development of what he calls the "evil demi-urge," a figure created by the

misuse of technology in such works as *Frankenstein, The Island of Dr. Moreau,* and even Wagner's *Ring* cycle operas. As Friedlander sums it up, "at the very moment when man affirms that unlimited progress will put an end to the natural movement of civilizations, a fear develops, the fear that nature will take its revenge and destroy man, who denies its laws and transgresses the limits imposed on him" (Friedlander, "Themes of Decline and End in the Nineteenth Century Imagination," in *Visions of Apocalypse,* edited by Friedlander, Holton, Marx, and Skolnikoff [New York: Holmes and Meier, 1985], 80).

34. Susan Napier, "Panic Sites: The Japanese Imagination of Disaster from *Godzilla* to *Akira*," in *Contemporary Japan and Popular Culture,* edited by John Treat (Honolulu, University of Hawaii Press, 1996), 255-256.

35. Kōtani, *Seibo Ebuangerion,* 27-28.

36. Ibid., 30.

37. I am indebted to Ezra Vogel for pointing out the possible connection between the sexual orgies of *Legend of the Overfiend* and the financial orgies of the period in which it was created.

CHAPTER TWELVE

1. For a discussion of nostalgia in the works of Yoshimoto Banana and the relation between nostalgia and *shōjo* culture, see John Treat's "Yoshimoto Banana Writes Home: The Shōjo in Japanese Popular Culture," in *Contemporary Japan and Popular Culture,* edited by John Treat (Honolulu: University of Hawaii Press, 1996).

2. Marilyn Ivy, *Discourses of the Vanishing: Modernity, Phantasm, Japan* (Chicago: The University of Chicago Press, 1995), 9-10.

3. Ibid., 2.

4. Frederic Jameson, "Postmodernism and Consumer Society," in *The Anti-Aesthetic,* edited by Hal Foster Port Townsend, WA: The Bay Press, 1983), 117.

5. Linda Hutcheon, "Post Modern Film," in *Postmodern After-Images,* edited by Peter Brooker and Will Brooker (New York: St. Martin's Press, 1997), 39.

6. Kitano Taiitsu, Nihon animeshigakukenkyūjōsetsu (Tokyo: Hachiman Shoten, 1998) 162.

7. Jennifer Robertson's description of what *furusato* means is very helpful here. According to Robertson, the "quintessential landscape features" of *furusato* include "forested mountains, fields cut by a meandering river, and a cluster of thatched-roofed farmhouses" ("It Takes a Village: Internationalization and Nostalgia in Postwar Japan," in *Mirrors of Modernity: Invented Traditions of Modern Japan,* edited by Stephen Vlastos [Berkeley: University of California Press, 1998] 116). All of these landscape elements are in ample evidence in the scenic images of *Only Yesterday.* Even more interesting and appropriate is Robertson's subsequent point about the more abstract features of *furusato.* As she says, "the recognition of a place as *furusato* is possible only once that place is, or is imagined as, distant, inaccessible, lost, forsaken, or

disappearing" (117). This sense of loss is precisely what the film's elegiac mode both plays up and ultimately resists in its insistence on a happy ending. Finally, Robertson points out that *furusato* names a place that exists in contrast to—and therefore amplifies the aimlessness and malaise—of the present moment (117). This implicit criticism exists as the narrative tension on the part of the film—the contrast between the spiritually rich country-side and the emotionally impoverished urban world.

8. The question of Taeko's "selfishness" is an interesting one, especially in relation to her father whose own actions, at least from some points of view, might be interpreted as equally selfish. It seems from the context of the film, however, that the father's actions, while not admirable, are meant to be justified in contrast to Taeko's selfishness. Unlike so many other films and fiction in contemporary Japanese culture, this father is seen at least as asserting his authority. Takahata seems to underline this point when he has the young farmer reassure Taeko at a time when she seems dubious about her father's actions that "all fathers are like that."

9. Jameson, "Postmodernism," 117.

10. David Harvey, "Time and Space in the Postmodern Cinema," in *Postmodern After-Images,* edited by Peter Brooker and Will Brooker (New York: St. Martin's Press, 1997), 72.

11. Ibid., 62.

12. For more on the East Asian tradition of ambiguity see Susan Napier, 1996, *The Fantastic in Modern Japanese Literature: The Subversion of Modernity* (London: Routledge: 1996), 226.

13. For a discussion of the relationship between Japan's concurrent *furusato* movement and internationalization movement in terms of their physical manifestations of traditional villages and foreign model–based theme parks, see Robertson, "It Takes a Village," especially 127-129.

14. Harry Harootunian, "Persisting Memory/Forgetting History: The 'Postwar' (*sengo*) in Japanese Culture or the Trope that Won't Go Away," paper presented at the Association for Asian Studies Annual Conference (March 1999), 2.

CONCLUSION

1. Paul Wells, *Understanding Animation* (London: Routledge, 1998), 16.

2. Eric Smoodin, *Disney Discourse: Producing the Magic Kingdom* (New York: Routledge, 1994), 12.

3. Arjun Appadurai, *Modernity at Large: Cultural Dimensions of Globalization* (Minneapolis: University of Minnesota Press, 1996), 33.

APPENDIX

1. For example Susan Pointon's discussion of the popularity of *Legend of the Overfiend* among American viewers wonders: "why a generation [of Ameri-

cans] should . . . engage so passionately with foreign imports suffused with an inordinately high content of sexual sado-masochism and graphic violence" ("Transcultural Orgasm as Apocalypse," *Wide Angle* 19.3 [1997]: 43).

2. Susan Pointon "Transcultural Orgasm," 44.

3. Ibid.

4. Annalee Newitz, "Anime Otaku: Japanese Animation Fans Outside Japan," *Bad Subjects* 13 (April 1994): 2 and 10, italics in original.

5. See Paul Willemen, "Letter to John," in *Screen's The Sexual Subject* [no editor] (London: Routledge, 1992), 174-175, 183.

6. John Tulloch and Henry Jenkins, *Science Fiction Audiences* (London: Routledge, 1995), 144.

7. Steve Pearl, "Anime Clubs in America," paper delivered at Japan Society Symposium on Anime, New York, January 1999.

8. Ibid., 3.

9. Henry Jenkins, *Textual Poachers* (New York: Routledge, 1992), 26.

10. For more information on the gender makeup of *Star Trek* fans, see Camille Bacon Smith, *Enterprising Women: Television Fandom and the Creation of Popular Myth* (Philadelphia: University of Pennsylvania Press, 1992), especially pages 1-22.

11. The gender gap may be becoming less intense, however. Although I do not yet have statistics on this, at a recent anime convention, Project A-kon, in June 2000, I noticed a large number of women participants, many of whom mentioned that they were initially attracted to anime by watching the *Sailor Moon* episodes, which aired on American television in the mid 1990s.

12. Jenkins, *Textual Poachers,* 110.

13. Newitz, "Anime Otaku," 6.

14. Pointon, "Transcultural Orgasm," 44.

15. Annalee Newitz suggests that the very absence of fan discussion on the subject of anime's origins is actually symptomatic of its unacknowledged importance but I am unable to substantiate this assertion in my own research (Newitz, "Anime Otaku," 10).

16. Ella Shohat and Robert Stam, "From the Imperial Family to the Transnational Imaginary: Media Spectatorship in the Age of Globalization," in *Global/Local*, edited by Rob Wilson and Wimal Dissanayake (Durham, NC: Duke University Press, 1996), 165.

17. Jenkins, *Textual Poachers,* 282.

BIBLIOGRAPHY

Allison, Anne. *Permitted and Prohibited Desires: Mothers, Comics and Censorship in Japan.* Boulder, CO: Westview Press, 1996.

Animerica Staff. "Anime Dream Girls." In *Animerica* 7, no. 10 (1995): 8-27.

Appadurai, Arjun. *Modernity at Large: Cultural Dimensions of Globalization.* Minneapolis: University of Minnesota Press, 1996.

Arai, Hiroyuki. "Shinseiki Ebuangerion no baransu shiito." *Pop Culture Critique* 0 (1966): 67-79.

Ashkenazi, Michael. *Matsuri: Festivals of a Japanese Town.* Honolulu: University of Hawaii Press, 1993.

Awaya, Nobuko, and David Phillips. "Popular Reading: The Literary World of the Japanese Working Woman." In *Re-Imagining Japanese Women.* Edited by Anne Imamura. Berkeley: University of California Press, 1996.

Bachelard, Gaston. *The Poetics of Space.* Boston: The Beacon Press, 1969.

Bacon-Smith, Camille. *Enterprising Women: Television Fandom and the Creation of Popular Myth.* Philadelphia: University of Pennsylvania Press, 1992.

Bakhtin, Mikhail. *Problems of Dostoevsky's Poetics.* Minneapolis: The University of Minnesota Press, 1984.

Baudrillard, Jean. "The Ecstasy of Communication." In *The Anti-Aesthetic: Essays on Postmodern Culture.* Edited by Hal Foster. Port Townsend, WA: The Bay Press, 1983.

Beller, Jonathan. "Desiring the Involuntary: Machinic Assemblage and Transnationalism in Deleuze and *Robocop 2*." In *Global/Local.* Edited by Rob Wilson and Wimal Dissanayake. Durham, NC: Duke University Press, 1996.

Bell-Metereau, Rebecca. *Hollywood Androgyny.* New York: Columbia University Press, 1993.

Belton, John. Introduction to *Movies and Mass Culture.* New Brunswick, NJ: Rutgers University Press, 1996.

Bhabha, Homi K. *The Location of Culture.* New York: Routledge, 1994.

Blacker, Carmen. "Millenarian Aspects of the New Religions in Japan." In *Tradition and Modernization in Japanese Culture.* Edited by Donald Shively. Princeton: Princeton University Press, 1971.

Boronoff, Nicholas. *Pink Samurai: The Pursuit and Politics of Sex in Japan.* London: Grafton, 1992.

Boss, Peter, "Vile Bodies and Bad Medicine." *Screen* 27 (1986): 14-24.

Bowring, Richard. *Murasaki Shikibu: Her Diary and Poetic Memoirs*. Princeton: Princeton University Press, 1982.

Brophy, Philip. "Horrality—the Textuality of Contemporary Horror Films." *Screen* 27 (1986): 2-13.

———. "Ocular Excess: A Semiotic Morphology of Cartoon Eyes." *Art and Design*, Profile 53 (1997).

Buckley, Sandra. "'Penguin in Bondage': A Graphic Tale of Japanese Comic Books." In *Technoculture*. Edited by Constance Penley and Andrew Ross. Minneapolis: University of Minnesota Press, 1991.

Bukatman, Scott. "X-Bodies." In *Uncontrollable Bodies: Testimonies of Identity and Culture*, Rodney Sappington and Tyler Stallings. Seattle: Bay Press, 1994.

Burke, Frank. "Fellini's *Casanova*: Male Histrionics and Phallocentrism." In *Crisis Cinema*. Edited by Christopher Sharrett. Washington DC: Maisonneuve Press, 1993.

Buruma, Ian. *Behind the Mask*. New York: Pantheon, 1984.

Butler, Judith. *Bodies That Matter*. London: Routledge, 1993.

Cavanaugh, Carole. "A Working Ideology for Hiroshima: Imamura Shōhei's *Black Rain*." In *Word and Image in Japanese Cinema*. Edited by Dennis Washburn and Carole Cavanaugh. Cambridge: Cambridge University Press, 2001.

Ching, Leo. "Imaginings in the Empires of the Sun: Japanese Mass Culture in Asia." In *Contemporary Japan and Popular Culture*. Edited by John Treat. Honolulu: University of Hawaii Press, 1996.

Cholodenko, Alan, ed. *The Illusion of Life*. Sidney, Australia: Power Institute of Fine Arts, 1991.

Chūjō, Shōhei. "Tatakai no ronri to hishō no kairaku: *Kaze no tani no Nausicaä*." *Eureka*, Special Issue: "Miyazaki Hayao no sekai" 29, no. 11 (1997): 104-109.

Clover, Carol. "Her Body, Himself." In *Gender, Language, and Myth: Essays on Popular Narrative*. Edited by Glenwood Irons. Toronto: University of Toronto Press, 1992.

———. *Men, Women and Chain Saws: Gender in the Modern Horror Film*. Princeton: Princeton University Press, 1992.

Corliss, Richard. "Amazing Anime." *Time* 154 (22 November 1999).

Cornyetz, Nina. *Dangerous Women, Deadly Words: Phallic Fantasy and Modernity in Three Japanese Writers*. Stanford: Stanford University Press, 1998.

Creed, Barbara. "From Here to Modernity." In *Postmodern After-images*. Edited by Peter Brooker and Will Brooker. New York: St. Martin's Press, 1997.

———. *The Monstrous Feminine: Film, Feminism, Psychoanalysis*. London: Routledge, 1993.

Desser, David. "*Blade Runner*: Science Fiction and Transcendence." *Literature/Film Quarterly* 13, no. 3 (1985): 173-178.

Endō, Toru. "Konna Kitanai kirei na hi ni wa: fujori to iu sukui." *Pop Culture Critique* 0 (1997): 80-93.

Felski, Rita. "Fin de siècle, Fin de sexe: Transsexuality, Postmodernism, and the Death of History," *New Literary History* 27 no. 2 (1996): 337-349.

Fowler, Roger. *A Dictionary of Modern Critical Terms*. London: Routledge and Kegan Paul, 1987.

Freiberg, Freda. "Akira and the Postnuclear Sublime." In *Hibakusha Cinema*. Edited by Mick Broderick. London: Routledge and Kegan Paul, 1996.

Freud, Sigmund. *Totem and Taboo*. London: Routledge and Kegan Paul, 1983.

Friedlander, Saul. "Themes of Decline and End in the Nineteenth Century Western Imagination." In *Visions of Apocalypse: End or Rebirth*. Edited by Friedlander, Holton, Marx, and Skolnikoff. New York: Holmes and Meier, 1985.

Galbraith, Stuart. *Japanese Science Fiction, Fantasy, and Horror Films: A Critical Analysis*. Jefferson, NC: McFarland and Co., 1994.

Garber, Marjorie. *Vested Interests*. New York: Routledge, 1997.

Gibson, William. *Neuromancer*. New York: Ace Books, 1984.

Gluck, Carol. "The End of the Postwar: Japan at the Turn of the Millennium." *Public Culture* 10, no. 1 (1997): 1-23.

―――. "The Past in the Present." In *Postwar Japan as History*. Edited by Andrew Gordon. Berkeley: University of California Press, 1993

Gomarasca, Alessandro. "Mechanized Bodies, Exoskeletons, Powered Suits: The Metaphors of Techno-dress in Japanese Animation." In *Re-Orienting Fashion*. Edited by Brian Moeran and Lise Skov. Richmond, Surrey: Curzon Press, Forthcoming.

Grosz, Elizabeth. *Volatile Bodies: Toward a Corporeal Feminism*. Bloomington: Indiana University Press, 1994.

Hall, Stuart. Introduction to *Questions of Cultural Identity*. London: SAGE, 1996.

Hardacre, Helen. "Aum Shinrikyō and the Japanese Media: The Pied Piper Meets the Lamb of God." New York: Columbia University East Asian Institute, 1995.

Harootunian, Harry. "Persisting Memory/Forgetting History: The 'Postwar' (sengo) in Japanese Culture or the Trope That Won't Go Away." Paper presented at the Association for Asian Studies Annual Conference, Washington DC, March 1999.

Haraway, Donna. *Simians, Cyborgs and Women: The Reinvention of Nature*. New York: Routledge, 1991.

Harvey, David. "Time and Space in the Postmodern Cinema." In *Postmodern After-images*. Edited by Peter Brooker and Will Brooker. New York: St. Martin's Press, 1997.

Hibbett, Howard. *The Floating World in Japanese Fiction*. Tokyo: Tuttle Books, 1976.

Hirashima, Natsuko. "*Tonari no totoro:* fuantaji ga umareru kūkan." In *Eureka* 29, no. 11 (1997): 164-169.

Hurley, Kelly. "Reading Like an Alien: Posthuman Identity in Ridley Scott's *Alien* and David Cronenburg's *Rabid.*" in *Posthuman Bodies*. Edited by Judith Halberstram and Ira Livingston. Bloomington: Indiana University Press, 1995.

Hutcheon, Linda, "Post Modern Film?" In *Postmodern After-images*. Edited by Peter Brooker and Will Brooker. New York: St. Martin's Press, 1997.

Inaga, Shigemi. "*Nausicaä in the Valley of the Wind:* An Attempt at Interpretation." *Japan Review* 11 (1999): 113-128.

Ishihara, Ikuko. "*Majo no takyūbin:* koko kara asoko e no aida no shōjo." *Eureka* 29, no. 11 (1997): 193-199.

Ito, Kinko. "Sexism in Japanese Weekly Comic Magazines for Men." In *Asian Popular Culture*. Edited by John Lent. Boulder, CO: Westview Press, 1995.

Ivy, Marilyn. *Discourses of the Vanishing: Modernity, Phantasm, Japan*. Chicago: The University of Chicago Press, 1995.

Iwao, Sumiko. *The Japanese Woman: Traditional Image and Changing Reality*. Cambridge, MA: Harvard University Press, 1993.

Jackson, Rosemary. *Fantasy: The Literature of Subversion*. London: Routledge, 1981.

Jameson, Fredric. "Postmodernism and Consumer Society." In *The Anti-Aesthetic*. Edited by Hal Foster. Port Townsend, WA: The Bay Press, 1983.

Jenkins, Henry. *Textual Poachers*. New York: Routledge, 1992.

Kamata, Tōji. "'Nagare' to 'chikara' no hate ni." *Eureka* 20, no. 10 (1988): 54-67.

———. *Ōdōron*. Tokyo: Shinyōsha, 1988.

Kasabe, Jun. "Mokushiroku e no shottai." In *Zenryaku Oshii Mamoru*. Edited by Noda Makoto, Tokyo: Futtowaku, 1998.

Kato, Shuichi. *Japan: Spirit and Form*. Rutland, VT: Charles Tuttle Company, 1994.

Kawamoto, Saburo, and Itō Shunji," *Akira*: Mirai toshi no arushību." *Eureka* 20, no. 10 (1988): 74-97.

Keirstead, Thomas, and Deirdre Lynch. "*Eijanaika*: Japanese Modernization and the Carnival of Time." In *Revisioning History*. Edited by Robert Rosenstone. Princeton: Princeton University Press, 1995.

Kellner, Douglas. *Media Culture*. London: Routledge, 1995.

Kelsky, Karen. "Flirting with the Foreign: Interracial Sex in Japan's 'International' Age." In *Global/Local*. Edited by Rob Wilson and Wimal Dissanayake. Durham, NC: Duke University Press, 1996.

Kelsky, Karen. "Gender, Modernity, and Eroticized Internationalism in Japan," *Cultural Anthropology* 14, no. 2 (1999): 229-255.

Kidd, Kenneth. "Men Who Run with Wolves and the Women Who Love Them: Child Study and Compulsory Heterosexuality in Feral Child Films." *The Lion and the Unicorn* 20, no. 1 (1996): 90-112.

Kinoshita, Sayoko, "Japon: à côté de Goldorak . . ." In *Sommaire,* special issue "Le Cinèma d'animation" (1993): 157-163.

Kinsella, Sharon. *Adult Manga*. Richmond, Surrey: Curzon Press, 2000.

———. "Cuties in Japan." In *Women, Media and Consumption in Japan*. Edited by Brian Moeran and Lise Skov. Richmond, Surrey: Curzon Press, 1995.

Kitano, Taiitsu. *Nihon animeshigakukenkyūjōsetsu*. Tokyo: Hachiman Shoten, 1998.

Kobayashi, Kyūzo, "Shichinin no samurai kara no ketsubetsu o kuwadate." In *Mononokehime o kaku, kataru*, Comic Box 3 (January 1998): 152-153.

Komatsu, Kazuhiko. "Mori no kamikoroshi to sono noroi." *Eureka* 29, no. 11 (1997): 48-53.

Kōtani, Mari. *Seibo Ebuangerion*. Tokyo: Magajin hausu, 1997.

Kristeva, Julia. *Powers of Horror.* New York: Columbia University Press, 1982.

Langer, Lawrence, ed. *Art from the Ashes*. New York: Oxford University Press, 1995.

Ledoux, Trish, ed. *Anime Interviews*. San Francisco: Cadence Books, 1997.

Ledoux, Trish, and Doug Ranney. *The Complete Anime Guide*. Issaquah, WA: Tiger Mountain Press, 1997.

Levi, Antonia. *Samurai from Outer Space: Understanding Japanese Animation*. Peru, IL: Open Court Publishing, 1997.

Lewis, Dina. "Nihon anime ga sekai e tobu." *Newsweek Japan*. (30 July 1997): 43-49.

Lewis, Jon. "The Road to Romance and Ruin: The Crisis of Authority in Francis Ford Coppola's *Rumble Fish*." In *Crisis Cinema: The Apocalyptic Idea in Postmodern Narrative Film*. Edited by Christopher Sharrett. Washington DC Maisonneuve Press, 1993.

Lifton, Robert. "The Image of 'The End of the World': A Psychohistorical View." In *Visions of Apocalypse: End or Rebirth*. Edited by Friedlander, Holton, Marx and Skolnikoff. New York: Holmes and Meier, 1985.

Lyman, Rick. "Darkly Mythic World Arrives from Japan." In *The New York Times* (21 October 1999): sec. B, 1.

Masters, Patricia Lee. "Warring Bodies: Most Nationalistic Selves." In *Colonialism and Nationalism in Asian Cinema*. Edited by Wimal Dissanayake, Bloomington: Indiana University Press, 1994.

McCarthy, Helen. *The Anime Movie Guide*. Woodstock, NY: The Overlook Press, 1997.

McCarthy, Helen, and Jonathan Clements. *The Erotic Anime Movie Guide*. Woodstock, NY: The Overlook Press, 1999.

Minamida, Misao. "Kindai animeshigairon." In *Nijūseikianimetaizen*. (No editor). Tokyo: Futabasha, 2000.

Misono, Makoto. *Zusetsu terebianime zensho*. Tokyo: Hara Shobo, 1999.

Miyazaki, Hayao. "Araburu kamigami to ningen no tatakai." Introduction to *The Art of The Princess Mononoke*. Tokyo: Studio Ghibli, 1997.

———. "Hikisakarenagara ikite iku sonzai no tame ni" (interview with Yamaguchi Izumi). *Eureka* 29, no. 11 (1997): 29-47.

Modleski, Tania. *Loving with a Vengeance: Mass Produced Fantasies for Women*. Hamden, CT: Archon Books, 1982.

Moeran, Brian. "Reading Japanese in *Katei Gahō*: The Art of Being an Upperclass Woman." In *Women, Media and Consumption in Japan*. Edited by Lise Skov and Brian Moeran. Richmond, Surrey: Curzon Press, 1995.

Morimoto, Marie. "The 'Peace Dividend' in Japanese Cinema: Metaphors of a Demilitarized Nation." In *Colonial Nationalism in Asian Cinema*. Edited by Wimal Dissanayake. Bloomington: Indiana University Press, 1994.

Morley, David, and Kevin Robins. *Spaces of Identity*. London and New York: Routledge, 1995.

Mraz, John. "Memories of Underdevelopment: Bourgeois Consciousness/Revolutionary Context." In *Revisioning History*. Edited by Robert Rosenstone. Princeton: Princeton University Press, 1995.

Mulvey, Laura, "Visual Pleasure and Narrative Cinema." In *The Sexual Subject: A Screen Reader on Sexuality*. London: Routledge, 1992.

Murase, Hiromi. "Kumorinaki sunda manako de mitsumeru 'sei no yami': Miyazaki anime no joseizō." In *Pop Culture Critique* 1 (1997): 53-66.

Napier, Susan. *The Fantastic in Modern Japanese Literature: The Subversion of Modernity*. London: Routledge, 1996.

———. "Panic Sites: The Japanese Imagination of Disaster from *Godzilla* to *Akira*." In *Contemporary Japan and Popular Culture*. Edited by John Treat. Honolulu: University of Hawaii Press, 1996.

————. "Vampires, Psychic Girls, Flying Women and Sailor Scouts: Four Faces of the Young Female in Japanese Popular Culture." In *The Worlds of Japanese Popular Culture*. Edited by D. P. Martinez. Cambridge: Cambridge University Press, 1998.

Nash, Cristopher. *World-Games: The Tradition of Anti-Realist Revolt*. London: Methuen, 1987.

Natsume, Fukanosuke. *Sensō to manga*. Tokyo: Kodansha, 1997.

Nelson, John K. "Freedom of Expression: The Very Modern Practice of Visiting a Shinto Shrine." In *Japanese Journal of Religious Studies* 23, no. 1-2 (1996): 118-153.

Nelson, John W. "The Apocalyptic Vision in American Popular Culture." In *The Apocalyptic Vision in America*. Edited by Lois Zamora. Bowling Green, OH: Bowling Green University Popular Press, 1982.

Newitz, Annalee. "Anime Otaku: Japanese Animation Fans Outside Japan." *Bad Subjects* 13 (April 1994): 1-12.

Ogasawara, Yuko. *Office Ladies and Salaried Men: Power, Gender, and Work in Japanese Companies*. Berkeley: University of California Press, 1998.

Oshii, Mamoru, Ueno Toshiya, and Itō Kazunori. "Eiga to wa jitsu wa animēshon datta." In *Eureka* 28, no. 9 (1996): 50-81.

Ōtomo, Katsuhiro. *The Memory of Memories*. Tokyo: Kodansha, 1996

Ōtsuka, Eiji. "Yugama ba yagate yonaoshi." *Eureka* 20, no. 10 (1988): 68-71.

Painter, Andrew. "The Telepresentation of Gender in Japan." In *Re-imaging Japanese Women*. Edited by Anne Imamura. Berkeley: University of California Press, 1996.

"Panoramic Miyazaki." (No author.) *Eureka*. Special Issue, "Miyazaki Hayao no Sekai," 29, no. 11, 1997

Pearl, Steve. "Anime Clubs in America. Paper delivered at Japan Society Symposium on Anime. New York, January 1999.

Penley, Constance. *Close Encounters: Film, Feminism and Science Fiction*. Minneapolis: University of Minnesota Press, 1991.

Penley, Constance, and Andrew Ross. "Cyborgs at Large: Interview with Donna Haraway." In *Technoculture*. Minneapolis: University of Minnesota Press, 1991.

Pippin, Tina. *Death and Desire: The Rhetoric of Gender in the Apocalypse of St. John*. Louisville, KY: Westminster Press, 1992.

Plutschow, Herbert. *Matsuri: The Festivals of Japan*. Richmond, Surrey: Curzon Press, 1996.

Pointon, Susan. "Transcultural Orgasm as Apocalypse: *Urotsukidōji:* The Legend of the Overfiend." *Wide Angle* 19, no. 3 (1997): 41-63.

Poitras, Gilles. *The Anime Companion: What's Japanese in Japanese Animation?* Berkeley, CA: Stone Bridge Press, 1999.

Prindle, Tamae. "A Cocooned Identity: Japanese Girl Films: Nobuhiko Oobayashi's *Chizuko's Younger Sister* and Jun Ichikawa's *Tsugumi."* *Post Script* 15, no. 1 (Fall 1998): 24-36.

Raffaeli, Luca. "Disney, Warner Bros., and Japanese Animation: Three World Views." In *A Reader in Animation Studies*. Edited by Jayne Pilling. Sydney, Australia: John Libbey and Co., 1997.

Rayns, Tony. "Apocalypse Nous." In *Time Out* (16 January 1991).

Reader, Ian. "Japanese Religion Looks to the Millennium." Paper presented at the Symposium on Crisis and Change in Japan, University of Washington, 1995.

Richie, Donald. *Japanese Cinema: An Introduction.* New York: Oxford University Press, 1990.

Robertson, Jennifer. "It Takes a Village: Internationalization and Nostalgia in Postwar Japan." In *Mirror of Modernity: Invented Traditions of Modern Japan.* Edited by Stephen Vlastos. Berkeley: University of California Press, 1998.

———. *Takarazuka: Sexual Politics and Popular Culture in Modern Japan.* Berkeley: University of California Press, 1998.

Rosenstone, Robert. Introduction to *Revisioning History: Film and the Construction of a New Past.* Princeton: Princeton University Press, 1995.

Rushing, Janice, and Thomas Frentz. *Projecting the Shadow: The Cyborg Hero in American Film.* Chicago: University of Chicago Press, 1995.

Russell, Catherine. "The Spectacular Representation of Death." In *Crisis Cinema: The Apocalyptic Idea in Postmodern Narrative Film.* Edited by Christopher Sharrett. Washington, DC: Maisonneuve Press, 1993.

Saeki, Junko. "Nijūisseiki no onnagami, saibogu=goddesu." In *Hayao Miyazaki (Filmmakers* vol. 6). Edited by Yoro Takeshi. Tokyo: Kinema Junpōsha, 1999.

Saito, Minako. *Kōitenron.* Tokyo: Bireiji senta, 1998.

Saito, Tamaki. *Sentobishōjo no seishin bunseki.* Tokyo: Ota Shuppan, 2000.

Sato, Ikuya. *Kamikaze Biker: Parody and Anomy in Affluent Japan.* Chicago: The University of Chicago Press, 1991.

Satō, Kenji. "More Animated than Life: A Critical Overview of Japanese Animated Films." *Japan Echo* (December 1997): 50-53.

Satō, Tadao. *Currents in Japanese Cinema.* Tokyo: Kodansha International Press, 1982.

Schaffer, Scott. "Disney and the Imagineering of Histories." *Post Modern Culture* 6, no. 3 (1996): 1-33.

Schodt, Frederik. *Dreamland Japan: Writings on Modern Manga.* Berkeley, CA: Stone Bridge Press, 1996.

———. *Manga! Manga! The World of Japanese Comics.* Tokyo: Kodansha International, 1983.

Sedgewick, Eve Kosofsky. *Between Men: English Literature and Male Homosocial Desire.* New York: Columbia University Press, 1985.

Shapiro, Jerome. "Atomic Bomb Cinema: Illness, Suffering, and the Apocalyptic Narrative." In *Literature and Medicine* 17, no. 1 (1998).

Sherif, Ann. "Japanese Without Apology: Yoshimoto Banana and Healing." In *Oe and Beyond.* Edited by Stephen Snyder and Philip Gabriel. Honolulu: University of Hawaii Press, 1999.

Shimizu, Yoshiyuki. "Sukoyaka naru bōsō: *Tonari no totoro* no opunu endingu o megutte." In *Pop Culture Critique* 1 (1997): 92-101.

Shimotsuki, Takanaka. "Anime yo Anime! Omae wa dare da!?" *Pop Culture Critique* 0 (1997): 7-18.

Shohat, Ella, and Robert Stam. "From the Imperial Family to the Transnational Imaginary: Media Spectatorship in the Age of Globalization." In *Global/Local*. Edited by Rob Wilson and Wimal Dissanayake. Durham, NC: Duke University Press, 1996.

Smoodin, Eric. *Disney Discourse: Producing the Magic Kingdom*. New York: Routledge, 1994.

Sobchak, Vivian. "Child/Alien/Father: Patriarchal Crisis and Generic Exchange." In *Close Encounters: Film, Feminism, and Science Fiction*. Edited by Constance Penley. Minneapolis: University of Minnesota Press, 1991.

Sontag, Susan. "The Imagination of Disaster." In *Film Theory and Criticism*. Edited by Gerald Mast and Marshall Cohen. New York: Oxford University Press, 1985.

Spigel, Lynn. "From Domestic Space to Outer Space: The 1960s Fantastic Family Sit-Com." In *Close Encounters: Film, Feminism and Science Fiction*. Edited by Constance Penley, et al. Minneapolis: University of Minnesota Press, 1991.

Sponberg, Alan, and Helen Hardacre, eds. *Maitreya, The Future Buddha*. Cambridge, Cambridge University Press, 1988.

Springer, Claudia. *Electronic Eros: Bodies and Desire in the Postindustrial Age*. Austin: University of Texas Press, 1996.

Standish, Isolde. "*Akira*, Postmodernism and Resistance." In *The Worlds of Japanese Popular Culture*. Edited by D. P. Martinez. Cambridge: Cambridge University Press, 1998.

Swinfen, Ann. *In Defense of Fantasy*. London: Routledge and Kegan Paul, 1984.

Tachibana, Reiko. *Narrative as Counter-Memory: A Half Century of Postwar Writing in Germany and Japan*. Albany, NY: State University of New York Press, 1998.

Takada, Akinori. "Animeeshon kōzō bunseki hōhōron jōsetsu." In *Pop Culture Critique* 0 (1997): 19-39.

Takeuchi, Melinda. "Kuniyoshi's *Minamoto Raiko and the Earth Spider*: Demons and Protest in Late Tokugawa Japan." *Ars Orientalis* 17 (1987): 5-37.

Tanner, Ron. "Mr. Atomic, Mr. Mercury and Chime Trooper: Japan's Answer to the American Dream." In *Asian Popular Culture*. Edited by John Lent. Boulder, CO: Westview Press, 1995.

Telotte, J. P. *Replications: A Robotic History of the Science Fiction Film*. Urbana and Chicago: University of Illinois Press, 1995.

Theweleit, Klaus. *Male Fantasies*. Minneapolis: University of Minnesota Press, 1989.

Todorov, Tzvetan. *The Fantastic: A Structural Approach to a Literary Genre*. Ithaca, NY: Cornell University Press, 1975.

Totman, Conrad. *The Green Archipelago: Forestry in Pre-Industrial Japan*. Athens: Ohio University Press, 1998.

Treat, John, ed. *Contemporary Japan and Popular Culture*. Introduction by John Treat. Honolulu: University of Hawaii Press, 1996.

———. *Writing Ground Zero: Japanese Literature and the Atomic Bomb*. Chicago: University of Chicago Press, 1995.

———. "Yoshimoto Banana Writes Home: The *Shōjo* in Japanese Popular Culture." In *Contemporary Japan and Popular Culture.* Edited by John Treat. Honolulu: University of Hawaii Press, 1996.

Tudor, Andrew. *Monsters and Mad Scientists: A Cultural History of the Horror Movie.* Oxford: Basil Blackwell, 1989.

Tulloch, John, and Henry Jenkins. *Science Fiction Audiences.* London: Routledge, 1995.

Twitchell, James B. *Dreadful Pleasures: An Anatomy of Modern Horror.* Oxford: Oxford University Press, 1985.

Ueno, Kōshi. "Tenkū no shiro Raputa: eiga no yume, jitsugen to sōshitsu." *Eureka* 29, no. 11 (1997): 158-163.

Ueno, Toshiya. *Kurenai no metarusutsu anime to iu senjō/Metal Suits the Red Wars in Japanese Animation,* Tokyo: Kodansha, 1998.

Uno, Kathleen S. "The Death of Good Wife, Wise Mother?" In *Postwar Japan as History.* Edited by Andrew Gordon. Berkeley: University of California Press, 1993.

Viswanathan, Mira. "In Pursuit of the Yamamba: The Question of Female Resistance." In *The Woman's Hand: Gender and Theory in Japanese Women's Writing.* Edited by Paul Schalow and Janet Walker. Stanford: Stanford University Press, 1996.

Wells, Paul. *Understanding Animation.* London: Routledge, 1998.

———. "Hayao Miyazaki: Floating Worlds, Floating Signifiers." In *Art and Design,* Profile 53 (1997): 22-26.

Willemen, Paul. "Letter to John." In *Screen's The Sexual Subject* [no editor]. London: Routledge, 1992.

Williams, Linda. *Hardcore: Power, Pleasure and the Frenzy of the Visible.* Berkeley: University of California Press, 1989.

Wood, Robin. "Papering the Cracks: Fantasy and Ideology in the Reagan Era." In *Movies and Mass Culture.* Edited by John Belton. New Brunswick, NJ: Rutgers University Press, 1996.

Yamada, Tadon. "Animekai no Kein to Aberu: Miyazaki to Takahata Isao wa Fujiko Fujio datta." *Pop Culture Critique* 11 (1997): 37-42.

Yomota, Inuhiko. *Mangaron.* Tokyo: Chikuma Shobo, 1994.

Yoshimoto, Mitsuhiro. "Real Virtuality." In *Global/Local.* Edited by Rob Wilson and Wimal Dissanayake. Durham, NC: Duke University Press, 1996.

BOOKS IN JAPANESE ON ANIME
(NO EDITORS OR AUTHORS)

The Analysis of Kōkakukidōtai. Kodansha: Young Magazine, 1995.
Anime hiroingahō. B Media Books. Tokyo: Takeshobō, 1999.
The Art of the Princess Mononoke. Studio Ghibli, 1997
Ebuangerion: Owari to hajimari 255. Studio Voice, 1997.
Mononokehime. Animage, 1997.
Mononokehime o kaku kataru. Tokyo: Comic Box, no. 3, 1997.

INDEX